Saving Our Children
from the First Amendment

CRITICAL AMERICA

General Editors: Richard Delgado and Jean Stefancic

*In the Silicon Valley of Dreams:
Environmental Injustice,
Immigrant Workers,
and theHigh-Tech
Global Economy*
David N. Pellow and
Lisa Sun-Hee Park

*Mixed Race America and the Law:
A Reader*
Kevin R. Johnson

*Critical Race Feminism:
A Reader, Second Edition*
Edited by Adrien Katherine Wing

*Murder and the Reasonable Man:
Passion and Fear in the
Criminal Courtroom*
Cynthia K. Lee

*Success without Victory:
Lost Legal Battles and the
Long Road to Justice in America*
Jules Lobel

*Greasers and Gringos: Latinos, Law,
and the American Imagination*
Steven W. Bender

*Saving Our Children
from the First Amendment*
Kevin W. Saunders

Saving Our Children from the First Amendment

Kevin W. Saunders

NEW YORK UNIVERSITY PRESS

New York and London

NEW YORK UNIVERSITY PRESS
New York and London
www.nyupress.org

Library of Congress Cataloging-in Publication Data
Saunders, Kevin W.
Saving our children from the First Amendment / Kevin W. Saunders
p. cm. — (Critical America)
Includes bibliographical references and index.
ISBN 0–8147–9835–7 (cloth : alk. paper)
1. Freedom of speech—United States. 2. Obscenity (Law)—
United States. 3. Internet and children—United States.
I. Title. II. Series.
KF4772.S28 2003
342.73'0853—dc21 2003014383

New York University Press books are printed on acid-free paper,
and their binding materials are chosen for strength and durability.

Manufactured in the United States of America

10 9 8 7 6 5 4 3 2 1

In memory of my parents,
 Morton (1916–98) and
  Eleanor (1920–2003) Saunders.

Contents

Acknowledgments

Several of the ideas contained in this book were discussed in earlier work. One of the approaches to violent depictions presented was discussed more fully in an earlier book, *Violence as Obscenity*, and in articles in the *William & Mary Bill of Rights Journal* and the *Oklahoma Law Review*. Earlier analysis of problems raised by the Internet was published in the *Drake Law Review*.

I wish to express my thanks to several individuals for their comments on earlier drafts of this book. Rod Smolla of the University of Richmond and Richard Delgado and Jean Stefancic of the University of Colorado all provided extensive and valuable comments, as did the anonymous referees for New York University Press. Their efforts and the work of NYU Press itself are greatly appreciated. I would also like to thank the library staff at Michigan State University—DCL College of Law for their research support. Finally, I would like to thank my wife, Dr. Mary Scott, and our daughter, Molly Saunders-Scott, not only for their support of my efforts but also for the psychological and teenage perspectives they provided on the issues addressed.

Introduction

> [A]t the confluence of two streams of concern which flow through our polity—our concern for the protection of our First Amendment freedoms and our concern for the protection of our children[—]we expect to hear a roar rather than a purr.[1]

In 1949, Justice Jackson wrote: "There is danger that, if the Court does not temper its doctrinaire logic with a little practical wisdom, it will convert the constitutional Bill of Rights into a suicide pact."[2] Similarly, writing for the Court in 1963, Justice Goldberg stated: "[W]hile the Constitution protects against invasions of individual rights, it is not a suicide pact."[3] The position that the Constitution is not a suicide pact finds support in other opinions of the Supreme Court[4] and lower courts.[5]

Yet, how better for a society to commit suicide than to fail in its duty to raise its youth in a safe and psychologically healthy manner. We are so failing. While rates fluctuate, violent crime by youths is unacceptably high. Homicide is the second leading cause of death for fifteen to twenty-four-year-olds and the leading cause among African American males of that age.[6] Teenage pregnancy rates are also too high. Although down 11 percent from its 1994 high, the birthrate for unwed fifteen- to nineteen-year-olds was 41.5 births per thousand in 1998.[7] Children also use tobacco and alcohol at unacceptable rates.[8] The Campaign for Tobacco-Free Kids cites government reports showing that more than 5 million children are current smokers, and 43.8 percent of high school boys used tobacco in the month preceding a 2001 survey.[9] The Campaign for Alcohol Free Kids reports that 10 million American teenagers drink monthly; 8 million drink weekly, with half a million of those binge drinking; that alcohol consumption is not uncommon at ages eleven and twelve; and that a majority of grade five through twelve students say that advertising encourages them to drink.[10] We are failing in our duty to society and its coming generations, and the First Amendment's limitations on our ability to restrict the influences children face are among the roots of that failure.

The First Amendment does contain the most important of our political freedoms. Stating those freedoms very succinctly, the amendment says: "Congress shall make no law respecting an establishment of religion, or prohibiting the free exercise thereof; or abridging the freedom of speech, or of the press; or the right of the people peaceably to assemble, and to petition the Government for a redress of grievances." The importance of the amendment to adults is obvious, but its importance to children is less clear. Even if children should enjoy some First Amendment rights, the benefits these rights provide may well be limited by a child's developmental stage. Rather than concluding that the rights of children and adults should be equal, we should consider the possibility of limiting children's rights to correspond to children's capacities.

Free expression also has its costs. While there are limitations on adult expression, those limitations are narrow. Only when a clear and present danger attends the speech or when the speech falls within certain categories—obscenity, fighting words or libel—may adult speech be limited. When the recipient of the speech is a child still developing psychologically, the costs of unrestrained speech may be too high. Shielding children from harms that adults may have to tolerate protects children in their development. This same shielding also serves to protect the rest of society. Any negative effects that free expression has on children affect not only children but society as a whole.

The thesis of this work is that the First Amendment should function differently for children and for adults. For communication among adults the amendment should be fully robust, perhaps even more so than under current law. Where children are concerned, however, the amendment should be significantly weaker. Society should be allowed to limit the access of children to materials not suitable to their age. Legal prohibitions on distributing sexual materials to children are now constitutional, and this treatment should extend to violent materials, vulgar or profane materials, and the hate-filled music used to recruit the next generation to supremacist organizations. No good reason requires that we recognize a right on the part of children to such access. Nor should the free-expression rights of adults be seen as including a right to express themselves to the children of others. The full development and autonomy of adults may require the right to express themselves on a wide variety of topics, but that right should not include access to children who are not their own.

Perhaps no one should tell authors, producers or computer programmers what they can create. But that is not the same as saying that they have a right to a juvenile audience for their books, films or video games.

A. *The Specter of Censorship*

The immediate response to this thesis is certain to be, "Isn't that censorship?" Yes, it is. But, is censorship always an evil? Even with adults, there are arguments that censorship is sometimes positive. Some feminists argue that the harm pornography does to women outweighs the free-expression rights of the producers and even adult consumers of pornography. Advertising tobacco and alcohol causes harm, even if the ads could be restricted to adults, and advertising prescription drugs to the end consumer increases the cost of health care and may cause needless danger to those consumers. Hate speech, even when directed toward adults, may have strongly negative effects on those adults, even having medical consequences.

These are real costs to free expression. For adults, however, the costs are worth bearing. The lines between hate speech and the advocacy of a political position may be too difficult to draw to allow a prohibition on such speech. Commercial speech also has value. Consumers need to know the differences among products or the varying prices of the goods they purchase. Not only men, but women and couples may use pornography, and the right to obtain such material and for the producers to express themselves may be worth retaining. Generally, the dangers of government censorship provide reason to treat with skepticism any efforts to censor communication among adults. Even if some censorship might have overall positive value, the great dangers of censorship to political freedom, the attainment of truth and autonomy rights justify a strong freedom of expression that includes a strong presumption against censorship.

Children, however, are different. The values behind the First Amendment that make the costs worth bearing are not as strong when children are involved. The costs are also greater. Children are in the process of development. Influences that might be minor for adults can have a seriously negative impact on children. The lessened benefits of free expression for or toward children and the greater costs attendant to such expression reduce the strength of the presumption against all censorship and should leave open the possibility of providing more protection for children.

These ideas will be more fully developed in the chapters that follow, but a brief discussion of the foundational benefit and the costs of free expression and of the differences between children and adults regarding expression would be useful at this point.

Justice Holmes explained his view of the theory behind the First Amendment's speech and press clause in *Abrams v. United States*.[11] Holmes recognized the desire to suppress the expression of opinion regarded as incorrect, but he questioned the reasonableness of the surety with which the determination of truth or falsity can be made.

> [W]hen men have realized that time has upset many fighting faiths, they may come to believe even more than they believe the very foundations of their own conduct that the ultimate good desired is better reached by free trade in ideas—that the best test of truth is the power of thought to get itself accepted in the competition of the market, and that truth is the only ground upon which their wishes safely can be carried out. That at any rate is the theory of our Constitution.[12]

Holmes's "marketplace of ideas" justification for the freedoms of speech and of the press reflects that offered by John Stuart Mill in his 1859 work *On Liberty*.[13] While other theories also explain or justify the protection given expression, theories that will be discussed in the next chapter, this "marketplace of ideas" has a firm historical basis.

This theory's central import to the political process is reason enough to maintain a strong freedom of expression, but it is most clearly of importance for those who are actual participants in the political system. If children are not allowed to vote, this rationale at least partially evaporates. Adults who wish to influence political or social change should direct their efforts to other adults, those who can vote for that change. Children should be influenced by their parents and by society, with the role of other adults limited to trying to affect the political community in its decisions on the influences to which children will be exposed.[14] Expression by children, as it relates to social and political change, may have value, but again its value must be less than that of adults, or there would be no justification for denying children the vote.

Other rationales for free expression are discussed in chapter 1 along with further discussion of the marketplace of ideas. None of those theories speak particularly strongly to children. While society benefits, despite occasional costs, from the strong free-expression rights it recognizes for adults, the benefits are simply not as strong in allowing equivalent free expression for children, either in their own communication or in the information they receive from adults other than their own parents or guardians.

The desire to censor is, of course, based on the perceived costs of expression. But, even where the freedoms of speech and press have their costs, the benefits may clearly outweigh those costs. For example, excesses by the press may be criticized. Sensational headlines may sell papers but may also inaccurately attribute behavior to an individual damaging the person's reputation. At least for public officials, the cost is worth bearing, and plaintiffs must show not only falsity but that the media organ knew of that falsity or recklessly disregarded a known risk that the report was false. A public official may then have to tolerate false reports that injure his or her reputation, but the failure to protect the press would have significant negative effects. The press, faced with potential liability, would not report on public officials unless they were very sure of their news gathering. The public would be deprived of reports that might be both true and very relevant to voting decisions and public accountability. Where a public official is involved, the balance runs in favor of protecting the public's need to know, even in the face of some possible cost to that official.

In other situations, the benefits may not as clearly outweigh the costs. It has been argued that pornography exposes women to unequal treatment. Hate speech, either on the basis of race or gender, has been said to have similar effects. Violence in media depictions may be argued to lead to violence in the real world. Campaign contributions, seen as a protected expression of opinion, may have a corrupting effect on the political process. The Internet, in opening channels of communications among adults, may expose children to material that is certainly inappropriate and may be damaging. Advertising may mislead consumers. Protection of profane speech and shock media may have a coarsening effect on society.

These issues will be addressed in chapter 2, but generally the balance has been properly struck in favor of providing First Amendment protection. In some cases the benefits outweigh recognized costs. In other cases, fear that difficulties in drawing lines aimed at eliminating speech with little or no value would lead to the suppression of speech that has value and ought to be protected for its own sake limits the inclination to regulate. This, for example, is sometimes offered as a rationale for the protection of shock media. While there may be little value other than that some find such programming entertaining, once limits are imposed on shock media, where is the line to be drawn? Where is the cut to be made along the continuum ranging from programs that present shocking material for purely entertainment purposes, at one end, through confrontational reporting and on to the evening news, at the other?

Concern over drawing lines is less compelling where children are involved. This is particularly so if parents retain the right to second-guess society and make available to their children materials that others may not provide them directly. Furthermore, the costs of free expression are experienced more through their effects on children than on adults. Reducing those costs by imposing limitations only in this area of primary negative effect can benefit society while leaving the greatest benefits, adult-to-adult communication, free.

Children are different. Their abilities to analyze conflicting visions of society are not fully developed. While we may believe that through free and open exchange adults will eventually arrive at the truth, the argument is not as convincing for children. Without the experiential basis of adults, children are more likely to be led astray. And, we may be more confident in the fact that the direction is, in fact, wrong. While it may be unreasonable to claim general infallibility, it is more reasonable to claim a better grasp of the situation than that enjoyed by children.

The harms done by speech or press protected by the First Amendment may also be more severe when children are exposed to objectionable expression. Children may be more affected by material such as pornography or depictions of violence. Those in the process of developing psychologically may have that development harmed by depictions that would not negatively affect adults. Certainly, the child's beliefs as to the violence present in the world or of the variety of sexual activity practiced by the average adult may, in the absence of real life experience, be affected by a view of the world formed primarily through television and the movies.

John Stuart Mill himself, the champion of freedom of expression and strong proponent of libertarianism, recognized that children may be treated differently. Mill was willing to allow society to shape the thinking of children in a way that would be unacceptable for adults. In considering possible rationales for society acting paternalistically toward adults, Mill agreed that punishment for the sake of the actor is preferable to punishment for failure to provide benefits to society. But, he said that society has other ways of bringing its "weaker members" up to the expected standards of conduct. Mill noted that society has power over these "weaker members" during their youth and may attempt, in that period, to teach them rational conduct.[15] Mill recognized the primary role of parents in raising their children but concluded that, when parents fail to provide training, the state has a role to play.[16]

The period of childhood is that in which, even for Mill, society has the opportunity to teach the values it hopes children will accept as they become adults. Teaching opposing values to children would defeat society's right to educate. Children simply do not have the competency to determine which of the competing theories of values is preferable. That is not to say that there cannot be debate over values, but it is one that must occur on an adult level. Adult expression of opinion over the values to teach children should be robust and open, but not all the proponents of competing positions should have access to society's children. Parents, of course, play a primary role in teaching values, and society should not punish parents for teaching values that disagree with those of the majority. But that does not mean that society must leave children at the mercy of all others who wish to teach children values that differ from those of the majority and of their parents. Society has the right and duty to limit the access of adults to other people's children.

B. *The Role of Parents*

The second response to the thesis that society has a role in the protection of children from expression that may be harmful to them is likely to be, "Shouldn't that be the job of parents?" Again, yes it should. Not only should parents have the right to control the influences to which their children are exposed, it is a part of the job of parenting. But parents need help in discharging that responsibility. It may have been easy to make sure that children were exposed to the right influences in an earlier era. Children are now subjected to far more influences, from videos to cable television to video games to the Internet, than when the issues were simply what books to read or which of the television network broadcasts to watch. The greater explicitness of both sex and violence in the current media also make the concern over inappropriate exposure far more pressing.

That this is the parents' job does not mean that the state has no role. It only means that the governmental role should be a supportive role rather than one that supplants the parents as the determiner of the values to which children are exposed. The decisions the government makes will have an effect on the child's ability to obtain exposure to various forms of media, but it should only be an effect on third parties' direct provision of these products to the child. Parents must still be allowed to disagree with the state, purchase the material and provide it to their children themselves.

To conclude that, because controlling the influences on children is the parents' job, the state should have no such role is unreasonable. Consider a similar argument for cigarettes. It should also be the parents' job to teach their children not to smoke. But from that premise, no one would argue that the state should not be allowed to prohibit sales of tobacco to minors. Parents need the support of the state in their efforts. While tobacco laws may not assure that children will not smoke, making it more difficult to purchase cigarettes provides at least some help to parents.

The response to that is likely to be that expression is different. While the Constitution does not protect cigarette smoking, the First Amendment does protect the freedom of expression. Expression is, admittedly, different. Values behind free expression are not just different but more important than any values behind letting people make their own choices regarding the consumption of tobacco. Nonetheless, as just discussed, the values of free expression are less when children are concerned. This is most clear for the autonomy interests represented by the guarantees of free expression. Even if one accepts that one value behind the First Amendment is allowing the individual to be the person he or she wants to be, that does not mean that such a laissez faire attitude toward children is appropriate. If children were to be allowed the same autonomy rights as adults, that would seem to extend to tobacco use. There are differences in the sort of harm caused, but cigarettes and violent media both cause harm: the health associations, such as the American Medical Association, and the surgeon general have found this to be true, and the disagreement over that point in both cases comes primarily from the industries themselves.

The major difference between the tobacco and free expression issues, with regard to the rights of children or of nonparental adults with regard to children, is in what occurs when the child reaches the age of majority. When the child turns eighteen, there is no sudden need for the new adult to be a competent smoker. Thus, the child need not be a smoker in training. On turning eighteen, however, the child is suddenly a member of the voting part of the political community, and it is necessary that the new adult be a competent voter. Exposure to political debate and the issues that face the community are then needed, at least during the latter part of the individual's minority.

The need for children to learn about politics does not mean that society must throw up its hands and allow children to experience all possible forms of expression. It is a part of our tradition that parents are primarily responsible for instilling values in their children, and we must recognize that such influence is likely to carry over to the choices of young voters. It should only be the influences of government, as they affect the future voting choices of children, that should raise concern. That influence is likely to come through the schools, and it is there that caution should be exercised. Limitations on video tapes and games or the music children can purchase directly are of less concern, since parents can obtain any material they believe appropriate. Schools, however, could be used to inculcate values that the parent finds objectionable. They could be used to skew the political process. If the schools take one side on a political issue, children whose parents are on that side will have their values reinforced. Children whose parents are on the opposite side will have the values their parents are trying to inculcate called into question. One side may then be able to use the schools to help implant its political position in the upcoming generation of voters.

This concern over the political savvy of the next generation does not mean that there can be no limitations on speech to children. Limitations that do not absolutely prohibit all exposure of children to legal, such as nonobscene, expression should be acceptable. If the only limits are on direct sales, parents can still obtain materials they think suitable for their children, even if society disagrees. The only change such a regulation mandates is a sort of change in presumption. Without such limits, the presumption seems to be that it is acceptable for children to have access to the material, but this presumption is at least theoretically rebuttable by the parent who tells a child not to purchase a particular CD or see a particular film. With limitations, the presumption is that children should not watch, read, listen to or play particular material, but again the presumption is rebuttable by the parent who provides the material for his or her child.

Again, the issue of speech limitations in school is more serious. Care must be taken that the societal political debate is not skewed. But even here, it does not mean that all regulation is foreclosed. Limits on sexual indecency certainly are allowed, but the schools should not shut off one of the two positions on the political debate over whether obscene material should be proscribed. Limits on speech that degrades another person on the basis of race, color or gender should be allowed, but the debate on affirmative action should not be skewed. Discussion of war, crime or the First Amendment should be vital, but that does not mean that violent video games must be allowed in the cafeteria, even if the school allows nonviolent games.

C. A Matter of Common Sense?

The suggested likely first responses already discussed would have come from those who disagree with the proposed thesis, but there is also a dismissive response that could come from a supporter. That response would be: "They're only children. Of course their First Amendment rights are different from those of adults. Isn't that just common sense?" The answer, as with the answers to the "Isn't that censorship?" and "Isn't that the parents' job?" is again "Yes." But, common sense and the dictates of the law, including the Constitution, are not always the same thing, and there are certainly interpretations of the First Amendment that are contrary to the position taken here.

The American Civil Liberties Union has consistently taken a contrary position. Sometimes, as in the case of the Communications Decency Act's attempt to prevent minors from accessing indecent material on the Internet, the legal claims of those who, along with the ACLU, successfully sought to enjoin the act, were based at least in part on the effect the attempt to shield minors would have on the access rights of adults.[17] But, even when adult access has not been threatened, the ACLU has taken positions against measures intended to protect minors. The v-chip was criticized as a variety of censorship that violates the First Amendment.[18] The ACLU argued that the v-chip legislation was a "governmental usurpation of parental control" over what their children see on television,[19] despite the fact that parents were not required to activate the filter. If they wanted help in limiting their children's viewing, the scheme provided that opportunity, while parents who were less concerned with media violence could simply choose not to avail themselves of the aid the v-chip would provide.

The ACLU was similarly unimpressed by efforts to label musical recordings to warn parents of objectionable content. Once again, some of the concern regarded the likelihood that retail chains would opt not to carry recordings labeled as unsuitable for minors and the negative effect this would have on adult access. But the organization also generally questioned the wisdom of shielding children, saying "scapegoating artistic expression as a cause of social ills is simplistic. How can serious social problems like violent crime, racism or suicide be solved by covering children's ears?"[20] Despite this skepticism, there are serious concerns over negative media effects on children, and once again, the labeling would not prohibit parents who do not share that concern from providing labeled recordings to their children. Parents would simply be provided the information necessary to make an informed decision.

The American Library Association has taken a similar position regarding attempts to require filtering on computers in schools and libraries that received federal funding to provide Internet access.[21] Again, the concern was not solely that adults might lose access to valuable material on the Internet. In an explanation of their concerns, the association said: "People of all ages and backgrounds come to libraries seeking connection to a world of ideas via books, magazines and the Internet. Providing access to the broadest spectrum of information possible is the heart of America's public libraries."[22]

Probably the strongest assertion of the expression rights of minors may be found in Marjorie Heins's recent book, *Not in Front of the Children*.[23] Heins is a free-expression activist, former ACLU litigator and current director of the Free Expression Policy Project of the National Coalition Against Censorship. She describes, as a major theme of her book, "the intellectual freedom interests of young people . . . a concept too often impatiently dismissed by child protectionists[, who think m]inors insufficiently mature or socialized to understand and resist the ideas that a majority of adults think are not good for them."[24] She goes on to question the wisdom of this protectionist approach:

> But is this really the best way to prepare youngsters for adult life in a democratic society? The simultaneous titillation, anxiety, and confusion spawned by forbidden speech zones may do more harm than good. Certainly healthy upbringing, education and community values are likelier than taboos to immunize them against violent, degrading, or simpleminded ideas. Censorship may also frustrate young people's developing sense of autonomy and self-respect, and increase their feelings of alienation. Some older children and adolescents are able to process

information and make coherent decisions at the same level as many adults. They *need* access to information and ideas precisely because they are in the process [of] becoming functioning members of society and cannot do so if they are kept in ideological blinders until they are 18.[25]

But younger children clearly are insufficiently mature to understand what is good for them. A very young child is unlikely to understand sound nutrition and may need to be told that a diet consisting entirely of fast food is unacceptable and to eat his or her vegetables, whatever this may do to a "developing sense of autonomy." While the negative effects of certain expressive influences may be less clear, they do exist and children should be shielded.[26] Parents are in the best position to recognize the developing good sense of their children, and their judgment should be backed up by the sort of restrictions advocated here, which leave those parents free to provide materials that may not be directly available to children. If it is accepted that younger children should be protected, the issue is simply one of where to draw the line. If Heins's argument is only that children should not be shielded right up until their eighteenth birthdays, there is some strength to the position, as discussed below.

Turning to the legal precedents, support in opposition to the thesis of this work is also available, although as the chapters to follow will show, those precedents, at least at the highest level, are not dispositive. The first, important case in this line is *Tinker v. Des Moines School Dist,*[27] a case that will receive in-depth treatment throughout but particularly in chapter 12. *Tinker,* in recognizing First Amendment protection for student arm bands worn in school in protest of United States actions in Southeast Asia, said, "First Amendment rights, applied in light of the special characteristics of the school environment, are available to teachers and students. It can hardly be argued that either students or teachers shed their constitutional rights to freedom of speech or expression at the schoolhouse gate."[28] In a later case, *Erznoznik v. Jacksonville,*[29] striking down a ban on nudity in films visible from the street, as at a drive-in movie, the Court again recognized First Amendment rights of minors but also recognized that those rights are weaker than those of adults. The Court said: "It is well settled that a State or municipality can adopt more stringent controls on communicative materials available to youths than on those available to adults. Nevertheless, minors are entitled to a significant measure of First Amendment protections, and only in relatively narrow and well-defined circumstances may government bar public dissemination of protected material to them."[30]

The *Tinker* case is an important recognition of expression rights involving children, but it must be recognized that the issue there was political speech that should enjoy the strongest protection. The promised later treatment of the case must be sensitive to that variety of speech even though arguing for, as recognized by later cases on schools and expression,[31] lesser expression rights where children are concerned. *Erznoznik* is also of limited application. The Court had already recognized, in *Ginsberg v. New York*,[32] that a lesser level of sexuality will justify bans on dissemination to children, as obscene for that audience, of materials that would not be obscene when distributed to adults. *Erznoznik* concluded that not all nudity, potentially reaching "a picture of a baby's buttocks, the nude body of a war victim, or scenes from a culture in which nudity is indigenous,"[33] rather than solely sexually explicit nudity, is swept within the state interest recognized in *Ginsberg*. Nor could the Court find any other governmental interest that would justify the ban. There is, however, additional language that is contrary to the position taken here. The Court said that speech "cannot be suppressed solely to protect the young from ideas or images that a legislative body thinks unsuitable for them. In most circumstances, the values protected by the First Amendment are no less applicable when government seeks to control the flow of information to minors."[34]

A more recent lower court decision recognized free expression rights of children with a vengeance, or at least with a strong use of rhetorical hyperbole. *American Amusement Machines Ass'n v. Kendrick*[35] enjoined the enforcement of an Indianapolis ordinance limiting the ability of minors to play violent games in video arcades without a parent or guardian present. Judge Posner, writing for the three-judge panel, said:

> Children have First Amendment rights. . . . This is not merely a matter of pressing the First Amendment to a dryly logical extreme. The murderous fanaticism displayed by young German soldiers in World War II, alumni of the Hitler Jugend, illustrates the danger of allowing government to control the access of children to information and opinion. Now that eighteen-year-olds have the right to vote, it is obvious that they must be allowed the freedom to form their political views on the basis of uncensored speech *before* they turn eighteen, so that their minds are not

a blank when they first exercise the franchise. And since an eighteen-year-old's right to vote is a right personal to him rather than a right to be exercised on his behalf by his parents, the right of parents to enlist the aid of the state to shield their children from ideas of which the parents disapprove cannot be plenary either. People are unlikely to become well-functioning independent-minded adults and responsible citizens if they are raised in an intellectual bubble.[36]

This view seems in conflict with that of the Supreme Court. In *Ginsberg* the Court found two state interests that justified the limitations on selling indecent material to minors. The second of the two was the state's interest in the well-being of its youth. The first was the interest of parents. The Court said "constitutional interpretation has consistently recognized that the parents' claim to authority in their own household to direct the rearing of their children is basic in the structure of our society" and that parents are entitled to the support of the laws in discharging their responsibility.[37] It is true that *Ginsberg* addressed sexual material, but the interest cited was not limited to sex. If children have independent First Amendment rights, the *Ginsberg* result might still be reached by concluding that the material was obscene when viewed by children, a conclusion the Court did reach, but the interests of the parents would not have been relevant to that conclusion. The Court clearly recognized the rights of parents to determine that material is inappropriate for their children, and that is a far cry from children having fully independent rights under the First Amendment.

On the other hand, Judge Posner does point to a real issue regarding older minors, and if his analysis were limited to that concern, his view may not as directly conflict with *Ginsberg*. While *Ginsberg* recognized parental rights to control the influences their children confront, the statute at issue there addressed distribution to children under seventeen. The statute in *Ginsberg* had also been enacted in an era in which eighteen-year-olds did not have the right to vote. With the eighteen-year-old vote and the Indianapolis statute's extension to all those under eighteen, Posner's concern carries more weight. While it may be difficult to argue with a straight face that playing violent video games is necessary to casting an intelligent vote, the line between political speech and entertainment has been recognized as difficult to draw.[38] Despite the rhetoric and the specter of Nazis emerging due to efforts to limit the exposure of children to objectionable media influences, Judge Posner's concern does point to the possibility that an age below full adulthood should be taken as the point at which expanded, or perhaps full, First Amendment rights are enjoyed.

D. *The Plan of Analysis*

These claims, certainly not convincingly established by the discussion presented, are the themes that will be developed through the chapters to follow. Chapters 1 and 2 will discuss the values and costs behind or implicit in the Free Expression Clauses. Chapter 1 will demonstrate that the admittedly strong values embodied in the First Amendment do not have as great strength where children are concerned. Chapter 2 will look to the costs of free expression, costs that are worth bearing for adults but may not be as justifiable for expression to children.

Chapter 3 examines the attempts of others to balance the costs and benefits of free expression. These attempts have generally been along the lines of providing less protection for certain varieties of speech, sometimes motivated out of a fear that requiring the First Amendment to protect too much speech will weaken the amendment in the eyes of the people. Drawing lines based on age, even though content is central in determining what is fit for children, is less likely to lead to slippery-slope concerns presented by content lines for the general population. Furthermore, lines based on age and the protection of children remove the greatest objections to free expression. The "Would you want your child to see that?" response to claims of protection is removed from the debate over what is acceptable for adult communication, allowing a stronger First Amendment for adults than presently exists.

Chapter 4 looks at the need to inculcate values in children. The psychological development of children is briefly examined to show that the experiences children face do affect what kinds of people they become. The values to be inculcated and the role of parents and the government in that developmental task are also examined.

Chapters 5 and 6 look to the current state of children's rights under the Constitution. Chapter 5 examines constitutional provisions outside the Free Expression Clauses that treat children differently, adopting a more protective stance for children than for adults. Chapter 6 looks to a particular aspect, the obscenity exception, of the Free Expression Clauses, and examines the difference in the treatment of material distributed to children compared to material available to adults. The chapter also argues that recognizing differing standards for adults and children can provide greater freedom for adults than currently exists.

Chapter 7 argues that the provisions of obscenity law can be carried over to depictions of violence. But it also argues, in the alternative, that the recognition of a two-tier First Amendment, based on the age of the communicants, would allow protection of youth without adding a new or extended exception affecting adult communication. Any concerns that abuse of obscenity law affecting adult communication would carry over to violent material can be addressed by this alternative approach that speaks only to communication involving children.

Chapter 8 may be viewed as an aside. In this chapter we will consider the medium of the Internet, rather than addressing particular content. It is important, nonetheless, because there is a current tendency to believe that all attempts to regulate the exposure of children to negative media influences are bound to fail, since the Internet is seen as uncontrollable. It is actually controllable, and whatever content decisions are made as a result of the other considerations presented can be applied to that medium as well.

Chapters 9, 10 and 11 return to the consideration of content. Chapter 9 examines hate speech, an area in which the battle over adult communication seems to have been lost by those favoring restrictions. An argument is provided that children can still be shielded from such speech. Chapter 10 turns to the issue of indecent or profane speech and the possibility of limiting the exposure of children to such expression. Chapter 11 looks at the issue of advertising and children.

Chapter 12 looks at the issue of free expression in the schools. The seemingly conflicting case law is examined, and an attempt is made to draw conclusions as to what varieties of speech may be limited in that context. It is argued that the schools are not Hyde Park, where all views must be heard. They must not, however, become the tools of the government in furthering the side of the political debate it prefers. But, that does not mean that the schools cannot teach, and require adherence to, basic values such as respect for others, nonviolent resolution of disputes and honesty.

Finally, the Conclusion summarizes the sorts of regulation justified by the arguments presented. The arguments are all legal, in the sense that they assert that the First Amendment should be interpreted to allow the conclusions they present. The conclusion also recognizes, however, that the arguments have a political dimension. Even if the claim that they justify the interpretation of the First Amendment put forward is not accepted, the arguments do present ends worth pursuing. If the courts refuse to recognize the need and right of parents and society to raise safe and psychologically healthy children and conclude that such attempts violate the First Amendment, the arguments presented herein provide a political argument that the Constitution should be amended to allow society to meet those essential goals.

Before going on to the substance of the argument, a word should be said about the use of case law in the analysis and the relevance it may have to different audiences. Readers of this book are likely to be, primarily, those interested in public policy regarding children and media influences. An audience not trained in the law may well underestimate the obstacle the First Amendment can place in the way of reform. Constitutional arguments are not just policy arguments to be rebutted by other interests, and those who would simply point to psychological evidence to support the governmental interests in limiting youth access to violent images or their exposure to hate speech don't recognize what is required when the First Amendment is involved. If children have full First Amendment rights, limitations must be shown necessary to, or narrowly tailored to, a compelling governmental interest. While courts have recognized a compelling interest in the psychological and physical well-being of youth, they have been unconvinced by the need to restrict the media to meet that interest.[39] For that audience, the cases presented show the obstacles to achieving the goal of protecting children.

The cases may provide too much detail for the other potential audience, those trained in law. Lawyers know the obstacles and may want to skim or omit the explanations of the holdings of the cases. I do, however, also present analysis for this audience. While recognizing the stumbling blocks the First Amendment cases place in the way of recognizing differing levels of protection for adults and children, a closer look at those cases allows for a reinterpretation that can accept the distinction. But, once again, if the reinterpretation of the cases is held to be too radical, the arguments in favor of the reinterpretation can also serve as arguments for a change in the Constitution.

1 | The Most Important Freedom

The First Amendment was originally the third of the amendments sent to the states for ratification, but it is fitting that it enjoys the place and title it does. The first to be ratified, it contains the most important of our freedoms—the freedoms of speech and of the press. A people cannot be free and self-governing unless they are free to discuss the issues facing their society and to debate the direction society should follow or to protest actions the government may have taken.

The First Amendment states that "Congress shall make no law . . . abridging the freedom of speech, or of the press," but the amendment has never been understood as providing the absolute protection the language seems to convey. The Supreme Court has said time and again that certain classes of speech, such as obscenity, fighting words and libel are outside the scope of the amendment's protections.[1] Actually, the First Amendment may have been intended to do nothing more than remove prior restraints and licensing requirements present in English law in the pre-Revolutionary era. Leonard Levy, a noted historian of the issues surrounding the American Revolution and the Constitution, takes this position.[2] He notes that John Milton, an early champion of free expression, attacked licensing but would have allowed criminal sanctions to punish the abuse of that freedom and that John Locke took a similar position.[3] Levy also quotes Blackstone's statement of the law in the Revolutionary era:

> The liberty of the press is indeed essential to the nature of a free state; but this consists in laying no previous restraints upon publication, and not in freedom from censure for criminal matter when published. Every freeman has an undoubted right to lay what sentiments he pleases before the public; to forbid this is to destroy the freedom of the press; but if he publishes what is improper, mischievous, or illegal, he must take the consequences of his own temerity.[4]

Whatever may have been the intent behind the First Amendment, the more restrictive view certainly has not survived. The evolved First Amendment includes within the protections of free expression the right to criticize the government without facing the possibility of a seditious libel charge. The free expression of views regarding governmental action is now recognized as essential to self-government and to a free society. Without such freedom, without the right freely to express one's political opinions, government cannot take account of the various opinions of the populace, and government cannot be said to be by the people.

Furthermore, the scope of First Amendment protection has broadened beyond political debate. A wide variety of entertainment, including pornographic films, video games and rap music, have come under its umbrella. A number of theories have also developed to explain the protection of other than political speech and press. Some build on ideas derived from John Stuart Mill, the marketplace of ideas and its role in the search for truth in all areas of inquiry and theories of autonomy in personal development. Others are based on free expression as a method of social control or as a way of building tolerance in society. Nonetheless, the core of the First Amendment is the protection of political speech, and that value will be considered first.

A. Political Speech

Alexander Meiklejohn, in his book *Free Speech and Its Relation to Self-Government*, argues that the basis for the First Amendment is the same as the basis for the Constitution as a whole. Both must be understood as being built on, and are justified by, the idea that the people are both governors and the governed. For Meiklejohn, "What is essential [to the freedom of speech] is not that everyone will speak, but that everything worth saying shall be said."[5] Equality of voice across divergent opinions is necessary to self-government. If a people are to govern themselves, they must have all the information necessary to that task. If some opinions are barred as unwise or incorrect, the decisions of the community will not be well considered and the policies adopted well balanced. As Meiklejohn put it,

It is that mutilation of the thinking process of the community against which the First Amendment to the Constitution is directed. The principle of the freedom of speech springs from the necessities of the program of self-government. It is not a Law of Nature or of Reason in the abstract. It is a deduction from the basic American agreement that public issues shall be decided by universal suffrage.[6]

A more recent analysis of the role of the First Amendment in protecting the part the people play in government is found in the work of Vincent Blasi. The checking value referred to in his article *The Checking Value in First Amendment Theory* is the role that "free speech, a free press, and free assembly can serve in checking the abuse of power by public officials."[7] The major difference between the theories of Blasi and Meiklejohn seems to be Meiklejohn's more regular active role of the citizen, as opposed to the exceptional role played by Blasi's citizen, and Blasi suggests that his checking value is a more realistic view of what the framers expected of the people and of the actual participation of the people in government.[8]

While other values have come to be included in the explanation of the protection that the First Amendment provides for the freedoms of speech and the press, the role free expression plays in self-government, either in regular participation or as a check on abuse, is central to the First Amendment. Political speech is at the core and deserves the strongest of protection.

Turning to the issue of the First Amendment and children, it is important to look at one remaining comment by Meiklejohn. In explaining the need for all views to be heard, he says, "Just so far as, at any point, the citizens who are to decide an issue are denied acquaintance with information or opinion or doubt or disbelief or criticism which is relevant to that issue, just so far the result must be ill-considered, ill-balanced planning for the general good."[9] The importance of free speech to self-government is that those who are to make the decisions have all the information and will be able to convince each other of the wisest course. Children are not among those who make the decisions, so it is at least questionable how strongly the First Amendment, at least on this justification, applies to children.

Actually, a distinction should be drawn between two types of communication necessary for self-government. Intelligent participation in self-government requires the receipt of information. It also requires the ability to communicate one's thoughts to others involved in the process. It is this first form of communication that has the more questionable application to children. If children are not allowed to vote or otherwise participate in society's determination of governmental policies, it is not as important that children be able to receive all the information that adults may need for rational self-government. Certainly, as children approach the age of majority and will soon become voting members of the polity, the interest in their ability to cast an intelligent vote grows. But until that point their access may be balanced against other interests that are also important to helping them develop into intelligent, psychologically healthy members of the political community.

The second aspect of political communication may seem more applicable to children. Even if children do not participate directly in the decision-making process, they have interests that society ought to take into account. It may be important that children be able to communicate those interests. The strength of that claim, however, varies greatly with the context in which it is made. We have come to realize that it is important, for example, to listen to the claims of children that they have been victims of abuse. The child victim may be the only witness, and protecting children requires that their claims not be dismissed simply because they are children.

The abuse claim is, however, not political or policy-oriented speech. Determining how to treat child-abuse cases and how to examine the testimony of child victims are political issues, but they are decided by adults. The factual assertions of children are relevant input to the decisions adults must sometimes make, but the political opinions of at least young children are not considered to be of great importance. On political issues, as opposed to factual inquiries, the child has no particular knowledge, and the child's opinions are reasonably considered uninformed. The general questions of the role and rights of children in society are addressed by including the opinions of adults who have responsibility for, or interests in, children.

That is not to say that minors may never play a role in self-government. Those below the voting age, which was twenty-one at the time, played a central role in changing U.S. policy in Southeast Asia. Their insights, or at least their protests, proved important to those who could vote and those who directly made policy. There is a great difference, however, between an elementary school campaign to eliminate homework and serve pizza daily in the cafeteria and concerns of seventeen-year-olds over foreign policy or a curfew for minors. The elementary school campaign is reasonably ignored, while the opinions of teenagers should be more strongly considered. In both cases adults will make the decision, but the elementary school child is seen as having little rational debate to offer, while the seventeen-year-old is capable of offering a reasoned position that should at least be heard. "Because I said so" is only a reasonable response up to a certain age.

There is one additional reason for according an increasing role to minors as they approach the age of majority. While most high school students cannot actually participate in self-government, on their eighteenth birthdays they are suddenly so empowered. It would be for the good of society for these soon-to-be participants to learn how to participate. Their debate, as they approach majority, should receive more respect and response. Straw votes and mock political campaigns, as well as campaigns for school government, serve to prepare minors for participation in self-government.

John Garvey refers to such practices as "spring training,"[10] and the appellation is apt. Spring training, so far as the team is concerned, counts for nothing, but the players get the opportunity to prepare for games that will count. The same is true of the political activities of minors. They count for nothing in the actual decision-making process, but it is important to society that they be ready to step in when they do become a part of self-government. The respect given the views of older minors is likely to be the model for the respect these young people will show for the views of others as young adults. There are, then, self-government interests in the speech of minors, but the interests are training interests and can be made to yield to other interests in a way that adult interests could not be sacrificed.[11]

A somewhat different metaphor was employed by Franklin Zimring. He viewed adolescents as being at a "learner's permit" stage between infancy and adulthood.[12] They deserve greater freedom than younger children but may have restrictions on their rights that would be unconstitutional restrictions on adults. Again, the label and theory speak to the thesis argued for here. Children, including teenagers, are developing the knowledge and critical and expository skills required of active participants in the political process. Just as student drivers need to spend time behind the wheel to become competent, nascent voters need time involved in thinking about and arguing over political issues. But, once again, they are learners rather than actual participants, and the rights granted to further the process of political education need not be coextensive with the rights necessary to actual participation.

The use of phrases such as "spring training" and "learner's permit" should not be taken to deny the importance of the rights involved. As Garvey explains, expressive rights of children are important, though different from those of adults:

> Freedom of speech for children is instrumentally important, not intrinsically so—it is a right that we protect in order to help kids become real First Amendment players. Because it has no intrinsic value for children it can be limited in ways that we wouldn't tolerate for adults. But it has real meaning, and within proper limits can be enforced against government.[13]

When he turns to an analysis of constitutional limitations on child speech restrictions, he focuses on the educational setting. That is unsurprising, since the school is the locus of the greatest interaction between most children and the state.

Much of the scholarship on the expression rights of children has a similar focus on schools. Amy Gutmann's book *Democratic Education* discusses generally the education of young people to be participants in a democracy and devotes a great deal of attention to the role of the schools.[14] She argues that even in primary school, "[c]hildren must learn not just to *behave* in accordance with authority but to *think* critically about authority if they are to live up to the democratic ideal of sharing political sovereignty as citizens."[15] Nonetheless, she says that schools must, at the same time, help develop the moral character of their students and, indeed, can't help but do so through their everyday practices.[16] Suzanna Sherry also recognizes a need to educate children for republican citizenship, but such education goes beyond the ability to think critically about political issues to include "moral character . . . and cultural literacy (that is, a knowledge of and attachment to their own culture)."[17] While recognizing society's interest in raising children prepared to participate in democracy, she allows moral education and limitations that would be inappropriate for adults. For example, she says that "hate speech regulations, . . . while intolerable if imposed on adults, may be appropriate to teach young children tolerance and sensitivity."[18]

There is then a balance to be reached. As Stanley Ingber put it, "Society must teach values, thereby molding character, if children are to have conceptions of the public good as adults. . . . [But, s]tudents who receive nothing but predigested ideas throughout their childhood cannot miraculously transform into autonomous, free-thinking individuals upon reaching adulthood."[19] This balance is most tenuous where political speech by and toward older children is involved, and care must be taken that the schools not be used to indoctrinate children beyond basic political values and to stifle their abilities to think about issues that are debated by the adult community. Outside the schools, the balance is more easily struck. Limits on the exposure of children to excessively graphic sexual or violent images or to hate speech would seem to raise few, if any, of the concerns raised by the case of in-school limitations reaching political debate.

B. Entertainment

The First Amendment protects more than debate at political conventions and the distribution of political tracts. Entertainment also comes under the amendment's protective umbrella. While children may not participate in self-government, they are consumers of entertainment at a rate at least equal to that of adults. Furthermore, concerns over the First Amendment as an impediment to the protection of children have focused primarily on entertainment. An analysis of the basis for the protection of entertainment is then important to the issue of children's rights under the First Amendment to receive, and adults to distribute to those children, expressive material.

The Supreme Court's rationale for extending the protections of free expression to entertainment is found in a 1948 case, *Winters v. New York*.[20] *Winters* grew out of an arrest for the distribution of a magazine titled *Headquarters Detective, True Cases from the Police Blotter*. The sale was in violation of a statute barring the sale of publications that massed stories of bloodshed and crime in a way that incites crimes against the person.[21] The statute was held to be unconstitutionally vague, but before reaching that issue, the Court had to consider whether such magazines enjoyed any First Amendment protection. On that issue, the entirety of the Court's analysis was as follows:

> We do not accede to appellee's suggestion that the constitutional protection for a free press applies only to the exposition of ideas. The line between the informing and the entertaining is too elusive for the protection of that basic right. Everyone is familiar with instances of propaganda

through fiction. What is one man's amusement, teaches another's doctrine. Though we can see nothing of any possible value to society in these magazines, they are as much entitled to the protection of free speech as the best of literature.[22]

Thus, entertainment is not protected simply because it is expression. It is protected because of the chance that it could contain information or views related to political and social issues. Not all entertainment is valuable in that way, but the lines are too difficult to draw.

Entertainment may contain political or socially important ideas. Film and music readily lend themselves to uses that are as highly protected as explicit criticism of government. It is also true that lines would be difficult to draw. Perhaps even more importantly, any attempts to draw lines leave open the possibility of abuse. A government allowed to decide what entertainment contains ideas important enough to be protected may be unlikely to find such importance in works that may be seen as critical of that government.

With regard to children, the rationale for protecting entertainment is weakened at least to the degree that the need to protect political speech is lessened. If political factors do not justify complete First Amendment protection for the distribution of political materials to younger children and the protection of entertainment is tied to its possible political or socially important content, entertainment should not have full protection for young children. Again, as children approach the age of majority, society's interests in their exposure to and engagement in political debate may include an interest in their exposure to such content in the form of entertainment. But this interest is not equal to the full interest that motivates the First Amendment protection of political speech. It is, again, of the spring-training variety. Nonetheless, society may conclude that children, as they approach majority, would benefit from gaining some experience with political speech in its guise as entertainment.

Interestingly, the Court's rationale in *Winters* would seem to put the entertainment industry in a difficult position with regard to negative effects of media depictions, for example with regard to media industry assertions that violence in the media has no effect on violence in society. The only rationale offered by the Court for the protection of entertainment is the possibly positive aspects of the content involved. Recognition of this positive role of content seems to require recognition of potential negative effects. Conversely, the industry denial of the possibility of negative effects implies the rejection of positive effects, and the argument that material should be protected loses its force.

C. Autonomy

If the only reason for protecting entertainment was its possible relationship to self-government, it should again be less protected when distributed to minors. There is, however, another important rationale offered for the protection of expression. Edwin Baker argues that the self-governmental value recognized by Meiklejohn and Blasi is only one of two fundamental purposes behind the First Amendment. The second fundamental purpose is fostering "individual self-fulfillment."[23] Baker's argument for this self-fulfillment rationale rests on an assertion that our system of government recognizes the equality and autonomy of the individual. Each individual has the right to self-realization and self-determination. Part of self-definition is tied to the freedom to express any thoughts one may have. A First Amendment justified by this value would certainly protect speech not protected by a solely self-government-focused First Amendment. In fact, the expression that Professor Baker would protect need not even involve communication of the speaker's ideas. He includes telling stories purely for entertainment, as well as singing purely to demonstrate the accomplishment of the singer.[24]

David Richards[25] relies on values seemingly similar to the autonomy Baker invokes in an analysis modeled on the work of John Rawls.[26] Like Rawls, Richards considers the question of what rational contractors would agree on as the structure of society, if they had no knowledge of their own personal situations. In addressing freedom of expression as the sort of general good that rational contractors would adopt, Richards explains the moral principles involved:

> [P]eople are not to be constrained to communicate or not to communicate, to believe or not to believe, to associate or not to associate. The value placed on this cluster of ideas derives from the notion of self-respect that comes from a *mature person's* full and untrammeled exercise of capacities central to human rationality. . . . Freedom of expression . . . supports a *mature individual's* sovereign autonomy in deciding how to communicate with others; it disfavors restrictions on communication imposed for the sake of the distorting rigidities of the orthodox and the

established. In so doing, it nurtures and sustains the self-respect of the *mature person.*[27]

Richards seems to recognize that autonomy interests do not apply, at least with the same strength, to children. While the potential of children should be respected and nurtured, the ideas of children need not be treated with the same respect as those of adults. An adult may be presumed to be in the best position to determine what is in his or her own best interest and how best to communicate his or her ideas to others. Younger children simply are not in that same position. Others may far better know the child's best interests and are in the better position to communicate those interests.

Both Baker and Richards justify protection of free expression as part of a broader right to be free of government interference in making decisions that define one's life. Autonomy rights, and libertarian positions generally, grew out of, or at least gained popularity with, the work of John Stuart Mill. Mill's *On Liberty* justifies free speech based on its usefulness, its utility, in reaching truth. The aspect of Mill's theory on which autonomy arguments build, however, is found elsewhere in *On Liberty*. Mill discusses societal attempts to control the lifestyle decisions of the individual. Mill finds those attempts unjustified, except to prevent harms to others. Where there is no such harm, Mill says "neither one person, nor any number of persons, is warranted in saying to another human creature of ripe years, that he shall not do with his life for his own benefit what he chooses to do with it."[28]

Mill recognized a difference between children and adults. He does speak of persons "of ripe years," and despite his arguments for individual choice, Mill was willing to impose greater restrictions on children. In considering possible rationales for society acting paternalistically toward adults, Mill argued against punishment for purely self-regarding behavior by adults in part because society has other ways of bringing its "weaker members" up to the expected standards of conduct.

> Society has had absolute power over them during the early portion of their existence: it has had the whole period of childhood and nonage in which to try whether it could make them capable of rational conduct in life. The existing generation is master both of the training and the entire circumstances of the generation to come. . . . If society lets any consider-

able number of its members grow up mere children, . . . society has itself to blame for the consequences.[29]

While Mill would place the primary role of teaching children to become adults on the child's parents, he does recognize the propriety of society providing that training when parents fail to do so.[30] This position can only hold with greater strength when the state and parents are not in conflict. If the issue is, as it often is in First Amendment cases involving children, the state's ability to limit nonparental distribution of materials to minors without parental permission,[31] society's right must be even stronger.

Similarly, while Richards found free expression important as a bulwark against "the distorting rigidities of the orthodox and the established,"[32] his concern was over the imposition of those rigidities on the "mature person." While Richards may be right with regard to such mature persons, society has a right, perhaps even a duty, to impose at least some of those orthodox and established modes of thought on children. While there may be difficulty in determining just which specific beliefs must be taught to children,[33] there is a core of values involving nonviolence in human interactions and respect for others that must be imparted. For noncore values, there will be sufficient diversity among parents to provide continued diversity in the succeeding generation.

D. The Marketplace of Ideas

Mill's ideas on the role of free expression in the search for truth have also strongly influenced First Amendment theory. While the central concern of the First Amendment may be the protection of political opinion, the search for truth has broader application. Science involves a search for the truth, even in areas that do not have immediate and specific application to political or social issues. Depending on what "truth" means, even such areas as art may be seen as attempts at seeking truth.

The search for truth rationale for free expression rests on a marketplace metaphor. The test of truth is seen as the acceptance of a position in the marketplace of ideas. A parallel is drawn to the marketplace for goods, where in an open market, better products drive out poorer-quality goods. The product that dominates the market, determined by individual decisions as to which product to choose, is the best product. Carrying over to the marketplace of ideas, the theory is that the accumulation of individual decisions as to what position to accept is more likely to reach the truth than an imposed orthodoxy. It is this free market in ideas that Justice Holmes had in mind in his dissent in *Abrams v. United States,* when he wrote that the free expression view behind the Constitution is that society benefits from such free trade in ideas and that "the best test of truth is the power of thought to get itself accepted in the competition of the market."[34]

This marketplace-of-ideas justification also finds expression in Mill's *On Liberty.* Mill argues that expression must be protected, whether the position asserted is true, false or a bit of both. The possibility that the assertion may be true provides the easiest justification for protection. If it is true and the received opinion is false, suppression will lead away from the truth. To argue against possible truth would be, says Mill, to assume the infallibility of those holding the received position. Where the received opinion is partially true and partially false, the process of clash between thesis and antithesis leads to successively better approximations of the truth. Even where the received position is true, Mill still sees value in allowing the expression of contrary views. If the received opinion is unopposed, it comes to be held on the same basis of prejudice or assumption as untested, false views. The rational basis for asserting the position need never be reconsidered and may be lost as the exercise of rationality fades into the profession of dogma.

The free-market metaphor also lies at the foundation of Justice Brandeis' concurrence in *Whitney v. California,* where he says that the remedy for bad speech is correcting speech, not suppression. "If there be time to expose through discussion the falsehood and fallacies, to avert the evil by the process of education, the remedy to be applied is more speech, not enforced silence."[35] For children, however, more speech may not be an adequate remedy for bad speech. The adult, having heard both sides of an issue, is called on to analyze the positions offered and is trusted to come to the right result. Not all adults may be capable of the rational thought such a theory requires, but the First Amendment and our societal concepts of equality require that we assume all adults so capable. The same position need not be taken with regard to children. There are differences in the abilities of children and adults to make rational decisions, and principles of equality would not be violated by allowing free expression for adults while restricting the exposure of children to expression that may prove harmful.

Suppression of an idea seems to imply the assumption that the received position is a closer approximation of the truth than its opposition. Where the opposition is offered by another person of mature years, the only basis for such a claim can be the belief in superior insight or intelligence. Such a claim must come from a sense of superiority at odds with principles of equality. When the opposing position comes from a child, it is less in conflict with principles of equality to impose the adult's position. The belief in superior insight and experience is reasonable. Similarly, a child's contribution is less likely to contribute to a new synthesis more closely approximating the truth or to serve as an important test for the received position.

That is not to say that children are never capable of contributing to a debate. It is important for parents to listen to their children's beliefs, concerns and positions. At the very least, the parent may learn of a misapprehension behind the child's stance that should be addressed. At the best, the child may turn out to be right. On the public front, again where the issue concerns facts about something that happened to the child, the child's testimony is important. Nonetheless, where issues of politics and public policy are involved, the contributions of minors are unlikely to serve as the test of, or make the contribution to, the truth that Mill envisions.

Of course, as a child approaches majority, the likelihood of valuable contribution increases, and the thoughts of a more mature minor should not be dismissed simply because they come from a child. Listening to the arguments of children and treating them more seriously as they approach majority also serves the "spring training" function. The power of a position to affect the outcome of either political debate or the search for the truth depends, to a great degree, on how well that position is asserted. Giving children the opportunity to voice their positions helps them develop skills in argumentation and will make them more valuable contributors to the search for the truth.

What has been said, so far, on the issue of children and the marketplace of ideas has concerned the voices of children. However, the issue more commonly of concern in the balance between the freedom of expression and the psychological well-being of children is that of the expression experienced by children. While children stating their positions may or may not serve as a contribution to the truth, those statements do not cause psychological harm. They may be symptomatic of difficulties, but a child's verbal or written self-expression is unlikely itself to damage the child. Indeed, suppression of such self-expression, while not doing injury to the truth, may contribute to psychological harm and provide a non-First Amendment argument for listening to the concerns of children.

In considering the issue of speech to children in the approximation of the truth, the role of third-party adults should be limited. A working model of the truth is fed to the younger child, and the issue is that of who has the right to determine the child's intellectual diet. Mill would have placed that role primarily on the parents, with the state stepping in when parents failed to provide an education.[36] The role of society in providing an education may be far greater now than in Mill's time, but parents still fill the primary role. Parents get to impart their belief system to their children, even if dangerous acts motivated by those beliefs may be limited. The government, through its schools, also cannot help but impart some sorts of beliefs to children. However, parents, when they disagree with those beliefs, have the right to provide alternative education for their children.

Given the primacy of the parental role, supplemented by the school system, there is little to no room to argue that individuals other than the parents have any right to offer their own ideas to children. A musical group or a motion picture production company should have no right to insist that its offerings be directly available to children to help those children eventually see the truth. That argument may hold for adults, but parents should have the right to determine the factors that contribute to the psychological development of their children. They may choose to allow their children to hear the music or see the film at issue, but restrictions on sales or rentals to children should be upheld in support of the parents' rights.

E. Social Control

Thomas Emerson proposed an additional rationale justifying the freedom of expression, suggesting that it serves an important role as an instrument of social control.[37] Society achieves stability through the safety valve of expression. If the state suppresses expression, it "substitutes force for logic." In a country in which dissent is restricted, there will exist an undercurrent of distrust and doubt. Such a society will also be less able to adapt to new situations or generate ideas for its own improvement.

> [S]uppression of expression conceals the real problems confronting a society and diverts public attention from the critical issues. It is likely to result in neglect of the grievances which are the actual basis of the unrest, and thus prevent their correction. For it both hides the extent of the opposition and hardens the position of all sides, thus making a rational compromise difficult or impossible. Further, suppression drives opposition underground, leaving those suppressed either apathetic or desperate.[38]

Moreover, those who have had their positions heard are more likely to accept a contrary decision. Having had a fair hearing, they are more likely to accede to the wishes of the majority.

Emerson recognizes that there may be costs to bear in this full hearing of dissent. There may be delay, the best result may not be obtained and spirited discussion may "tend to loosen the common bonds that hold society together and may threaten to bring about its dissolution,"[39] but it is worth the risk. "Change is inevitable; the only question is the rate and the method. The theory of freedom of expression offers greater possibilities for rational, orderly adjustment than a system of suppression."[40]

It is important to note that this approach applies most forcefully to the expressive side of the freedoms of speech and press. It is the restriction on the ability to present one's thoughts that leads to apathy or revolution. The failure to hear all that might be heard is less likely to be the basis of such feelings. Of course, for adult speech the two are tied together. One who is allowed to speak but not allowed an audience will not feel that he or she has had a full hearing and will be left to means other than expression to obtain change. It is not clear, however, that the same should hold true with regard to children.

Children are regularly frustrated. They have to go to bed, when they want to play, and they can't have ice cream as their only food source. Not getting a full hearing for their ideas is only one such source of frustration. Of course, venting their feelings is less likely to do harm than a lack of adequate rest or an ice cream diet, and that might be a good reason for choosing expression as an area in which to allow greater latitude and decrease overall frustration. On the other hand, part of bringing up children is teaching them what their parents view to be acceptable forms of expression. Learning good manners includes learning when to speak and when not to speak and what to include in the content of that speech. It may be dangerous for the government to limit adult speech in the name of good manners,[41] but parents should be able to so limit their children. The role of the schools in training youth would also provide schools with similar authority to limit the speech of children in schools.[42]

The safety valve Emerson sees for free expression is, for children, present in the attainment of majority itself. The frustration an adult would feel in the inability to express his or her views is in the belief that they will never be heard. Only then do the proponents have to go underground or resort to insurrection. A delay in presenting one's views causes frustration that matches the length of the delay or the necessity of immediate expression to meet an urgent concern. For youth, there is delay rather than complete repression. Once the minor reaches majority, he or she will have the same expression rights as adults. The degree of frustration is likely to be greater for older children, as is the danger of alternative channels for making their positions known. However, as the child gets older, the length of the delay to reaching full expression rights decreases, and that may decrease frustration.

There is, of course, the other dimension to the relationship between children and the First Amendment. It has been the right of adults to speak to children and the right of children to receive information or expression from others that has been the most controversial. But here too, there is less need for a safety valve than there is with adult-to-adult speech. An adult who is shut off from communication to other adults has no opportunity to make his or her position known to those who are participants in the political process. A democratic system cannot take into account the interests of those it fails to hear, so an adult whose message to other adults is limited may feel the need to resort to nonpolitical action. Children are, however, not direct participants in the political process. They have no vote, and the ability of an adult to sway the majority is not cut off by the refusal to allow access to the minds of children.

It is, of course, true that the ability to mold the minds of children can have a strong future political effect. Nonetheless, leaving the task of molding those minds to the children's parents and to the state, through the schools, should not lead to the frustration of concern to Emerson. Adults still have a role in the current political debate, and a part of that debate will be the educational process. If an individual believes that the educational system should be changed, the arguments of that person should be directed toward other adults rather than directly to children.

The only adult who should feel frustrated by such a route is one whose arguments are incapable of winning a majority and who wants to subvert the political process by appealing to less rational youth in hopes of a future triumph.

Finally, there is the issue of a safety valve to stem the frustrations of youth who are not able to gain access to materials they may wish to see or hear. Rebellion in this area is likely to be limited to attempts to get around the regulations limiting such access. Children do try to get into motion pictures rated for an older audience, or try to defeat filters on Internet access—and may well succeed. Indeed, the rating or filter may, for some, serve as an additional attraction. That level of rebellion is not, however, the danger to society that is the concern of the safety valve or social control rationale. The likelihood of a rebellion by youths deprived of the ability to attend "R"-rated films seems remote.

Young children regularly encounter limits and expect their parents and teachers to tell them what is appropriate or acceptable. As children mature, they expect, and should be given, more freedom. They may feel more frustration, but the length of time for which they must endure that frustration decreases as the age and frustration increase. As children approach majority, preparation for full participation in society would be furthered by lessening limitations on the material they may see or hear, but certainly the safety valve concern does not mandate that children have access to all the material they might find interesting.

F. Toleration

Lee Bollinger, in his book *The Tolerant Society*, offers yet another argument for the freedom of expression, an approach that explains current free expression law that includes the protection of extremist speech.[43] While the protection of extremist speech may not be justifiable because of any role it may have as a part of the search for the truth or because it is essential to the democratic process, Bollinger does find positive value in the protection of speech, even when that speech has little or no value.

Bollinger's theory grows out of his observation that people are commonly intolerant of differences they find in other individuals. It is a struggle for many individuals, if not most or all, to tolerate people who act differently, people who hold different views, or those who are different in almost any other way. For Bollinger, it is concern over the tendency toward intolerance that justifies the protection of free expression. Society has developed a position of tolerating even extremist speech, not because of any inherent value in that speech but in hope that the attitude of toleration so developed will carry over to other areas in which there is concern that people might tend toward intolerance.

Toleration is an important quality to develop in children as well as in adults, and speech is an area in which such toleration may be taught. Children were once taught that, while sticks and stones might break their bones, names would never hurt them. Nonetheless, names do hurt. The lesson one really hopes children will learn is that name-calling should not be met with violence. Interestingly, this attempt to teach tolerance in children is in an area recognized as an exception to free speech rights in adults. *Chaplinsky v. New Hampshire*[44] held that fighting words, "those which by their very utterance inflict injury or tend to incite an immediate breach of the peace,"[45] are unprotected because their minimal value is so outweighed by society's interest in maintaining order. Bollinger explains this exception as a recognition that the tolerance function of the First Amendment must sometimes yield to the realities of human nature.[46] The name-calling to which the sticks and stones ditty is supposed to be a response would seem to be such fighting words, given the likelihood of the target responding with violence, and the reality of the nature of children is such that an aggressive response is likely.

While it is important to teach children this sort of toleration, name-calling by children should be met with negative reaction from adults. Our refusal, because of First Amendment concerns, to place limits on marches by neo-Nazis or the Klan need not be matched by a refusal to respond negatively to hate speech from children. Parents and schools should teach children directly that others should not be treated with disrespect due to race, gender, handicap, or any of a number of other reasons beyond their control. Schools should be free to require that children respect others or at least that they not act, physically or verbally, in a manner showing any disrespect they may actually feel.[47] Part of raising children is teaching civility, and civility is the polar opposite of the behavior shown in name-calling toward other children or disrespect toward adults.

Here again, what has been said addresses the less controversial aspects of the relationship between First Amendment rights and children. Few, if any, would argue that parents must tolerate any speech their children may utter. Most would also allow the public schools some latitude in enforcing speech codes that require students to treat other students and teachers with respect. That is not to say that schools should be able to quiet all criticism, but complaints should be voiced with civility. The more controversial aspects of free expression and children is adult expression toward children. Parents are free to communicate with their children, as are the schools, within certain broad limits. But, does Bollinger's toleration justification require that parents and society tolerate other, third-party speakers to have access to children? It would seem not, on two grounds.

First, at least one part of Bollinger's rationale for selecting speech as the area through which to teach toleration is the view that speech does less harm than other activities.[48] That may be true for adults, but for children speech may well be seen to cause greater harm. Children in their formative years may have their psychological development affected in ways that can reasonably be characterized as injuries. While there are good reasons why the state should not interfere with parental communication with their children on the basis of potential negative effects on the children's psychological development, particularly where those effects on a particular child are not certain, there is less reason why the state should allow third-party access to those children. Building tolerance for others does not require that those others be given access to children. Parents and the schools, to the degree that the parents accept public education, should have access not allowed others.

The second argument rests on what toleration of speech is intended to teach. Bollinger's theory is that it teaches us general toleration, the toleration of others as to their characteristics and actions. That is, there are actions by others that deviate from the norm, and by learning to accept speech we may not like from others, we come to tolerate those acts. But, with regard to our children, we don't want to and have no reason to tolerate deviant actions by others. While speech toleration in others may teach toleration of acts generally, the parallel that tolerating speech toward children would teach toleration of other acts toward children, though it may be true, proves nothing. There is no reason to tolerate undesired acts of others toward our children, so there is no toleration-based reason to accept undesired speech directed at our children. Parents and schools, again to the degree accepted by the parents, have the opportunity to provide the atmosphere within which children are raised. They need not tolerate video rental stores' and music sellers' contrary judgments as to what is suitable.

G. The First Amendment and Children

It used to be said that a child should be seen and not heard. In fact, it is important that children be heard, but it is not as important as it is that adults be heard. Children must be heard when they have evidence to offer or to help adults understand their situations and feelings. In such situations, they may be the only ones with access to the experience or evidence involved. The same is, of course, true for adults. The difference between children and adults lies in the areas the First Amendment is thought to further. In those areas, the interests of children are not as great, and society should be able to impose limitations that would be unacceptable interferences with adult communication.

Children are not allowed to participate directly in the political process by electing representatives or voting in referenda. This can only be justified by recognizing that children are not capable of making the rational decisions required. All adults were once children and may remember some frustration in not having their opinions accepted, but almost all come to the position that what they wanted as children may not have constituted the wisest of choices.

If children cannot participate directly in the political process because of a lack of capacity, there is no great loss to society in children not playing a regular active role in the political debate. It is, again, to the good of society that children do become involved before they actually obtain the right to vote. Participating in political discussion will sharpen their political skills and prepare them for active roles. This "spring training" function is an important part of development, but it may be balanced against other factors in that process.

The same lessened importance in hearing the expression of children is also present under the other offered justifications for free expression. Children are not as freely engaged in self-definition as adults. Indeed, not even adults have free rein in self-definition; behaviors that could serve such a role are sometimes restricted. Children need to be taught acceptable and unacceptable behavior. They need to be given the broad outlines of definition for human beings. As adults they can fine-tune that definition, but a foundation is required. The call to accept adults as they are and to allow them the behavioral latitude to define themselves rings hollow when applied to children. Children need to be taught what society expects of them. If society fails in its teaching, it may be left having to accept undesirable self-regarding, self-defining behavior, but it need not give up the effort to raise its children to behave in an appropriate manner. If speech has its value as a part of that self-definition, society can also regulate the speech of children in its effort to teach them societal values. If society fails, it may have to live with adult speech it views as improper, but again that does not mean that children must be given the same self-definition protection as adults.

Similarly, the contribution of children to the attainment of truth in the marketplace of ideas lacks the significance of that of adults. While a child might, theoretically, have some unique and important contribution to make to that marketplace, the likelihood of having such insight and of being the best spokesperson for that view is minimal, at least where the issue is not one of facts to which the child has best access. Again, as children approach majority, they may make greater contributions, but the contributions of younger children are not sufficiently important to require that children have the same rights as adults.

Children need not be given free-expression rights to avoid revolution. The social control rationale for protecting adult speech is lacking. Children will rebel. It seems to be a part of the teenage role to reject adult values and rules. But the frustration over speech issues would seem no greater than the frustration over other limits on behavior. Children live with a variety of restrictions, and speech restrictions may be included. There may be less reason to include speech, since less direct harm is involved, but restrictions deemed necessary as a part of raising civil children are acceptable.

Finally, the toleration rationale does not really apply to speech by children. The toleration role is aimed toward increasing toleration for differences in individual characteristics and behavior. Toleration of speech may be an important step toward toleration of adult behavior. But it is not a social goal to tolerate undesired child behavior. It is instead a duty of society to teach proper behavior. A belief that it is not proper to limit speech in children may carry over to a belief that society need not fill that behavioral role either.

Again, however, the real issue in the most controversial cases is not the speech offered by children but the speech offered to children. Here too, none of the rationales for adult free expression apply. Protection of political speech requires not only that the speaker have freedom to offer his or her ideas but that others have the right to hear those ideas. Only then can the one vote of the speaker become a majority position in the democratic process. But children do not have the right to vote; they are not direct participants in democracy. The one vote of the speaker does not become a majority position, at least in the short term, by having children as an audience. It may have long-term effects, if children internalize the positions heard, but this should not lead to open season on the minds of children. Adults who want change in society should offer rational arguments that convince other adults, not statements that rely on a nonrational attraction to children that carries over to their adult lives. While society may have the advantage in teaching values in the child's formative years, the debate over what society, as opposed to the parent, should teach is open to political debate. Those who want a change in the values children learn should, when the issue is children other than their own, engage in that political debate rather than claim a right to espouse those values directly to the children of others.

Similarly, the marketplace-of-ideas rationale is best viewed as an adult market. The test of an idea found in the power of the idea to gain acceptance in the marketplace requires the free-market decisions of rational adults. Offering the idea to children too young to make such rational decisions does nothing to test the rational power of the idea but only its superficial attraction. Allowing attempts to convert children to a particular position, before they are capable of consumer wariness, is to allow a subversion of the marketplace rather than protecting the free market in ideas.

The protection of expression as a part of protecting self-definition also has no application when applied to speech toward children. Whatever autonomy rights may exist with regard to behavior do not protect the actions of adults toward other people's children. Self-definition, unlike parenthood, simply provides no warrant to intervene in the lives of children. Nor do children have self-definition rights that would allow them to obtain expression offered by others and not acceptable to their parents. During their minority, they must live with their parents' rules, and those rules may include limitations on the films they see and the music they hear. Other adults have no right to subvert those rules by insisting on providing the objectionable material. Where these third parties attempt to expose children to material that is sufficiently contrary to societal views as to what is acceptable, society should be able to impose legal restrictions.

Neither does the free-expression role in maintaining social control or a safety valve carry over from speech to adults to speech to children. Where people have complaints about society, they should voice these complaints to those who can do something about them. They must be free to complain to the government. They must also be allowed to offer their concerns to other adults to have the opportunity to change the conditions they find objectionable. The only safety valve application to children would seem to invoke a right to reach future voters before they develop their full capacities. Rather than being a way around revolution, this appeal at least to younger minors could be viewed as a form of revolution. It is the attempt to change government or society by other than rational argument. While the social control rationale is based in part on not driving dissent underground, directing dissenting speech at children is itself such an underground tactic.

The same differences between adult and youth speech are present under the toleration rationale. Society need not tolerate the objectionable speech of others to children. While parents may have wide latitude in what they present to their own children, either with regard to their own speech or the expression in videos or recorded music they make available to children, the producers and distributors of these videos and CDs need not be tolerated, as they make their own decisions on what to make available to youth. Society is not a better place if we learn to tolerate the undesired behavior of others toward our children, so there is no reason to tolerate undesired speech as a road to that toleration of behavior.

The rights of adults to offer their expression to children depends on who those adults are. Parents have great discretion in the upbringing of their children. The Supreme Court has recognized the parents' right to select the schools and education their children attend and receive.[49] That right would seem to include making decisions on the expression parents make available to their children. Any formal societal limitations in that regard should be suspect. Parental limitations should be available only to the degree that the expression they offer their children is abusive or otherwise presents a certain and significant danger to the child or others.

Limitations on the schools may be somewhat stronger. Where there is conflict between the schools and parents as to what is appropriate, parents may seek other educational opportunities. Schools might also be required to offer some options to avoid specific topics or views. Formal civil sanctions should also sometimes be available. While parents are free to speak positively of one political party and negatively of the other(s), the same practice by schools would be unacceptable and could be legally enjoined. Public schools are also clearly limited on the religious speech they may deliver to students.

Those who stand in neither relationship to children have no right of access to children. Their political rights are limited to addressing other participants in the process. Their marketplace rights are limited to offering their visions of truth or good to those mature enough to evaluate rationally their offerings. Their self-definition rights include no right to affect the lives of other people's children, and their expression need not be tolerated under either a safety valve or toleration approach. Statutes that help parents enforce their decisions on the third-party expression to which their children will be exposed should be constitutional. There is simply no reason, among those offered as justifications for the First Amendment's freedoms of expression, to allow a video rental store or music distributor to make directly available to children material that their parents and society both find objectionable.

It is true that any statutes, particularly if they are to impose criminal liability, must be clear as to what may and may not be distributed to children. Distributors of media products must be given fair warning, and courts should continue to strike down statutes that are unacceptably vague. On the other hand, the chilling-effect concerns that surround limitations on distribution to adults—that is, the concern that individuals will choose not to make available expression that is actually protected because of fear of prosecution—are less important in statutes that limit only expression made available to children. If a distributor, in an excess of concern, decides not to make a particular video available to children, parents can still rent or purchase the video and allow their children to view it. Expression is not completely cut off. The distributor simply decides to let the parents make the decision, and that ought to be the parents' role.

2

The Costs of Free Expression

Free speech, despite the essential role it serves in a politically free society, does have its costs. For the most part, those costs are worth bearing. But, before concluding that they are always worth bearing, it is important to examine the evils that may be seen to flow from expression. With an appreciation of the issue, it may be more likely that a reasonable balance, particularly with regard to free expression and youth, may be drawn.

Some First Amendment absolutists would contend that no one has ever been harmed by a bad book or film. If that were the case, it would logically seem to follow that no one has ever been improved by reading a good book or viewing a good film. If we are not so affected, then sermons, inspirational or patriotic speeches and the entire advertising industry are a wasted effort. The books we read and the films and television we watch do influence us. Of course, they are not the totality of our influences. They act against a cultural background of values and relationships. Violent media in one culture may have little to no effect on actual violence. In another, with greater alienation and a breakdown in community or with more access to weapons, such an effect may exist. Expression is not the sole cause of any societal problems, but it may be seen to contribute in a number of areas.

A. *Images of Violence*

Perhaps the greatest concern over effects of expression in recent times has been the exposure of youth to depictions of violence. In 1986, the Task Force on Television and Society of the American Psychological Association presented amazing conclusions on children's exposure to televised violence. The task force concluded that, by the time the average child finishes elementary school, the child has seen more than eight thousand murders and more than 100,000 other acts of violence.[1] Children who view television more than the average may have viewed up to 200,000 acts of violence before they become teenagers.[2] Even these statistics don't measure the true degree of childhood exposure to media violence, since the estimates were based only on depictions of violence on broadcast television. Cable programming, which is often more violent, films, videotapes and video games were not included but make up an increasing proportion of media use by both adults and children.

This exposure of children to violence as entertainment raises the question of possible psychological effects. Does media violence lead to aggression and real-world violence? Forty years of study in the passive media—television and film—indicate a positive response.[3] There has not been the opportunity for such long-term study of the more active developing medium of violent video games, but the greater player involvement in the game and the skills taught make reasonable the conclusion that the results will carry over with equal, if not greater, strength.

1. The Passive Media

Laboratory studies—observations in a controlled environment—comprised most of the early research on the effects of media violence. The classic Bobo doll study, by a group led by Albert Bandura, involved a group of nursery school children and demonstrated imitative aggressive behavior.[4] Similar results were obtained in a series of studies led by Leonard Berkowitz, who looked at the behavior of male university students and, in particular, looked at the effect of meaning or context of the violent depictions.[5] Subjects seeing a film with "aggressive meaning" were themselves significantly more aggressive in a situation after the viewing. The study also concluded that observing aggression especially leads to aggression against those whom the actor sees as similar to the observed victim. The laboratory studies are reinforced by field studies, involving real-world settings, that lead to the same conclusion.

Still more backing comes from correlational studies—also real-world studies but in this case of broader populations in search of relations between demographic variables. An example is provided in a study by Brandon Centerwall, who found a relationship between the increase in access to television and a rise in the homicide rate ten to fifteen years later.[6] Another example is provided by a longitudinal study by Lefkowitz, Eron, Walder and Huesmann of children as they progressed from third grade through the year after high school; it found a correlation between consumption of violent media and aggressiveness, particularly later-developing aggressiveness.[7]

While any of these studies may be criticized,[8] together they form a strong basis for the claim that media violence causes violence in the real world. Six major professional organizations in the health field, after examining the science, have so concluded. In a July 2000 joint statement, the American Psychological Association, the American Academy of Pediatrics, the American Academy of Child and Adolescent Psychiatry, the American Medical Association, the American Academy of Family Physicians and the American Psychiatric Association concluded "well over 1,000 studies . . . point overwhelmingly to a causal connection between media violence and aggressive behavior in some children."[9] The American Academy of Pediatrics had already said, in an earlier policy statement, that "[t]he vast majority of studies conclude that there is a cause-and-effect relationship between media violence and real-life violence."[10] It called the link "undeniable and uncontestable."[11] A representative of the same pediatrics group, also in 2000, testified before the United States Senate Commerce Committee that there are now more than 3,500 studies examining the relationship between media and real-world violence and that "[a]ll but 18 have shown a positive correlation between media exposure and violent behavior" and that epidemiological studies conclude that "exposure to violent media was a factor in half of the 10,000 homicides committed in the United States in the [year studied]."[12]

The view of the scientific community seems to be that the debate is over and that it is clear that there is a connection between media violence and aggression in the real world. The Surgeon General's report *Youth Violence*, while noting that ethical considerations bar the use of the sort of randomized studies that are best used to determine causation, nonetheless concluded that "a diverse body of research provides strong evidence that exposure to violence in the media can increase children's aggressive behavior in the short term."[13] While less secure in concluding that there is a causal connection to violence in the long term, the report does find a "small but statistically significant impact on aggression over many years."[14]

Given the evidence on the causal effects of media violence, the disjoint between science and what seems to be the perception of at least a portion of the public that there is no causation is puzzling. On the other hand, it is not surprising that the media continue to deny any causation. Media executives will, as with tobacco executives and lung cancer, be the last to accept such a connection. The difference between the effectiveness of the denials on the part of these two industries may be that the media industry also controls the outlets through which the public gains the information necessary to form its views. A recent study, published in the American Psychological Association's journal *American Psychologist*, finds a "disheartening" discrepancy between the scientific results and media reporting.[15] "As it became clearer to the scientific community that media violence effects were real and significant, the news media reports actually got weaker."[16]

2. Video Games—Teaching Kids to Kill

Lt. Col. Dave Grossman, who formerly taught psychology at the United States Military Academy, draws chilling conclusions from an analogy between military training and the conditioning and training that media violence and video games provide our youth.[17] Grossman notes that in World War II only a small minority of American riflemen—15 to 20 percent—were willing to fire their weapons at the enemy. The military found this rate unacceptable and took steps to change training and increase the firing rate. By the Korean War, the firing rate had increased to 55 percent, and with refinements in training the rate increased to between 90 and 95 percent for the Vietnam War.[18]

The greatest improvement in training has been the use of computer simulations. Trainees using computers "learn how to shoot, where to shoot, how to maneuver through possibly deadly combat situations, how to tell enemy from friend, and, most important, how to kill. The entire event of killing in combat can be simulated by a computer."[19] These computer simulations employed by the military are very similar to the video games available to our society's children.[20] And apparently these video games provide equivalent training in how to kill. Grossman and his coauthor Gloria DeGaetano examined the killings by fourteen-year-old Michael Carneal at a school in Paducah, Kentucky:

> [He] never moved his feet during his rampage. He never fired far to the right or left, never far up or down. He simply fired once at everything that popped up on his "screen." It is not natural to fire once at each target. The normal, almost universal, response is to fire at a target until it drops and then move on to the next target. This is the defensive reaction

that will save our lives . . . [n]ot to shoot once and then go on to another target before the first threat has been eliminated. But most video games teach you to fire at each target only once, hitting as many targets as you can as fast as you can. . . . And many video games give bonus effects . . . for head shots. It's awful to note that of Michael Carneal's eight shots he had eight hits, all head and upper torso. . . . And this is from a kid who, prior to stealing that gun, had never shot a real handgun in his life![21]

Video games appear to supply the skill necessary to be an efficient killer.

Video games also seem to be a part of overcoming the reluctance to kill. The military use of simulators helps to develop a conditioned response in which the soldier fires when faced by a particular set of circumstances. That response is reinforced by rewards for high scores, the dropping of the target, marksmanship badges and other rewards, ranging from praise to three-day passes.[22] Dropping targets and attaining high scores reinforce the efficient performance of children on the civilian equivalent simulators.

A further requirement in developing the willingness to kill is the desensitization of the shooter to the harm being caused. Training with human-shaped targets may help the soldier think of opponents in combat as targets rather than as people, making it easier to kill. Indeed, it seems common, in descriptions of those fired upon, to refer to "targets" rather than "persons." On the civilian side, our youth, at the same impressionable age or a younger age than that at which soldiers are trained, also become desensitized by both video games and the violent passive media.

Grossman's concerns are beginning to be borne out by scientific studies, although research on the effects of violent video games has not developed to match that on the effects of film or television. Video games, particularly violent, first-person shooter games in a realistic graphics environment, are too new a medium to have led to the extensive research available on the older media. Such research has, however, begun. Craig Anderson and Karen Dill recently published the first scientific comparison of the aggressiveness-producing effects of violent and nonviolent video games,[23] with results similar to studies comparing violent and nonviolent television or film. Their effort consisted of both a correlational/demographic variable study and a laboratory experiment.

Anderson and Dill conclude that the combination of correlational and laboratory results support the causal claim. "The convergence of findings across such disparate methods lends considerable strength to the main hypothesis that exposure to violent video games can increase aggressive behavior."[24] They also believe violent video games to be of more concern than violent television or films because of the identification with the game aggressor that players experience and the active participation in the virtual violence of the game. "In a sense, violent video games provide a complete learning environment for aggression, with simultaneous exposure to modeling, reinforcement, and rehearsal of behaviors. This combination of learning strategies has been shown to be more powerful than any of those methods used singly."[25]

Anderson, with Brad Bushman, more recently published a meta-analysis of the current, developing research on the effects of violent video games.[26] They identified thirty-five research reports, most of them experimental, laboratory studies but including some field studies. Longitudinal studies were lacking, but that is unsurprising given the recent genesis of a specific interest in violent video games. The authors concluded from the meta-analysis that "[v]iolent video games increased aggression in males and females, in children and adults, and in experimental and nonexperimental settings."[27] The experimental studies showed that "short term exposure to violent video games *causes* at least a temporary increase in aggression,"[28] while the nonexperimental studies demonstrate that "exposure to violent video games is correlated with aggression in the real world."[29] The study also showed that violent video games cause a decrease in prosocial behavior and are correlated to an unwillingness to help others in the real world, cause aggressive thoughts and increase aggressive feelings.[30]

3. Defending the Social Science

Those who would deny the causative relationship between media violence and violence in the real world can always fall back on the claim that all the scientific evidence shows is correlation rather than causation. While that may seem like a reasonable argument, it does not really weaken the scientific conclusion. As empiricists since David Hume note, one never observes causation but only a form of correlation that Hume called constant conjunction.[31] Because of the constancy of that conjunction, the perfect correlation, one may be more secure in drawing the causal conclusion, but there is a jump from observation to conclusion. The similar jump may be less justified when the conjunction is not constant, but it is one science makes with regularity. The correlations between smoking and lung cancer, between unprotected sex and AIDS, and between low calcium intake and osteoporosis are all imperfect. That is, not everyone who smokes gets lung cancer and some who get lung cancer did not smoke, and the same is true for the other relations involving AIDS and osteoporosis. Yet, those relations are seen confidently as causal.

The failure to accept the correlation as causation in the case of media violence can't be explained by the degree of correlation. The correlation between media violence and aggression is stronger than that of failure to use a condom and HIV, secondhand smoke and lung cancer, lead exposure in children and lower IQs, use of the nicotine patch and smoking cessation, calcium intake and bone mass, homework and academic achievement, asbestos exposure and cancer of the larynx and self-examination and early detection of breast cancer.[32] While the correlation between smoking and lung cancer is more significant than that between media violence and aggression, the acceptance of all these lesser correlations as indicating causation leads to the conclusion that the correlation in the case of the media ought also to be considered sufficient to allow society to proceed on the assumption that there is causation.

A further objection regarding causation has to do with the mechanism involved. There may be a greater willingness to conclude that there is causation in the case of secondhand smoke or lack of condom use because the mechanism bringing about the result is more easily understood. The brain is, to most if not all of us, mysterious. But so is the rest of science, if the analysis is sufficiently deep. It is clear to all that gravity causes objects to fall to the earth, but try explaining, even to yourself, why it is that objects with mass attract each other. Those of us who have experienced even mild visceral effects from viewing violence would have a better understanding of how such exposure might lead some to have a sufficiently strong response to lead them to violence, or to experience a sufficiently long lasting effect to make them more aggressive in the future.

Finally, those who would deny the science may resort to the claim that media violence has a cathartic effect, that it may serve a therapeutic role and reduce real-world violence. Marjorie Heins makes this point, arguing that social science has not disproved catharsis. She writes: "Rarely do the debaters note that the same work may induce imitation in some viewers and catharsis in others—or that the same person may respond differently to different violent or sexual content."[33] She may well be correct. In an experiment, some in the group that saw the violent film or played the violent game may be less aggressive as a result. The laboratory experiments measure effects on sample populations, and some individuals may have become less aggressive while others have become more aggressive. What the science does show is that, overall, there is an increase in aggression, so it would appear that a society with less violence in its media would experience less violence in total, even if some individuals become more violent.

While the science would seem to disprove the overall benefit of catharsis, the claim has a long pedigree. It comes from Aristotle's argument that viewing tragedy, including violence, could lead the viewer to identify with the victim, feel pity and purge negative emotions.[34] Sissela Bok has, however, explained why the catharsis theory, even if valid for Greek tragedies, is not relevant to much of what appears in modern violent media. While she accepts that there are films and television that "arouse both fear and pity in ways that can have transformative effects on viewers," where the predominant reaction to a depiction is thrill rather than pity, there is no cathartic effect.[35] She also argues that, for Aristotle, catharsis was "only for adults mature enough to derive the fullest benefit from such an experience."[36] Even accepting catharsis, then, it would seem that the view only reinforces the thesis of this work. If media violence serves a positive, cathartic role for adults and not for children, that is all the more reason to accept differing First Amendment protection for the two groups.

B. Obscenity and Pornography

Some objections to obscenity, or to less explicit or offensive pornography, are based on considerations of morality. In the case of obscenity, that may be enough to justify the exception to the First Amendment that leaves such material unprotected, although there are certainly arguments to the contrary.[37] Moral costs are, however, more difficult to measure than the costs discussed for violent material. Indeed, there would be disagreement as to what is to count as a moral cost, as well as whether the morality of other adults should be the subject of legal prohibitions. There may, however, be other costs to society that are more objective.

There are those who argue that pornography causes violence against women. Catharine MacKinnon, using a definition of pornography that speaks not purely in terms of erotic content but combines eroticism with treatment of women in a degrading manner, takes such a position.[38] In particular, she notes that, when explicit sex is combined with violence, the evidence shows that violence against women increases.[39]

MacKinnon also argues that pornography is a form of discrimination against women and that it is behind the discrimination women face in the workplace and elsewhere. It is both a symptom of sexual inequality and patriarchy and a cause of both. MacKinnon sees the effect as so pervasive that it defines reality. "[Pornography] institutionalizes the sexuality of male supremacy, fusing the erotization of dominance and submission with the social construction of male and female. . . . Men treat women as who they see women as being. Pornography constructs who that is."[40] Pornography is, in this view, a civil rights issue, one that affects all aspects of women's lives by causing and perpetuating discrimination, trivializing women's contributions, and encouraging sexual harassment. While the argument is limited to images that degrade and dehumanize women, material that depicts women as objects to be sexually exploited or in "postures or positions of servility, or submission or *display*"[41] is included as pornographic, so it is less than clear how far the approach extends.

There are feminists who disagree with MacKinnon's stand against pornography. ACLU president Nadine Strossen argues that pornography should be protected, and her argument is not based solely on her strong commitment to the First Amendment. She argues that feminism itself should oppose the suppression of pornography because censorship would affect material that is important to women, particularly to feminists and lesbians, and would perpetuate stereotypical views of women as victims for whom sex is a harm, limiting the ability of women to develop their own sexuality and strengthening patriarchy.[42]

While Strossen sees enough value in pornography to be willing to bear the costs,[43] the purported costs can also be questioned. Certainly not all sexual relations involve the objectivization of either or both partners, and that would seem to hold true even if a couple used pornography as a part of that relationship. While the images on a screen may be seen as objects, that does not mean that the partners are objects to each other. The images are in fact objects, in this case light or electronic effects, even though what is depicted are real people. That does not necessarily lead to a confusion between those objects and the real sexual partner. It is knowing one's partner as a person that keeps one from objectivizing that person. The more one cares for another, the less one is likely to see that person as a sexual object rather than as a sexual partner.

Turning to the more general use of pornography, the same relationship would seem likely to hold. Just as knowing an individual woman makes it less likely that one would treat her as an object, knowing women in general makes it less likely that one will treat women generally as objects. That is to say that the more one knows women as persons, the less likely it would seem that images of women involved in sexual activities would lead to a one-dimensional view of women as sexual objects and to the discrimination MacKinnon sees as flowing from that view.

If that is so, then the concern should be with those who use pornography but have not had any significant relations with members of the opposite sex. While there are certainly adults who fall into this class, minors are more likely to be included. If there is an objectivizing effect, it is less likely to occur in adult males than among boys whose only relationship with females is their unreal experiences with objective images. The argument that pornography leads to discrimination would seem then of far more concern when minors are exposed to such material. The costs of adult exposure would seem far less significant.

There is another potential cost to sexual depictions, including those that might not even be strong enough to be considered pornographic, and that cost too falls more heavily on the young. The cultivation hypothesis, the theory that heavier media consumers' views of the world are constructed through that experience, has application to sex content in the media. The authors of a study on media exposure and perceptions of sexuality came to the conclusion that "[h]igh exposure to televised portrayals of sexual behavior tended to be associated with increased perceptions of frequencies of those behaviors in the real world."[44] The authors recognize that those heavier media users who perceive higher rates of sexual activity in the real world may have a more accurate worldview than those low-incidence users who perceive lesser rates of activity.[45] The relationship, however accurate it may be, does exist, and adolescents whose sexual activities are less than the level portrayed may feel deprived. Furthermore, an "everybody is doing it" attitude may well counter the abstinence messages presented children by parents, schools and churches. At any rate, "[a] case can be made . . . that consumption of sexually oriented media probably has some influence on sexual permissiveness in some individuals."[46] Furthermore, adolescents themselves report that the media play a major role in sexual education,[47] so any media emphasis on casual sex and media failure to concern itself with safe sexual practices would also appear likely to have a negative impact.

C. Advertising, Media Image and Substance Abuse

The use of alcohol, tobacco and controlled substances among American youth are at unacceptably high levels. A study published in 2001 showed that 80 percent of high school seniors, 71 percent of tenth-graders and 52 percent of eighth-graders have experimented with alcohol.[48] Even more troubling, when students were asked about their activities in the previous two weeks, binge drinking, the consumption of five or more drinks, was reported by 30 percent of high school seniors, 26 percent of sophomores and even by 14 percent of eighth-graders.[49] Tobacco use has also grown within the high school population; more than one-third currently smoke and two-thirds have tried smoking.[50] The use of illicit drugs is also of concern. The need for middle school programs such as D.A.R.E. and television ad campaigns to induce parents to talk with their sixth-graders about drugs point to concern with drug experimentation by younger and younger children.

Commercial advertisements for the products involved are an obvious target for those upset with these youth consumption patterns. Cigarette ads employing cartoon camels and beer ads involving animated frogs would seem to be attractive to minors. While the industries involved participate in programs promoting responsible use and the prevention of illegal distribution to minors, they are interested in the market share they will enjoy when age cohorts reach the legal ages for the products they manufacture. Ads that appeal to youth can have that future legal effect, but it would seem that they would also have a parallel potential for inducing illegal use by those who are still too young. Advertising has been limited in fora aimed specifically at youth, but the general presence of such ads cannot help but have some spillover effect on the environment of children.

Advertising, referred to in First Amendment law as commercial speech, does enjoy constitutional protection, although at a lesser level than other varieties of speech.[51] Thus, this would appear to be one of the more addressable concerns growing out of free expression. Advertising is not, however, the only free-expression-based genesis of the problem. If it were, the use of illegal drugs would not have any free-expression roots, since such substances are not advertised. Illicit drugs, as with alcohol and tobacco, are portrayed in the entertainment media in ways that might lead to use by minors, and those portrayals enjoy the stronger protections of noncommercial speech. While there is not as much specific research on the effect that media consumption of alcohol, tobacco and illegal drugs has on actual consumption by minors as there is for the effects of violence, the research on violence makes it likely that there would be such an effect. The studies that do exist indicate that television viewing generally is a risk factor in adolescent alcohol use.[52]

Mediascope, a media research and policy organization, recently published studies examining the frequency and nature of substance use in the top-rated, prime-time programming for the fall 1998 television season and in the two hundred most popular rental videos for the period of 1996–97, and one thousand songs drawn from the most popular listings of various music categories.[53] The television study found tobacco use in 19 percent of the episodes and alcohol use in 71 percent.[54] The percentages were higher in motion pictures, with tobacco appearing in 89 percent and alcohol in 93 percent.[55] While both tobacco and alcohol use were more prevalent in films rated for older audiences, their presence was significant at all levels, with tobacco use at 79 percent in G or PG movies, 82 percent in PG-13 movies and 92 percent in R-rated films, while alcohol appeared in 76 percent of G or PG, 97 percent of PG-13 and 94 percent of R-rated films.[56] The same increase is found as TV rating ages increase, with tobacco use increasing from 6 to 20 to 24 percent as the ratings move from TVG to TVPG to TV14, and alcohol increasing from 38 to 77 to 84 percent for the same ratings levels.[57]

The studies also examined the nature of the portrayals. In the television episodes that portrayed alcohol use, drinking was commonly shown in humorous contexts, accounting for 45 percent of such use.[58] Overall, the television episodes containing alcohol use depicted alcohol use as a positive experience 40 percent of the time and as promoting relaxation or good times 29 percent of the time.[59] Only 10 percent of the alcohol-use episodes made alcohol use appear as a negative experience.[60] In the film study, alcohol use was associated with parties in 49 percent, humor in 24 percent, wealth in 34 percent, and sexual activity in 19 percent of the sample, while tobacco use was less likely to be associated with these activities or properties.[61] On the other hand, negative contexts for both alcohol and tobacco were depicted, with alcohol associated with crime or violence 38 percent of the time and tobacco so associated in 34 percent of the films portraying tobacco use.[62]

Certainly, media portrayal of substance use is not the sole cause of substance use by minors. Peer pressure and parental use and attitude also influence minors' attitudes toward substance use. Nonetheless, generations of young people imitating everything from 1950s movie stars carrying cigarettes in a rolled tee shirt sleeve to the hairstyles of music, film and television favorites show that the media influence the social choices minors make. When television and film frequently depict tobacco and alcohol use, and particularly if they do so in a positive way, imitative behavior is likely. These depictions are positive; even in film use by minors, there were few depictions of consequences of substance use.[63] While most depictions were of adult use, minors often want to act the way they see adults act, particularly popular or wealthy ones, and may well imitate the substance use they see.

While at least older adults, who presumably are no longer as deeply involved in searching for their own identities as minors and young adults are, might be less influenced by television and motion picture depictions of substance use, the advertising concerns discussed earlier turn out to be not only addressed to effects on minors. A recent series of "Policy Forum" advertisements have addressed the issue of advertising prescription drugs. One entry in the series questioned ads for the drug Viagra.[64] While recognizing the value of the product for addressing impotence in people with serious impairments, such as those with advanced diabetes or who are paraplegic, the drug is promoted for use by those with "erectile dysfunction." The author finds no use or definition of that term in medical textbooks, and suggests that it appears to be defined as dissatisfaction by either partner with sexual intercourse. The implication is that the advertising of the drug leads to its use to enhance sexual intercourse, rather than to cure impotence.

While the author's interests might be questioned, since he is senior vice president of the Blue Cross and Blue Shield Association and as such concerned with insurance and the costs of prescription drugs, he does raise interesting concerns. The pharmaceutical industry sees a need to educate the consumer as to the availability of alternatives to treat medical conditions they may have. Taking a more active role in one's own health care would seem to be a wise course, and these ads can help in that active role. The ads can also, however, lead to requests for prescriptions that are inappropriate and perhaps dangerous.

The author uses fen-phen as an example. While not advertised for weight loss, the combination gained a popular reputation as a diet combination. The combination could help if there was a medical need to lose weight, but it was requested by those with a cosmetic desire for weight loss, even if there was no medical need. Patient pressure on physicians led to overuse. "Patients demanded it. We physicians often prescribed it."[65] Fen-phen turned out to have dangerous side effects on the valves in the heart. If only those who needed the drug had used it, fewer would have been affected, and even for those affected, the risk may have been less than the risk associated with the weight that had been lost. When used by those who did not need the drug but still wanted it, more people faced the heart risks and did so without a reduction in other risks.

This nonadvertised case may not seem relevant to drug ads, but it is. If this inappropriate use occurred with no commercial impetus, the pressure produced by an advertising campaign can only be greater. A television ad extolling the virtues of a drug, even if it contains a line saying that your physician will want to conduct liver tests because of possible side effects, or a magazine ad that is followed with a page of information too small to read regarding side effects or contraindications, will produce demand. People who might have controlled their cholesterol through diet and exercise may instead demand a pharmaceutical. They will then face unnecessary risks that might have been acceptable for those whose conditions were addressable only through pharmaceuticals.

While there may be costs to the degree of First Amendment protection afforded commercial speech, the benefits of such speech, at least for adult consumers, makes the protection worth keeping. There are limitations on commercial speech that address concerns over the potential of such speech to mislead. In particular, in the drug ads that have been the focus of most of the concern over advertising to adults, the Food and Drug Administration requires disclosures to accompany the advertising. While the disclosures may be seen as inadequate, at least adults are put on notice that they should seek further information. Our assumption of adult competence to make individual decisions demands access to accurate expression that would inform that decision.

Here, too, the decision for children can be different. We do not take as an article of faith the ability of children to make such competent decisions. There may be situations in which commercial speech makes products such as tobacco and alcohol seem sufficiently attractive and in which children are unable to appreciate the physical costs of such product use. While adult decisions on this balance are accepted as an exercise of autonomy, we are not as neutral on the decisions of children. As a part of the effort to prevent children from using such products, children should be shielded from such commercial speech.

D. The Coarsening of Society

Society seems to lack the decorum and politeness it had in the not too distant past. Some may view the past as having been overly restrictive and the new laxity as a good thing. Others find the coarseness of our current society an unpleasant change. Certainly, language that was simply not used in public, or at least in mixed company, in the past is now commonly heard. It is a change to which a date can reasonably be assigned. The date is 1971, and the significance of that year is that it was the year in which the Supreme Court handed down its opinion in *Cohen v. California.*[66]

Cohen grew out the conviction of an individual under a California Penal Code provision prohibiting maliciously and willfully disturbing the peace by offensive conduct. Cohen had worn a jacket bearing the words "Fuck the Draft" in a corridor of the Los Angeles County Courthouse. For this expression, which was intended to convey his feelings against the Vietnam War and the draft, he was sentenced to thirty days' imprisonment. The conviction was based solely on the jacket and there was no indication of any disturbing noise or other unlawful act. The Supreme Court overturned the conviction, saying that "while the particular four-letter word being litigated here is perhaps more distasteful than most others of its genre, it is nevertheless often true that one man's vulgarity is another's lyric."[67] With the *Cohen* decision, language that had been unacceptable and even subject to criminal sanction became constitutionally protected. Furthermore, it was not the private use of such language that gained protection but the public use of words that many, certainly at that time if not at present, would find offensive and unsettling.

The effect of *Cohen* has gone beyond the protection of profanity in the expression of political dissent. Words that were, prior to *Cohen*, seldom heard in public now seem to be the most frequent words in the speech of many. While the broadcast media have not gone as far in the use of offensive speech, the general use of offensive or suggestive speech has led the way to greater latitude in the media as well. It might be thought that *Cohen* would have little or no effect on the broadcast media. After all, Cohen's expletive was one of the seven "filthy words" used in the George Carlin routine in *Federal Communications Commission v. Pacifica Foundation.*[68] That 1978 case held that the FCC could require that the broadcast media channel indecent material into hours when children are less likely to be in the audience. *Cohen* is then limited in the context of the broadcast media, and the use of various words, including Cohen's, must be limited to late-night hours. Furthermore, it is not only Carlin's words that must be channeled but any material, at least any sexual material, that doesn't meet societal standards for morality. As society generally is forced to tolerate profanity, the standards for what is acceptable change, and the media can, under the revised standards, say things that may formerly not have been acceptable. The current use of sexual innuendo or outright sexually suggestive speech may be seen to flow from *Cohen*'s change in the law.

Of course, with the media, the consumer has some choice in programming, even if one easily offended may be left with little to watch. Exposure to offensive terms in public places has become common. Individuals, including children, cannot avoid profanity except by remaining at home. Walking on the street, attending a football game or sitting in a public park, both adults and children are regularly exposed to language many find offensive. The Court in *Pacifica* noted that indecency in the broadcast media reaches children too young to read the offending words. Words said in public, as opposed to the written word on Cohen's jacket, also reach children too young to read, and having to stay at home to avoid such offensive language is a price attributable to free expression, even if it is believed to be a cost worth bearing.

Certainly not all the loss of civility in society can be laid at the doorstep of *Cohen*. The case was decided in an era in which there was a general rejection of the mores of the older generation, and changes in speech patterns may better be seen as a part of that more general change. The fact that *Cohen* protected profanity would not have led to its widespread use without an accompanying change in social mores. Nonetheless, even if the greater acceptance of profane language grew out of a more general change in our culture, *Cohen* gave sanction to that change in mores and cannot be completely detached from the coarsening of society.

E. Hate Speech

Hate speech, whether directed at individuals because of their race, ethnicity, gender or sexual orientation, also has costs.[69] Richard Delgado writes that "[r]acist speech damages the dignity, pecuniary prospects, and psyches of its victims (particularly children), while it impedes the ability of colleges to diversify their student bodies. When severe or protracted, it can even cause physical sickness, including high blood pressure, tremors, sleep disturbance, and early death."[70] Mari Matsuda finds similar costs.

> Victims of vicious hate propaganda have experienced physiological symptoms and emotional distress ranging from fear in the gut, rapid pulse rate and difficulty in breathing, nightmares, post-traumatic stress disorder, hypertension, psychosis, and suicide. . . . In order to avoid receiving hate messages, victims have had to quit jobs, forgo education, leave their homes, avoid certain public places, curtail their own exercise of speech rights, and otherwise modify their behavior and demeanor. The recipient of hate messages struggles with inner turmoil. One subconscious response is to reject one's own identity as a victim-group member. . . . [T]he price of disassociating from one's own race is often sanity itself.[71]

Delgado argues that the First Amendment should not stand in the way of governmental attempts to provide relief from or remedies for hate speech.[72] He argues that the danger against which the First Amendment is intended to shield society is the suppression of the weak, the voiceless dissident. The government should not be allowed to use its considerable power to protect itself from criticism. But that is not what happens with proscriptions against hate speech. Instead, the government acts on behalf of a disempowered group to protect that group from more powerful tormentors. The government is not preserving its own power; it is giving strength to the voice of a minority.

Hate speech might seem to differ from many of the other costs of free expression in the mode of delivery. Much hate speech is the product of individuals, often anonymous or even hooded. The media seem less involved. There are complaints over the lack of representation of minorities on television network programming and sometimes over stereotyping of minority roles, but the major media do not provide the sort of hate speech that would be the electronic equivalent of a cross burning or of painting a swastika on a temple. The media are, however, not wholly uninvolved.

The Anti-Defamation League has identified a record label, Resistance Records, as "a thinly disguised mouthpiece for the most dangerous organized hate group in America," the National Alliance.[73] The National Alliance is a group organized by William Pierce, the author of *The Turner Diaries*, a book describing an attack on the federal government and read by Timothy McVeigh before the Oklahoma City bombing.[74] Resistance

Records has a catalog of approximately 250 titles of hate-filled music CDs. The music groups represented include Aggravated Assault, Nordic Thunder, Angry Aryans, Brutal Attack, Plunder & Pillage, Blue-Eyed Devils, and RaHoWa, a contraction of "Racial Holy War." CD titles include *Racially Motivated Violence, Holocaust 2000, Retribution, Born to Hate* and *On the Attack*. Song titles include "Race Riot," "Third Reich" and "White Revolution."

Resistance Records has, in its distribution of materials, also recently combined its hate speech with all the dangers raised by violent video games. The game "Ethnic Cleansing" lets the player choose whether to be a skinhead or a member of the Klan. The player then roams the streets of a virtual city, killing gangs of "subhumans," African Americans and Hispanic Americans. The player works his way to the subway to search out and destroy the subhuman's Jewish masters, thereby thwarting their plans for world domination and saving the white race.[75]

The cost of this expression is greater than a cross burning or a swastika. It represents not just hate speech but a perpetuation of such speech. Again according to the Anti-Defamation League, "Pierce believes hate music—with its racist, anti-Semitic and anti-government messages—can be used effectively to attract troubled youths. His stated goal is to fill the ranks of the National Alliance with a new generation of haters."[76] The founder of Resistance Records, RaHoWa member George Burdi, is quoted as saying "Music alone cannot save our Race, granted. . . . But our music is precious to us, and highly effective as a recruiting tool."[77] The ADL again quotes Pierce in explaining the process of using music to recruit.

> As hate rock bands subtly infiltrate mainstream youth culture, they capitalize on teen-age rebelliousness and channel it into enmity and fury against "non-Aryans." Pierce has explained, "My aim with resistance music is to give them a rationale for alienation, to help them understand why they're alienated, to help them understand the programs and policies behind these alienating conditions, and to give them a target, a purpose for their anger and rage." Coupled with these organizations' slick and enticing Web sites, hate rock is part of a multimedia approach that packs a powerful and seductive punch. Therein lies the most dangerous threat.[78]

That is, indeed, the most dangerous threat. It is the danger of perpetuation of racism by reaching youth still in the process of developing their personalities and moral compasses. It also reaches youth before they may have had sufficient contact with individuals of other races and religions to learn not to think in generalities.

F. The Price We Must Be Willing to Pay—But at What Cost?

1. Minimizing the Costs

It bears repeating, or re-repeating, that having been willing to recognize that free expression has its costs is not the same as concluding that free expression rights are not worth retaining. The law involving the treatment of public officials and public figures as libel plaintiffs provides an example in which there are free expression costs that fall on those public officials or figures but in which the costs are worth tolerating. The Supreme Court, in *New York Times v. Sullivan*,[79] required that a public official plaintiff demonstrate "actual malice," a defendant's knowledge that the defamatory statement was false or reckless disregard of the statement's possible falsity, to prevail in such a suit. The actual malice rule was extended to public figures in *Curtis Publishing Co. v. Butts*.[80]

A related example is found in *Hustler Magazine v. Falwell*.[81] That case involved a parody of a series of ads for a liquor that appears to be an acquired taste. In the ad series, celebrities were asked to describe their first times, ostensibly tasting the liquor but with sexual undertones. The parody, which was labeled "ad parody—not to be taken seriously," described the Reverend Jerry Falwell's "first time" as having been with his mother in an outhouse. Falwell, at the trial level, won a $150,000 judgment for the intentional infliction of emotional distress. The Supreme Court reversed unanimously, concluding that recovery for intentional infliction of emotional distress, when a public figure such as Falwell is the plaintiff, also requires the actual malice standard of knowledge of falsity or reckless disregard for falsity of the statement causing the distress.

Clearly, these aspects of the freedom of expression have their costs. Those who are defamed suffer injury to reputation. They may lose business or social opportunities. People may also suffer an emotional cost in knowing that others may think less of them as a result of false statements made about them. The emotional aspects of the injuries that may result from defamatory statements are at the heart of the issue in the *Hustler* case. There, Falwell was certainly harmed emotionally by the ad parody.[82] Indeed, the purpose of the parody seems to have been to hold Falwell up to ridicule, and the inclusion of his mother in the parody maximized both the ridicule and the injury. The protection from suit enjoyed by the magazine makes the infliction of this sort of injury in the future more likely.

Despite these costs, the constitutional limitations on recovery for defamation or the intentional infliction of emotional distress are worth retaining. The *Times v. Sullivan* case itself demonstrates the importance of protecting the media from suits by public officials. The criticism contained in the ad at issue was aimed at the city government, and the right to criticize government is at the heart of the First Amendment. Any criticism of a public official, at least for acts performed in his or her official capacity, is also a criticism of government. In fact, if the public is to make informed choices about the best candidates standing for election, all information bearing on the candidates' fitness for office is important. While false statements may not be legitimate criticism of government and may not really contribute to informed election choices, even false statements must be protected to leave breathing room for legitimate criticism. The Court's position was that requiring anything less than actual malice would result in media self-censorship of even true statements. The resulting loss of information would damage the ability of the public to choose governmental leaders and to criticize their actions once chosen. Public figures must also be subject to public scrutiny and criticism. Since they have power to affect the lives of people and are not answerable in any elections, critical expression is the only road to assuring that their power is not abused.

Even the protection from intentional infliction of emotional-distress suits serves an important purpose. A long history of editorial cartoons shows this medium to be an effective means of criticizing those who are public officials or public figures. These cartoons are often parodies, making statements not literally true and not likely to reasonably be taken as true, but certainly ridiculing their targets and perhaps causing emotional distress. The acceptance of this mode of sometimes hurtful criticism from the early days of the Republic through the present attests to its importance and effectiveness and the need to provide it the protection of the First Amendment. As the *Hustler* Court said, if it were to allow recovery for nondefamatory statements that were intended to cause emotional injury, there can be little doubt that political cartoonists and satirists would be subjected to damage awards without any showing that their work falsely defamed its subject. . . . [T]he appeal of the political cartoon or caricature is often based on exploration of unfortunate physical traits or politically embarrassing events—an exploration often calculated to injure the feelings of the subject of the portrayal. The art of the cartoonist is often not reasoned or evenhanded, but slashing and one-sided.[83]

This, too, is a First Amendment cost worth bearing.

Even accepting the need to pay a price to retain the great benefits of free expression, there may still be the possibility of lessening that cost. One approach to cost cutting would be to limit the protection of free expression to the core areas that motivate the First Amendment, to political expression, to speech aimed at discussing social change. The response to this suggestion would likely be the invocation of a slippery slope argument. Delgado may take solace in his observation that other Western democracies that have banned racist speech have not come to deny the freedom of expression in other more vital areas,[84] but not all may be as confident of that result being replicated or being permanent. To many, the risk of a continued erosion of free expression is real enough that any step down the slippery slope must be avoided.

There is, however, another approach to lessening the costs that would not seem to lead to the same slippery-slope concerns. If the freedom of expression were limited not based on topic or type of speech but on the age of the speaker or audience, a firmer line is drawn. While regulation of obscenity might lead to regulation of pornography and then to other varieties of speech, the tradition of the law drawing lines at specific ages seems less susceptible to unacceptable sliding. There may be debate over whether seventeen or eighteen is the appropriate age at which to apply different rules of expression, but there would seem to be no likelihood that the age would eventually slip up to twenty-six or forty. We recognize the age of majority as being eighteen, with an exception of twenty-one for alcohol consumption and other ages for election to federal office. The fact that the right to vote obtains at eighteen means that the political basis for free expression becomes vital at that age, and all who reach eighteen should have the full expression rights of our society. Even before the age of eighteen, some rights might obtain, but there is no reasonable basis for allowing the age at which expression rights mature to slip to ages older than eighteen.

Not only would an age-based limitation not lead to a slippery slope problem, it would go a long way to solving many of the problems that are the costs of free expression. The violence that is caused by exposure to media violence is a particular problem among youth.[85] If pornographic material has a negative influence with regard to equality for women, that influence seems greater when it is youth who are exposed. While we all may be influenced by advertisement for alcohol, tobacco or drugs, there is a greater harm in children being so influenced at an age where society does not recognize a right to engage in such use. The coarsening of society might be reduced by limiting language of and toward children, while allowing adult-to-adult conversation to be as coarse as the participants might wish. Similarly, for racial hatred to be perpetuated, it must be taught, and it is best taught to children. If such speech were limited to an already corrupted adult audience, adult rights could be protected while children would be less likely to continue to maintain an atmosphere of racism. Thus, the major costs of free expression can be limited while retaining the major benefits by limiting free expression where children are involved, while allowing strong protection for adult-to-adult communication.

2. The Strength of the Evidence and the Need for a Two-Tier First Amendment

A last word with regard to costs must be addressed to readers who are not convinced of the existence of, or extent of, the costs discussed. Even those who are convinced also need to understand why the approach advocated here with regard to free expression and children is necessary to attempts to shield children from those costs. If expression is protected by the First Amendment, that does not mean that it must be tolerated at all costs, but it does mean that any limitations will be tested against an extremely strict standard. The government will bear the burden of demonstrating that it was addressing a compelling governmental need and that the regulation was necessary to, or narrowly tailored to, that end.

The difficulty in meeting this test is demonstrated by cases addressing state attempts to limit the exposure of minors to violent material. The negative effects of violent media seem to be the best established of the costs discussed. While social scientists find those costs clear, the courts have been generally unwilling to accept the evidence as sufficient to allow an infringement on expression rights. A Missouri statute prohibiting the rental to minors of violent videos provides an example. The statute was challenged by a group of video dealers and distributors and by the Motion Picture Association of America in *Video Software Dealers Association v. Webster*.[86] The court applied the strict scrutiny test but was willing to recognize a compelling interest in protecting the physical and psychological well-being of minors. Nonetheless, the court decided that the statute had not been shown to be narrowly drawn to serve that interest. Since the statute did not state exactly what types of violent depiction are detrimental to minors, and indeed since the studies are not so definite, the court could not conclude that the statute was narrowly drawn to ban only that sort of expression.

The burden the court put on the state seems impossible to meet. Studies involving exposure to violence necessarily involve a variety of depictions. A laboratory study of short-term effects may focus on a particular type of depiction, but real-world studies of general exposure to violence and long-term effect are just that: general. Children cannot be placed in different groups and exposed only to particular types of violence over an extended period to determine the effects of each variety. Only general conclusions can be reached regarding the overall effect of violence. Yet, without this unacceptable variety of experiment, the "narrow tailoring" requirement will be unmet. Given that violence has received the most attention and study, the inability to justify other limitations is apparent. And this is not a conclusion that only the skeptic regarding the social science may reach. Even accepting the conclusions of the studies presented, the nonskeptic should probably recognize the lack of specificity in the conclusions, and that it will be difficult to satisfy any strict scrutiny analysis the First Amendment may mandate.

The difficulty discussed explains the need to accept an approach to the First Amendment that allows strong protection for adults and much more limited protection for speech to children, if children are to be protected. If a variety of expression is unprotected, when children are the recipients, there is no need to justify a restriction under a strict scrutiny standard. For unprotected expression, only a rational basis is required. The regulation will be upheld if it addresses a permissible governmental objective and is rationally related to that goal. Since maintaining the physical and psychological well-being of youth is certainly a permissible objective, the remaining question is that of rational relationship. The studies cited and arguments presented are sufficient to meet that requirement. The narrow tailoring and scientific certainty of strict scrutiny are not required, so long as it is rational to believe that the media influences addressed have a negative impact on the youthful mind. Even the social science skeptic, while disagreeing with the conclusions of the studies, should at least admit that it is not irrational to believe those results.

3

Relieving the Strain
on the First Amendment

The costs associated with free expression raise the serious concern that society will be tempted to conclude that the free-expression clauses are not worth retaining. While the question of costs versus benefits should be taken seriously, the importance of the speech and press clauses to a free and democratic society counsels in favor of protecting the First Amendment from reductions in strength that would do injury to the political system. The other values that serve to justify free expression, while perhaps not as essential or central, are also important, and an effort should be made to maintain them in spite of the harms that may flow from expression.

There are two concerns over the scope of the protection that the First Amendment offers free expression. One has to do with the range of the protections, that is, with the varieties of materials that come under the umbrella of the amendment. The second has to do with the strength of the protection offered. Should the commitment to free expression be absolute, at least in those areas in which it applies, or should it be balanced against other societal values?

A. Concerns over Range

1. Public versus Private Speech Interests

The issue of the range of the protections afforded by the free expression clauses was the subject of a 1940s debate between Zechariah Chafee and Alexander Meiklejohn. Chafee maintained, in his book *Free Speech in the United States*,[1] that the First Amendment protects two sorts of interests in free expression. There is, in his view, "a societal interest in the attainment of truth, so that the country may not only adopt the wisest course but carry it out in the wisest way."[2] This interest matches the values generally recognized to be at the core of the First Amendment. Chafee, however, also recognized another interest, "an individual interest, the need of many men to express their opinions on matters vital to them if life is to be worth living."[3] This interest seems to match more closely the values asserted by theories based on autonomy. Both interests, in Chafee's view, are protected by the First Amendment.

Meiklejohn, in his subsequent book *Free Speech and Its Relation to Self-Government*,[4] agreed that there were two types of interests in free expression, a public interest and a private interest, but he took Chafee to task for protecting both sorts of interest through the First Amendment. For Meiklejohn, it is the public interest that is protected by the First Amendment, and including private interests within that protection weakens the protection afforded public speech. Meiklejohn did recognize that private speech merits protection, but he would find this protection in the Due Process Clauses that provide protection in the Fifth Amendment against federal deprivation and in the Fourteenth Amendment against state infringement. The difference, as he saw it, was that the protection afforded by the First Amendment should be absolute, while the protection afforded by the Due Process Clauses is subject to balancing against other governmental interests.

If the two sources of protection were not kept distinct, rather than lifting the protection for private speech to the level that must be provided for public speech, Meiklejohn believed that vital public, political speech would be negatively affected. "The right of citizens of the United States to know what they are voting about, by an unholy union with a private desire for private satisfaction, is robbed of its virtue. The constitutional defences of public discussion have been broken through."[5] Meiklejohn explained that it was only a "single-minded" First Amendment that could serve the vital purpose of furthering self-government. The First Amendment could not be concerned with the individual need to express oneself but must focus on the public interest. "[P]ublic discussion . . . has a constitutional status which no pursuit of an individual purpose can ever claim. It stands alone, as a cornerstone of the structure of self-government. If that uniqueness were taken away, government by consent of the governed would have perished from the earth."[6] Only a First Amendment aimed solely at the protection of public speech could, for Meiklejohn, have the strength to protect the political role of the people in our society.

Chafee quickly responded in his review of Meiklejohn's book.[7] He argued that the line between public and private speech is "extremely blurred" and gave as an example a novel dealing with race relations. It was not clear to Chafee whether, under Meiklejohn's scheme, the book should be considered public or private speech.

> The truth is that there are public aspects to practically every subject. The satisfactory operation of self-government requires the individual to develop fairness, sympathy, and understanding of other men, a comprehension of economic forces, and some basic purpose in life. He can get help from poems and plays and novels. . . . This attitude, however, offers such a wide area for the First Amendment that very little is left for his private speech. . . . On the other hand, if private speech does include scholarship (as the author suggests . . .) and also art and literature, it is shocking to deprive these vital matters of the protection of the inspiring words of the First Amendment.[8]

Meiklejohn never does really clear up this blurred distinction between public and private speech. He continued to assert that the First Amendment protects not a freedom to speak but a freedom to engage in the thought and communication that are a part of government, that it protects a public power rather than a private right.[9] On the other hand, he recognized that "there are many forms of thought and expression within the range of human communications from which the voter derives the knowledge, intelligence, sensitivity to human values: the capacity for sane and objective judgment which, so far as possible, a ballot should express."[10] While he concludes that literature and the arts are protected, it is not because of the value of self-expression. It is because people need novels, dramas, poems, and even paintings, "because they will be called on to vote,"[11] and casting that vote requires that people be stimulated and challenged by ideas rather than be terrified by them.

Meiklejohn, then, rejects what might easily have been taken as the conclusion of his earlier work that entertainment is not protected by the First Amendment.[12] But he does not reject that position because of a commitment to the individual's autonomy interest. He simply recognizes that entertainment may have the public value of contributing to the knowledge necessary for meaningful participation in the discussion of public issues. On the other hand, he continued to maintain a distinction between public and private speech, at least as a theoretical difference, if one without clear differences in extension.

2. The Pathological Perspective

The assertion of a limited view of subject-matter coverage has found a more recent champion in Vincent Blasi. Meiklejohn and Blasi were likely to take similar positions, given their similar views as to the purpose of the First Amendment. While Meiklejohn found his rationale for the amendment and his model for how it should operate in self-government and in the town meeting, Blasi views the amendment as protecting the right of the people to place a check on governmental abuse.[13] While Blasi's view of the central role of the amendment as a check may be more limited than Meiklejohn's protection of more regular active participation, the general contours of the protections afforded and those not provided by the amendment were likely to be similar.

Blasi advocates a "pathological perspective" on the First Amendment.[14] It is not that he views the First Amendment as itself a pathology but rather that the courts should be guided in their interpretations of the amendment by a concern for the strength those protections must have in pathological periods. Pathological periods are, for Blasi, exceptional and time-bound periods in which there is a strong shift away from the tolerance of ordinary periods toward an intolerance for the unorthodox.

> In pathological periods, at least some of the central norms of the constitutional regime are indeed scrutinized and challenged. The core commitments that derive from those norms are viewed by many as highly burdensome and controversial. In such periods the times seem so different, so out of joint, the threats from within or without seem so unprecedented, that the Constitution itself is perceived by many persons as anachronistic, or at least, unrealistically formalistic. In times when those misgivings take hold, the central norms of the constitutional regime are in jeopardy.[15]

Blasi finds the constitutional norms regarding free expression to be particularly likely to suffer during pathological periods. Pathological periods may be precipitated by events that bring about a perceived need for conformity, rather than honoring dissent, and such a strong identification of the people with the position of the government that distrust of the government by others is not tolerated.[16]

What the pathological perspective theory requires is that, during ordinary periods, the free-expression clauses be interpreted in such a way as to make them as strong as possible in the critical pathological periods. A tradition of adjudication directed at the role of the clauses in normal times, without employing this perspective, is seen as unlikely to protect free expression in pathological periods, because the central norms in those ordinary times are not themselves challenged but instead serve as starting points for examining the periphery of the First Amendment. In pathological periods, those central norms, then under challenge themselves, are not helped by a tradition of ordinary interpretation not based on concern for pathology.

When it comes to what direction the pathological perspective dictates, Blasi recognizes that there are a variety of issues and approaches. Whatever decisions are made, concern must be directed toward instilling in the populace "an attitude of respect, devotion, perhaps even reverence, regarding those central norms."[17] With regard to the scope of First Amendment protection, Blasi sees two possibilities. One is as broad an extension of First Amendment rights as possible in normal times. Then, in a pathological period, any paring of First Amendment coverage would trim only "doctrinal fat." A broadly interpreted First Amendment would also provide a wider constituency benefiting from First Amendment values that might be expected to support the amendment in turbulent times. Such broad coverage could also lead to a more active specialized bar in ordinary times that would step in to defend the First Amendment, when pathology demands. On the other hand, Blasi suggests that "[b]etter equipped for the storms of pathology might be a lean, trim First Amendment that covered only activities most people would recognize as serious, time-honored forms of communication."[18] In weighing the benefits of broad versus more limited coverage, he sees the stronger arguments as being on the side of narrower scope. "In pathological periods, courts need to present the forces of repression with strict, immutable legal constraints. That kind of implacable judicial posture is easier to assume when the basic reach of the First Amendment is modest and compatible with widely shared intuitions regarding the natural ambit of the commitment to expressive liberty."[19]

The decision in favor of a lean, trim First Amendment leads to the question of what is to be included within, and what excluded from, the amendment's coverage. What, for example, of obscene materials?[20] An analysis from the pathological perspective may not be completely clear. On the one hand, a decision not to protect obscenity requires that lines be drawn, and line drawing in this matter may invite the drawing of other lines that may fence out material whose protection is vital in our political system.

On the other hand, the inclusion of hard-core pornography within the protection of the First Amendment may well erode the respect for the amendment necessary to protect it in pathological periods. In ordinary periods, the most common invocations of the First Amendment seem to be by those who seek to claim protection for their right to make money by providing materials many find morally, not politically, objectionable. If the First Amendment comes to be seen as having as a primary role the protection of profiteering on what many view as immoral activities and materials, it is unlikely to foster respect. The image of the pornographer, or the producer of violent, racist or misogynistic material, cloaked in the First Amendment, seems unlikely to produce respect for the doctrine of free expression. If the amendment comes to be seen as little more than a provision that protects such commercial exploitation, public attitudes toward free expression may not be sufficient to protect the core values of the First Amendment during a pathological period.

3. Drawing a Different Line

Both Meiklejohn and Blasi raise legitimate concerns. Sometimes a great strain is put on the First Amendment, when individuals protest the actions of the government. The freedom of expression, to survive such challenges, must be robust, and the question of the effect of broad coverage on the strength of protection is interesting and important. While Blasi's thesis has not been, and probably cannot be, confirmed with any surety, it does make an important point. Any public disrespect for the First Amendment that develops during normal times has to have an effect on the perception of the amendment and its ability to withstand the challenges of pathological times. Even the development of an active First Amendment bar may not be sufficient to overcome the effects of that decreased respect. Limiting the role the First Amendment must serve allows it to do so with strength and respect and keeps our commitment to it strong enough to do its necessary job of protecting political dissent.

There are, nonetheless, line-drawing problems in limiting the role of the amendment. While it might seem simple to eliminate obscene materials from protection, a judgment of obscenity requires decisions as to offensiveness, appeal to the prurient interest and the value of the material involved. Lampooning of public officials or religious personages by portraying them in sexual contexts has served an important critical role at various times,[21] and a loss of this ability to criticize would be unfortunate. It is also not always easy to distinguish commercial from noncommercial speech, as in the case of a public utility including inserts discussing energy policy along with its bills.[22] Furthermore, while a democratic society may survive with free-expression rights limited to political speech, it is not the open society to which we seem committed.

There are, however, still real concerns over the damage that free expression may do. That concern seems strongest when children are involved. While there is debate over the propriety of limiting adult access to obscene materials, most would agree that children should be shielded from pornography. Concerns over violence and misogyny in rap music lyrics also center on their effects on youthful listeners. If the First Amendment is to protect more than political speech, it is possible that the expanded role it is asked to play may lead to a loss of necessary respect for the core values of free expression. That possibility would seem much greater if the amendment were seen as protecting the exposure of children to such objectionable material.

If it is a concern for children that would lead to a First Amendment unfit for pathological times, the solution should be limiting negative effects on children. If a line is to be drawn, it should be between children and adults. Expanded First Amendment protection for adult expression may still have the effects that concern Blasi, but societal reaction will not be as strong as it would be if the same amendment is seen as responsible for the protection of objectionable expression aimed at children. The pathological perspective should lead to a First Amendment that protects expression by or toward adults differently than when children are involved, whether or not it also calls for limits on adult expression.

The decision to limit protection for free expression, where children are involved, leaves adults free to communicate with one another. There should not be a concern with the lines that would otherwise have to be drawn based on subject matter. There would be no slippery slope that could lead to less and less protection for adult speech. The line between children and adults, even if there were to be debate over whether sixteen, seventeen or eighteen is the place to draw that line, will not slowly change into one that limits the expression of those under twenty-five, then thirty, and so on. There will be subject matter issues and lines to be drawn with regard to the application of the amendment to youth, but that line will not have an effect on adult communication. It is also a line that, as already argued, does not implicate the values that ought to be protected by the First Amendment.

B. *The Strength and Direction of First Amendment Protections*

1. The Communitarian Movement

Communitarianism calls into question the strength of our commitment to individual rights, at least to the extent that such rights serve to trump all appeals to other values. While few, if any, view the protections of expression as absolute, the strict scrutiny of government regulation of expression that the First Amendment requires is not accepted by all. Communitarians do not deny a role for individual rights but do call for a balancing rather than a trump card approach. As Amitai Etzioni puts it,

> [t]he communitarian quest . . . is to seek a way to blend elements of tradition (order based on virtues) with elements of modernity (well-protected autonomy). This, in turn, entails finding an equilibrium between universal individual rights and the common good (too often viewed as incompatible concepts), between self and community, and above all how such an equilibrium can be achieved and sustained.[23]

For the individual, Etzioni proposes a new golden rule: "Respect and uphold society's moral order as you would have society respect and uphold your autonomy."[24]

Communitarians also criticize the rhetoric of individual rights as cutting off debate that would be valuable to society. In an ongoing debate on the direction society should take, the assertion of an individual right serves as the playing of a trump card. It overrides the value of any other cards offered. Mary Ann Glendon complains that the features of our rights dialog

> make it difficult to give voice to common sense or moral intuitions, they also impede development of the sort of rational political discourse that is appropriate to the needs of a mature, complex, liberal, pluralistic republic. Our rights talk, in its absoluteness, promotes unrealistic expectations, heightens social conflict, and inhibits dialogue that might lead toward consensus, accommodation, or at least the discovery of common ground. . . . [T]hese traits promote mere assertion over reason-giving.[25]

Even if it is appropriate for the assertion of a right to cut off debate when adults are concerned, it is of particular concern when the debate over protecting children from objectionable expression is truncated by the assertion of rights more appropriate for adults.

Communitarianism is usually seen as conservative, but as defined by Etzioni, that is true only in a fairly liberal, individualist society. Where there is already strong respect for individual rights, the direction the communitarian will urge is toward a commitment to the traditional values of the society. If, on the other hand, a society has tilted in the direction of strong, perhaps enforced, adherence to traditional values, the communitarian should be on the side of individual rights.

> A good communitarian society . . . calls on those who are socially aware and active, people of insight and conscience, to throw themselves to the side opposite that *toward* which history is tilting. This is not because all virtue is on that opposite side, but because if the element that the society is neglecting will continue to be deprived of support, the society will become either oppressive or anarchic, ceasing to be a good society, if it does not collapse altogether.[26]

The goal is an equilibrium between an ordered society and individual liberty.

Not only is there a difference between Etzioni's communitarian balance and social conservatism in that social conservativism will always argue in favor of societal values, there is also a difference in how those goals are to be achieved. While social conservatives may be willing to resort to law to enforce values, Etzioni urges adopting nonlegal methods to further the acceptance of traditional societal values. His version of the good communitarian society is one in which normative effect is achieved not through law enforcement but instead through education, moral leadership and role models, peer pressure and exhortation and the willingness of society to take moral stands on issues and give voice to those positions.[27] Coercive methods should be used only when society faces a clear and present danger and has already been unsuccessful in addressing that danger through noncoercive methods, and even then the coercive methods should be minimally intrusive with any side effects minimized.[28]

Etzioni also argues that the scope of communitarian values to which these noncoercive methods will be addressed is narrower than the social conservatives' broad imposition of values. The success of noncoercive means requires that "most members of the society, most of the time, *share a commitment to a set of core values*, and that most members, most of the time, will abide by the behavioral implications of these values because they believe in them, rather than being *forced* to comply with them."[29] Further, in Etzioni's view:

> Communitarians . . . limit the virtues the society favors to a set of core values while legitimating differences on other normative matters, the scope of values social conservatives promote is much more pervasive and unitary. Social conservatives see few areas of behavior which they are willing to leave open to personal and subgroup choice. If the individualists are virtue-avoiders, strong social conservatives are virtue-monopolizers.[30]

Etzioni also argues that society is protected from majoritarianism by both moral and legal restrictions on majority action. As he notes, the Bill of Rights recognizes certain areas as removed from majority control. *The Responsive Communitarian Platform: Rights and Responsibilities*, developed by Etzioni, Mary Ann Glendon and William Galston, sets out the communitarian position on the First Amendment.

> The First Amendment is as dear to Communitarians as it is to libertarians and many other Americans. Suggestions that it should be curbed to bar verbal expressions of racism, sexism, and other slurs seem to us to endanger the essence of the First Amendment, which is most needed when what some people say is disconcerting to some others. However, one should not ignore the victims of such abuse. Whenever individuals or members of a group are harassed, many *non-legal measures* are ap-

propriate to express disapproval of hateful expressions and to promote tolerance among the members of the polity.[31]

As an example of such nonlegal methods, a teach-in on tolerance could be a reasonable response to incidents indicating bigotry on a college campus.

While Etzioni's variety of communitarianism may grant sufficient deference to First Amendment concerns, there are those who invoke similar community-based values to limit speech that would otherwise be protected. Prominent among those who would limit speech are scholars concerned over the effects of free expression on minorities and women. Richard Delgado considers university campus hate speech codes and recognizes that they often pit two groups against each other—advocates of free expression on the one hand, and the members of minority groups subjected to such speech on the other.[32]

> The white . . . insists on the freedom to say whatever is on his mind. The black or brown insists on the right not to hear what is on the white's mind when it takes the form of a vicious racial slur. One interest is balanced against another, one emanating from one part of the Constitution (the First Amendment), the other from a different part (the Fourteenth Amendment)—seemingly a perfect standoff.[33]

Delgado, joined by Jean Stefancic, recognizes that this balance between speech and community is particularly difficult to strike, because the two depend on each other. Speech, to serve as a real dialog, requires some equality among those engaged in that exchange. If that equality is lacking, the result is a sermon or order, rather than a dialog; thus, speech requires equality. Speech also requires community, a group of speakers and listeners who accept the same linguistic conventions and assign similar meanings to utterances. "Speech requires community—without it communication is virtually impossible. At the same time, community requires speech because it is our only way of doing what communities must do."[34] In striking the balance, advocates of limits on racist speech do recognize the concerns of free-speech advocates. Mari Matsuda writes that "[t]he image of book burnings should unnerve us and remind us to argue long and hard before selecting a class of speech to exclude from the public domain,"[35] even while arguing for a hate speech exception aimed at messages of racial inferiority directed toward a historically oppressed group that are persecutorial, hateful, and degrading.[36]

Leaving the issue of racist speech,[37] feminist scholars have made many of the same points in their attacks on pornography. Catharine MacKinnon and Andrea Dworkin believe that, just as racist speech may marginalize those at whom it is addressed, sexist speech, including in their view pornography, can marginalize women. An Indianapolis ordinance mirroring their concerns, held unconstitutional in *American Booksellers Association v. Hudnut*,[38] presented an insight into their concerns. The target of the ordinance was not all erotic material. It concentrated on pornography, defined as encompassing sexually explicit images of the subordination of women that also depict women as enjoying pain, assault, humiliation or certain other forms of degradation, as being filthy or inferior, dominated, exploited, possessed or presented in positions of servility or display.[39]

It is clear that the concern behind this ordinance was the effect certain depictions of sexuality may have on the lives of women.[40] Supporters of the ordinance maintained that "pornography influences attitudes, and the statute is a way to alter the socialization of men and women rather than to vindicate community standards of offensiveness."[41] The concern over pornography is not simply moral or aesthetic; it is seen as both a symptom of sexual inequality and patriarchy and a cause of both. The effect is seen as so pervasive that it defines reality. Pornography is said to affect all aspects of women's lives by suggesting that women are "a lower form of human life defined by their availability for sexual use."[42] MacKinnon argues that pornography decreases inhibitions on, and increases acceptance of, aggression against women, reduces the desire of both males and females to have female children and fosters a belief in male domination.[43]

The Seventh Circuit addressed the argument that pornography changes people and contributes to the subordination of women, saying

> this simply demonstrates the power of pornography as speech. All of these unhappy effects depend on mental intermediation. Pornography affects how people see the world, their fellows, and social relations. If pornography is what pornography does, so is other speech. Hitler's orations affected how some Germans saw Jews. Communism is a world view, not simply a Manifesto by Marx and Engels or a set of speeches.[44]

The court was clear in its conclusion that the ordinance violated the First Amendment, and the expression remained protected. It is also a conclusion that would carry over to race-based hate speech.

While free speech prevailed, at least in this instance, the passing of the ordinance may give pause to the acceptance of the communitarian approach. While Etzioni disavows coercive measures to enforce community values, the arguments he uses in support of his noncoercive means are similar to those raised by the advocates of legal limits on hate speech and pornography. All point to other values as strong enough to stand alongside the value of free expression, and at least for the proponents of hate speech codes and pornography ordinances, strong enough to allow legal limits on expression. In the cases of racist speech and sexist speech or pornography, the argument of the proponent of regulation is strengthened by being able to point not only to a community value but a community value enshrined in the Constitution. The Equal Protection Clause of the Fourteenth Amendment provides not just a value, but arguably, although not yet to the satisfaction of the courts, another trump to counter the playing of the trump card of the First Amendment.

2. Unidirectional Rights

Another theory that could serve to limit the strength of the First Amendment, by channeling the direction in which the amendment's protection leads, is presented by the perfectionists. Perfectionists argue that among the acceptable roles for government is making its citizens better, more moral people. Robert George takes this sort of perfectionist stand and sees a more active role for the law than that envisioned by theorists who argue for individual autonomy. George recognizes that laws do not make men moral, even if they punish immoral behavior. Only freely making morally correct choices makes the individual moral,[45] but the law, he believes, can help individuals be or become moral. The law may do so by preventing the increase in corruption that can result from morally bad decisions, by preventing bad examples, by preserving a positive moral environment within which people make their decisions, by removing temptation, and by serving as a form of moral education.[46] For George, these effects justify the enforcement of morals. "[A] social environment abounding in vice threatens [people's] moral well-being and integrity. A social environment in which vice abounds (and vice might . . . abound in subtle ways) tends to damage people's moral understandings and weaken their characters as it bombards them with temptations to immorality."[47]

While George, like the communitarians, places the primary role in moral education on parents, teachers and the clergy, he clearly argues for a stronger role for the government, to the point of allowing it to coerce moral behavior.[48] He also has another important point of departure from the communitarians. Communitarian arguments find the values to be furthered in attitudes shared in the community; it is simply the fact that the values are shared that makes them important in making a group a true community. Since George would allow coercion, he accepts that moral laws cannot be justified on any basis that does not require that the enforced morality be "true."[49]

Questions of morality and truth are always difficult, but this may be particularly so when the issue is free expression. The role the First Amendment is supposed to play in self-government, criticism of the government or the search for truth is compromised if the government is allowed to assert an official version of the truth and to prevent expression that runs contrary to that "truth." Despite this difficulty, George would allow his perfectionist theories to apply to expression and would seem to justify government regulation of material that the First Amendment protects. He discusses pornography, and does not limit his analysis to pornography that reaches the level of obscenity. George concludes that "anti-pornography legislation need neither violate anyone's rights, nor sacrifice anyone's welfare, for the sake of advancing collective interests."[50] The collective interest he identifies is "[t]he human interest in dignity and beauty in sexual relationships, and in the creation and maintenance of a 'cultural structure' which supports these goods."[51] He goes on to say that anti-pornography legislation serves even the interests of those inclined toward the use of pornography. "Dignity and beauty in sexual relationships (and a supporting cultural structure) are no less goods for them than for anyone else. To the extent that it preserves these (truly common) goods, anti-pornography legislation preserves and advances, rather than harms, *their* interests as well as the interests of everyone else."[52] Of course, that argument rests on the assumption that the majority is the best judge of the real interests of the individual who might believe the availability of pornography to be in his or her actual interest.

Another view, which might also be labeled "perfectionist," is John Garvey's theory that rights are not two-way streets. They do not protect all choices, even in an area they address, but protect the ability to make the right choice. Garvey explains the difference between liberal, autonomy-based theories and his own:

[I]n liberal theory the right is prior to the good. . . . I think that some actions are better than others. And the whole point of freedoms is to let us do these things. The law leaves us free to do *x* because it is a good thing to do *x*. This might seem pretty obvious. But it inverts the first principle of liberalism—it makes the good prior to the right.[53]

Garvey does not see freedom as being about making individual choices between actions that are not—but that the government must consider to be—morally equivalent. He sees some choices as better than others, and the role of freedom is to allow individuals to follow these morally superior paths. If religion is good, that will explain the First Amendment's freedom of religion, but it would not explain any value or protection for irreligion. Some other value, such as free expression, would have to serve as a justification for the protection of irreligious views.

Garvey addresses an aspect of free expression as an example of how to apply his theory. To do so, he must first identify the good toward which the freedom of expression is directed. That is, since rights follow goods, the dimension of the right can only be understood once the good is identified. The purpose behind protecting speech, for Garvey, is that the freedom of speech allows people to pursue knowledge.[54] If that is the purpose of free expression, that freedom would not protect all expression. His good explains the protection afforded speech involved in coming to public policy decisions and scientific inquiry. Both involve aspects of the pursuit of knowledge. A somewhat wider understanding of the knowledge being pursued can extend protection to the artistic and literary.

The tie of the freedom of speech to the good of the pursuit of knowledge rests on the recognition that the pursuit of knowledge is a social activity. As a social activity, it requires communication among those engaged in the pursuit. Even the seemingly solitary scholar builds on the work of others, found in materials protected by the freedom of the press. The scholar presents his or her results to colleagues for reaction and correction, as a part of the process of developing or discovering knowledge. The scholar also, once arriving at a firm conclusion, will try to spread the truth by convincing others of the correctness of his or her results. Speech is required for the pursuit of knowledge, not just in the sense that a language may be required for complex thought but because of the interpersonal communication required in the social activity of the pursuit of knowledge.

The conclusion Garvey draws is that the protections justified by the good of the pursuit of knowledge is both broader and more narrow than that currently recognized by the law. He argues that activities other than speech or expression are vital to the pursuit of knowledge and provides as an example the currently unprotected activity of the collection of bugs by one who is interested in the classification of insects. Garvey also considers commercial speech, such as publishing the prices of pharmaceuticals. He argues that there is a difference between a pharmacist stating the price of a particular drug as part of an offer of sale and a professor who publishes the price of the same drug as a part of a research project examining drug costs. The former is the first step toward a sale; the latter is part of the pursuit of knowledge. While there may be mixed cases and difficult lines to draw, Garvey concludes that the government should be allowed to limit speech when it is attempting to regulate sales but not when it wants to limit the pursuit of knowledge.

3. Rebalancing and Redirecting First Amendment Protection

Those who argue for strong individual rights or autonomy consider the imposition of morality through the law illegitimate, but it is important to understand the nature of the objections. However complex or sophisticated the way in which the argument is presented, it seems to come down to the complaint that society's attempt to enforce morality is paternalistic. That is, when the state forbids behavior that has its effects only on consenting, competent participants, the only basis for the intervention is the state's belief that it knows better than the individual what is best for that individual. There are, of course, contingent arguments over who is affected by the behavior, but the jurisprudential issue is over the right of the state to limit the individual's ability to make decisions having an effect solely on that individual.

When the charge of paternalism is raised against a proscription regarding adult behavior, it has some impact. Clearly, it would further the individual's own best health interests if the state were to forbid smoking. But our society believes that individuals should be able to make their own decisions in such cases. The same applies to the use of alcohol, although drug laws seem to indicate the limits the culture has for such autonomy arguments.

When it comes to issues of free expression, the antipaternalistic feeling is particularly strong. Through the first half of the twentieth century, adult use of obscene materials was routinely suppressed and suppressed largely on the theory that such use was not good for the individual. While obscenity laws continue to exist, their enforcement has become more lax, and the likelihood that a particular work will be found obscene has decreased. The decreasing acceptability of paternalism was central in *Stanley v. Georgia.*[55] In that case, the Supreme Court reversed a conviction for the possession of obscene materials in the privacy of the defendant's home. The state argued that it had the right to protect the mind of the individual from the effect of obscenity, but the Court flatly rejected the claim, concluding that "if the First Amendment means anything, it means that a State has no business telling a man, sitting alone in his own house, what books he may read or what films he may watch."[56] The Court went on to say that the state "cannot constitutionally premise legislation on the desirability of controlling a person's private thoughts."[57]

Since many arguments against restrictions on free expression, like many arguments against the enforcement of morality generally, are based on antipaternalistic feelings, it is important to understand just what is wrong with paternalism. Paternalism, when it is wrong, is wrong because it is an affront to equality. When the state tells the individual what is in the individual's best interest, the state discounts the individual's own view as to how to balance his or her own interests. It treats the individual as less able to make such a decision than the majority the state represents, and numbers alone should not resolve such disagreements over individual goods.

Children, however, are not equals in this regard. Knowing what one's best interests are requires an ability to make judgments that children, depending on their age, may completely lack or may be insufficiently developed. "Paternalism" means acting like a father. That may be inappropriate, when the action is toward an adult, but it is completely appropriate, when a father or mother acts that way toward his or her child. Children need to be taught how to act, both when the acts involved may have an effect on others and when the issue is what is in the child's own best interests. The same is true when the issue is what to read or see. There may be no right to interfere with an adult's decisions as to the materials he or she believes contribute to understanding or happiness. With children, however, it is appropriate for parents to decide what materials run counter to their child becoming the sort of person they think the child should be and to refuse to allow the child access to those materials.

The state also serves a role with regard to children that is, in a sense, parental. The state may act in its *parens patriae* role in the way parents may act. When it does so, its role is paternalistic, but not in the pejorative sense in which the word is usually used. The role of the state, so long as the parents are not unfit, is secondary to the parents, but just as preventing nonparents from selling tobacco to minors is not objectionably paternalistic, limiting the ability of nonparents to distribute harmful media to children should not, whatever First Amendment issues may be involved, be objectionably paternalistic.

Allowing the state to limit third-party expression to children would do some of what the communitarians and the perfectionists want without imposing majority views on or limiting the personal autonomy of adults. The communitarians would have the period of the child's minority to transmit the community's values from generation to generation.[58] This fits also with Mill's recognition that society has the period of childhood to teach its children how to act. At the same time, once a child reaches adulthood, individual rights can come into full bloom. Such individual rights may still interfere with or run counter to community values, but the community had its opportunity to teach those values. If it has failed to do so, the value may simply be of insufficient strength to override the commitment to individual rights that society also recognizes.

Similarly with the perfectionists, society may have a right to make people morally better, but it has the period of minority to do so. Children must be trained, morally as well as in other areas. They need to be made into the morally best people they can be, but the project should be relatively complete by the time the child reaches the age of majority. To carry it on beyond that age is disrespectful of the equality of the individual. To engage in the task before the age of majority is to recognize that there is, in fact, an inequality and that the child needs help in his or her development.

The acceptance of a strong First Amendment for adults and a weaker First Amendment for children would help relieve the pressure against the freedom of expression presented by its having to do the difficult to odious job of protecting those who would disseminate sex, violence and hate to children. The balance between community and perfectionism on the one hand and individual rights on the other can also be struck by allowing the community interests and the belief that there are goods toward which the community may direct its citizens to prevail for children, while allowing the individual-right position to dominate for adults. Recognizing the differences between adults and children would go a long way to relieving the strain on the First Amendment that, without such relief, could weaken the protection of free expression for adults.

4

Inculcating Values

Children are not just miniature adults. This is not another case of technology having found a way to cram all the computing power, understanding of values and judgment of a full-size adult into a smaller package. Children, rather than miniatures, are projects under construction. Like all construction projects, supervision is required to be sure the pieces fit together well and the final result is nondefective. Random inputs as experiences that develop a child's personality are no more likely to produce a result with character than the random placing of bricks will lead to an inhabitable building. Parents and society have the responsibility to provide value training for children to make it more likely that they will become responsible adults, capable of functioning in society and understanding and meeting their own needs while respecting others.

A. The Need to Teach Children Values and Judgment

Psychologists have long recognized that children are less than complete as moral agents.[1] Adults, passing on their moral standards during the child's development, maintain the group as a civil society. Children need to learn the ethical standards of their culture.

One may examine moral development from a variety of psychological perspectives. Psychodynamic theories concentrate on affective features and look at moral development as an outgrowth of children's emotional attachment to their parents and the resulting influence parents have on the moral standards children take as their own.[2] Freud's theories are an example. For Freud, the development of morality takes place early in childhood, through the age of five or six. The period appears to be at least similar to religious views on when children reach the age of reason and can be guilty of sin and near the age at which the criminal law will allow for criminal liability. Before five, six or seven, the child is not capable of moral analysis and should not be viewed as sufficiently culpable to face societal punishment or divine retribution.

Freud tied moral development in boys to the phallic stage and the resolution of the Oedipal complex.[3] For that resolution to occur, the male child must suppress his instinctual urge toward his mother and hostility toward his father and become allied with that same-sex parent. Part of that alliance and identification with the father is the adoption of the father's moral values. For young girls, the resolution of the analogous Electra complex was seen as less traumatic and would lead to a weaker moral sense.[4] This aspect of the theory has been, quite naturally, controversial and presages controversy in sex differences postulated in later theories of moral development.

Freud's theory may well be the least supportive of the position taken here. If the inculcation of moral values arises in the identification of the child with his or her same-sex parent, outside influences from the media or peers would seem not to have the sort of influence necessary to justify restrictions on the access of others to children. However, that position may have been more easily asserted in an earlier era in which the child was raised and educated in the home with little outside influence. The modern child may still look for models in same-sex characters, but the availability of such characters in the media, particularly if the same-sex parent is absent, should still raise concern over the images to which children are exposed.

The second variety of moral development theories are social learning theories, which emphasize the acquisition of learned moral behavior.[5] Parents play a role in these theories, but so do others. Children learn standards of morality through rewards and punishments for their behaviors and through observing the behavior of others and reactions to that behavior. Moral behavior, in these theories, is learned like other behaviors and should lead to increasing conformity with standards expected by society.[6] "Children who observe a model committing a prohibited act, such as touching a prohibited toy, are more likely to perform the act themselves, whereas children observing a model who resists temptation commit fewer transgressions themselves."[7] Social learning theories fit well with the results of social science experiments on the effects of observed violent behavior on the willingness of children to aggress. Certainly, for social learning theories, the influence of the media and exposure to at least unpunished inappropriate behavior will have a negative effect on the moral development of youth.

The third variety of moral development theories are the cognitive-developmental theories that focus on the development of moral reasoning, that is, the child's ability to think about moral problems and make moral decisions.[8] One of the major theorists of this genre was Jean Piaget.[9] He studied moral development through presenting a series of scenarios to children of various ages and listening to their reactions. The stories involved the actions of a character doing something that caused a harm, but the intentions of the character and the severity of the harm varied from story to story. Piaget found that children younger than ten focus on consequences and that the degree of fault or wrongfulness is determined for them by the extent of the damage done rather than on the intention of the actor; for older children, motives come to play a role.[10] This changing focus can occur only when the child has developed the ability to understand motives and intentions and thus the development is cognitive. This ability to understand others requires experience with such others. "Peer interaction forces the child to consider the thoughts and feelings of others and eventually leads to an understanding of their intentions and motives. Thus, both maturation and social experience play a role in the child's move toward maturity in moral understanding."[11]

The extended period of moral development is clear in Piaget's work. The importance of peers also comes through. Here too, though, the differences between Europe in an earlier era and the modern United States are important. In an earlier era, one's understanding of motives and intentions and the propriety of those motives and intentions may have come from actual peers, and that is reflected in long-standing concerns over the companions one's child has. In a modern era, models and understanding can come from media representations as well as from real people, and concern over the behavior those actors model is quite reasonable.

Lawrence Kohlberg has done more recent, and very influential, work in the cognitive-developmental theory of moral development.[12] Like Piaget, Kohlberg presented children (and young adults) of various ages with a situation that raises moral questions. The most often described situation involved an individual whose wife was dying of cancer, but a new drug might be able to save her. It was developed by a local pharmacist, who was charging far in excess of the cost of manufacture and far more than the husband could afford. The husband had asked for a reduced price, had done everything he could to raise the money to pay the asking price, and had asked the pharmacist to provide the drug on the promise to pay later. All these efforts failed, and the husband broke into the pharmacy and stole the drug. The children were asked if the husband should have done what he did.

Kohlberg found that children at differing ages, ten to sixteen in his original study, responded differently. More accurately, children progressed through stages of moral development, although they did so at varying rates. His interest was not so much in the yes-or-no answer the children provided but in how they supported their conclusions, their moral reasoning. Children were seen to progress from the preconventional to the conventional to the postconventional levels of moral reasoning, each stage with two substages.[13] At the preconventional level, children are concerned with punishment and reward. In the "punishment and obedience orientation" substage, children focus on what it takes to avoid punishment. In the second "naive instrumental hedonism" substage, the focus shifts to reward.

At the conventional level, the child recognizes the existence of societal rules and social order, and the intentions, motives and perspectives of others play a role in the child's moral reasoning. At the "good boy morality" substage, the stress is on avoiding disapproval rather than simply avoiding punishment. At the "authority-maintaining morality" substage, the stress is on adherence to rules and avoiding harm to others.

At the postconventionalist level, the child, or more likely, the young adult, has developed an understanding of the nature of rules and laws. "They are now seen as the result of a social contract that all individuals must uphold because of shared responsibilities and duties. The individual recognizes the relative and sometimes arbitrary nature of rules, which may vary from group to group. Certain principles and values, however, such as justice and human dignity, must be preserved at all costs."[14] In the "morality of contract and democracy" substage, the stress is on self-respect and earning or keeping the respect of others. The individual recognizes that laws, while they should be obeyed, may be in conflict with the demands of morality. In the second "morality of individual principles of conscience" substage, a stage that few people, even as adults, seem to reach, the concern is faithfulness to one's own moral principles, even if such adherence demands a departure from the rules.

For Kohlberg, as well as for earlier theorists, children are in the process of developing their moral sense and abilities to reason about moral issues, and the experiences of children and observation of others and the behaviors of others play a role. If children are to come to consider themselves in the context of society, their understanding of that context, the understanding of the kind of society in which they find themselves will be affected by the expression of others. It is the only way they can gain that understanding. While the expression of parents and the models they provide will be of great importance and peers will play a role, other less directly involved parties, including the media, would seem also likely to play an important role. Furthermore, that development does not end with early childhood but progresses well into adolescence and even into adulthood, with Kohlberg suggesting that few ever reach his highest stage.[15]

Recent studies in neuroscience back this development through adolescence by demonstrating that actual physical changes occur in the brain, during puberty and adolescence, that appear related to judgment.[16] Neuroscience had formerly believed the brain to have completed its basic wiring—the formation of connections between nerve cells—in early childhood, as early as three, and to be mostly finished by age five. It had also been known that there was an overproduction of neural connections in early childhood, with a massive pruning after the age of eighteen months. This pruning creates a more efficient central nervous system and seems associated with the greatest period of cognitive development. What is new is the discovery that there is a second overproduction of gray matter at puberty as new connections among nerve cells are formed. That is followed by a second pruning occurring through the teen years. This second growth and pruning occurs in the regions of the brain that are associated with "executive function," self-control, impulse inhibition and emotion regulation, as well as organization, planning and goal setting.

This second pruning also promotes efficiency but in areas more central to morality and values. Which neural connections remain and wire the brain for its future responses are determined by what the environment tells the brain is necessary to adapt to the environment. It is becoming clear that the environment in which the teenager lives has physical effects on that teenager's brain development. This demonstrates a route through which environmental factors cause later behavior and that the environmental causes occur throughout the teenage years. The influences to which a child is exposed do matter. The remaining issue is that of who should be allowed to provide that input.

B. *The Role of Parents*

Primary responsibility for teaching children values must lie with the child's parents or guardians. There is certainly no guarantee that a child will end up sharing his or her parents' values and concerns, but parents are the greatest influence in the lives of young children. The outside world of schools, peer attitudes and the culture children experience will certainly influence the outcome, but parents build the foundation. Parents can also at least try to limit the effects of those outside influences by continuing to interact with their older children, perhaps with a shift to discussion rather than mandates.

Teaching values is also unavoidable for parents in custody of their children. Even if values are not discussed, they are demonstrated. The least verbal of parents still interacts with others. That parent's children will learn from the parent's example how to treat others, whether or not to put off immediate gratification in favor of a greater, though later, good, if and when to depart from the truth, the keeping of promises and any of a variety of other character issues.

In addition to responsibility and inevitability of teaching values to one's children, there is also a right to do so clearly established by the Supreme Court. *Meyer v. Nebraska*[17] considered the authority of the state of Nebraska to prohibit teaching foreign languages prior to the ninth grade. The statute did not simply control the curriculum of the state's public schools but prohibited any school from teaching foreign languages, other than the "dead languages," Latin, Greek and Hebrew, to younger students. The state viewed the statute as justified by a concern that allowing immigrant populations to teach their children in their native languages would lead to the children always thinking in that language and inclining them toward foreign ideas and sentiments that were not in the best interests of the United States. In striking down the statute, the Supreme Court noted the importance of education to the American people and "the natural duty of the parent to give his children education suitable to their station in life."[18] The Court recognized the right of the state to take measures to improve its citizens physically, mentally and morally but rejected intrusions into the raising of children that remove control from the parents of those children.

Pierce v. Society of Sisters[19] raised similar issues. That case involved Oregon's compulsory education laws, which required not just that parents provide their children an education but that the children, until they reach the age of sixteen or complete the eighth grade, be sent to public schools. The effect, of course, was to do away with private or parochial elementary education, and the act was challenged by both a religious order and a private military school. The challenge argued that the statute violated the rights of parents to choose their children's schools, as well as the right of the schools and teachers to engage in their businesses and professions.

As the Court noted, no issue was raised as to the right of the state to supervise schools, teachers and students to be sure that the children of the state were adequately educated. Nor did the state claim that the plaintiff schools were failing to meet their obligations. The issue then was purely one of whether the state had the authority to require that children be educated in contravention of their parents' wishes to have them educated in otherwise acceptable nonpublic schools. The Court held, citing *Meyer v. Nebraska*, that the statute unreasonably interfered with the rights of parents to direct their children's education.

> The fundamental theory of liberty upon which all governments in this Union repose excludes any general power of the state to standardize its children by forcing them to accept instruction from public teachers only. The child is not the mere creature of the state; those who nurture him and direct his destiny have the right, coupled with the high duty, to recognize and prepare him for additional obligations.[20]

This unwillingness to allow the state to interfere with the rights of parents in determining how their children are to be raised was carried to what some might think extreme lengths in *Wisconsin v. Yoder*,[21] although the decision mixed that right with the free exercise of religion. The case involved Wisconsin's compulsory school attendance laws for children under sixteen. The challenge was brought by members of the Old Order Amish religion, who refused to send their children to any school beyond the eighth grade. They believed that their children attending high school was contrary to their religion's insistence on insulation from worldly influence, would result in censure from their religious community and would endanger their and their children's salvation. The Supreme Court held that the compulsory attendance laws violated the rights of the Amish in removing their children from the community during critical periods in the formation of Amish attitudes toward community and work. In place of a high school education hostile to Amish values, the Amish would be allowed to substitute the informal vocational training required for the lives their children would lead.

The Court's analysis primarily relied on the free exercise of religion, also protected by the First Amendment, but elements of parental rights to direct the upbringing of their children were intermixed. The Court cited *Pierce* and *Meyer* in determining that the state's valid imposition of educational rules and regulation must sometimes give way to the rights of parents. The Court did recognize that parents have no right to cause their children harm, but the long, successful history of the Amish community and the preparation given their children for participation in that community meant that no harm was done to Amish youth. In the Court's view,

> this case involves the fundamental interest of parents, as contrasted with that of the State, to guide the religious future and education of their children. The history and culture of Western civilization reflect a strong tradition of parental concern for the nurture and upbringing of their children. This primary role of the parents in the upbringing of their children is now established beyond debate as an enduring American tradition.[22]

An additional insight on this issue, and one clearly in the arena of First Amendment rights and children, is presented by *Ginsberg v. New York*.[23] That case involved the sale of a "girlie magazine" to a teenage boy, in violation of a state law prohibiting the sales of such material to children under seventeen. The magazine would not be considered obscene for adult consumption, but the Supreme Court allowed a variable obscenity standard under which the measure of obscenity would take into account the age of the person to whom the magazine was sold.[24] Thus, material protected by the First Amendment for adults lacked such protection for children.

In its analysis, the Court discussed parental rights, citing to Professor Louis Henkin as a commentator who, while disagreeing generally with obscenity laws, "would give effect to the parental role and accept laws relating only to minors."[25] Henkin based this difference in treatment on the role of the state to "'support the right of parents to deal with the morals of children as they see fit.'"[26] The Court also recognized an "independent interest" on the part of the state in the well-being of its youth, but even that interest seemed less than truly independent. The Court quoted an opinion by the New York Court of Appeals that makes the state's interest seemingly subordinate to and built on the foundation of the parents' interests: "While the supervision of children's reading may best be left to their parents, the knowledge that parental control or guidance cannot always be provided and society's transcendent interest in protecting the welfare of children justify reasonable regulation of the sale of material to them."[27]

If it was not clear in *Ginsberg* that the result rested on the importance of recognizing the rights of parents, a more recent case makes it more clear. The case is the 1997 challenge to the Communications Decency Act[28] found in *Reno v. American Civil Liberties Union*.[29] The statute, aimed at indecency on the Internet, prohibited the knowing transmission to a person under eighteen years of age of any obscene or indecent message or sending or displaying offensive material in a way available to persons under eighteen. In defense of the statute the government relied in part on *Ginsberg*, but the Court distinguished this case in several ways. Importantly, for the purposes of the issue under discussion, the Court said "we noted in *Ginsberg* that 'the prohibition against sales to minors does not bar parents who so desire from purchasing the magazines for their children.' Under the CDA, by contrast, neither the parents' consent—nor even their participation—in the communication would avoid the application of the statute."[30] The right of parents to control the upbringing of their children, at least as long as their decisions do not endanger the health or safety of their children, is thus clearly established in Supreme Court case law. Furthermore, that right extends to choosing the material they are allowed to see, read or hear, even when the government believes that this material may be inappropriate for consumption by children.

The focus of the Supreme Court in these cases has been on the Due Process Clause's fundamental rights of parents to make vital decisions in the upbringing of their children. There are, however, additional reasons why parents should play this primary role, reasons that rest not on the rights of parents but instead on societal goods related to the First Amendment. This additional rationale was touched on by the *Meyer* Court when it said: "The fundamental theory of liberty upon which all governments in this Union repose excludes any general power of the state to standardize its children by forcing them to accept instruction from public teachers only."[31] Just as allowing education in private schools serves to prevent the standardization of children, the active role of parents in choosing values for and imparting them to their children also limits standardization.

Certainly the most effective way for a government to perpetuate its power would be to teach the children the wisdom and goodness of that government and to prevent them from hearing any contrary views. Nazi and communist youth movements ingrained the beliefs of their government sponsors in children and encouraged children to turn in parents for subversive thoughts. Lenin is said to have said: "Give me four years to teach the children and the seed I have sown will never be uprooted."[32] And, Hitler is reported to have said something akin to: "Give me your children today, and I will give you the world tomorrow."[33] Add to the government's teaching the potential threat of being turned in by one's children for expressing views contrary to the government's, and parents will be unwilling to offer views that might buffer the effects of the government's propaganda on children.

Of course, not all inculcations of values in children by others than their parents are necessarily evil. St. Francis Xavier expressed thoughts similar to those of Lenin and Hitler, in saying, "Give me the children until they are seven, and anyone may have them afterwards."[34] And, all the expressions are variations on Virgil's "As the twig is bent the tree inclines."[35] Every country tries to instill its cultural and political principles in its children. The difference between Lenin's and Hitler's governments on the one hand and a free government on the other is not just a difference in the values taught. In a free society, the scope and strength of indoctrination are limited by other, particularly parental, influences that prevent the government from becoming the sole teacher of values to the children of that society.

C. A Role for Society

1. What Values to Further

Not surprisingly, the communitarians have discussed how to determine the community values they would allow society to further in a noncoercive manner. Etzioni looks to shared values, those values to which most of the members of society are committed. These communitarian values are handed down from generation to generation. They are not the invented or negotiated momentary positions taken by the current generation.[36] Identifying those heirloom values and resolving conflicts among them is the subject of "values talks." To keep those talks from breaking down, Etzioni suggests rules to prevent a deterioration into a culture war.[37] He says that those engaged in values talks should avoid demonizing one another, and they should recognize the positive aspects of the other's values. They should also avoid attacking one another's deepest moral commitments and some issues should even be left out of the debate.

Etzioni argues that societies, including large societies, do engage in the moral dialogs he suggests. These societal debates, what he calls "megalogues," may be found in combinations of local conversations among couples or coworkers, at pubs or coffeehouses, in meetings of associations, and at the national level in magazines, televised debates and on call-in radio programs.[38] "Megalogues are often extensive, disorderly (in the sense that there is no clear pattern to them), have an unclear beginning, and no clear or decisive conclusion. Nevertheless, in societies that are relatively communitarian, megalogues lead to significant changes in core values."[39] He offers examples of changes in the definition of death and in views as to the importance of preserving the environment, changes that would seem to go beyond simply enacting legislation and that affect views about individual autonomy and property rights.

It would seem clear that the results of megalogues, the core values handed down from generation to generation, are likely to have the form of general principles rather than the detail of a civil code. There is certainly great disagreement in our or any other diverse society regarding many specific issues. There is also strong, and at least close to universal, agreement on other values, values that may be said to be at the core. Our society is committed to the value of human life even if there is disagreement as to what constitutes human life, either at the early developmental stages or in the terminal stages, and with regard to the acceptability of the death penalty. Our society is also committed to the resolution of disagreements by other than physical force and to certain rights of property owners. These values may conflict, and an extended, strong disagreement may require resolution through a megalogue.

For other values, a significant part of society may be committed, while the remaining, also significant, part of society is opposed. The moral status of the unborn and the right of the individual to make her own decisions regarding an abortion are issues over which there is great disagreement. Issues regarding the existence of God and more so over the nature of God and God's relationship to humans also divide society. We may be in agreement as to the importance of a free, vigorous political debate, but there is certainly disagreement as to the correct conclusions that should emerge from that debate.

If society is to teach or otherwise further values, it must be limited to those truly core values widely, preferably almost universally, shared. Society can teach respect for the religions and political views of others, without teaching specific religious or political positions.[40] Universality need not be required. Respect for the property of others can be taught, despite the existence of some who may not believe in private property. The existence of a number of sociopaths does not prevent teaching the wrongfulness of murder.

The difference between the core values and the specifics over which there is wider and legitimate disagreement drives home again the importance of parents retaining a strong and protected role in imparting values to the younger generation. Society may play a role in inculcating its core values. Indeed, when what parents teach is at odds with core values to the point of encouraging criminality, parents might be prevented from passing on their values. Where the issues are not core and disagreement must be acceptable, parents determine which values they will at least try to pass on. With regard to religion, it is the parents who make initial decisions that may later be adhered to or rejected by their children. Parents, and not the formal state or the less formal society, should be the primary teacher of political values for children as well.

2. Using the Schools to Teach Values

Since the concern of this work is raising children and the development of values in the new generation, the front along which any government action takes place is likely to be in the schools, the locus of interaction between the child and the government. While some may argue that schools should not be in the business of teaching values, that is an impossibility. Whatever a school does or does not do, values will be learned. A school may take actions to prevent cheating on tests or it may ignore such cheating. If it takes action, it teaches honesty. If it takes no action, it teaches doing whatever serves the individual's immediate desires. It must teach one of the two, and it would seem difficult to argue that, of the two, it should choose against teaching honesty. Amy Gutmann suggests even more subtle ways in which schools teach values. She notes practices in Japanese elementary schools in which students who have mastered the day's material help those who have not, and in which students, faculty and administration share in doing the chores that keep the school running. These actions serve as lessons in egalitarianism, and she argues that the lack of such practices in the United States teaches different lessons.[41]

Etzioni also gives his communitarian view about the role of schools in the teaching of values and the values the schools should teach. He argues that schools are more important than ever in teaching values, because families are currently less likely to fill this role.[42] Not that there is a conflict between the values present in families and those the school would teach, but parents simply have or take less time in teaching values. At the same time, schools are seen as less willing to teach values or character.[43] This is, perhaps, because of a reasonable desire to avoid value issues that are too specific and perhaps tied to a religious view. But that is not what Etzioni has in mind. His concern and the role he sees for the schools is in the development of character.

> From a communitarian viewpoint, to draw on public schools as developers of character (for a stronger higher self) it is most important that they focus on development of personality capabilities that enable people to act civilly and morally. First among these capabilities is the ability to control one's impulses. The underlying assumption is that aggressive and other antisocial impulses cannot be extinguished; a mature person needs to learn to recognize urges—anger, for instance—and acquire ways to curb them or channel them toward socially constructive outlets. Second a well-formed person must have what Adam Smith called "sympathy": roughly, the ability to put oneself in the other person's shoes, what we would refer to as empathy. Without this quality, there is little likelihood that children will develop charity, fairness, respect for other people, or the other virtues. When a person possesses these twin capacities, the psychological foundations for abiding by internalized values are in place.[44]

Etzioni elsewhere emphasizes character development and the acquisition of core values as the most important requirements in the development of youngsters. With regard to character development, he places the development of self-control at the center. "[C]haracter development . . . is acquiring the capacity to control one's impulses and to mobilize oneself for acts other than the satisfaction of biological needs and immediate desires."[45] Self-control leads to the empathy and toleration he considers important and to the self-discipline necessary for success. It is hard to disagree with the character qualities put forward by Etzioni. Self-control, empathy, charity, fairness and respect for other people are so fundamental and so clear that one who does not accept them as good qualities must be seen as lacking character in a way that one who disagrees with another's views on abortion or the death penalty is not.

These values are also so basic that many everyday actions must be seen as either reflecting or rejecting them. A school cannot be neutral about whether or not its students should respect other people. Either it requires respect for one another among its students, or its failure to do so reflects a position that others are not worthy of respect. If self-control is not expected of students, sanction is given to acting on impulse. If schools tolerate hate speech directed by one student against another,[46] they will be seen as implicitly approving the value conveyed. Concerns over imposing more controversial values should not prevent schools from imparting at least these sorts of core values.

It is when the schools go beyond basic character building and turn to the second of these steps in moral development, the acquisition of core values, that controversy can, and indeed does, arise. Etzioni suggests that the schools begin selecting values by starting with the values we all share. There should be little controversy raised by teaching the impropriety of murder, robbery, rape, discrimination or disrespect for others. Properly done, values education may be widely supported. Etzioni reports on the experience of the Baltimore County, Maryland, schools, where a core of twenty-four values, including truth telling and due process are taught. A survey of participants showed support for the program at levels of 98 percent of the administrators, 85 percent of the parents and 75 percent of the students.[47] Neither, he says, need we worry about teachers "brain washing" children, given the wide exposure children have to other moral viewpoints presented by the media and their peers. Rather than the possibility of brainwashing by teachers, Etzioni says:

> [T]he opposite is true: if typical educators, whose values tend to be well within the community range, refrain from adding their moral voice to the cacophony of voices the students hear anyhow, the students would miss one perspective—and remain exposed only to all the other voices, many of which are less committed to values the community holds dear. It makes little sense to muzzle the educators and let everyone else spout their messages without inhibition.[48]

Many would, however, see some sense in limiting the educator, even when children are exposed to other voices. Educators have day-long access to children that others may lack, though television may be at least a close second. They also enjoy a sort of imprimatur from the state. Furthermore, parents are required to send their children to school, and for many, public school is the only real option for meeting that requirement.

If the values taught were limited to the truly core values, there might not be controversy, but schools do sometimes address issues on which there may be less agreement. An example is presented by the controversy, several years ago, regarding the use of the book *Heather Has Two Mommies*,[49] a story of a girl raised by a lesbian couple and the natural child, through artificial insemination, of one of them. The book explains how a child can "have no daddy" and teaches that the important thing about families is that the members love and support one another. The use of the book drew criticism, interestingly from many of the same quarters that called for the resurrection of teaching moral values in the schools in the wake of the Columbine High School shooting.

Presumably all should agree that children ought to be taught not to discriminate against Heather because of her two mommies. But the issue of the status of traditional families in comparison to the varieties of nontraditional family groupings is subject to more lively debate. What some would view as honoring loving, supporting relationships, others would see as an attack on values that make our society what it is. Schools may need to be careful in how they address these somewhat more controversial topics. There is much to be said in favor of schools taking on issues such as those presented by *Heather*. Children recognize that they live in a variety of circumstances, and the schools may not be able to avoid the issue. If the arrangements in which some live are ignored, the message will be that these families are not to be considered acceptable, and many will object to such a stance. If the arrangements are discussed openly, a positive message may emerge that others will find objectionable. Since a position must be taken, the schools should look to the values of the community and present those values, while being careful not to demonize those who disagree.

If the schools are going to teach values in the way discussed, the importance of opting out must be recognized. Parents must still be the principal teachers of values. If the values the schools teach conflict with those of the parents, the parents should be given the right to have their children excused from the lessons with which they disagree. Schools are often quite cognizant of this need to offer an opt-out. Notices are sent home explaining the content of the materials to be offered and asking parents to indicate any desire that their children be excused. In the extreme, we have the ultimate opt-out guaranteed by *Pierce* that allows parents to remove their children from the public schools and provide their children with an education in a values environment more like the one accepted by the parents. As long as the values taught are not so identified with religion as to constitute an establishment and parents are left the opportunity to opt out, the schools' role in inculcating values should not be a violation of the Constitution.

3. Limiting Exposure to Negative Experiences

While society can teach values, it may be even more effective if it limits the exposure of children to materials that have negative effects. The idea of limiting materials for adult consumption on the basis of a government belief that they are objectionable is unacceptable under the First Amendment, but children are different. As long as parents are free to obtain and provide for their children the material the government believes objectionable, limits on the provision of those materials to children by third parties simply help the parents in their right and duty to teach their children values.

The causative effect of media violence was discussed in chapter 2, but violence studies indicate an additional effect that may well carry over to other areas. Children may simply get the wrong idea as to what the world is actually like, which will affect their reactions to the world and their abilities to interact effectively with others. Again, there would be danger in allowing the government to decide what the "right idea" is as to what the world is like and limit the exposure of adults to materials that conflict with that idea. But as long as parents are free to provide other exposure, limits on materials that reach youth are of less concern.

Mistaken assessment of the world was examined by George Gerbner and his associates several decades ago.[50] Gerbner's cultivation hypothesis suggested that heavy television viewers, since they are exposed to more violence and more depictions of crime, would see the world as being more violent and as having more crime than it really is or does. Such viewers would be alienated, would be generally more fearful, and would be excessively cautious in living their everyday lives. The explanation offered for his hypothesis was that television would provide a major experiential structure through which its heavy viewers would interpret reality. Gerbner's studies found evidence confirming his hypothesis: heavy television viewers were more fearful of walking alone at night, even in their own neighborhoods, and were more likely than nonviewers or light viewers to believe that they would be the victim of violence. His hypothesis and conclusions also found support in studies conducted by others.[51]

A study by W. James Potter looked at Gerbner's work but added controls for beliefs about or attitudes toward television. He concluded that individuals who consider television to be a "magic window" on the world, that is, an accurate, unaltered picture of real life, and those who seek instruction from television or identify with television characters particularly exhibit the effects of cultivation. They have a stronger belief than others that the world is a mean and violent place.[52] Ronald Slaby ties this result to children. "Particularly high levels of unrealistic television violence are presented to those most vulnerable to its distorting effects—children. Children are generally more susceptible than adults because they lack the real-world experience and the critical judgment necessary to evaluate how unrealistic and irrelevant to their own lives the distorted portrayals of violence may be."[53] Since children lack the real-world experience of adults, they would seem more likely to consider television a "magic window" on the world and to take television to be instructional. There are, then, additional special reasons to shield children from images of violence, reasons that speak to the issue of the kinds of persons they are to become and what their psychological health will be.

A correlation between identification with the victim of media violence and the development of a belief that the world is more violent than it actually is may be of even more special concern for the psychological development of girls. While the generally greater likelihood of boys to resort to violence might lead some to conclude that media violence has little effect on girls, the cultivation hypothesis and the sort of victim portrayed in some forms of violent media depictions raise particular concerns for girls. The victims of many "slasher" films are women who show an inclination toward independence and autonomy.[54] The lesson to girls is that they are in danger if they are independent and autonomous, a lesson contrary to that which society is trying to teach in an era in which opportunities for women are supposed to be equal to those of men.

The cultivation hypothesis has received the most attention for violence in the media, but there is no reason why it should not also apply to other varieties of depiction. To whatever degree the sexual activity of television characters is of greater frequency than people of similar age in the general population, children are likely to grow up with unreasonable expectations regarding healthy sex lives, an expectation that may lead to more sexual experimentation at an earlier age than might exist without such media influences, or perhaps disappointment over their levels of sexual activity failing to meet their expectations. To the extent that media images depict more faithlessness in marriage, children may grow up believing that they are not expected to remain faithful and believing that their marriage vows have little binding effect on themselves or their partners. To the degree that the media depict unprotected sexual activity, children may grow up believing that AIDS is not the serious health problem it is.

Sex is also not the only additional area of concern. Conservative groups have complained about the depiction of drug use in film and to a lesser degree in television. Complaints also arise from the smoking and drinking of characters featured in the media. Among the strongest complaints regarding cigarette advertising was the Marlboro man presenting the image of cigarette smoking as a part of being the strong, independent man. Alcohol and cigarette ads generally use attractive young characters in an effort to portray those activities as a part of the desirable lifestyle of young adults.

There is a difference between the causation discussed in chapter 2 and the cultivation hypothesis at issue here, but the difference may be subtle, and it would seem that cultivation could contribute to causation. An individual who sees the normal operation of the world as more violent, more sexual or more involved with alcohol, tobacco or other drugs than it is would seem likely, in trying to adapt to or fit in with that world, to mirror the behavior believed to be so prevalent. If parents, and to a lesser degree the state, are to have an effective role in raising psychologically healthy children, the parents need to have the right to limit the unhealthy influences their children encounter. In this they need the help of the government in preventing third parties from foisting on children the most extreme of these negative influences, such as the hate-filled music available on CDs and the violence found in the video arcade and on film.

5

Children and
Other Constitutional Rights

The suggestion of a First Amendment with less strength, when children are concerned, coupled with a strong First Amendment protecting adult-to-adult communication is not without at least analogical constitutional authority. Adults enjoy a variety of constitutionally protected rights that have different strength when applied to children. In some cases the child has less right to make what would be constitutionally protected decisions if the individual were an adult. In other cases, constitutional limitations on the government are greater because of concerns over children. Thus, to whatever degree novelty counsels against the adoption of the thesis of this work, that negative counsel is mitigated by these analogous treatments.

A. Abortion and Contraception Rights

The Supreme Court, in *Roe v. Wade*,[1] established that a woman has a constitutional right to decide whether or not to obtain a previability abortion. While the right to abortion, or the more general right to privacy, is not mentioned in the text of the Constitution, the *Roe* opinion recognized that the Court, in *Griswold v. Connecticut*,[2] had already found constitutionally protected zones of privacy. In *Roe*, then, the issue was whether this privacy right extended to the decision to obtain an abortion, and the Court so concluded.

Abortion may seem an unlikely place to search for a parallel to lessened First Amendment rights, since minors have more rights regarding abortion than in other medical situations, but there is relevance. States have attempted to require parental consent before a minor can obtain an abortion. In 1976, the Court struck down a Missouri statute requiring the written consent of a parent or guardian for an unmarried woman under the age of eighteen to obtain an abortion not necessary to preserve the mother's life.[3] In that decision and a series of later decisions, the Court established that a parental consent requirement is constitutionally valid only if there is a judicial bypass procedure. The minor wishing to obtain an abortion, without getting consent from her parents, must be allowed to demonstrate to a judge that she is mature enough to make the decision for herself or that the abortion would be in her best interests.[4]

The treatment of abortion decisions by minors provides these minors more rights than other situations would call for but less than the full rights of adult females. A minor seeking any number of medical procedures, cosmetic surgery as an example, would not receive such services without the consent of the minor's parent. Yet an abortion may be obtained by following the judicial bypass procedure. The difference is perhaps best explained by the magnitude of the decision involved. A decision whether or not to obtain an abortion has lifelong consequences. It is the decision about whether or not to be a parent, and while putting the child up for adoption may address some of the consequences of the decision, the minor will still be a biological parent. The decision to have cosmetic surgery may also have lifelong consequences, but it is a decision that in most cases can be put off until the minor reaches the age of majority. The abortion decision is one that must be made in the short term, and the minor must be given the opportunity to demonstrate that she is mature enough to make the decision or that it is in her best interests.

Minors have more rights in making decisions regarding abortions than they may have in other areas, but that decision-making authority clearly has less strength than it does in the adult context. An adult female cannot be required to obtain the permission of her spouse, or any other person, before obtaining an abortion.[5] Even adding a judicial bypass procedure, in which the woman would be required to demonstrate maturity or that the abortion would be in her best interests, could not save such a requirement. An adult, unless ruled incompetent, is simply assumed to have the maturity to make her own decisions. Minors are not so assumed and must demonstrate that maturity.

This bifurcation might seem to be called into question by the decisions in the related area of contraceptive use. *Griswold* established the right of a married couple to use contraceptives. The Court there concluded that

the marital relationship falls within the zone of privacy it found established in the "penumbra" of the Constitution. It further noted that regulation of the use of contraceptives, rather than their manufacture or sale,
sought to achieve whatever goals the state might have by the means most
destructive to this protected relationship. This right to contraceptive use
was later extended to nonmarried persons in *Eisenstadt v. Baird*.[6] The
Court said,

> [T]he rights of the individual to access to contraceptives . . . must be the
> same for the unmarried and married alike. . . . It is true that in *Griswold*
> the right of privacy in question inhered in the marital relationship. Yet
> the marital couple is not an independent entity with a mind and heart of
> its own, but an association of two individuals each with a separate intel-
> lectual and emotional makeup. If the right of privacy means anything, it
> is the right of the *individual*, married or single, to be free from unwar-
> ranted governmental intrusion into matters so fundamentally affecting a
> person as the decision to bear or beget a child.[7]

The right to use contraceptives, while originally found in the protection
of the marital relationship, was also upheld for the sexual relationships
of the nonmarried. While the decision lacks the laudatory language of
Griswold, which had said that marriage is "a right of privacy older than
the Bill of Rights . . . a coming together for better or worse, hopefully en-
during, and intimate to the degree of being sacred,"[8] the Court in *Eisenstadt* provided clear recognition of a privacy right of unmarried persons
to the use of contraceptives.

It is true that the Court struck down, in *Carey v. Population Services*,[9]
a New York statute banning the distribution of contraceptives to those
under the age of sixteen. However, the talk of privacy rights present in the
extension to unmarried adults lacked any of the prominence of the earlier
decision. Rather than rejecting the state's goal of limiting sexual activity
by minors, the Court held that furthering that goal by banning the distribution of contraceptives to minors lacked rationality. The four-justice
plurality opinion said that it would be unreasonable to believe that the
state was making pregnancy the punishment for fornication. Justice
Stevens, in a concurrence, said that the state banning the distribution of
contraceptives to minors in order to communicate its disapproval of minors' engagement in sexual activities would be the same as expressing disapproval of motorcycles by prohibiting the use of protective headgear.[10]

As Justice Stevens said, there need not be a constitutional right to ride a motorcycle to conclude that the ban on helmets is irrational. Access to contraceptive by minors, then, is on a different basis than for adults. The rights of adults are stronger, but the punishment handed down to minors, even when no privacy right is involved, must still be rational.

Thus, the Court appears to treat contraceptive rights for adults differently than for children. There is an unwillingness to allow interference with marital sexual relations, and there is talk of rights inherent in the Constitution for a couple to make its own decisions as to the procreative probability of that relationship. Such rights talk carries over to the right of unmarried adults to make similar decisions. When it comes to children, however, the contraceptive decision, while allowing such use, does so by a different analysis. The state can express its view that sex among minors is morally unacceptable. Indeed, it can impose criminal liability through statutory rape laws. What it cannot do is express its position through a statute that requires minors to accept the greater risk of pregnancy that accompanies sex without contraceptives.

B. *The Free Exercise of Religion*

While it might be countered that arguing for different treatments of adult and minor free speech rights based on differences in contraception and abortion rights lacks force because free speech is explicit in the Bill of Rights and reproduction rights are nontextual, differing treatment is also found involving explicit provisions. In fact, the religion clauses, also in the First Amendment, are seen as having differing strengths depending on whether adults or children are involved. One of those clauses will be considered in this section, and the other will be the subject of the next.

The Free Exercise Clause, speaking of religion, provides: "Congress shall make no law . . . prohibiting the free exercise thereof." While nothing stated in the amendment would limit its application to adults, where children are involved the clause lacks the strength it has enjoyed for adults. The use of the past tense in the preceding sentence is due to a relatively recent decision limiting the strength of the clause generally.[11] As the clause loses vitality for adults, the difference between adult and minor application lessens.

Despite the weakening of the Free Exercise Clause, a history of differing treatment, when the clause served a stronger role, still serves as an analogical argument for differing treatment in the area of free expression. The most important earlier case for the issues addressed here is *Prince v. Massachusetts*.[12] *Prince* involved the conviction of a Jehovah's Witness who distributed *Watchtower* and *Consolation*, two publications of the church. Her legal problems grew out of the fact that she allowed her nine-year-old niece, of whom she was the legal guardian, to accompany her and to engage in that religious work. This was held, by the state courts, to be a violation of Massachusetts laws prohibiting furnishing goods to a minor knowing the minor intends to sell the goods and prohibiting a parent or guardian from permitting a minor under his or her control to be so employed. Mrs. Prince and her niece both testified that they were ordained ministers, and both aunt and niece believed it to be their religious duty to spread their religious message through this street ministry.

Mrs. Prince appealed her conviction to the Supreme Court, claiming violations of her First Amendment right to the free exercise of religion and her parental rights to raise her children as she saw fit, including teaching them the principles and practices of her religion. She also asserted her niece's own right to engage in the religious practice of preaching the gospel and distributing religious literature. The Court recognized a conflict of rights and interests. On the one side were the parental and religious freedoms just mentioned. On the other was the interest of society in protecting the welfare of children, "the interest of youth itself, and of the whole community, that children be both safeguarded from abuses and given opportunities for growth into free and independent well-developed men and citizens."[13] While the Court noted that it had earlier recognized the rights of children to free exercise, citing to its decision in *West Virginia v. Barnette*,[14] protecting Jehovah's Witness children who attend public schools from being forced to salute the flag, and *Pierce v. Society of Sisters*,[15] which struck down a law banning education in other than public schools, it stated that the family could not place itself beyond state regulation in the public interest by invoking the Free Exercise Clause.

It is clear that the Court found differing strengths in the free-exercise rights of adults and children or certainly differences in the state's ability to override those rights. The Court conceded that a statute like the one at issue but directed against adult distribution of materials under the same circumstances would be invalid. But, the Court said: "[T]he mere fact a state could not wholly prohibit this form of adult activity . . . does not mean it cannot do so for children. . . . The state's authority over children's activities is broader than over like actions of adults. . . . A democratic society rests, for its continuance, upon the healthy, well-rounded growth of young people into full maturity as citizens."[16] The Court then concluded, in language that seems overwrought for the degree of harm involved, "Parents may be free to become martyrs themselves. But it does not follow that they are free, in identical circumstances, to make martyrs of their children before they have reached the age of full and legal discretion when they can make that choice for themselves."[17]

While talk of martyrdom may have been overblown in *Prince*, in some of the cases in which the lower courts have applied the principles laid down in *Prince* the language was appropriate. There are religious sects that reject medical treatments commonly accepted by the rest of the population.[18] Jehovah's Witnesses, for example, will not accept blood transfusions. They view transfusions as the ingestion of human blood prohibited by the Bible. Christian Scientists rely on prayer and God for healing. They may seek the help of a Christian Science practitioner, but such help is spiritual rather than conventionally medical.

Where an adult refuses medical treatment, that adult may have the free-exercise right to what could be considered martyrdom. The Supreme Court has not decided such a case, but in *Cruzan v. Director, Missouri Dept. of Health*[19] the Court assumed for purposes of argument that there was a right to refuse medical treatment, including nutrition and hydration. The patient in *Cruzan* was in a persistently vegetative state and the issue was merely whether the state could require clear and convincing evidence of the wishes of the patient with regard to her continuing care. Even if such a right exists, based in decisional privacy or free exercise, the Court simply concluded that the state did have the right to require clear and convincing evidence that the patient did in fact wish to refuse medical care.

There are lower court cases that are more on point, cases in which courts have considered religiously inspired decisions to refuse medical care necessary to preserve the life of the patient. Where the patient is an adult, the cases may be seen as split on the constitutionality of ordering such treatment, but in the cases in which treatment is ordered, the courts may have been skeptical regarding the firmness with which the patient held his or her religious belief or the competence of the patient, or it had found a basis for an overriding interest on the part of society.[20] Where no such factor is present, the courts seem unwilling to order medical treatment for an adult patient.[21] When children are involved, however, courts have drawn strong guidance from language found in *Prince*. "The right to practice religion freely does not include liberty to expose the community or child to communicable disease or the latter to ill health or death."[22]

People ex rel. Wallace v. Labrenz[23] presents one such case. There the Supreme Court of Illinois considered the propriety of ordering treatment for an eight-day-old infant. Physicians testified that, without a blood transfusion, the child would die or at least be so brain damaged that she would be permanently mentally impaired. The parents, who were Jehovah's Witnesses, refused to consent to the transfusion. The lower court concluded that the refusal constituted neglect, appointed a guardian and authorized the guardian to consent to a transfusion. The parents appealed the lower court's orders, arguing that their freedom of religion and their rights as parents had been violated. The state supreme court had no trouble dismissing those claims, finding the governing principles so "well settled" that no extensive discussion was required. While the freedom of religion and parental rights merit the highest respect, neither is without limitation. The court noted the Supreme Court's *Prince* decision and found the facts of the case it was facing far stronger justification for intervention by the state.

Criminal convictions have even been obtained and affirmed based on parental failure to provide medical care to their critically ill children. In *Commonwealth v. Barnhart*[24] the parents of a two-year-old child were convicted of involuntary manslaughter and endangering the welfare of a child. The child had a tumor in the abdominal area whose continued growth caused weight loss and, ultimately, death by starvation. The defendants admitted awareness of the child's medical condition, but as lifelong members of the Faith Tabernacle church, they followed church teachings and relied solely on prayer for a cure.

On appeal to the Pennsylvania Superior Court, the parents asserted their free-exercise rights under the First Amendment to raise their child according to the tenets of their religion. The court did not treat the claim lightly, calling the issue and outcome "troublesome" and adding:

> Our decision today directly penalizes appellants' exercise of their religious beliefs. Appellants ask how we can hold them criminally liable for putting their faith in God. No easy answer attends. A central tenet of appellants' faith is that life rests ultimately in God's hands. Three generations of appellants' family have adhered to that belief. . . . [M]ore than

concern for the child's physical well-being, the church's "greater concern" was for the child's spiritual interest or eternal interest.[25]

Nonetheless, the court decided that the real question was whether or not parents can "impose" their religious beliefs on their children. The court, again citing *Prince*, held that right limited where the beliefs exposed the child to illness or death. Children also have rights, and since a child of two cannot speak for himself or herself, the state may require the parents to provide medical care necessary to preserve the child's health or life.

It is clear that the court was concerned about the effect of its decision on religious freedom but felt it necessary for the protection of children. The court stated:

> We recognize that our decision today directly penalizes appellants in the practice of their religion. We emphasize that the liability attaches not to the appellants' decisions for themselves but rather to the decision effectively to forfeit their child's life. . . . Admittedly, the distinction is not a happy one. An integral part of family life is the transmission of values from one generation to the next.[26]

Nonetheless, the court was clear in its conviction that criminal liability may attach to the failure to provide necessary medical care to children and that the religious basis for a failure to so provide is not protected by the Free Exercise Clause.

A similar case is presented by *State v. Norman*.[27] In that case the defendant father was convicted of manslaughter for failing to provide medical care for his ten-year-old son. Defendant, his wife and family were members of the "No-Name Fellowship," a group that believed all illness is caused by sin, that the medical establishment was to be avoided and that healing must come through God. The parents became aware, from his symptoms, that the son had diabetes and prayed for his cure but did not seek medical help, and the son died. Mr. Norman appealed his conviction as a violation of the Free Exercise Clause and of the religious protections of the state constitution. The Washington Court of Appeals dismissed the claims with ease. The court found the analysis of *Prince* dispositive and also noted that, by 1991, the claim of free-exercise protection for the religiously inspired refusal to obtain medical care for a critically ill child "has been addressed and dismissed by numerous courts across the land."[28]

While it seems clear that the courts will not accept the claim that parental free exercise rights protect their decisions not to provide medical care for their children, there is a developing area that may limit the application of the line of cases to the situations of some minors. The development is the suggested emergence of a mature minor rule that would allow older children to reject medical care.[29] However, this emergence has not gained much in size or vigor. Nor, for that matter, is it clear that even a mature minor exception is developing, at least in the sort of case relevant to this analysis. An adult may refuse medical treatment on religious grounds, even when treatment would result in a return to normal health. The cases that may be argued to represent a right for mature minors to make such a decision to refuse medical care involved, with one exception, minors who would never return even to consciousness and for whom the decision was made by the parents.[30] The exceptional case, *In re E.G.*,[31] did allow an exceptionally mature minor to forgo medical treatment, but it did so not on constitutional grounds but on the basis of state common law. The case further noted that a different result might have obtained had the child and her parents disagreed.

In summary, then, an adult, except under exceptional circumstances, may assert a right based in the Free Exercise Clause to refuse medical treatment necessary to preserve his or her life. Parents who wish to assert such rights regarding or on behalf of their minor children are not protected by the Free Exercise Clause. An order for treatment may be obtained, and failure to provide treatment may lead to criminal prosecution. An immature minor may not assert a Free Exercise Clause right to refuse necessary care, and even in the case of a mature minor, the existence of a constitutional right is questionable. The Free Exercise Clause rights of adults regarding themselves are stronger than their rights regarding their children or the children's own religious rights. The state's interest in protecting the lives of children overrides a right, while a similar interest in the life of adults cannot override the same right in adults.

Before leaving the Free Exercise Clause, we must admit that there are cases prior to the weakening of the clause in which Free Exercise Clause and parental rights in raising their children have served as protection against state statutes regarding practices in school and requirements on school attendance. In *West Virginia Board of Education v. Barnette*[32] the

Court recognized a right on the part of Jehovah's Witness children not to salute the flag and pledge allegiance, as required under state law. While the decision was based on a right not to speak, as a sort of negative corollary to the First Amendment's free-expression rights, the reason for the student's refusal was religious.

The second case is *Wisconsin v. Yoder*.[33] This case concerned a state law requiring that children attend school until the age of sixteen. The law was challenged by an Amish family that refused to send their children to school past the eighth grade. The refusal was based on a religious belief in a community withdrawn from worldly matters. While an elementary school education was viewed by the community as valuable, education at the high school level would involve acts and activities incompatible with their Amish beliefs and would undermine the Amish community. The Court declared the law, as applied to the Amish children, unconstitutional. The state's interest in compelling an additional year or two of formal high school education instead of the informal education the children received in the community was held inadequate to justify the perceived harm to the children and the community.

Neither of the cases counters the view that adult claims under the Free Exercise Clause are treated more strongly than claims asserted by, or on behalf of, minors. The state interest in *Barnette* in requiring an orthodoxy of belief, or at least statement of orthodox belief, was simply inadequate to override the rights of either adult or child. The state's interest in *Yoder* was stronger, and the decision that the attendance requirement was unconstitutional was argued by Justice Douglas to put Amish children who might want to attend high school in a position in which they would be unable to choose any future other than as a member of the Amish community. The Court suggested that the result might have been different if a minor did wish to attend high school. The state's interest, at least where parent and child agreed, was still inadequate. Had the issue been a state requirement that Amish adults attend classes that would expose them to materials and activities harmful to their religion, the *Yoder* Court would certainly have had no difficulty in finding such a requirement unconstitutional. The degree of argument required in concluding that the children's religious rights were sufficient to overcome the state's interest certainly indicate that the state's interest was stronger and that a free-exercise clause right that would easily be held to have protected adults was at least a closer case for children.

C. The Establishment Clause

The Establishment Clause states "Congress shall make no law respecting an establishment of religion." This constitutional guarantee differs from those already discussed in that the reproductive and Free Exercise Clause rights are asserted in an effort to allow the individual to make a decision free of government interference. A violation of the Establishment Clause occurs not when the government interferes with an individual's actions but instead adopts, or appears to adopt, a religious position of its own. Even here, however, the fact that the audience before whom the seeming religious adoption takes place is youthful has an effect. An action by the government might not be seen as a violation of the Establishment Clause, when the audience is adult, but may be a violation when the audience consists of children.

Supreme Court references to the impressionability of youth appear in relatively early cases considering the interaction of religion and the schools. *Lemon v. Kurtzman*[34] involved state programs that provided aid to religious schools. One program paid a salary supplement to teachers in nonpublic schools teaching secular subjects, courses such as mathematics or Spanish, and the other reimbursed nonpublic schools for the salary and materials costs of teaching such secular subjects. The case is primarily known for the test the Court developed for analyzing Establishment Clause issues. That test requires that the statute or program have a secular purpose, not have the advancement or inhibition of religion as its primary effect and not foster excessive entanglement of government and religion.[35]

The programs in question would seem to have had secular purposes in providing for the secular education of nonpublic-school children. While the programs did help religious institutions by reducing the costs of teaching subjects that would have to be included in the curriculum of any secular or religious school, the principal or primary effect may not have been religious. Nonetheless, the programs were declared unconstitutional, because they fostered an excessive entanglement of government and religion. The Court adopted district court findings that parochial schools are an integral part of the Catholic Church's religious mission. The schools serve as a powerful tool in passing on the Catholic faith from one generation to another, and the Court said, "This process of inculcating religious doctrine is, of course, enhanced by the impressionable age of the pupils, in primary schools particularly."[36] Concern over this impressionability required care that the aid provided under the program not carry over to the religious mission of the schools. This required a level of monitoring of schools operations that was an unacceptable entanglement of the government in this essential part of a religious mission.

Similar concerns are found in *Grand Rapids v. Ball*.[37] There, teachers hired by the public school system were sent into classrooms at nonpublic, including religious, schools to teach remedial and enrichment courses in secular subjects. The classrooms in which they taught were not to contain religious objects, were technically leased to the public school system and were required to contain a sign stating that the room was a public school classroom. A second program in the same school district provided after-school courses in such subjects as gymnastics, home economic, drama, chess and yearbook production. The same requirements were in place regarding the classrooms involved. While the teachers in the school day program were full-time employees of the school district, the teachers in the after-school program were part time employees of the school system, and almost all were also full time employees of the nonpublic schools.

The Court applied the *Lemon* test, saying: "We have particularly relied on *Lemon* in every case involving the sensitive relationship between government and religion in the education of our children. The government's activities in this area can have a magnified impact on impressionable young minds."[38] While the Court found a clear secular purpose, the programs ran afoul of the requirement that the primary or principal effect be other than the advancement or inhibition of religion. There, again noting the involvement of young minds, the Court said that "the programs may provide a crucial symbolic link between government and religion, thereby enlisting—at least in the eyes of impressionable youngsters—the powers of government to the support of the religious denomination operating the school."[39] The Court also considered the issue of government endorsement of religion, an Establishment Clause test argued for by Justice O'-Connor.[40] The issue, under that test, is whether the statute, act or program in question is likely to be perceived by adherents of the controlling religion as an endorsement of their religious position and by nonadherents as a disapproval of theirs. In that regard, the Court said,

> The inquiry into this kind of effect must be conducted with particular care when many of the citizens perceiving the governmental message are children in their formative years. . . . The symbolism of a union between church and state is most likely to influence children of tender years,

whose experience is limited and whose beliefs consequently are the function of environment as much as of free and voluntary choice.[41]

References to age differences also may be found in cases involving
prayer. The Court decided, in *Marsh v. Chambers*,[42] that beginning a legislative session with a prayer was not a violation of the Establishment
Clause. Two more recent cases examining prayer in the school setting but
outside the classroom itself provide an interesting counterpoint to *Marsh*.
Lee v. Weisman[43] considered the constitutionality of invocations and
benedictions as part of graduation ceremonies in the public schools. The
prayers involved were "nonsectarian" and were delivered by a member of
the clergy selected by the school board. The Court, in declaring the practice to be in violation of the Establishment Clause, noted that it was concerned over protecting freedom of conscience in the schools from even
subtle coercive pressure. When prayer occurs in the school context, it may
be more likely to be seen as an attempt to use the state to inculcate religious belief.

The ceremonial use of prayer at graduation might well seem equivalent
to the ceremonial legislative invocations approved of in *Marsh*, but the
Lee Court found the situations to differ. Speaking of *Marsh*, the Court
said: "The atmosphere at the opening of a session of a state legislature
where adults are free to enter and leave with little comment and for any
number of reasons cannot compare with the constraining potential of the
one school event most important for the student to attend."[44] Formality
and teacher control left fewer options for the student, and the role of peer
pressure was seen as stronger. While adults might choose not to participate, "[r]esearch in psychology supports the common assumption that
adolescents are often susceptible to pressure from their peers towards
conformity, and that the influence is strongest in matters of social con-
vention."[45]

The Court came to a similar conclusion, when students rather than the
school board chose the individual to deliver the prayer and when the situation was not as central to the educational mission as graduation. In
Santa Fe Independent School Dist. v. Doe[46] the Court considered prayers
delivered over the public address system before a high school football
game. The students had decided to have such a prayer and chose a student to lead or offer the prayer. Despite the student initiation and delivery, the Court held that the prayer was still school sponsored. The school
had not opened the public address system as a public forum, and the

prayer could then not be viewed as private speech. The Court also quoted the language from *Lee*, quoted above, on peer pressure and concluded that there was as much social pressure and real desire to be involved in an extracurricular activity as central as football or activities such as cheerleading and band as to make attendance almost as psychologically compulsory as for graduation.

The Court has recognized that there is a need to provide more protection for children from practices that might constitute violations of the Establishment Clause than when only adults are involved. The impressionability of youth requires particular vigilance regarding school activities that might serve to inculcate religious beliefs. Even as the impressionability of youth fades with adolescence, the peer pressure to attend and act like one's peers at events such as graduation and football games requires that school-sponsored prayer be banned. It is clear that age has played a role in setting the dimensions of this constitutional protection.

D. Other Rights

Other constitutional rights are also of lesser strength for minors. In *Parham v. J.R.* [47] the Supreme Court considered Georgia statutory provisions for the commitment of minors to mental hospitals. The statute provided that parents could apply to have their children admitted. The hospital, on such application, could admit the child for observation. If the hospital superintendent then determined that there was evidence of mental illness and the child was suitable for treatment, the child was admitted. There was also a statutory duty imposed on the superintendent to release the child, once the child recovered or improved sufficiently so that hospitalization was no longer required.

This procedure was far short of the procedural guarantees due adults facing involuntary commitment. Adults had the right to full and fair adversary proceedings and the need to commit them had to be demonstrated to the satisfaction of a neutral tribunal.[48] Adults had the right to representation, to confront the witnesses against them through cross-examination and to put their own evidence in the record.[49] None of these procedures were afforded minors, with the arguable exception of the neutral decision maker, since the hospital superintendent had to agree to admission.

It was argued that the Georgia provisions for minors violated their Fourteenth Amendment rights not to be deprived of life, liberty or property without due process of law. The Court recognized that there was a liberty interest involved, both in terms of bodily restraint resulting from confinement and in the emotional and psychological harm that could result from commitment. Recognition of a life, liberty or property interest is, however, only the first step in analyzing a claimed violation of due process. The remaining task is to determine what process is due, that is, what procedure is required. In making that determination, courts consider, among other factors, the private interest affected.[50]

Turning to an analysis of the private interest, the Court did consider the child's interest in not being committed, but instead of treating that interest in isolation, the Court said "since this interest is inextricably linked with the parents' interest in and obligation for the welfare and health of the child, the private interest at stake is a combination of the child's and parent's concerns."[51] The Court agreed that the child, like an adult, has a substantial interest in avoiding unnecessary confinement for medical treatment and that there could be social consequences resulting from knowledge by others that a child has been committed. The Court, however, recognized that children lack the maturity, experience and judgment to make difficult decisions. Furthermore, the Court recognized interests on the part of parents who had decided that their child needed treatment and rejected the contention that the child's interests were so overriding that the parents' interest must be subordinated at least to the degree of requiring an adversarial hearing prior to commitment. Children's procedural rights are simply not as strong in this area as those of adults.[52]

An additional area in which adults' and minors' rights differ is that of firearm possession. The Second Amendment provides: "A well regulated Militia, being necessary to the security of a free State, the right of the people to keep and bear Arms, shall not be infringed." There is a great deal of debate over the meaning of the Second Amendment,[53] including the issue of whether the amendment applies only to the militia or is an individual right, but even advocates of individual rights seem willing to accept restrictions on possession by minors. Don Kates notes several restrictions on minors, without criticizing those restrictions, and notes that a federal statute that restricts gun ownership by minors was drafted and promoted by the National Rifle Association.[54] Glenn Reynolds offers an explanation for denying the right to bear arms to minors, along with criminals and the mentally unbalanced. He suggests that bearing arms was a part of being the virtuous citizen and that those incapable of or unwilling to be virtuous citizens did not share in the right.[55]

It might be argued that this particular restriction of a constitutional provision to adults does not support the general thesis that children may be less protected, because of the wording of the amendment. There is the lead clause of the amendment that ties the right to the need for a militia. That might lead to a conclusion that only those considered a part of the historical militia, adult males between a minimum and a maximum age, enjoy the right. But Reynolds notes that the right had always been extended to those, such as women, clergymen, seamen and older men, who were not part of the militia.[56] Thus, the exclusion of children is on a basis other than their nonmembership in the militia.

As a last example, consider the Fourth Amendment search and seizure rights of schoolchildren, addressed in *New Jersey v. T.L.O.*[57] A teacher discovered T.L.O., a fourteen-year-old female freshman, smoking in a high school lavatory. When taken to the principal's office, she denied to the assistant vice principal that she had been smoking or that she smoked at all. He demanded her purse, opened it and found and removed a pack of cigarettes. He also noticed a pack of cigarette-rolling papers, which he took to be associated with marihuana use. Suspecting such drug use and that a further search would yield more evidence, he searched more thoroughly, finding a small amount of marihuana, some money, a list of what appeared to be students owing T.L.O. money, and two letters implicating her in marihuana dealing. The evidence was turned over to the police, and delinquency charges were brought.

The issue of the admissibility of the seized evidence eventually reached the United States Supreme Court. The Court first considered whether or not the Fourth Amendment applies in the context of searches by school officials and concluded that it does. "In carrying out searches and other disciplinary functions pursuant to such policies, school officials act as representatives of the State, not merely as surrogates for the parents, and they cannot claim the parents' immunity from the strictures of the Fourth Amendment."[58]

Despite school officials being state actors and the Fourth Amendment applying to searches in schools, the Court found no violation in the search of T.L.O.'s purse. The Fourth Amendment demands that searches be reasonable, but reasonableness is, the Court said, dependent on the context of the search. While the child had a privacy interest, it must be balanced against the substantial interest of the schools in maintaining security and order. In striking the balance, the Court said:

> It is evident that the school setting requires some easing of the restrictions to which searches by public authorities are ordinarily subject. The warrant requirement, in particular, is unsuited to the school environment: requiring a teacher to obtain a warrant before searching a child suspected of an infraction of school rules (or of the criminal law) would unduly interfere with the maintenance of the swift and informal disciplinary procedures needed in the schools.[59]

The Court also held that there is a difference in the level of suspicion of illicit activity needed to justify a search. Probable cause would not be required but only reasonableness both at the inception of the search and in the way it was carried out.

> Under ordinary circumstances, a search of a student by a teacher or other school official will be "justified at its inception" when there are reasonable grounds for suspecting that the search will turn up evidence that the student has violated or is violating either the law or the rules of the school. Such a search will be permissible in its scope when the measures adopted are reasonably related to the objectives of the search and not excessively intrusive in light of the age and sex of the student and the nature of the infraction.[60]

Applying the rule to the search at issue, the Court found nothing unreasonable.

What is particularly interesting is that T.L.O.'s possession of cigarettes was not illegal and was not even a violation of school rules. This was not a case of suspicion of possession of a weapon or even of contraband. In those cases, the security of the school would certainly justify an intrusion that would not be tolerable in most other circumstances. The only justification for the search, a justification the Court found acceptable, was the expectation of securing evidence of violation of a school rule, a rule against actually smoking in the school. It seems inconceivable that the search of a teacher's briefcase to find evidence of a teacher's violation of school policy would be justified under these circumstances. It would seem that, lacking a security or safety interest in the presence of cigarettes in T.L.O.'s purse, the acceptance of the search, not only without a warrant but without an insistence on probable cause, must be taken as an indication that the Fourth Amendment rights of schoolchildren are simply not as strong as those of adults.

E. Considering Children

As the examples presented demonstrate, in a variety of areas of constitutional law, guarantees are interpreted differently for adults and for children. While the theory of our government is that there are areas in which the individual is free to make decisions without interference from that government, the theory simply does not apply with the same strength to children. Adults, at least competent adults, must be assumed to be equal in their capacities to make decisions and to enjoy the autonomy to act on those decisions in the areas of life protected by the Constitution. The dangers inherent in unrestrained government control of expression, religion, reproduction and detention are too great to allow unfettered majority control.

On the other hand, children are not equal to adults in their capacity to make decisions and need not enjoy the same levels of autonomy. Children may have to obtain parental consent for an abortion or they must demonstrate to a judge that they have sufficient maturity to be allowed to make their own decision or that the decision to obtain an abortion is in the child's best interests. This view clearly recognizes that children are not the equal of adults in their decision-making capacity or autonomy rights.

Differences in the procedures required for commitment to a mental hospital also demonstrate a constitutional rift between adult and child rights. The Court may have been correct in its view that parents will generally act in the best interests of their children, but that is not always the case. Furthermore, even if a parallel claim could be made for spouses caring for each other, certainly the Court would not be willing to lessen the procedural rights required for adult commitment when the commitment was at the request of a spouse.

The Establishment Clause also demonstrates a recognized difference in the capacity of adults and children to withstand societal influence in forming or retaining their belief systems. The Court has recognized that children may be more easily influenced by the public display of religion. The *Lemon* and endorsement tests for violations of the Establishment

Clause should be influenced by the likelihood that the act or display will further religion or that the audience will take that act or display as an endorsement, and in that regard youth matters.

Perhaps the best support for the thesis of this work is that found in the cases revolving around the Free Exercise Clause. That area provides a clear case of not only a constitutional right but a First Amendment right that is far stronger for adults than for children. Adults have been guaranteed the right to make religious decisions that most would consider to be against their best interests or at least against their best temporal interests. Adults with strong religious convictions dictating that they must forgo a particular form of medical treatment are allowed to choose prayer over medicine, even when the choice is likely to result in death. While there have been courts, either in questioning the competence of the patient or noting the needs of the patient's children, that have appointed guardians authorized to consent to treatment for the afflicted adult, adults generally are allowed to make decisions they see as vital to the soul at the expense of the body. With children the opposite situation holds. Courts have proven quite willing to step in to appoint guardians for purposes of countering parental decisions and allowing medical treatment necessary to protect the health or life of children.

The application of the Free Exercise Clause cases to the issue of free expression, at least with regard to the position argued for here, would seem strong. The Free Exercise Clause cases involved situations in which the parents' and child's wishes were aligned, with the state in opposition. The state's position should be more easily justified when there is not such a unity between the parents' and the child's desires. If the parents and child are not on the same side, the state's support for the parents' position is not only a lesser infringement on any rights but is also a recognition of the parents' role in the upbringing of their children.

The situation in which parent and child are on opposite sides, or at least not actively on the same side, is the case in the issue addressed here. The argument is that third parties can be barred from distributing materials to minors that the state believes are harmful to the children or to others. If parents disagree, they are still free to obtain the materials for their own children. But, the video game dealer or motion picture theater owner may be prohibited from providing the objectionable material directly to youth, without that parental decision and role. Thus, the state prohibits expression to children only when it is in agreement with the child's parents. That is a far lesser infringement on rights that ought to be protected than in the case where the state refuses to honor a religiously based decision agreed to by both parent and child. Society should be allowed to come down on the side of protecting its own and parental values at the expense of the values that unrelated third parties might wish to impart to children who are not their own.

6

Obscenity

The treatment of obscenity provides an example of how differing standards may be used for material distributed to children compared to material distributed to adults. The Supreme Court has held that material not obscene for an adult audience may be considered obscene when the audience consists of minors. For the most part, the result of this different treatment is to provide for the balance argued for here. Adults generally have access to material without government interference, while children are protected from unsuitable images. There are, however, negative effects on adult access that would be addressed by recognizing the more general differing applications of the First Amendment to adults and to children. Chilling effects on materials even for adult audiences would be lessened by a general recognition of the principle that the First Amendment rights of children should not be as strong as those of adults.

To understand the differing standards, the obscenity exception to the First Amendment must be examined. The doctrine that already provides for a lower standard for youth will then be addressed. The positive effects of this distinction, as well as the negative effects of the obscenity exception on adult availability will then be considered. Finally, the results of a restructured First Amendment, with limited protection for material distributed to children, will be discussed.

A. The Obscenity Exception

The obscenity exception to the First Amendment was recognized in *Roth v. United States* in 1957.[1] It is important to note, however, that this does not mean that obscene material was protected until 1957 and was suddenly swept from under the umbrella of the First Amendment. The Court stated that it had always been assumed that obscene material was not protected and also noted that, at the time of the framing of the Constitu-

tion and Bill of Rights, there was no absolute protection for all speech utterances, citing statutes from thirteen of the then fourteen states that punished certain types of speech.[2] Furthermore, there was said to be sufficient
evidence in a variety of statutes and cases, roughly contemporaneous with
the Bill of Rights, to show that obscenity was not intended to be within
the scope of First Amendment protection.[3]

Having declared obscene material to be unprotected, the Court turned
to the problem of definition. Not all sexual material is obscene. "Obscene
material is material which deals with sex in a manner appealing to the
prurient interest,"[4] material that incites lustful thoughts. The Court further defined "prurient" as "'Itching; longing; uneasy with desire or longing; of persons, having itching, morbid, or lascivious longings; of desire,
curiosity, or propensity, lewd.'"[5] Perhaps recognizing inadequacy in
drawing the distinction between sexual and obscene material, the Court
went on to say that it saw no difference between its definition and the one
found in the American Law Institute's Model Penal Code, which stated:
"'A thing is obscene if, considered as a whole, its predominant appeal is
to prurient interest, i.e., a shameful or morbid interest in nudity, sex, or
excretion, and it goes substantially beyond customary limits of candor in
description or representation of such matters.'"[6]

After *Roth*, the Court handed down a line of cases eventually producing, in *Miller v. California*,[7] the current test for obscenity. This test asks

(a) whether "the average person, applying contemporary community
standards" would find that the work, taken as a whole, appeals to the
prurient interest; (b) whether the work depicts or describes, in a patently
offensive way, sexual conduct specifically defined by the applicable state
law; and (c) whether the work, taken as a whole, lacks serious literary,
artistic, political, or scientific value.[8]

Even with *Miller*, obscenity law may not have progressed much beyond Justice Stewart's 1964 assertion that, while he could not define
obscenity, he knew it when he saw it.[9] The *Miller* test does require that
the statute at issue state the specific sexual activities that may be the
subject of obscenity prosecutions. Nonetheless, there is still the issue of
whether or not the depictions of those activities go beyond community
standards for prurience and are sufficiently offensive. The Court seems
untroubled by this issue. In examining the question of scienter, the defendant's knowledge required for a conviction, the Court has decided

that the defendant need not have recognized that the materials were legally obscene. The prosecution is only required to show that the defendant knew of the nature or character of the materials involved.[10] Foreknowledge on the part of the defendant as to the result of a legal determination of obscenity does not have to be shown.

One last case should be discussed before turning to the issue of juveniles and sexual material. The case is important, not because it itself involved minors but because it established a theory later used to allow differing standards for material distributed to minors. The case, *Mishkin v. New York*,[11] affirmed an obscenity conviction. What differentiated the case from other obscenity cases was the nature of the material involved. Mishkin was prosecuted for his role in hiring writers to produce particular material and in distributing the resulting product.

> Fifty books are involved in this case. They portray sexuality in many guises. Some depict relatively normal heterosexual relations, but more depict such deviations as sadomasochism, fetishism, and homosexuality. Many have covers with drawings of scantly clad women being whipped, beaten, tortured, or abused. Many, if not most, are photo-offsets of typewritten books written and illustrated by authors and artists according to detailed instructions given by the appellant. Typical of appellant's instructions was that related by one author who testified that appellant insisted that the books be "full of sex scenes and lesbian scenes. . . . [T]he sex had to be very strong, it had to be rough, it had to be clearly spelled out. . . . I had to write sex very bluntly, make the sex scenes very strong. . . . [T]he sex scenes had to be unusual sex scenes between men and women, and women and women, and men and men. . . . [H]e wanted scenes in which women were making love with women. . . . [H]e wanted sex scenes . . . in which there were lesbian scenes. He didn't call it lesbian, but he described women making love to women and men . . . making love to men, and there were spankings and scenes—sex in an abnormal and irregular fashion." Another author testified that appellant instructed him "to deal very graphically with . . . the darkening of the flesh under flagellation. . . . " Artists testified in similar vein as to appellant's instructions regarding illustrations and covers for the books.[12]

The nature of the material involved allowed an interesting defense to the obscenity charges.

Mishkin argued that at least some of the material at issue could not be considered obscene. To be obscene, material must appeal to the prurient interest, measured by the average person and contemporary community standards. Mishkin took the position that "some of the books involved in this prosecution, those depicting deviant sexual practices, such as flagellation, fetishism, and lesbianism, do not satisfy the prurient-appeal requirement because they do not appeal to a prurient interest of the 'average person' in sex, that 'instead of stimulating the erotic, they disgust and sicken.'"[13] The appellant's theory was that, since the average person would be turned off by the material rather than stimulated, it could not be held obscene.

The Court rejected Mishkin's gloss on obscenity law's prurient-appeal requirement, concluding that "[w]here the material is designed for and primarily disseminated to a clearly defined deviant sexual group, rather than the public at large, the prurient-appeal requirement of the *Roth* test is satisfied if the dominant theme of the material taken as a whole appeals to the prurient interest in sex of the members of that group."[14]

The Court explained that its requirement in *Roth* that prurient interest be judged by the average or normal person was not intended to foreclose conviction when material was aimed at a population with sexual interests that might be viewed as other than normal. Rather, the use of "average" and "normal" in *Roth* was intended for a very specific purpose. The Court had intended specifically to reject the *Hicklin* test, derived from the British case *Regina v. Hicklin*.[15] That test judged obscenity based on its impact on the most susceptible person. Material would be obscene, under a test based on the *Hicklin* approach, if it appealed to the prurient interests of anyone. *Roth*'s use of "average" or "normal" was intended to remove the most susceptible person as the measure of obscenity and allow material First Amendment protection or not, based on its effect on the general population.

The Court would not allow the *Roth* definition to stand in the way of prosecuting the production and distribution of sexual material that was intended for and marketed to a group with different sexual interests.

> We adjust the prurient-appeal requirement to social realities by permitting the appeal of this type of material to be assessed in terms of the sexual interests of its intended and probable recipient group; and since our holding requires that the recipient group be defined with more specificity

than in terms of sexually immature persons, it also avoids the inadequacy of the most-susceptible-person facet of the Hicklin test.[16]

While *Roth*'s change from *Hicklin* should require that materials not be considered obscene based on appeal to the most susceptible member of the group at which they were aimed, appeal is relative to the group at which the material is aimed or at which it is marketed. If material marketed to sadomasochists appeals to the prurient interests of the average sadomasochist and meets the other requirements of *Roth*, or now *Miller*, it is obscene and outside the protection of the First Amendment.

With regard to the material at issue in *Mishkin*, the Court concluded that there was no claim that the material, which depicted "sexually deviant practices" was lacking in prurient appeal to "sexually deviant groups" and that the books had been specifically produced and marketed for such groups.

> Appellant instructed his authors and artists to prepare the books expressly to induce their purchase by persons who would probably be sexually stimulated by them. It was for this reason that appellant "wanted an emphasis on beatings and fetishism and clothing—irregular clothing, and that sort of thing, and again sex scenes between women; always sex scenes had to be very strong." And to be certain that authors fulfilled his purpose, appellant furnished them with such source materials as Caprio, Variations in Sexual Behavior, and Krafft-Ebing, Psychopathia Sexualis.[17]

The theory resulting from *Mishkin* is known as variable obscenity, and while it found its Supreme Court case law origins in the consideration of depictions of sexual deviation, its academic seeds were found in an article by Lockhart and McClure regarding material distributed to youth.[18] This application of the theory as it applies to youth would come a mere two years later in the case discussed below.

B. Pornography and Children

Pornographic material has sexual content but is not necessarily obscene. To be obscene, pornographic material must be not merely sexual but also meet the requirements of *Miller*. It must go beyond community standards for prurience, be offensive and lack serious value. If pornographic material is not obscene, it enjoys the protection of the First Amendment. Thus, less explicit material is protected, as is explicit material that also has serious value. While adults may produce and distribute nonobscene pornographic material, the Court has limited the First Amendment protections of pornographic material when it is distributed to minors.

1. Obscenity as to Children

Ginsberg v. New York involved the sale of a magazine to a minor.[19] Sam Ginsberg and his wife ran Sam's Stationery and Luncheonette on Long Island. As part of that business, they sold magazines. Ginsberg was charged with having, on each of two occasions, sold two copies of what the Court characterized as "girlie magazines" to a sixteen-year-old boy. All the magazines contained pictures of female nudity. None were argued to be obscene if distributed to adults.

Ginsberg was charged with violating a New York statute making it a crime "'knowingly to sell . . . to a minor . . . any picture . . . which depicts nudity, sexual conduct or sado-masochistic abuse and which is harmful to minors.'"[20] The statute defined material "harmful to minors" as material that depicts nudity, sexual conduct, sexual excitement, or sado-masochistic abuse and which "'(i) predominantly appeals to the prurient, shameful or morbid interest of minors, and (ii) is patently offensive to prevailing standards in the adult community as a whole with respect to what is suitable material for minors, and (iii) is utterly without redeeming social importance for minors.'"[21] The statute also defined nudity as "the showing of the human male or female genitals, pubic area or buttocks with less than a full opaque covering, or the showing of the female breast with less than a fully opaque covering of any portion thereof below the top of the nipple, or the depiction of covered male genitals in a discernibly turgid state."[22] "Sexual conduct" was defined as "acts of masturbation, homosexuality, sexual intercourse, or physical contact with a person's clothed or unclothed genitals, public area, buttocks or, if such person be a female, breast."[23] Further defined were "sexual excitement" as "the condition of human male or female genitals when in a state of sexual stimulation or arousal" and "sado-masochistic abuse" as "flagellation or torture by or upon a person clad in undergarments, a mask or bizarre costume, or the condition of being fettered, bound or otherwise physically restrained on the part of one so clothed."[24]

The statute, which employed a minor-specific variant of the then relevant obscenity test, was far from unique. The Court cited obscenity statutes from thirty-five states containing provisions regarding distribution to minors.[25] Ginsberg was found guilty and, while he could have been fined up to $500 and imprisoned for up to one year, he received a suspended sentence.

It is important to note, though not an issue in *Ginsberg*, that the statute did contain provisions regarding knowledge or belief with regard to content of the magazines and the age of the purchaser. The statute presumed that a vendor knows the content and character of the magazines he or she sells, as long as there was reasonable opportunity to examine the content of the material. The Court said that it intimated no view on the constitutionality of that presumption. The statute also provided a defense:

> [I]t is an affirmative defense that: (a) The defendant had reasonable cause to believe that the minor involved was seventeen years old or more; and (b) Such minor exhibited to the defendant a draft card, driver's license, birth certificate or other official or apparently official document purporting to establish that such minor was seventeen years old or more.[26]

The defense was not asserted in *Ginsberg* but is important in addressing any concern that the New York statute could have set a trap for unwary merchants.

The Court recognized that the New York state legislature had employed the then recent theory of variable obscenity and quoted Lockhart and McClure's explanation of that concept. "'Variable obscenity . . . furnishes a useful analytical tool for dealing with the problem of denying adolescents access to material aimed at a primary audience of sexually mature adults. For variable obscenity focuses attention upon the make-up of primary and peripheral audiences in varying circumstances, and provides a reasonably satisfactory means for delineating the obscene in each circumstance.'"[27] The theory implies that material protected for adult distribution is not necessarily protected for dissemination to children.

Directly confronting this theory, Ginsberg took the position that "the scope of the constitutional freedom of expression secured to a citizen to read or see material concerned with sex cannot be made to depend upon whether the citizen is an adult or a minor."[28] That is, of course, also directly contradictory to the thesis of this work, the position that the First Amendment should apply differentially to adults and minors, not only in the obscenity area but in other areas of expression as well. The Court specifically determined not to consider the general issue of minors and freedom of expression but restricted itself to the issue of whether or not the legislature could limit the rights of minors with regard to sexual material. On that limited issue, the Court concluded that the statute did not violate whatever free expression rights the Constitution does grant minors.[29] The Court found the New York statute to be merely an adjustment to the definition of obscenity to minors by allowing the assessment of the appeal of the material in terms of minors' sexual interests. Just as flagellation may appeal to the prurient interests of sado-masochists and should be assessed on that basis when marketed to such an audience, material included in the statute may appeal to the prurient interests of minors, while not so appealing to adults, and may be assessed on that basis.

The Court noted the position of scholars in First Amendment theory that the state may regulate access of children to material that would be protected for adult consumption.

> Many commentators, including many committed to the proposition that "[n]o general restriction on expression in terms of 'obscenity' can . . . be reconciled with the First Amendment," recognize that "the power of the state to control the conduct of children reaches beyond the scope of its authority over adults," and accordingly acknowledge a supervening state interest in the regulation of literature sold to children. . . . "Different factors come into play, also, where the interest at stake is the effect of erotic expression upon children. The world of children is not strictly part of the adult realm of free expression. The factor of immaturity, and perhaps other considerations, impose different rules. Without attempting here to formulate the principles relevant to freedom of expression for children, it suffices to say that regulations of communication addressed to them need not conform to the requirements of the First Amendment in the same way as those applicable to adults."[30]

The Court recognized that the state has interests in the well-being of its children that do not extend to adults.

One of those interests is preserving the authority of parents to direct the basic upbringing of their children. The Court said that the legislature could conclude that parents need support for their decisions regarding their children. The statute provided such support for parents by limiting the material that others could furnish their children. As the court noted, the statute did not prohibit parents from supplying their own children with the varieties of material addressed. Once again, the Court drew support from a scholar, this time Louis Henkin, who while skeptical regarding adult obscenity laws, found a difference where children were involved.

> One commentator who argues that obscenity legislation might be constitutionally defective as an imposition of a single standard of public morality would give effect to the parental role and accept laws relating only to minors. . . . "One must consider also how much difference it makes if laws are designed to protect only the morals of a child. While many of the constitutional arguments against morals legislation apply equally to legislation protecting the morals of children, one can well distinguish laws which do not impose a morality on children, but which support the right of parents to deal with the morals of their children as they see fit."[31]

In addition to supporting parental rights, the Court said that the state has its own, independent interest in the well-being of its youth. It quoted with approval an opinion of a New York Court of Appeals judge in a case considering an earlier version of the New York statute.

> "While the supervision of children's reading may best be left to their parents, the knowledge that parental control or guidance cannot always be provided and society's transcendent interest in protecting the welfare of children justify reasonable regulation of the sale of material to them. It is, therefore, altogether fitting and proper for a state to include in a statute designed to regulate the sale of pornography to children special standards, broader than those embodied in legislation aimed at controlling dissemination of such material to adults."[32]

The legislature had declared that the variety of material addressed by the statute is "a basic factor in impairing the ethical and moral development of our youth and a clear and present danger to the people of the state."[33] While the Court expressed doubt that the legislative finding expressed accepted scientific fact, it was not irrational for the legislature to have found harm to minors. Since obscenity is not protected expression, the Court said that such a rational basis was all that is required, and the Court refused to demand that the legislature act only pursuant to scientifically certain criteria.[34]

Turning to other issues, the Court also addressed a vagueness challenge with regard to the "harmful to minors" definition. The Court noted that, as construed by the state courts, the definition was virtually identical to the then applicable obscenity test. That definition gave adequate notice of what was prohibited and did not violate the Constitution. Finally, the Court rejected an argument that there was not an adequate scienter requirement. The Court noted a state court construction of the statute that made it clear that a knowledge of the character of the material was required, and the statute specifically provided a defense of honest mistake as to the age of the purchaser.

2. Indecency

Ginsberg involved material that was not obscene when distributed to adults but that the Court was willing to consider obscene when provided to minors. It did not seem to see the decision as breaking really new ground. Instead, it recognized that it is easier to appeal to the prurient interest of a teenager than to the prurient interest of an adult, and it matched the ascription of obscenity to the potential prurience of the material to the audience. A greater extension of the power to protect children, or the shrinking of the protection of the First Amendment where children are involved, is found in the broadcast indecency case *Federal Communications Commission v. Pacifica Foundation*.[35]

Pacifica grew out of the broadcast of comedian and social satirist George Carlin's "Filthy Words" monologue. The twelve-minute monologue discusses "the words you couldn't say on the public, ah, airwaves, um, the ones you definitely wouldn't say, ever." While Carlin's performance was in a theater, the Pacifica Foundation played a recording of the performance on its New York City radio station. The words "you definitely wouldn't say, ever" over the airwaves were repeated, time and again, in a variety of contexts, over those airwaves. The performance was not obscene. It was a commentary on language and social taboos regarding the use of particular words. Its broadcast was in the context of a program on society's attitude toward language and the audience was advised, at the beginning of the broadcast, that the upcoming program included "sensitive language which might be regarded as offensive to some."

The Federal Communications Commission received a complaint from a listener. The listener had been driving in his automobile with his young son, at two o'clock in the afternoon, when the program aired. Pacifica was given a chance to respond to the complaint and explained the context in which the monologue aired. The FCC found the complaint valid but decided not to impose sanctions. Instead, it determined to associate the order with the station's file, so that if later complaints were received, sanctions could be imposed. The position the FCC took in its decision was not in fact that you "definitely [c]ouldn't say, ever" the words in the monologue but that such language must be channeled into time slots when children are less likely to be in the audience.

Pacifica appealed the FCC ruling and the case reached the Supreme Court. The Court's First Amendment analysis began by noting that the broadcast media enjoy less First Amendment protection than other media. This lesser protection was said to be justified by several characteristics that distinguish the broadcast media. The broadcast media were seen as a uniquely pervasive presence in American life. The broadcast of indecent material confronts the individual not only in public, but in the privacy of his or her home. While the Carlin monologue was preceded by a warning, simply requiring such warnings does not provide adequate protection, if someone turns on the radio after the program has begun, and turning off the program after hearing the indecent language was said not to be an adequate remedy. The Court also noted the accessibility of radio broadcasts to children, even those children who are too young to read. While children might be protected from indecency in other media by a requirement that the material not be distributed to children, the only effective protection for children from broadcast indecency is channeling such material into hours when children are unlikely to be listening.

What is of particular interest here is that the FCC's attempt to protect children also would limit the access of adults to the material at issue. It is settled First Amendment law that the law may not reduce adults to hearing or seeing only that which is fit for children,[36] but the Court said that adults could still purchase tapes or go to theaters or clubs to hear the monologue and that the FCC had not foreclosed the possibility of broadcasting the material in the late evening.[37] Once again the Court allowed the protection of children from material that was less than obscene. In this case it did so even at some expense to adult rights, since adult access is at least reduced, even if not shut off.

More recently, the Supreme Court refused to extend the *Pacifica* rationale to cable television. In *United States v. Playboy Entertainment Group*,[38] Playboy complained about statutory requirements that cable signals of channels dedicated primarily to sexually explicit material be either completely scrambled for nonsubscribers or limited to the hours when children are less likely to be in the audience. Since complete scrambling was not feasible, Playboy limited its programming to late-night hours. The Court found this burden on the right of adults to receive pornographic, but nonobscene, material and on the revenues of Playboy unacceptable. The statutorily required availability of complete blocking of channels at the subscriber's request made cable less invasive and less available to children if parents so desired. The refusal to extend *Pacifica* does not mean that the Court has backed down from its willingness to protect children but only recognizes that, if children can be protected without limiting adult access to protected expression, this less restrictive route must be followed.

C. A Better Approach

While the state of First Amendment theory would allow prosecution for the distribution of obscene materials to adults, such prosecutions are not very common. Cass Sunstein argues that the requirement of both offensiveness and appeal to the prurient interest, a combination he finds unlikely, along with the requirement of a lack of serious value makes the *Miller* test very protective of sexual materials.[39] If that is so and at the same time prosecution does occur for distributing to children material that is obscene as to minors, that would seem to provide the combination argued for here—a robust First Amendment for adults and a more limited First Amendment for the distribution of material to children.

Obscenity as applied to adults, however, presents other problems. Since the *Miller* test relies on community standards, results will vary from jurisdiction to jurisdiction. That was the Supreme Court's intent. In *Miller* the Court said that it would not require that the people of Maine or Mississippi accept depictions tolerable in New York City or Las Vegas.[40] It may well be that the citizens of New York will be willing to tolerate more than those in a smaller town, and smaller towns should be able to impose community standards. Allowing such variation, however, makes it more likely that there will be abuses of obscenity law that will suppress protected material. Furthermore, obscene material may be thought to have value other than serious literary, artistic, political or scientific value. Any such value behind offensive material appealing to the prurient interest will not serve to protect the material. A dual approach to the First Amendment could allow adult access even to obscene material, while still protecting children. Such an approach would prevent abusive prosecution, at least for distribution to adults, and would protect whatever value obscene material may have for adult audiences.

1. A History of Abuse

It is clear that obscenity prosecutions have, at least in the past, been brought against serious and valuable works of literature. Edward de Grazia chronicles this abuse in his book *Girls Lean Back Everywhere.*[41] His concern is conveyed by the book's subtitle, "The Law of Obscenity and the Assault on Genius." Given the events he presents, the subtitle would appear not to be an exaggeration. He notes English prosecutions against the works of Zola, Flaubert, Bourget and de Maupassant and that among the targets for the American antiobscenity crusader Anthony Comstock were works by Balzac, Tolstoy and D'Annunzio, with a publisher of Balzac's *Droll Stories* serving two years' imprisonment.[42]

Among the assaults on genius discussed by de Grazia was a prosecution growing out of the 1888 English translation of Emile Zola's *La Terre.*[43] The publisher was found guilty and served time in prison. The book trade stopped handling books his company published, and England did not see the republication of *La Terre* until 1954. Also discussed in detail are prosecutions in the United States based on the publication of James Joyce's *Ulysses.*[44] A 1920 prosecution grew out of the publication of an excerpt from that book. The episode was printed, on the recommendation of Ezra Pound, in Margaret Anderson and Jane Heap's literary journal, *The Little Review.* Anthony Comstock's successor, John Sumner, had Anderson and Heap charged with publishing obscenity. They were convicted and fined one hundred dollars, and no more installments of *Ulysses* appeared in their magazine.

Ulysses was not, however, suppressed for as long as *La Terre* had been in England. In 1932 Random House, led by Bennett Cerf and Donald

Klopfer, won the rights for the American publication of *Ulysses*. The fact that there was a contest for the rights indicates a belief that there was a likelihood that an American court might be convinced that the book, which had been well received in Europe, was not obscene. The publishers, to obtain a prepublication ruling on obscenity, arranged to have a copy seized by United States Customs. Random House was represented by Morris Ernst, a well-known lawyer and scholar in the area of freedom of expression. At trial in federal court, the book was held not to be obscene, and the holding was affirmed on appeal, with Judges Learned and Augustus Hand providing the majority votes in a two-to-one decision.[45]

While the *Ulysses* decision was a victory for serious literature and would have seemed to indicate that the works of other literary figures would also be protected, this was not the immediate result. De Grazia notes that D. H. Lawrence's *Lady Chatterley's Lover* and Henry Miller's *Tropic of Cancer* and *Tropic of Capricorn* had already been declared obscene, and Theodore Dreiser's *An American Tragedy*, Erskine Caldwell's *God's Little Acre* and Edmund Wilson's *Memoirs of Hecate County* were later banned.[46] The *Ulysses* case had had the benefit of judges more protective of freedom in literary expression than other works had previously enjoyed or were yet to enjoy.

It might be thought that these old cases are now irrelevant. The *Miller* test now provides protection for works which, taken as a whole, have serious literary, artistic, political or scientific value. Works by authors such as Zola, Joyce and Lawrence certainly have serious literary value and merit protection under the First Amendment. Nonetheless, more recent prosecutions indicate the potential for continued abuse in obscenity prosecutions.

The rock musical *Hair* may not have the lasting value of the works discussed, but it was hardly equivalent to an "adult film." The musical appealed to and conveyed younger-generation attitudes in the cultural struggles of the late 1960s and early 1970s. It contains a brief scene in which the cast appears nude. That nude scene led to refusals by local officials to allow the staging of the play in government-owned facilities. In the view of these officials, the play was obscene. Legal challenges to these denials initially met with mixed success. Denials of the use of municipal facilities in Atlanta and Charlotte were declared unconstitutional,[47] but a refusal by the City of Chattanooga was upheld by the district court because the production would violate local nudity and obscenity laws.[48] This latter decision was later reversed by the United States

Supreme Court.[49] The Supreme Court held that the denial of the application for the use of the municipal facilities was an unconstitutional prior restraint and lacked the procedural safeguards necessary to any such system of licensing. The Court specifically did not reach the issue of the lower court's finding of obscenity. While the play could be staged, there was a long delay between the original application and the final determination, and the Court's decision left open the possibility that the producers could be charged with promoting obscene material, when the play would be presented.

The litigation surrounding *Hair* may also serve as an example of another form of abuse of obscenity laws. It is hard to say how much of any negative reaction to the musical was based on the brief nude scene and how much was based on the musical's broader attack on the values of the older generation. It would not be the first time that obscenity laws had been used to suppress or punish the speech of those who have also attacked society in other ways. Iconoclasts are not one dimensional and criticism of societal sexual mores through the production of material that defies those standards is often a part of an attack on other values or on the political structure more generally. As an example, the prosecution of John Wilkes in one of the early English obscenity cases was ostensibly based on the publication of Wilkes's poem "Essay on Woman."[50] It has, however, been suggested that the real motivation for prosecuting Wilkes grew out of other work in which he exposed corruption in the government, impliedly questioned the mental capacity of King George III, and suggested the existence of a relationship between the mother of George III and the prime minister, Lord Bute.[51]

Even more recent events indicate that, while concerns over suppression of expression to which adults should have access may not be as strong as they were in the past, there is still danger to work with serious value. The events of 1990 in Cincinnati demonstrate that there may be attempts to suppress not just expression but expression with serious value.[52] On April 7, 1990, the Contemporary Arts Center in Cincinnati opened an exhibit of photographs by Robert Mapplethorpe. The 175-piece exhibit, titled "Robert Mapplethorpe: The Perfect Moment," had already been displayed at the University of Pennsylvania's Institute of Contemporary Art and the University of California at Berkeley Art Museum. The Corcoran Gallery of Art had scheduled and then canceled the show, after protests of the use of National Endowment for the Arts funds, and the Washington Project for the Arts exhibited the works instead. The day of the

Cincinnati opening, the county grand jury visited the museum and in-
dicted both the museum and its director on obscenity charges.

It would seem, given the *Miller* test requirement that to be obscene material must, taken as a whole, lack serious literary, artistic, political and
scientific value, that the Mapplethorpe exhibit could not be considered
obscene. The very fact that the exhibit had been, and was being, shown
in art museums would indicate serious artistic value. Nonetheless, local
authorities brought obscenity charges based on seven photographs, five
depicting homoerotic activities and two involving nude or seminude, but
nonsexual, depictions of children.

When the case went to trial, the jury found both the museum and the
director not guilty. The exhibit also enjoyed a successful run. Over a
seven-week period, it drew a record 81,302 visitors. While efforts to suppress the material were unsuccessful, even victory had its costs. The legal
expenses of the Contemporary Arts Center, even with some free legal aid,
ran to nearly $325,000. These costs, along with statements by the county
prosecutor that the acquittal in the Mapplethorpe case would not deter
him from charging other arts organizations, could well deter at least
local arts organizations from presenting exhibitions that are at all controversial.

2. Value in Obscenity

Even obscenity law that is applied only to material lacking serious literary, artistic, political or scientific value may still raise concern. That is,
the nonabusive application of obscenity law, in the sense of applying the
law only to those instances clearly within the intended scope of the law,
may still be criticized. One such argument is based on the value that
pornographic material has long served as a vehicle for social criticism. As
an example, Boccaccio's *The Decameron*, published in 1371 and one of
the first printed books,[53] was placed on the Roman Catholic Church's
index of forbidden books in a mid-sixteenth century reaction to the Re-
formation.[54] The Church's concern was not solely over the sexual content
of the book but was instead due to the fact that the characters involved
in the sexual stories were Catholic clerics. The work, as an implied criticism of the Church, was seen as dangerous, but when the work was revised by changing monks to conjurors, nuns to noblewomen, an abbess
to a countess and the Archangel Gabriel to a Fairy King, the book was removed from the forbidden list.[55] The reaction to *The Decameron* shows

how effective the placement of leaders in sexual situations as a form of social criticism was seen to be. By portraying clerics or nobles as being as base, or more base, than the ordinary people, the authority of the prevailing leadership could be called into question.

Other examples of the use of pornography as social or political criticism may be found in Lynn Hunt's book *The Invention of Pornography*.[56] Hunt points to French pornographic pamphlets attacking Queen Mother Anne of Austria and her believed lover Cardinal Mazarin and similar material directed at Queen Christina of Sweden after she converted to Catholicism in 1654.[57] In the era leading up to the French Revolution, political pornography attacked the clergy and the nobility, including King Louis XV, and the revolution itself "let loose another cascade of pornographic pamphlets directly linked to political conflicts."[58]

A more recent example of at least similar genre may be found in the publication by Larry Flynt in *Hustler* magazine of a parody of a series of advertisements for Campari. In the real ads, celebrities described their first experiences, on the surface their first experiences of Campari but with clear undertones of first sexual experiences. Flynt published a similar-looking ad, labeling it a parody, that described Jerry Falwell's first experience as being in an outhouse with his mother. Falwell, understandably upset, sued and won a trial court judgment for the intentional infliction of emotional distress, later overturned by the Supreme Court in *Hustler Magazine v. Falwell*.[59] The Flynt-Falwell example and earlier uses of pornography as social criticism all use sexual conduct, or an inference of sexual conduct, to call into question the moral status of a leader and thus have value that might go unrecognized as serious.

Even beyond this role of pornography as criticism, there are uses of pornography that may have value that would not be recognized under the *Miller* test. Nadine Strossen, in her book *Defending Pornography*, notes that even the Meese Commission, in its study of pornography, found some value in such material in treating sexual dysfunction, diagnosing and treating some forms of preferences or addictions to unusual sex practices and improving marriages by teaching sexual techniques.[60] She goes on to say,

> To the extent that erotic publications and videos offer an alternative sexual outlet for people who otherwise would be driven to engage in psychologically or physically risky sexual relations, they serve a public

health function. . . . In the age of AIDS . . . sex itself is often fraught with risks. Yet sexually explicit materials *are* a safe alternative.

In addition, sexually explicit materials may well be the only source of sexual information or pleasure for many people who, for a host of reasons, do not have sexual contact with others—shy or inhibited people, people with mental of physical disabilities, people with emotional problems, gay people who are confused about their sexual orientation or are afraid to reveal or express it, people who are quite young or old, geographically isolated people, unattractive people. . . .

Even for individuals who generally have sexual relations with other people, pornography may well serve as a welcome alternative stimulus and outlet in situations where that is not possible. . . .[61]

With the possible exception of application to the young, depending on how young "quite young" is, Strossen has identified value in sexually explicit materials. There are individuals for whom such material may be their only source of information or their only outlet. Even for those with alternative outlets, pornography may be either a stimulus or a safe alternative. Indeed, even for the young adult or older minor, sexually explicit materials may be part of a safer alternative for those who would otherwise engage in more risky activities.

While these values are, at least arguably, important and serious, they are not the sort of value that protects sexually explicit material from being found obscene; the values are not serious literary, artistic, political or scientific values. They are, in fact, the very characteristics that have led some to conclude that obscene material does not deserve First Amendment protection. Some such material has been said to be nothing more than a sex aid and indistinguishable from a device for mechanical stimulation.[62] It would appear that Strossen's argument could be extended to such mechanical devices, so the two may not be distinguishable. If so, then the argument offered by Strossen is not so much a First Amendment argument as it is an argument for sexual liberty. That is not to say that it is not an important argument but merely that it is not based in the First Amendment.

Strossen's argument is a strong argument against enacting obscenity laws, even if not an argument that such laws would violate the First Amendment, although she certainly also takes that position. The possession and use of pornographic materials might be seen as constitutionally protected liberty interests. It might seem odd, however, for the First Amendment to have an exception allowing proscriptions against obscenity, while an argument under the Due Process Clauses of the Fifth and Fourteenth Amendments cuts against actually implementing obscenity laws. An argument against the obscenity exception to the First Amendment would avoid this seeming conflict.

3. A Dual Approach

A major impediment to erasing the obscenity exception from First Amendment law would be the effect such an erasure could have on children. The 1930 Massachusetts obscenity prosecution of Theodore Dreiser's *An American Tragedy* reflects this concern. The district attorney, in his closing argument, asked for each of the passages he had read to the jury if they were obscene and "if they would be harmful to the morals of a young girl: '*How, sirs, would you like to have your fifteen-year-old daughters read that?*'"[63] The jury returned a verdict finding the novel obscene. When the Massachusetts Supreme Court unanimously affirmed the lower court determination, that court too spoke to concerns over access by youth.

"Even assuming great literary evidence, artistic worth and an impelling moral lesson in the story, there is nothing essential to the history of the life of its principal character that would be lost if these passages were missed which the jury found were indecent, obscene, and manifestly tending to corrupt the morals of youth. . . . Furthermore, the seller of a book which contains passages offensive to our statute has no right to assume that children to whom the book might come would not read the obnoxious passages or that if they should read them would continue to read on until the evil effects of the obscene passages are weakened or dissipated with the tragic denouement of a tale."[64]

That is, indeed, the problem. While most may not, in this era, be concerned with the exposure of a fifteen-year-old daughter to material like Dreiser's, there are certainly scenes from adult-oriented material to which we would not want an eight-, ten- or twelve-year-old exposed.

Presumably most who favor the elimination of the obscenity exception would not espouse the free dissemination of hard-core pornography to children. What would seem to be the ideal position would be the current situation, but without the possibility of abusive prosecution. The elimination of the obscenity exception for adults would move from the current unlikelihood of prosecution for distribution to adults but the possibility of abuse to a guarantee that such distribution would not be punishable. If that result could be combined with the continued prohibition of the distribution of pornographic materials to minors, the outcome would include the ideal of free expression for adults and still include the protection of the psychological health and development of children. Government would stay out of the private lives of adults, and parents would be in greater control over the raising of their children, since they, rather than commercial purveyors of pornography, would control the materials to which their children have access.[65]

The difficulty, under current First Amendment theory, is in eliminating the adult obscenity exception without also eliminating the ability to prohibit distributing sexually explicit material to minors. The category "obscene to minors" was established on the basis of variable obscenity theory. But, if the obscenity exception is eliminated, material cannot be barred based on its prurient appeal, so the fact that minors' prurient interests are more easily piqued becomes irrelevant. The demise of the obscenity exception would be accompanied by the demise of variable obscenity generally and obscenity with regard to children specifically. Furthermore, given strong arguments that the concepts of obscenity and indecency must be tied together, prohibitions on the broadcast of indecent material might fall with the obscenity exception. Sexual content could become available during hours in which children are likely to be in the broadcast audience.

These ancillary effects of the elimination of the obscenity exception may well prevent such a repeal, again at least under current First Amendment law. The evolution of the position of Justice Brennan regarding the obscenity exception may serve as an example. Justice Brennan wrote the majority opinion in the 1957 *Roth* case recognizing the obscenity exception. By the time *Miller* was decided in 1973, Justice Brennan found himself in dissent. He expressed concern over sixteen years of instability in the law, the lack of fair notice to potential defendants, the chilling effect on protected speech and the stress on the courts. These concerns led him to conclude that government suppression of sexually explicit materials on the basis of obscenity violates the First Amendment. Justice Brennan, joined throughout by Justices Stewart and Marshall, recognized, in a case decided the same day, an exception to this conclusion. The material at issue should be protected, "at least in the absence of distribution to juveniles or obtrusive exposure to unconsenting adults."[66] If Justices Brennan, Stewart and Marshall had to have given up prohibitions on distribution of obscene materials to minors along with their proposed elimination of the obscenity exception for adult distribution, it is less than clear that they would have taken the position they did. Regardless of their individual positions, it would seem certain that the enthusiasm of many who would otherwise support the freedom to distribute obscene materials to adults would have that enthusiasm tempered, if their position must also allow distribution to minors.

The alternative to losing *Ginsberg* along with the obscenity exception, the alternative that Justice Brennan seemed to have in mind, is to divorce *Ginsberg* from its roots in the obscenity exception for adult First Amendment protection. As long as the same First Amendment applies to children and adults and the only basis for *Ginsberg* is the ease of appeal to the teenage prurient interest, that divorce cannot take place. The acceptance of the position that, generally, there should be a robust First Amendment for adults with significantly weaker protection for children allows the *Ginsberg* result to stand, while the *Roth* and *Miller* authorized restrictions on adult distribution of obscene material can be abandoned.

The regulation of indecent material, as allowed by *Pacifica*, should also remain in force. The material at issue in *Pacifica* was already protected material, since it was not obscene. The abandonment of the obscenity exception for adults would then have no effect on the status of the material relative to adults. The interests the Court found justifying the channeling of the material into hours when children are less likely to be in the audience remain the same and retain their same strength. The balance against adult speech interests should be unaffected.

It may be argued in response that the indecency at issue in *Pacifica* must be conceptually related to obscenity. Professors Krattenmaker and Powe, in an article published shortly after the *Pacifica* decision, took that position in arguing that *Pacifica* did not authorize the regulation of violence in the broadcast media.[67] The Krattenmaker and Powe argument should not prevent *Pacifica* from remaining in force if the adult obscenity exception is abandoned. The obscenity exception for minors would remain in force, and the distribution to minors of the type of material at issue in *Ginsberg* would still be barred.

The demise of the obscenity exception would end concerns over the chilling effect of the obscenity exception for adults, but one might still object that there remains a chilling effect on providing information or materials to minors. That chilling effect ought not, however, to be of as great concern. Importantly, it would only be a chilling effect on nonparents. If parents believe that their children would derive some benefit from materials that happen to contain sexually explicit material, a law like that in *Ginsberg* would not prevent them from providing such material to their children. Thus, a disagreement between the parents and the community about the value the material might have will not bring down criminal liability on the parents. It is only the third-party stranger to the family who will be chilled, and parents can overcome that chill by obtaining the material themselves and providing it to their children.[68]

That answer might be seen as inadequate in situations in which a *Ginsberg*-like law is used to suppress not sexually explicit material but informational material that might be important to a minor but of which his or her parents disapprove. Examples might include material on birth control, sexually transmitted diseases or even materials on human growth and development and sexuality. Some might find such a chilling effect to be of little concern, again being willing to live with the parents' decisions. On the other hand, minors may, even under a dual approach, have First Amendment interests in the receipt of information that ought to be protected. Maintaining the *Ginsberg* result should affect only material that appeals to the prurient interest, is offensive as to what is appropriate for minors and lacks serious value for minors. An organization that wants to make birth control information available to minors should be chilled only to the extent that it avoid making their materials appeal to the prurient interest of those minors. Information itself should remain protected in recognition of the First Amendment protection that minors should continue to have.

7

Violence

Doom is the best known of the "first person shooter" genre of video games. In these games the player holds a realistic hand gun and fires at people who pop up or come around corners on the video screen. Killing quickly and efficiently produces high scores. The games are such good training that adaptations are used by the armed forces and law enforcement agencies. Most users, however, are not soldiers but teenage boys.

In 1997, Michael Carneal was a fourteen-year-old freshman at Heath High School in Paducah, Kentucky.[1] He enjoyed playing *Doom* and similar video games. He had also seen the film *The Basketball Diaries* in which the film's hero, in a dream sequence, goes to school with a firearm under his trench coat and guns down a teacher and several classmates. One morning Carneal went to his school with a stolen pistol, arriving just as a prayer group was breaking up. He opened fire on the group, and with nine shots inflicted head or chest wounds on eight students, killing three.[2] He did so with no firearm experience other than on video games.

Two years later, Eric Harris and Dylan Klebold went to Colombine High School in Littleton, Colorado.[3] They were heavily armed, and by the time they were finished and committed suicide, they had killed a teacher and twelve students and had wounded twenty-three others. They too were avid *Doom* players. One had given his sawed-off shotgun the name of a character from the game. They also appear to have been influenced by *The Basketball Diaries*, going so far as to adopt the dress of the film.

In the wake of the shootings at Columbine, Congressman Henry Hyde introduced an amendment to a bill titled the Consequences for Juvenile Offenders Act of 1999. The amendment provided, in part:

> Whoever in interstate of foreign commerce knowingly and for monetary consideration, sells, sends, loans, or exhibits, directly to a minor, any picture, photograph, drawing sculpture, video game, motion picture

film, or similar visual representation or image, book, pamphlet, magazine, printed matter or sound recording, or other matter of any kind containing explicit sexual material or explicit violent material which —

(1) the average person, applying contemporary community standards, would find, taking the materials as a whole and with respect to minors, is designed to appeal or pander to the prurient, shameful or morbid interest;

(2) the average person, applying contemporary community standards, would find the material patently offensive with respect to what is suitable for minors; and

(3) a reasonable person would find, taking the material as a whole, lacks serious literary, artistic, political or scientific value for minors

may be fined or imprisoned for up to five years for a first offense and fined and imprisoned for up to ten years for subsequent offenses.[4] The amendment provided definitions of sexual material and violent material. "Violent material" was defined as "a visual depiction of an actual or simulated display, or a detailed verbal description or narrative account of—(A) sadistic or masochistic flagellation by or upon a person; (B) torture by or upon a person; (C) acts of mutilation of the human body; or (D) rape."[5]

The amendment, in its approach to sexually explicit material, tracked the language of the New York statute upheld by the Supreme Court in *Ginsberg v. New York*.[6] The Court's recognition, in that case, that material not obscene when distributed to adults may be obscene when distributed to minors, allows society to protect minors from exposure to sexual material to which adults should be allowed access. The statute in *Ginsberg*, adopted in the era of an earlier version of the obscenity test, was modified in the amendment to reflect changes in *Miller v. California*,[7] requiring that value be based on the serious value in the work taken as a whole, and in *Pope v. Illinois*,[8] requiring that value be judged on a national, reasonable-person basis rather than on community values.

The *Ginsberg* statute was also modified to include violent material. The intended effect was to protect minors from violent material while allowing adult access. Congressman Hyde, in explaining the need for legislation, expressed concern that exposure to media violence left children desensitized to real-world violence and unable to appreciate the tragic consequences of violent actions in which they might engage.[9]

The amendment was not well received. Representative Conyers called it "an unparalleled assault on the First Amendment."[10] He argued it was patently unconstitutional and an attempt to turn attention away from the gun safety legislation he favored. Representative Foley argued that the amendment "tramples on the First Amendment" and "tries to assume the role of parents."[11] The belief that parents' role would be usurped was also expressed by others.[12] In that regard, it is interesting to note that the amendment would only have addressed the provision of material to minors for monetary consideration. Parents could obtain videos for their children, and the amendment would have protected the parents' decisions by not allowing commercial distribution to children other than through their parents or other adults. Nonetheless, after debate, the House defeated the amendment.[13]

The House defeat of the amendment was based, at least in major part, on the belief that its treatment of violent material was unconstitutional. Most scholarly commentary agreed. The consensus was that, while the distribution of sexually explicit material to minors may be prohibited, violent material enjoys greater First Amendment protection. Distributing sexually explicit material to minors may be barred because of the obscenity exception and the variability of obscenity standards depending on the audience. The conclusion was that violent material cannot, based on its violent content rather than any additional sexual content, be considered obscene. There is, then, no standard to vary, when violent material is distributed to minors.

House opponents did have case law to support their position. Representative Conyers cited *Video Software Dealers Ass'n v. Webster*,[14] and that case does indeed provide the support claimed. *Webster* concerned a Missouri statute that, like the Hyde amendment, mirrored the test for obscenity modified to reflect concern over audiences composed of minors. The statute barred distribution to minors of material that "appeal[s] to morbid interest in violence for persons under the age of seventeen" and "[t]aken as a whole, . . . lacks serious literary, artistic, political, or scientific value for persons under the age of seventeen." When challenged, the statute was declared unconstitutional.

The federal district court opinion recognized that *Ginsberg* allowed variable standards as to what was acceptable for youth and for adults but held that case to be limited to obscenity and concluded that violent material enjoys First Amendment protection.[15] Any limitations on distribution would have to meet strict scrutiny by being narrowly tailored to promote a compelling governmental interest. While the court did recognize a compelling interest in protecting the physical and psychological well-being of minors, it concluded that the statute had not been shown to be narrowly drawn to serve that interest. Since the statute failed to state the types of violence that are detrimental to minors, the court could not determine if the statute was narrowly drawn to ban only that variety of expression.

While counsel for Missouri argued that the statutory language was similar to that approved for defining obscenity in *Miller v. California*, the court responded that obscene material is outside the protection of the First Amendment, while the material addressed by the statute was protected and restrictions on protected material require greater precision. The lack of precise definition was also held to make the statute unconstitutionally vague. Finally, the fact that the statute imposed strict liability with regard to the nature of the material, and the chilling effect such liability would have in an area of protected speech, also made the act unconstitutional.

On appeal, the United States Court of Appeals for the Eighth Circuit affirmed the district court on all three grounds. That court, like the district court, was troubled by the statute's lack of definition. The state tried to avoid the problem the lack of definition caused in meeting the narrow tailoring requirement by claiming that violent videos are obscene as to children. The state's position was that, since such material is obscene and unprotected, the ban on distribution to minors need not be narrowly tailored to a compelling purpose. While the court agreed with the state's assertion that under *Ginsberg* material not obscene as to adults may be obscene as to minors, it held that violence, without depictions or descriptions of sexual conduct, cannot be obscene.[16]

Clearly, attempts to limit access by children to violent materials have been, thus far, unsuccessful. They should, however, not be so easily dismissed. First, it should be noted that Congressman Hyde's approach was not intended to, and would not have had the effect of, removing the decision as to what is appropriate for children away from the control of their parents. Indeed, the amendment would have had the effect of protecting the parents' decisions. Without the amendment, strangers to the family can furnish material to children that their parents would find abhorrent. If the amendment had passed, only the parents could have made the decision that the children should be allowed to view the videos in question, or at least no one with a commercial motive could have supplanted the decision-making authority of the parents.

There are two approaches that would allow a statute like that proposed by Representative Hyde to pass constitutional muster. The first has been argued elsewhere[17] but will be recounted briefly herein. That approach is to recognize that material may be sufficiently explicit and offensive in the violence it portrays so that, regardless of its sexual content, it may come within the obscenity exception to the First Amendment. If such material can be obscene, then lesser levels of violence can be obscene for children, when distributed to children, as in the case addressed by Representative Hyde. Still lesser degrees of violence could be considered indecent for broadcast purposes.

The alternative is, once again, to recognize that there should be a dual First Amendment. Children simply should not have access to materials that may be fully protected for adults. As with sexually obscene material, the advantage to the dual approach is the access adults may have to the material without requiring that children be provided access to what may cause them physical or psychological harm.

A. Violence as Obscenity

If violent material meeting a test adapted from the *Miller v. California* test for sexual obscenity could be fit within the obscenity exception to the First Amendment, the shortcomings of the Missouri statute would be irrelevant. When material is unprotected, a restriction does not have to meet strict scrutiny. A statute drafted to meet the requirements of *Miller* would be constitutional, so long as it met a rational basis test. If the evidence of media violence causation of real world violence were inadequate to show that restrictions are necessary to prevent physical or psychological harm to our youth or the evidence is not sufficiently specific to limit restrictions to precisely those images that are harmful to youth, restrictions would fail strict scrutiny. It is, however, not unreasonable to believe that such a connection exists. The lack of scientific certainty as to effects that did not prevent limitations on sexually obscene material would similarly fail to prevent restrictions on violently obscene material from meeting the requirement that statutes be rationally related to permissible governmental interests.

It is important to note that the Supreme Court has never directly ruled that violent material cannot be obscene or at least regulable. In fact, *Winters v. New York*[18] specifically left the possibility open. *Winters* concerned a New York statute that was held unconstitutionally vague because of its failure adequately to define the violence addressed. It was vagueness rather than the target of violent material that was the flaw. The court warned against concluding that states could not address media violence, saying "[n]either the states nor Congress are prevented by the requirement of specificity from carrying out their duty of eliminating evils to which, in their judgment, such publications give rise."[19] Lower courts have, however, taken the *Miller* definition and the conclusion in *Cohen v. California* that offensive speech cannot be obscene without being erotic as indicating that only depictions of sex or excretion can be obscene.[20]

Despite the conclusions of lower courts, it may be argued that depictions of violence can reach such a level of explicitness and offensiveness as to be included within the obscenity exception. The current focus of obscenity doctrine on depictions of sexual or excretory activities, to the exclusion of any consideration of violent material, is an unwarranted product of Victorian era concerns with sexuality. An examination of the concept of obscenity unearths nothing that would require that it be limited to sexual or excretory activities. More importantly, nothing in history or case law, during any constitutionally important periods, requires the limitation of obscenity to erotic material. Finally, the policy grounds that have been offered to justify excluding sexually obscene materials from the protection of the First Amendment apply equally as well to sufficiently violent material. Sufficiently violent material may be obscene and unprotected due solely to its violence and without regard to its sexual content.

1. The Concept of Obscenity

Joel Feinberg, in his work on morality and criminal law,[21] examines the idea of obscenity. He sees obscenity as extreme vulgarity, sufficiently extreme as to produce disgust, shock or repugnance. Feinberg does not limit obscenity to sex, offering as an example of a proper use of the term the sentence: "The machine gunning of Bonnie and Clyde in the climactic scene of the film may have been morally and dramatically justified, but the blood spurting out of the bullet holes as bullets splattered the bodies was a naturally revolting sight—so offensive and shocking to the senses as to be obscene."[22] For Feinberg, obscenity may be found in a treatment of violence and death without any sexual content.

The etymology of the word also backs this view. There appear to be two suggested derivations of the word "obscene." One derivation is from ob caenum which translates to "on account of filth." The alternative derivation is from *ab scaena* or "off the stage," which could mean either "off the stage of life" or "off the theatrical stage." Under any of these derivations, the term applies as well to depictions of violence as to depictions of sex or excretion.

Harry Clor offers a definition of "obscenity" that speaks both to the idea of filth and the "off the stage of life" approach. He suggests that obscenity is "a degradation of the human dimensions of life to a sub-human or merely physical level."[23] Obscene literature "presents, graphically and in detail, a degrading picture of human life and invites the reader or viewer, not to contemplate that picture, but to wallow in it."[24] It is the concentration on the physical, animal aspects of sex that can make a depiction obscene, but the same can be said of violence. A Shakespearean death scene may be one thing, a slasher film another entirely.

Clor argues that we withhold from the view of others experiences in which only the subhuman aspects are observed.[25] This view explains the private nature of sex. If a depiction lacks any romantic content, the depiction is of a person governed by the same subhuman urges that affect animals. But treating humans as fodder for a chain saw is also to exclude all humanity with a focus solely on the physical, and under Clor's theory, it too should be removed from the stage of life.

If "obscene" derives from "off the [theatrical] stage," a look at the materials historically banned from the stage would be beneficial.[26] Beginning with the Greek origins of Western drama, one finds the Greeks quite tolerant of sexual themes but intolerant of violence, although the sexual content does not match that of modern "adult films." The Greeks did allow descriptions of violence, and even some audience exposure to violence was tolerated. What Greek drama did not accept was the visual depiction of violent death at the hands of another. If the plot required such an incident, the details were narrated by a messenger who had witnessed the event.

It is interesting to note that the current debate over media violence and its effects had a counterpart in the Greek era. Even with limitations on exposure to violence, there was disagreement over the worth of such tragedies. Cynthia Freeland, in her book *The Naked and the Undead*, compares the debate over horror films with the positions of Plato and Aristotle, with Plato placing violent spectacle low on his order of propriety and expressing concern over desensitization, while Aristotle found value in tragedies as providing intellectual engagement and catharsis.[27]

Roman theater appears to have treated sexual themes with at least as much toleration as had the Greeks. The Greek intolerance of violence, while present in early Roman drama, did not survive in the later Roman theater. In an era in which mortal combat became popular entertainment, theater also became more violent. It is claimed that in a performance of Catullus's *Laureolus* a prisoner was forced to play a role in which he was actually killed on stage by a bear.[28] While violence was not *ab scaena* in later Roman theater, neither was sex. Captives were available both to fight to the death and to engage in the dramatic staging of sexual acts.[29] It cannot be said that obscenity had shifted from violence to sex, rather, nothing was *ab scaena*.

Medieval drama also appears not to have been so averse to violence. Violence was common in religious plays portraying the lives of the martyrs. In a later era, many of Shakespeare's plays were set against a background of violence. Despite this violence, however, it is important to note that Shakespeare's plays were not as violent as they could have been and that some violence occurs off the stage.[30] Most of the on-stage violence in Shakespeare involves duels or other individual combat employing swords, avoiding the current theme of a slasher sadistically torturing and murdering helpless victims. In Shakespeare's swordplay the combatants are of similar age, rank and status, and the typical encounter has been said to have the character of a trial by combat.[31]

While there may have been an increased acceptance of violence, there also was, in some places, an increased tolerance for sexual displays. The psychologists Eberhard and Phyllis Kronhausen, in their study of the history, law and psychology of pornography, claim that exhibitions of human intercourse for the entertainment of select audiences were not rare in France from the Renaissance through part of the eighteenth century.[32] They further note that exhibitions of copulating animals were customary entertainment in that era in various European societies.[33] "Obscene" as "off the theatrical stage" does not apply solely to sexual activities. Such activities may only be talked about in some eras but shown in others. The same is true of violence, it could only be described in Greek drama but could be shown in gory detail in other eras. The ordinary language concept of obscenity is not limited to sexual and excretory activity and applies as well to depictions of violence.

2. Obscenity, Sex, and Violence in Case Law

The Supreme Court, in its *Roth v. United States* opinion recognizing the obscenity exception,[34] began by noting that the freedoms of speech and press were never considered absolute, citing thirteen statutes from the original colonies or states and from Vermont that predate the Bill of Rights and limit speech. The Court went on to say that "[a]t the time of the adoption of the First Amendment, obscenity law was not as fully developed as libel law, but there is sufficiently contemporaneous evidence to show that obscenity, too, was outside the protection intended for speech and press."[35] The statutes cited, all somewhat later than the Bill of Rights, did proscribe obscenity, but they failed to define what was obscene.[36]

Frederick Schauer notes a lack of definition for obscenity in English law, until 1868.[37] While in American law the focus on sex appeared to be developing in the mid- to late 1800s, Schauer finds it finally clear only with the Supreme Court's 1896 decision in *Swearingen v. United States*[38] that only sexually oriented material could be obscene.[39] The focus on sex then developed only in an era lacking in constitutional importance. An 1896 definition of obscenity should not be mistaken for a definition in the era of the Bill of Rights. If laws banning the obscene left such material unprotected in that era or shortly thereafter, it is not a later legal definition that sets the scope of that unprotected material. The broader concept should control.

It is also interesting to note the reaction of the states to the developing focus of obscenity on sex. While the Victorian era concerns over sex led to a limitation in the use of the word "obscene," the law did not cease to regulate other depictions that could formerly have been labeled "obscene." The New York group established by the anti-obscenity crusader Anthony Comstock also led the effort to establish a New York statute prohibiting the distribution of "any book, pamphlet, magazine, newspaper or other printed paper devoted to the publication, and principally made up of criminal news, police reports or accounts of criminal deeds or pictures, or stories of deeds of bloodshed, lust or crime."[40] While the statute was held to be unconstitutionally vague in *Winters*, it reflects a concern shared by a majority of the states in existence in the late 1800s and early 1900s, as shown by nineteen nearly identical and four substantially similar statutes.[41] Some of those statutes continued to use "obscene" in their titles and may be viewed as insisting that the category of the obscene is not so limited. Other states, by enacting statutes addressed to material no longer covered by obscenity statutes, may be seen as wishing to continue to ban such material without being concerned over the label to be applied.[42]

3. Policy Bases for Banning the Obscene

In addition to the historical bases for banning the obscene, the *Roth* Court and various commentators have presented policy reasons for denying the protection of the First Amendment to obscene materials. The policy analysis has been limited to the consideration of depictions of sexual activity, but the policy reasons carry over with equal weight to violence that might be considered obscene.

The *Roth* Court took the position that the First Amendment protections were intended to assure the free interchange of ideas to bring about political and social changes desired by the people, a rationale similar to Vincent Blasi's "checking value,"[43] or Alexander Meiklejohn's theory that for speech to enjoy First Amendment protection it should relate to self-governance.[44] These theories can justify denying protection to sexual obscenity, because while pornography may be used as a medium for political expression, pornography is only obscene if it "lacks serious literary, artistic, political, or scientific value." If obscene, it is not seriously political pornography.

The important point here is that, just as sexual obscenity may lack protection under these theories, so also should violent obscenity, if properly defined. If the *Miller* definition is adapted to allow a ban on explicit depictions of violence only when such depictions lack "serious literary, artistic, political, or scientific value," any work considered violent obscenity would by definition not have serious political value. Just as sexually obscene works without serious political value are unprotected under the "checking value" limitation, violently obscene works are similarly unprotected.

Even arguing for a far broader view of protected speech, Frederick Schauer still justifies the obscenity exception by arguing that sexual obscenity departs so completely from the sphere of the protected speech that it is nonspeech. He discusses what he admits is a hypothetical extreme example of hard-core pornography. The hypothetical ten-minute film is nothing but a close-up of sexual organs engaged in intercourse, with no dialogue, no music and no attempt at artistic depiction. Schauer argues that such a film is nothing more than a sex aid and that "any definition of 'speech' . . . that included this film . . . is being bizarrely literal or formalistic."[45] Since the film is designed to produce a physical, hormonal effect rather than to communicate, it is undeserving of First Amendment protection. This view, too, should carry over to violence. If material is violent enough to have a hormonal effect, Schauer's arguments would exclude such material from First Amendment protection.

There are First Amendment theories that speak against the existence of a sexual obscenity exception and would also speak against an exception for violent obscenity. Nonetheless, the obscenity exception is a part of the law. As long as it is a part of the law, the interesting theories are those that justify it. There appear to be no such theories that would not also justify an exception for violent obscenity.[46] Given the history, both in drama and law, the ordinary language uses of the term, and the inability to distinguish the two under First Amendment theory, the law could allow a refocusing of the obscenity exception to include violence and allow government to address the concerns reflected in Representative Hyde's amendment.

B. *The Benefits of Recognizing Violent Obscenity*

It may well be that major movie producers are unlikely to face a violent obscenity prosecution, but that does not mean that recognizing violent obscenity would have no effect. There are two important lines of cases that accompany the sexual obscenity exception to the First Amendment, and they should have parallels in the recognition of violent obscenity. Sexual obscenity law has been accompanied by a doctrine of variable obscenity and by the possibility of regulating broadcast indecency. Violent obscenity should have the same accompaniment, and these similar legal theories would be likely to have great effect.

The concept of variable obscenity allows the regulation of material not obscene—because it does not appeal to the prurient interests of the average person—to be considered obscene when marketed and distributed to a group for which there is an appeal to the prurient interest. *Ginsberg* allows material that would be protected, when distributed to adults, to be found obscene when distributed to youth if it appeals to the prurient interests of youth, is offensive and lacks serious value for youth. The recognition that material may be obscene because of the violence it contains should, by analogy to *Ginsberg*, speak to the distribution of violent materials to minors. A category of "violent obscenity as to minors" would allow the prohibition of the distribution to minors of violent material to which adults might still have access. This would apply not only to sufficiently violent videos but to the violent video games that have recently raised so much concern.

Recognizing violent obscenity also raises the possibility that material that is not explicit or offensive enough to be obscene either for adults or for minors is nonetheless still indecent. The broadcast of such indecent material could then be subject to regulation by the Federal Communications Commission. The Supreme Court, in *Federal Communications Commission v. Pacifica Foundation*,[47] upheld the FCC's authority to require channeling the broadcast of indecent material into hours when children are less likely to be in the audience. There are, however, strong arguments, raised by Thomas Krattenmaker and L. A. Powe, that the indecency at issue in *Pacifica* must be conceptually related to obscenity.[48]

The recognition that violence can be sufficiently explicit and offensive as to be obscene provides a response to the problem raised by Krattenmaker and Powe. If violent obscenity is recognized, then not only may lesser violence be obscene as to youth but still lesser degrees of violence can be considered indecent. Such material could then be subjected to FCC regulation limiting its airing to hours when children are less likely to be in the broadcast audience. The tie between indecency and obscenity, so important to Krattenmaker and Powe's analysis, is retained.

C. The Costs of Recognizing Violent Obscenity

While recognizing that sufficiently explicit violence can be obscene would help resolve the problems such materials cause in our culture, such recognition does have a down side. Presumably the eventual result would be a situation similar to that of sexual obscenity. Little, if anything—and nothing produced by major motion picture studios—would be considered obscene when distributed to adults. On the other hand, government would have the authority to do what Representative Hyde's effort attempted, and youths would not be exposed to material that may do them harm. The down side is in the effect such a recognition could have on adult access to materials that ought to be protected, even after the recognition of violent obscenity.

It took a period of some sixteen years for the law to move from the recognition of the obscenity exception in its 1957 *Roth* decision to the current statement of the test for obscenity found in the 1973 *Miller* case.

Even then, *Miller* was not the last word. Fourteen years later, *Pope v. Illinois* showed the continued need to interpret the *Miller* test.[49] There is, in fact, no assurance that even *Pope* will be the final and total explication of the test for obscenity.

Presumably, experience in developing the test for sexual obscenity would inform the development of a test for violent obscenity. The time for such a test to mature would likely be shortened. Nonetheless, some period of time would elapse in which guidance as to the acceptable levels of media violence would be less than complete. During that period, motion picture producers could suffer from the chilling effect on speech. That is, those who make decisions on what to produce and how to depict actions could decide, out of fear that the result would be held obscene, not to present material that would actually be held not to be obscene. While potential chilling effect and similar vagueness concerns have not led to the rejection of sexual obscenity but only require specificity in such statutes,[50] they are a cost of obscenity laws. The development of violent obscenity laws would impose a similar cost.

There is also the potential for abuse of violent obscenity laws. Just as prosecutions have been brought against sexual material that was not really obscene for political or other reasons, similar abuse could occur in the enforcement of violent obscenity laws. There are films that contain greater or lesser degrees of violence that are also important for their political content. A film such as Z, with its criticism of the Greek military junta, or *Missing*, which concerned the disappearance of dissidents in Chile, would not have been well received by the governments that were the subjects of the plots. If a film used violent depictions in a similar criticism of United States policy in some part of the world, it should be protected against any violent obscenity prosecution because of its serious political value. That does not mean, however, that a prosecution could not be brought. The costs of litigating the obscenity issue would itself be a penalty on the production of the film, and legitimate and important works might be self-suppressed.

D. A Dual Approach

Despite the costs of recognizing violent obscenity, if there were no other means of protecting children, the burdens might be worth bearing. The First Amendment should allow such regulation under the obscenity exception, but that does not necessarily imply that it would be wise policy to legislate against violent obscenity. On the other hand, if the protection of children from violent images can be accomplished only as a corollary to a general recognition of violent obscenity, that may be the best route to follow.

Fortunately, the alternative dual approach to the First Amendment would allow for the protection of children, without allowing limitations on adult access to material containing violence. If there is no violent obscenity exception for adults, films similar to *Z* or *Missing* face no suppression when shown to adult audiences. On the other hand, films such as *Natural Born Killers* or *Basketball Diaries*, films said to have been related to killings in Louisiana and Kentucky, could be barred for minors. Legislation such as that offered by Congressman Hyde would be constitutional and would provide protection for the psychological and physical well-being of youth. Additional legislation limiting use by minors of violent video games would also be justified.

There could still be a chilling effect resulting from the application of a dual First Amendment to the issue of youth exposure to depictions of violence. Any such statute would use an approach similar to statutes addressing material that is sexually obscene for youth. A statute would be required to list the types of violence addressed, but would then bar such depictions when they appeal to a morbid or shameful interest in violence and are patently offensive as to what is appropriate for children, under contemporary community standards. The statute should also protect material with serious literary, political, artistic or scientific value for minors.

There is enough fuzziness in those requirements that some speech directed at youth might be chilled. There is the possibility that a video dealer would refuse to rent a copy of *Schindler's List* to a fifteen-year-old, despite the value of the film. Nonetheless, the potential for chilling is the same as for sexual obscenity, and the balance that allows for the existence of those statutes should also be struck in favor of bearing the similar costs of statutes aimed at youth exposure to violent materials. In fact, the costs are less than they are for general obscenity statutes. The chilling effect of the potential prosecution for general sexual obscenity may be the complete suppression, by the producers, of the film at issue. Under a dual First Amendment, there would be no sexual or violent obscenity prosecutions for production or for distribution to adults. Films would not be suppressed. The only chilling effect would be the refusal to rent to minors. Minors could still see such films if parents decided that their children were mature enough to see the value in the material. The only chilling effect would be on third parties determining what is appropriate for other people's children.

The other corollary to sexual obscenity and to violent obscenity should also remain. Sexually indecent material may be channeled into hours when children are less likely to be in the audience. Under the violent obscenity thesis, lesser degrees of violence, like lesser degrees of sex, could be similarly channeled. The question remains whether, without recognizing violent obscenity but under a dual approach to the First Amendment, such channeling could be required by the Federal Communications Commission, assuming a congressional grant of authority.

The argument against such channeling would once again be that offered by Krattenmaker and Powe. They concluded that the indecency that was properly the subject of FCC regulation had to be conceptually related to obscenity. Recognizing violent obscenity was one response to that argument, but there is another. The Krattenmaker and Powe argument was that, unless the FCC's authority to channel was rooted in the obscenity exception, the protection of youth through such channeling would conflict with a number of cases recognizing First Amendment rights of children. Here, however, the entire thesis of this book is that there needs to be a new understanding of the First Amendment and of the Court's decisions on First Amendment issues involving minors.

The acceptance of a dual First Amendment would allow the rationale of *Pacifica* to carry over to violence. The broadcast media become no less pervasive in American life when violence rather than sex is involved. Similarly, the broadcast of violent material, just like the broadcast of sexual material, confronts the individual not only in public, but in the privacy of his or her own home. If warnings are inadequate for the George Carlin monologue at issue in *Pacifica*, they should also be seen as inadequate to provide protection against depictions of violence. If people turn on the television after the program has begun, they will be exposed, and as with the Court's conclusion regarding the Carlin monologue, turning off the program after seeing the violence would not be an adequate remedy. As with radio broadcasts, television is accessible to children, even those children who are too young to read. Just as children can be protected from broadcast indecency only by channeling, they can be protected from broadcast violence only by a similar channeling of televised violence into hours when children are unlikely to be watching.

If this call for a dual First Amendment and its application to the distribution of violent videos to minors means anything, it must mean that such distribution does not enjoy the level of protection the House of Representatives believed to be present in rejecting the Hyde legislation. To see what differences should exist, it would be useful to examine an additional part of the analysis offered by the court in the Missouri case discussed above in striking down the prohibition on distributing violent videos to minors.

The federal district court in *Video Software Dealers Association v. Webster*,[51] after asserting that *Ginsberg* did not apply to violent material, concluded that any restrictions on access by minors would have to meet strict scrutiny. The state would have to demonstrate that the restriction was narrowly tailored to a compelling governmental purpose. The court was willing to recognize a compelling interest in protecting the physical and psychological well-being of minors but determined that the statute had not been shown to be narrowly drawn to that interest. Since the statute failed to state the types of violence that are detrimental to minors, the court could not determine if the statute was narrowly drawn to ban only that specific detrimental expression. The language of the statute was similar to that in *Miller*, but the court noted that *Miller* addressed material that is outside the protection of the First Amendment, while the material at issue in the Missouri statute was protected. For protected material, narrow tailoring requires greater precision, and the lack of specificity was also held to make the statute unconstitutionally vague.

While social science studies indicate that exposure to media violence causes an increase in violence in the real world, the studies do lack specificity. Human studies are necessarily afflicted with this shortcoming. A particular film may be shown to have some effect on an audience's willingness to be aggressive, but the effects are small and not all viewers are affected. The factors that explain the differing effects must be determined, and, if the material itself is protected, those other factors must be the focus of any efforts to reduce violence. Other studies, studies that correlate television viewing habits to violence, must group programs into violent and nonviolent categories. If a study groups police dramas with slapstick comedy and finds that children who watch that combination are more violent than those who do not, it is unclear that all the program varieties in the violent category contribute to the effect. Yet, if the materials are protected, such specificity and narrow tailoring is required. An adequate study would seem to require separating a group of children into a variety of test groups and exposing each test group to a single variety of programming over a long period. Such an approach is obviously unacceptable.

Providing lesser First Amendment protection for children would mean a lowering of the strict scrutiny barrier. If access by minors to violent materials and adult distribution of such materials to minors are not protected by the First Amendment, legislation such as that offered by Congressman Hyde would have to meet only a rational basis test. Anyone challenging such a statute would be required to demonstrate that the statute was not rationally related to any legitimate government objection. The physical and psychological health of children, since they were accepted as compelling governmental objectives, would also serve as legitimate goals. The difference would result from regulations not having to be narrowly tailored to those objectives.

When employing the rational basis test, scientific certainty, whatever that may mean in the context of psychological studies, is not required. The Court so concluded in *Ginsberg v. New York*. The legislature had included in the statute a finding that the material addressed was "'a basic factor in impairing the ethical and moral development of our youth and a clear and present danger to the people of the state.'"[52] Although the Court expressed doubt that the legislature's finding was accepted scientific fact, it did not require that the finding be scientifically established. Because obscenity is unprotected by the First Amendment, it can be suppressed without establishing such a scientific basis. The Court only had to conclude that "it was not irrational for the legislature to find that exposure to material condemned by the statute is harmful to minors."[53] The Court then looked to the scientific studies available and concluded that, while a causal link between obscenity and the impairment of ethical and moral development had not been established, neither had such a link been disproved. Since the materials were unprotected, the Court refused to require "scientifically certain criteria of legislation" and was unwilling to find that a rational basis for the conclusion that such materials harm minors was lacking.[54]

Even if the studies on the real-world effects of youth exposure to media violence fail to establish narrowly the precise genre of violence that has negative effect, a ban on renting violent videos to minors can meet the rational basis test. Scientific certainty is not required under rational basis. It need only be shown that it is "not irrational for the legislature to find that exposure to material condemned by the statute is harmful to minors." The psychological studies on the effects of violence clearly meet this standard. The scientific evidence is far stronger for the proposition that violent images are harmful than it is for the proposition that sexually explicit images are harmful. If the state of science was adequate to support the statute at issue in *Ginsberg*, it is clearly sufficient to support the sort of ban sought by Congressman Hyde. It is equally the case that the science, while less fully developed, is sufficient to support a rational belief that violent video games are a danger to our nation's youth, and that limiting youth access would ameliorate that danger.

8 | The Internet

The Internet allows a school child to access more information to help on a homework assignment than can be found in all the other sources available to the child. But the same child may also be exposed to sites requiring no credit card or identification but containing sexual material of more than a mild variety. The child may not even be trying to find explicit material. Seemingly innocuous or valuable-sounding sites, such as "www.WhiteHouse.com," turn out to be pornographic. Furthermore, children are targets, in the initially anonymous world of the Internet, of sexual solicitations that might not have occurred in the real world.

The Internet does not raise any new content issues. The concerns are the same as in the older media: sex, violence, hate speech and all the other varieties of expression that cause concern when children are involved. The difference posed by the Internet has to do with access and delivery. While children would not be allowed in an adult book store, they may be exposed to the same sort of depiction via the Internet. With regard to book stores, adults may be allowed entry and children banned. Doing the same for the Internet has proven to be difficult. On the other hand, the advent of the Internet should not cause despair on the part of those who want to protect children from negative media influences. While the first attempts to regulate the Internet have been declared unconstitutional, that does not mean there can be no protection.

A. The Dangers of the Internet

The major concerns regarding the Internet have had to do with the sexually explicit material it contains, although the proportion of Internet addresses containing such material is actually very small. In a 1996 case, it was estimated that sexual material on the Internet comprises well under one-tenth of one percent of the total content.[1] Furthermore, with the exception of material sent to a recipient's e-mail, not an unheard-of event, some action on the part of the recipient is required before he or she is exposed to indecent material. While an affirmative act may be required to access Websites, that act need not have been one intended to search out sexual matter. In the proceedings in that same 1996 case an expert ran a search using the titles of popular children's movies: *Sleeping Beauty, Babe* and *Little Women*.[2] The search produced a small number of links to sexually explicit sites.

The concern that children would unintentionally stumble onto, or intentionally search out, indecent material has led to the development of screening mechanisms. Several varieties of filtering software are available, which can work in several ways. One way is to have it contain a list of sites containing objectionable material and block access to those sites. The difficulty here is again the great number of sites, as well as the regular changes the sites may undergo and the regular addition of new sites. Furthermore, the trial expert's searches using "Babe" and "Little Women" as key words both turned up links to sexually explicit sites, even with the screening software running.[3] Clearly, those sites were not listed as objectionable at that time.

While software can also screen for sexually suggestive words or phrases, such screening may block too little or too much. A program instructed to block sites containing the word "breast" would screen out sites discussing breast cancer. There are very few sexually suggestive terms that do not also have nonsexual uses. A program that simply blocks strings cannot distinguish these nonsexual uses from sexual ones. In addition to problems with words that have several meanings, blocking strings may eliminate words having nothing to do with sex. Blocking strings containing "sex" may block sites for Middlesex or Essex and other nonsexual sites containing the string.

Furthermore, software can only screen for text, leaving still or moving pictures unblocked, unless the site's address or textual material reveals sexual content.[4] The only approaches that can screen pictures involve a person examining the specific content of the sites.[5] Screening programs may then contain a list of sites that contain objectionable material and, when installed and activated by parents, prevent their children from accessing those sites. The problem with this approach again is the already massive size of the Web and the number of new sites added regularly.

B. Protecting Children While Allowing Adults Access

The test that any attempt to protect children will have to pass is presented in a relatively old case involving the print media. *Butler v. Michigan*[6] was a 1957 case growing out of a conviction for the sale of a book in violation of a Michigan statute that prohibited distributing to anyone material "'containing obscene, immoral, lewd or lascivious language, or obscene, immoral, lewd or lascivious prints, pictures, figures or descriptions, tending to incite minors to violent or depraved or immoral acts, manifestly tending to the corruption of the morals of youth.'" [7] The problem in *Butler* was that the book in question was not sold to a minor, but to a police officer. The statute was not limited to situations, as in *Ginsberg v. New York*,[8] in which materials were actually sold to a minor. The sale to the general public was banned on the basis of the undesirable influence the book could have on youth.

The state claimed a right to quarantine generally the books in question in order to protect its children. The Court responded, "Surely, this is to burn the house to roast the pig." [9] Michigan already had a statute similar to New York's, as well as one prohibiting the display of obscene materials on a public street or within view of such a street in a way visible to children, but did not prosecute under those laws, since the sale was in a store and to an adult. The Court's objection was that the statute that was the basis of the conviction had the effect of "reduc[ing] the adult population of Michigan to reading only what is fit for children." [10] The statute was, thus, a violation of the free-speech rights of adults.

The lesson to be learned from *Butler* is that any attempt to limit access by children to sexually explicit material must not limit the free-expression rights of adults. Adults must still be able to receive sexual content, at least so long as the material is not obscene. Any restrictions to adult access must meet strict scrutiny. They must be demonstrated to be narrowly tailored to a compelling governmental interest. It is this requirement that has made it difficult to protect children from objectionable material on the Internet.

C. The Communications Decency Act

Congress has attempted to provide children protection from exposure to Internet indecency, but these attempts have been declared unconstitutional. The first attempt was the passage of the Communications Decency Act of 1966 as a part of the Telecommunications Act of 1996.[11] The CDA made it a crime to transmit by any telecommunications service any "image or other communication which is obscene or indecent, knowing that the recipient of the communication is under 18 years of age."[12] The CDA also made it a crime to use an "interactive computer service" to "display in any manner available" to a person under age eighteen any "image, or other communication that, in context, depicts or describes, in terms patently offensive as measured by contemporary community standards, sexual or excretory activities or organs."[13] The statute also provided a defense for those providing only Internet access or connection and for content providers who restrict access by requiring use of "a verified credit card, debit account, adult access code, or adult personal identification number" or otherwise take "good faith, reasonable, effective, and appropriate actions under the circumstances to restrict or prevent access by minors."[14]

The statute was quickly challenged and reached the Supreme Court as *Reno v. American Civil Liberties Union*.[15] The Court had little difficulty deciding, in a relatively short opinion, that the act was unconstitutional. The Court considered three cases relied on by the government, *Ginsberg v. New York*, *Federal Communications Commission v. Pacifica*,[16] and *Renton v. Playtime Theatres, Inc.*,[17] and saw the actions behind all three as significantly different, and significantly more narrow, than that at issue in the CDA. With regard to *Ginsberg*, the Court noted that, while the statute at issue had limited the exposure of minors to certain sexual materials, the statute did not bar parents from exposing their own children to such material, applied only to commercial transactions, did not address material that had value for minors, and applied to minors under seventeen, rather than the eighteen years provided for in the CDA.

As for *Pacifica*, the Court noted that it had determined only when, rather than if, it was permissible to air indecent material; that is, it concerned channeling rather than a ban. The Court also noted that the medium that had been the subject of regulation in *Pacifica* was one that had been afforded the most limited First Amendment protection.

With regard to *Renton*, a case that upheld zoning regulations that limited the location of adult movie theaters, the Court noted that the ordinance there had been addressed to the secondary effects of such theaters, rather than at the content of the films. While the government tried to characterize the CDA as "cyberzoning," the Court said that the act applies to all of cyberspace, not only to certain neighborhoods. Furthermore, since the purpose behind the act was the protection of children from the primary effects of indecency, the act was content based. The precedents relied on by the government, therefore, failed to support the act.

The Court went on to address concerns over ambiguity. One part of the act addressed material that is "indecent," while another section addressed material that depicts or describes sexual or excretory activities or organs in a way that is "patently offensive as measured by contemporary community standards." The lack of definition, in the statute, for either the term or the phrase, combined with the different language used in the two sections, was seen as likely to lead to uncertainty among potential speakers as to how the standards relate to each other and what they mean. Such vagueness in a content-based regulation was said to be unacceptable because of the chilling effect it would have on protected speech.

In addition to vagueness concerns, the Court concluded that the act would have the effect of suppressing a great deal of speech that adults have the constitutional right to send to, and to receive from, other adults. This effect is unacceptable, where there are less restrictive alternatives, even accepting the governmental interest in protecting children from harmful materials. Even the prohibitions on sending indecent material, knowing the recipient to be a minor, would have an unacceptable effect, since if one member of a chat room is known to be a minor, the conversation of all the adult participants would be limited. Given the alternatives discussed in the briefs and presentations of the parties, and the lack of congressional findings or hearings on alternatives, the Court could not find that the CDA was narrowly tailored. Neither, said the Court, could the statutory defenses save the act, since the Court saw these defenses as being currently unavailable or economically unfeasible.

In addition to the majority opinion, there was also an opinion by Justice O'Connor, joined by Chief Justice Rehnquist, concurring in the judgment in part and dissenting in part. Justice O'Connor agreed with the Court with regard to its concerns over the act's effect on adult accessibility to protected material but wrote separately to explain her view that the CDA was "little more than an attempt by Congress to create 'adult zones' on the Internet [and that] precedent indicates that the creation of such zones can be constitutionally sound." [18] Nonetheless, she saw the CDA as having failed to meet the requirements for such zoning laws because of the effect it would have of unduly restricting access by adults.

Justice O'Connor did note the progress being made in screening software and tags on the addresses of indecent material and suggested that the development of such technology would make cyberspace more like the real world and therefore more amenable to a zoning-law approach. Nonetheless, the act must be assessed against the background of available technology, and at that point the only way to avoid liability was to refrain completely from indecent speech.

D. *The Child Online Protection Act*

The demise of the CDA led Congress to make a second attempt at limiting the exposure of minors to indecent material. The Child Online Protection Act (COPA) provided penalties for "[w]hoever knowingly and with knowledge of the character of the material, in interstate or foreign commerce by means of the World Wide Web, makes any communication for commercial purposes that is available to any minor and that includes any material that is harmful to minors."[19] The prohibition left several phrases to be defined. The statute provided that a person will be considered to be making a communication for commercial purposes only if he or she provides the communication as a business and intends to earn a profit, even if not actually making a profit.[20] Material harmful to minors was defined as

> any communication, picture, image, graphic image file, article, recording, writing, or other matter of any kind that is obscene or that—
> (A) the average person, applying contemporary community standards, would find, taking the material as a whole and with respect to minors, is designed to appeal to, or is designed to pander to, the prurient interest;
> (B) depicts, describes, or represents, in a manner patently offensive with respect to minors, an actual or simulated sexual act or sexual contact, an actual or simulated normal or perverted sexual act, or a lewd exhibition of the genitals or post-pubescent female breast; and
> (C) taken as a whole, lacks serious literary, artistic, political, or scientific value for minors.[21]

Furthermore, minors were defined as persons under seventeen. Like the CDA, COPA provided affirmative defenses to prosecution if the content provider required the use of a credit card, debit account, adult access code, adult personal identification number or digital certificate that verifies age or took other reasonable and feasible measures available under current technology.[22]

Before COPA was to go into effect, it was challenged and a temporary restraining order was issued. After taking evidence and hearing arguments, a federal district court in another case styled *American Civil Liberties Union v. Reno*,[23] issued a preliminary injunction based on its conclusion that COPA would likely be held unconstitutional following a full trial.

The court determined that setting up the credit card verification that would serve as a defense would cost at least $300 and perhaps run into the thousands in start-up costs plus transaction fees. Some Websites would have to move their operations to a new Internet service provider if their current provider's system could not support credit card verification, and that too would involve costs. The court also concluded that the loss of anonymity presented by any of these registration or verification devices would result in the loss of traffic to Websites containing material deemed harmful to minors. That would provide an economic disincentive toward carrying such material. Sites would be led to self-censorship, and speech that is protected for adults would be burdened.

The court concluded that the burden on protected speech required that COPA be tested under strict scrutiny analysis. The court was willing to concede that Congress had addressed a compelling interest in the protection of youth, even from material not obscene by adult standards. The means, however, were not narrowly tailored to that end. The requirements of COPA lacked efficacy in that some minors, for example minors with credit cards or those viewing foreign or noncommercial sites, would still gain access to material harmful to minors. While a statute need not be completely successful to meet strict scrutiny, COPA was seen as no more effective than filtering devices that do not limit adult access. Furthermore, since the concern seemed to be over pornographic images rather than text, the statute could have been more narrowly tailored by addressing only pictures or graphics. Finally, the affirmative defenses could have been incorporated in defining the elements of the crime in order to relieve defendants of the burden of establishing the defense.

The COPA case was heard by the U.S. Court of Appeals for the Third Circuit twice.[24] The first time the court affirmed the lower court grant of an injunction but on entirely different grounds. The appellate court's concern was directed entirely at COPA's use of contemporary community standards in assessing harmfulness to minors. This was despite the fact that the issue was not even addressed in the briefs submitted by the parties or amici and arose only at oral argument. The court noted that the Web has no geographical boundaries and concluded that a community standards test would force content providers to adhere to the standards of the most restrictive community or risk prosecution there. While the court expressed concern that the result would be a restriction on material available to adults, its concern carried over to minors in that minors nationwide would face limitations based on what the most restrictive community thought harmful for minors.

The community standard was the only part of COPA to reach the Supreme Court, and the Court rejected the Third Circuit's reasoning, holding that the act's reference to community standards did not, on its own, make COPA unconstitutional. [25] There was no majority opinion when it came to explaining that conclusion. A plurality saw no difference between the Internet and federal statutes regarding obscenity in the mail or on the telephone, concluding that "if a publisher wishes for its material to be judged only by the standards of particular communities, then it need only take the simple step of utilizing a medium that enables it to target the release of its material into those communities." [26] The plurality explained that, with regard to the statute at issue, this could be accomplished by placing the material behind an adult identification screen. Concurrences on this issue by Justices O'Connor and Breyer argued that a national standard should be adopted and applied to the Internet.

On remand the Third Circuit again concluded that COPA is unconstitutional. The court was concerned that the commercial limitation was still too broad, that the affirmative defenses were inadequate and that, despite the similarity of the "harmful to minors" standard to other constitutional statutes, the standard did not provide adequate guidance. Thus, other approaches to regulating access by children to objectionable Internet materials must still be addressed. It is important to note, before leaving COPA, that the Supreme Court opinion does remove one serious obstacle in that path, the stumbling block of community standards applied to a widely accessible medium.

E. More Recent Congressional Attempts

The Children's Internet Protection Act requires that any library receiving certain federal funds intended to foster Internet access employ filtering programs to prevent adult access to obscenity and child pornography and youth access to material that is harmful to minors. [27] The constitutionality of that act is in question. A federal district court recently declared the act unconstitutional, concluding that the available filtering programs bar access to a substantial amount of protected speech, and that it is currently impossible to develop a filter that does not suffer from underblocking or overblocking. [28] The Supreme Court will hear an appeal of this decision, and the act's future is unclear. Even if the Court reverses the lower court, children will still only be protected in facilities subject to the act. Further measures will be necessary to protect minors in other settings.

A still more recent attempt is found in the Dot Kids Implementation and Efficiency Act of 2002. [29] This act mandates the establishment of a second-level Internet domain name, within the "us" country code domain. The ".kids.us" domain would be limited to material that is appropriate for children under thirteen. Multiuser interactive services would be barred from the domain, unless they could show compliance with the goals of the statute, and links to sites outside the domain would be banned.

It is certainly likely that the Dot Kids act will be challenged, but the establishment of this limited forum may prove constitutional. Since adult speech is not affected, the thesis argued for here would certainly validate the approach. Nonetheless, other protective means are still required. The ".kids.us" domain is likely to become the province of content providers such as Disney or Children's Television Workshop. While a site with such material is a positive development, parents limiting children to such a domain will severely restrict the access of those children to important material available in other domains. If children are to have access to those other sites and still not face the harmful materials in the domains containing those sites, another approach is required.

F. An Alternative Based on Ginsberg

The difficulties faced by the first two attempts at protecting children from Internet indecency should not be taken as showing that nothing can be done. There is an alternative that could assist parents in making filtering an effective approach to protecting their children. It would filter out material that is unsuitable for minors, while leaving valuable material accessible. It would also treat the Internet as on a par with print media. It would enjoy all the First Amendment protection enjoyed by the most protected of media.

The key to an adequate and constitutional approach is to put the Internet publisher to a choice similar to the choice that must be made by the seller of magazines. As *Ginsberg* shows, a magazine seller must decide whether or not the magazine a minor wants to buy is appropriate for minors. If the vendor sells to a minor a magazine that is obscene as to minors, knowing the content of the magazine, the vendor is subject to criminal sanctions. If distributers of print material may be subject to such requirements, there is no reason why Web publishers, who in fact have more specific knowledge of the nature of the content of their own Web pages than the newsdealer has of the magazines on the store's shelves, should not face the same burden.

Web providers differ from the retail distributors of other media because Web providers cannot know who accesses their sites, while newsstand operators can identify their customers. Magazine vendors can make reasonable judgments about the age of customers and request more information if the customer might be a minor. On the Web all must be asked the same questions, and adults may be deterred from obtaining material which they have a constitutional right to access. If, however, a system did not put the requirement of actually determining the age of Web users on the site operator, and if neither minors nor adults actually had to identify themselves, those objections should be of no concern.

The key is to mandate the availability of the defenses suggested in the Internet cases, but found in those cases to be, as yet, unavailable. Much of the rationale of the CDA opinion was based on the inability of Internet publishers to limit the distribution of the material they provide. The implication in the opinions was that narrow tailoring would be met if providers could easily and inexpensively adopt one of the verification or screening approaches that were included in the statute, or explication of the statute, as defenses. Since the technology was unavailable, the defense was also unavailable, and the effect of the statute was overly broad in that publishers would be chilled into providing only what was fit for children.

The Platform for Internet Content Selection, developed by a consortium of Web publishers, allows tags that provide electronic ratings to be attached to Internet addresses. Just as Congress had mandated that all new televisions must contain a v-chip, Congress could require that all browser software and all mail and newsgroup reader software contain PICS sensitive technology. As with the v-chip, it would be the parents' prerogative to configure the software to block material accompanied by the signal. [30]

Once PICS is mandated, a defense to the distribution to minors of material obscene as to children would be the inclusion of a PICS signal. Each publisher of Internet material would be liable for the purposeful, knowing or reckless distribution to minors of material obscene as to children. Such obscenity would again be defined as it was in the statute at issue in *Ginsberg*, but with community standards defined relative to the Internet medium.

With regard to e-mail, list serve and bulletin board messages, the software used to write and send messages should be required to provide for each message transmitted a choice as to whether the message should be made available to minors. The best approach would be to have a default setting that limited the message to adults or non-PICS-activated receivers. The sender could toggle off the limitation if the sender intended to make the material available to children. This would reduce the negligent transmission of such material by senders who failed to toggle on the PICS tag, in a system where the default position allowed access by minors. This would eliminate the concern in the *Reno* Supreme Court opinion that the inclusion of a single minor in a chat room or on a mailing list would limit the speech of all participants. Participants may still offer any indecent, nonobscene speech but must accompany the message with a PICS signal. Minors using PICS-activated computers would not receive the message, but adults and minors whose parents allow their children to receive such material would still have access.

Returning to the Web, the publisher of a Web page should be liable for distribution to minors of material obscene as to children that appears on that page, just as any other publisher is so liable, unless a PICS signal is attached. Web pages, however, commonly contain hypertext links to other pages, and those other pages often contain links to still other pages. Holding the publisher of a Web page responsible for all information that could be linked from the publisher's page would constitute a substantial chilling effect. The only way in which a publisher could assure itself of protection would be to provide no links. Links, however, are often the best way to find the material the user is seeking.

Fortunately, it is not necessary to make the Web publisher responsible for all linked sites. If the publisher links to another site originating in the United States, that site is also subject to the requirements of the proposed statute. That site, if it contains material obscene as to children, will be required to contain a PICS-activating electronic tag. If the site does not contain such a tag, its publisher will be liable. Publishers whose own sites are not PICS activating and who link to the site should be allowed to rely on those other publishers adhering to the law and should still be allowed the defense. The only exception should be where a publisher purposely links to a site it knows to be obscene and not PICS activating with the intent to make that site available to children.

There are also, however, a significant number of sites that originate outside the United States. Those sites would not be subject to the statute requiring PICS tags for material obscene as to children, and a publisher could not rely on their inclusion of a PICS tag if their material were obscene as to children. If U.S. publishers were strictly liable for the material in non-U.S. linked sites, there would again be a chilling effect. Non-PICS-activated sites, that is, sites that are not indecent or are believed to have value for children, would likely be unwilling to link to non-U.S. sites, and children would lose the international and multicultural benefits the Internet can provide. The better approach here is to allow the government to prosecute for links to a non-U.S. site, only if it can prove that the site was obscene as to children at the time the U.S. provider included it as a link. The U.S. publisher is then under a duty to view any site to which it links and, if that site contains material obscene as to children, attach a PICS tag to its own page. If the non-U.S. linked site later adds material that is obscene as to children, the U.S. page publisher should only be liable if it becomes aware that it is now linking to a non-PICS-activating but obscene-as-to-children site.

This does still leave open the possibility that a foreign site containing material that is obscene as to children might be accessed, not as a link from a U.S. Web page but as a second-level link or as the result of a Web search. [31] A partial solution to this potential problem is for the browser software also to provide parents an option under which access will be limited to U.S. sites. Those sites will be subject to the statute and the sites to which they link will also either be subject to the statute or will have been checked by the publishers of the initial sites providing the links. It is, of course, possible that foreign sites with value will be inaccessible, but parents who wish their children to have access to such sites may choose not to activate the United States limitation on access, just as they may allow their children to use the Internet with no PICS screening at all.

This PICS-based approach puts the onus on the sender or publisher. It eliminates the massive, perhaps undoable, task of the government or an independent board examining and providing ratings for millions of Web-sites. It also brings e-mail and newsgroups within the scope of regulation. Furthermore, it does so in a way that does not prevent adults from com-municating with, or providing information for, one another. The pub-lisher or e-mail sender must determine whether or not the material being provided is obscene as to minors and may be liable if mistaken, but that is the same as it is for distributors of print material. Print distributors can still distribute indecent material to adults while being careful to refuse to provide minors material that is obscene to them. Electronic publishers and e-mail senders may also communicate indecent material to adults but must also be careful not to provide minors with material obscene as to children. The proposed defenses spell out what constitutes care, and the level of care required, including a PICS tag or examining non-U.S.-linked sites, seems minimal. The burden would seem no greater than—in fact, far less than—the seller of indecent magazines requesting evidence of age from one who purchases such a magazine.

There remains the community standards issue that some may see as making impossible the regulation of the Internet. Yet, the Court in its COPA decision concluded that variance in community standards did not, in itself, preclude regulation of an essentially national or international medium like the Internet. Furthermore, while the community standards aspect of the obscenity test was adopted in order not to require that the people of Maine or Mississippi accept depictions tolerable in New York City or Las Vegas,[32] the people of Maine and Mississippi would seem likely to be in more agreement with the people of New York City and Las Vegas over what violates standards of appropriateness for children than they are for adult standards. A national standard for what should be made available to children, at least in the context of the Internet, is not unrealistic.

Even if one does not accept the position that there should be a lessened First Amendment when the free-expression rights of or toward children are involved, the current existence of the obscenity exception and its corollary obscenity as to children doctrine should allow the restrictions on Internet accessibility already discussed. If the obscenity exception is held to extend to sufficiently offensive and graphic depictions of violence, then the corollary that should follow that extension would include a violent obscenity as to children doctrine. The Internet restrictions suggested would then also carry over to any violence on the Internet, although that appears currently to be less a concern than sexual material. Those who post or publish descriptions or depictions of violence that are unacceptable for minors would be required to attach the PICS signal to their content. Parents who did not want their children so exposed would have the opportunity to activate the PICS filter and protect their children.

If the basic thesis of this work is accepted—that is, that there should be a weaker protection for expression when children are involved—this thesis would lead to a broader application of the Internet restrictions suggested. For example, if it should be decided that profane language in the presence of other people's children is proscribable, then any Web page, e-mail or bulletin board posting involving such language would require the attachment of the PICS signal. Similarly, if hate speech directed toward or in the presence of other people's children is unprotected, then any Internet hate speech would require the attachment of a PICS signal. Again, if the default setting is to include such a signal in any publication or posting, it would be only intentional transmission without the PICS signal—that is, intentional publication to children—that would result in liability.

The protection of children on the Internet, however broad that protection may be, would be accomplished without limiting the right of adults to communicate with one another. The only chilling effect would be on adults who might choose to leave the PICS signal attached to a publication or posting that would in fact be acceptable to children. Even in that situation, however, parents who believe their children are sufficiently mature to receive more adult information could choose to leave their PICS filters inactivated or could help their children obtain adult information on a particular topic by working with them to access information that is valuable but, out of excess publisher caution, had a PICS signal attached.

The development of the Internet proposal as presented should not apply to parents' messages to their own children. Since parents could choose not to activate the PICS filter on their e-mail program and could thereby choose to allow their children to receive material more suited for adults, they should not be penalized for sending their children an e-mail that others might consider unacceptable for children. Of course, if parents, in an attempt to communicate with their children, post to a bulletin board or other site accessible to children generally, they must meet the requirements placed on other publishers or posters. The only restrictions placed on communication are on the intentional or reckless communication to other people's children of material that is inappropriate for children. It is a minor restriction on expression rights, more than justified by the interests parents have in determining the influences their children will experience as they grow into an adult world that has more robust expression rights.

9

Hate Speech

An Oscar Hammerstein song in the musical *South Pacific* makes the point that racial hatred is not natural but learned. Hammerstein wrote that hatred and fear of those with differently shaped eyes or skin of a different shade has to be "carefully taught."[1] It may be that children are not born altruists and exhibit some, or mostly, egocentric traits, but infants and very young children do not seem to display the racist attitudes some people develop later in life. Hammerstein went on to say that such hatred must be learned early, as a six- to eight-year-old. That may be less clear. Some seem to develop racist attitudes as teenagers or young adults, perhaps even as older adults. The moral development discussion in chapter 4 would seem to bear this out. Whatever may be the possibility of the later development of racism, childhood, given its status as the formative years in other areas, is likely to be of great importance.

If hate must be taught, there are those who are more than willing to provide the lesson plans. Resistance Records provides music useful in recruiting the next generation of white supremacists. The lyrics of the music they produce are hate filled. As an example, a 1992 offering of the label's group RaHoWa (a contraction of "Racial Holy War") calls on white people to wake up and save themselves from secret societies trying to bring the white race to its knees. They point to bloody street riots and "niggers run amok," calling on whites to "tremble in fear," save their children, and lock their doors.[2]

Should the First Amendment require society to tolerate such speech? If the answer for adults is "yes," must the nation's youth be allowed to purchase these recordings in record stores? Suppose a group of high school students plan to sing a RaHoWa song at a school talent show. Must the school allow the performance? What if the singing simply takes place in the halls between classes? Whatever the answer for adults, a two-tier First Amendment would allow a different answer for children. If children can be protected from this sort of racist expression, it may go a long way toward the elimination of, and certainly should contribute to the lessening of, racism in our culture generally.

A. Adult Hate Speech and the Courts

At an earlier time the prospect of the courts upholding attempts to limit racist or other varieties of hate speech looked promising. In 1952 the Supreme Court issued its opinion in *Beauharnais v. Illinois*,[3] a case that affirmed the conviction of an individual charged under an Illinois criminal statute making it unlawful to publish, present or exhibit material that "'portrays depravity, criminality, unchastity, or lack of virtue of a class of citizens, of any race, color, creed or religion which said publication or exhibition exposes the citizens of any race, color, creed or religion to contempt, derision, or obloquy. . . .'"[4]

The basis for Beauharnais's conviction was the distribution of a leaflet calling on the mayor and City Council of Chicago "to halt the further encroachment, harassment and invasion of white people, their property, neighborhoods and persons, by the Negro." The leaflet also contained a call for the "'[o]ne million self respecting white people in Chicago to unite'" accompanied by a statement that "If persuasion and the need to prevent the white race from becoming mongrelized by the negro will not unite us, then the aggressions . . . rapes, robberies, knives, guns and marijuana of the negro, surely will."[5] Also attached was an application for membership in the White Circle League of America, Inc.

The Court, with Justice Frankfurter writing and over the dissents of Justices Black, Douglas, Reed and Jackson, affirmed Beauharnais's conviction for publishing this "group libel." The Court noted that libel has, along with fighting words and obscenity, always been considered unprotected by the First Amendment. It was clear to the Court that the false assertion that an individual was a rapist, robber, carrier of knives or guns, or user of marijuana would be libelous. The only question was whether liability could attach when such allegations were directed at a group rather than an individual. On that issue, the Court concluded that "if an utterance directed at an individual may be the object of criminal sanctions, we cannot deny to a State power to punish the same utterance directed at a defined group."[6]

The applicability of *Beauharnais* may have been limited from the time it was handed down. It is clear that the Court, and in the Court's view the legislature, was particularly concerned with the allegations of fact contained in the publication. The Court cited instances of racial violence, murders, bombings and riots that had occurred in Illinois and elsewhere in the years preceding the enactment of the law and said that the state could conclude that "wilful purveyors of falsehood concerning racial and religious groups promote strife and tend powerfully to obstruct the manifold adjustments required for free, ordered life in a metropolitan, polyglot community."[7] The Court went on to say:

> In the face of this history and its frequent obligato of extreme racial and religious propaganda, we would deny experience to say that the Illinois legislature was without reason in seeking ways to curb false or malicious defamation of racial and religious groups, made in public places and by means calculated to have a powerful emotional impact on those to whom it was presented.[8]

The emphasis may, thus, have been on the falsehoods that may lead to strife and may not have extended to the use of racial epithets or abuse not including assertions of fact.

On the other hand, the Court also said: "'Resort to epithets or personal abuse is not in any proper sense communication of information or opinion safeguarded by the Constitution, and its punishment as a criminal act would raise no question under that instrument.'"[9] That language would not seem to require any assertion of fact, and the sort of insults that are of current concern may well have been within the ambit of the decision. Whatever the correct conclusion would have been, at the time of *Beauharnais*, a recent case calls any reliance on *Beauharnais* into question.

R.A.V. v. St. Paul resulted from a cross burning by several teenagers on the lawn of a black family living across the street from one of the teenagers.[10] R.A.V. was charged under a St. Paul, Minnesota, city ordinance providing

> whoever places on public or private property a symbol, object, appellation, characterization or graffiti, including, but not limited to, a burning cross or Nazi swastika, which one knows or has reasonable grounds to

know arouses anger, alarm or resentment in others on the basis of race, color, creed, religion or gender commits disorderly conduct and shall be guilty of a misdemeanor.[11]

The state courts had construed the statute to limit its application only to fighting words, words that "'inflict[] injury or tend[] to incite immediate violence,'"[12] or, as the Supreme Court had earlier defined them, words "ësuch as have a direct tendency to cause acts of violence by the person to whom, individually, the remark is addressed.'"[13] Furthermore, the state supreme court had said, in language seemed certain to protect the statute from challenges under the First Amendment, that the law "reached only expression 'that the First Amendment does not protect.'"[14] If that had been the state court's aim, it missed the target. The Supreme Court held that, even limited to fighting words, the ordinance was unconstitutional because "it prohibits otherwise permitted speech solely on the basis of the subjects the speech addresses."[15]

The Court recognized that fighting words, along with other forms of traditionally unprotected speech, are sometimes said to be outside the protection of the First Amendment. But, the Court said, such statements must be taken in the context in which they were written and are not literally true. "What they mean is that these areas of speech can, consistently with the First Amendment, be regulated because of their constitutionally proscribable content (obscenity, defamation, etc.)—not that they are categories of speech entirely invisible to the Constitution, so that they may be made the vehicles for content discrimination unrelated to their distinctively proscribable content."[16] While fighting words or obscenity may be banned without violating the First Amendment, it is not the case that the amendment had nothing at all to say about such materials. As an example, the Court said that a city council can ban obscene material altogether, but it cannot ban only obscene material that takes a position critical of the government.

The Court remained willing to allow some lines to be drawn within these categories of what had been called unprotected speech. For example, government could choose not to ban all obscene material but only obscene material that is the most lascivious. What must be avoided is the possibility that the government could drive particular ideas or viewpoints from the marketplace of ideas by banning only obscene material that presents views that government finds objectionable on dimensions other than obscenity.

The problem with the St. Paul ordinance, even when limited to fighting words, was that it did not regulate evenhandedly. It applied "only to 'fighting words' that insult, or provoke violence, 'on the basis of race, color, creed, religion or gender.' Displays containing abusive invective, no matter how vicious or severe, are permissible unless they are addressed to one of the specified disfavored topics."[17] Furthermore, the ordinance applied only to those taking a particular viewpoint.

> Displays containing some words—odious racial epithets, for example— would be prohibited to proponents of all views. But "fighting words" that do not themselves invoke race, color, creed, religion, or gender— aspersions upon a person's mother, for example—would seemingly be usable *ad libitum* in the placards of those arguing *in favor* of racial, color, etc., tolerance and equality, but could not be used by those speakers' opponents. One could hold up a sign saying, for example, that all "anti-Catholic bigots" are misbegotten; but not that all "papists" are, for that would insult and provoke violence "on the basis of religion." St. Paul has no such authority to license one side of a debate to fight freestyle, while requiring the other to follow Marquis of Queensberry rules.[18]

The Court did recognize another valid basis for differential treatment for subclasses of speech, if the government interest is in the secondary effects of the speech and not aimed at content. The most relevant example is a ban limited to sexually derogatory fighting words that violate prohibitions against sexual discrimination in employment. This, the Court said, is an example of speech that "can be swept up incidently within the reach of a statute directed at conduct rather than speech."[19] Where conduct is targeted because of some feature other than its expressive content, the conduct is not protected simply because it is expressive. Indeed, the city argued that it was addressing secondary effects. It was, it claimed, not trying to limit free expression but to protect individuals who are particularly vulnerable to victimization. The Court refused to accept this basis, concluding that the reaction of listeners to speech and the emotive impact of speech are not secondary effects.[20]

The Court also rejected the argument that a distinction can be drawn based on the view that the injuries caused by racist speech are qualitatively different from other injuries caused by speech. It saw any such claimed distinction as based on content. St. Paul claimed that, despite the ordinance's content or viewpoint discrimination, it was still constitutional because "the ordinance helps to ensure the basic human rights of members of groups that have historically been subjected to discrimination, including the right of such group members to live in peace where they wish."[21] The Court accepted that the interest is compelling and that the ordinance promoted that interest, but the dangers inherent in censorship require that content-based regulation be necessary to that interest, and it was on this requirement that the ordinance failed. While St. Paul's argued that "only a content-specific measure can communicate to minority groups that the 'group hatred' aspect of such speech 'is not condoned by the majority,'"[22] the Court would not allow this view to be expressed through the suppression of contrary speech.

There have also been attempts to limit hate speech on college campuses, but they too have not met with legal success. An example of that failure may be found in *Doe v. University of Michigan*.[23] The policies at issue in *Doe* were established after several incidents of racism and racial harassment that were believed to be increasing in frequency. Racist fliers had been distributed; racist jokes were told on a campus radio station, and a Ku Klux Klan uniform was displayed from a dormitory window during a demonstration protesting these incidents.

In response, the University of Michigan adopted its Policy on Discrimination and Discriminatory Harassment. The policy set rules for speech that depended on where the speech occurred. In the public areas of the campus, only physical violence and destruction of property were prohibited, and university-sponsored publications were not subject to the regulations. The limitations placed on speech applied to "educational centers," such as classrooms and classroom buildings, laboratories, libraries and study areas. In those areas, sanctions originally applied to:

1. Any behavior, verbal or physical, that stigmatizes or victimizes an individual on the basis of race, ethnicity, religion, sex, sexual orientation, creed, national origin, ancestry, age, marital status, handicap or Vietnam-era veteran status, and that
   a. Involves an express or implied threat to an individual's academic efforts, employment, participation in University sponsored extra-curricular activities or personal safety; or
   b. Has the purpose or reasonably foreseeable effect of interfering with an individual's academic efforts, employment, participation in University sponsored extra-curricular activities or personal safety; or

c. Creates an intimidating, hostile, or demeaning environment for educational pursuits, employment or participation in University sponsored extra-curricular activities.[24]

Similar provisions applied to behavior or speech stigmatizing or victimizing on the basis of sex or sexual orientation. Section 1(c) was later withdrawn, while the parallel section for sex-biased expression remained in force.

A graduate student in psychology challenged the policy. He alleged that he wanted to discuss sex and race differences in a Comparative Animal Behavior class in which he was a teaching assistant. He planned to present the theory that men are better, on average, at some spacial relation tasks because of biological differences between the sexes. He was concerned that some would consider the theory sexist and a violation of the policy. Since the policy would chill his intended speech, he asked the federal district court to enjoin its enforcement. The court found the policy to violate the First Amendment on both overbreadth, the potential of the policy to reach a substantial amount of protected expression, and vagueness grounds.

While the university insisted that the policy did not apply to protected speech, the court found instances in which it had been applied to such expression. A complaint had been filed against a social work graduate student, claiming he had harassed students on the basis of sexual orientation and sex. He had taken the position, in a research class, that homosexuality is a disease, that he planned to develop a counseling program to change gays to straight and was already doing so with some of his patients. The investigation concluded that there was sufficient evidence to proceed, and the case went to a formal hearing. While the hearing panel decided the comments on curing homosexuality were protected expression, the court was concerned that the university had forced the student to face a hearing growing out of speech made in the course of academic discussion and research. It was clear to the court that the university considered serious classroom comments potentially sanctionable and that the policy was therefore overly broad.

The court also found the policy unconstitutionally vague. The requirements that the expression "stigmatize" or "victimize" an individual lacked the clarity required to allow the person of average intelligence to know what language would violate the policy. It was also unclear what constitutes a threat to, or interferes with, an individual's academic efforts.

Furthermore, the court said, the fact that expression stigmatizes or victimizes does not necessarily deprive it of First Amendment protection.

Despite enjoining enforcement of the policy, the court did recognize the right of the university to limit some actions and expression. The university can sanction fighting words, including racial epithets that fall within that class and could address actual threats.[25]

> What the University could not do . . . was establish an anti-discrimination policy which had the effect of prohibiting certain speech because it disagreed with ideas or messages sought to be conveyed. . . . Nor could the University proscribe speech simply because it was found to be offensive, even gravely so, by large numbers of people. . . . These principles acquire a special significance in the university setting, where the free and unfettered interplay of competing views is essential to the institution's educational mission.[26]

Given the context in which the *University of Michigan* case arose, the claim that it would inhibit serious classroom discussion and the university's invocation of proceedings for remarks that did occur in the classroom, it might have seemed that there was still room for a more limited rule, one that did not interfere with "the free and unfettered interplay of competing views . . . essential to the institution's educational mission." A rule implemented by the University of Wisconsin served as an opportunity to test that distinction and was found wanting in *UWM Post v. Board of Regents of the University of Wisconsin System*.[27]

Also concerned over incidents of what it considered discriminatory harassment involving fraternities, a large caricature of a black Fiji Islander, skits performed in black face as part of a "slave auction," and a fight that may have involved racial issues, the system's Board of Regents adopted what it titled its "Design for Diversity." Each of the system's institutions was required to prepare policies against discriminatory conduct, with guidance from the Board's own policy contained in the "Policy and Guidelines on Racist and Discriminatory Conduct." The Regents also enlisted the help of several law professors at the Madison campus, including hate speech scholar Richard Delgado, to draft amendments to the student conduct code that would withstand First Amendment challenges.

The perceived key to the constitutionality of the rule was to include a requirement that the use of racist, sexist or other discriminatory speech be with the intent to make the educational environment hostile for the individual being addressed. A further, and seemingly important, distinction between the Michigan and Wisconsin rules was in the fact that the Wisconsin rule applied only "in non-academic matters." The rule addressed racist or discriminatory expression directed at an individual and that is demeaning on the basis of race, sex or a variety of other factors and creating an intimidating or hostile environment.[28] As had the University of Michigan, the Wisconsin system provided illustrations of conduct that would violate its rule. The illustrations included racist jokes or slurs made to an individual and equivalently demeaning visual material placed in the victim's living quarters or work area, but only if this was done with the intent to create a hostile environment. The illustrations also stated that there was no violation in the expression of a racially derogatory opinion in a class discussion, because such a remark is not directed toward an individual, and there would appear to be no intent to create a hostile environment. Further illustrations make it clear that the rule did not reach the academic discussion that seemed to come within the scope of the Michigan rule. Specifically said not to be actionable were situations such as the following: "In a class discussion concerning women in the workplace, a male student states his belief that women are by nature better equipped to be mothers than executives, and thus should not be employed in upper level management positions. . . . A faculty member, in a genetics class discussion, suggests that certain racial groups seem to be genetically pre-disposed to alcoholism."[29] On the other hand, it is clear that hurling racial epithets at an individual, with the requisite intent, was actionable.

Despite the attempt to draft a rule narrowly tailored to the particular concerns involved, the provisions were declared unconstitutional. The court rejected application of the "fighting words" exception, because that exception requires that the expression be such that its utterance is likely to provoke an immediate violent response and must be directed at the individual likely to so respond. There was no requirement of likely violent response in the Wisconsin rules. While willing to credit the Board of Regents' argument that demeaning a person based on "immutable characteristics . . . central to the person's identity" is likely to cause violent response in many cases, "[i]t is unlikely that all or nearly all demeaning, discriminatory comments, epithets or other expressive behavior which creates an intimidating, hostile or demeaning environment tends to provoke a violent response."[30]

The court also rejected the proposed use of a balancing approach comparing the efficacy of racist speech as a step toward truth and the costs of such speech on its victims. The court said that while the "fighting words" exception had been based on such an analysis, that was not an invitation for courts to employ such a test in other contexts involving content-based speech regulation. Furthermore, it disagreed with the Board of Regents about how any such balance would be struck, finding value in racial epithets to inform others of the speaker's views and the strength of those views. On the other side, rather than increase diversity, the court argued that this limitation on the expression of views limited diversity of ideas in the student population.

The court recognized the validity of the concerns that had motivated the Board of Regents but could simply not tolerate the limitations on expression imposed in response to those concerns.

> The problems of bigotry and discrimination sought to be addressed here are real and truly corrosive of the educational environment. But freedom of speech is almost absolute in our land and the only restriction the fighting words doctrine can abide is that based on the fear of violent reaction. Content-based prohibitions such as that in the UW Rule, however well intended, simply cannot survive the screening which our Constitution demands.[31]

As the above cases indicate, it may be difficult to impossible to erase hate speech from the adult world.[32] The Michigan and Wisconsin cases extend this difficulty to the university setting. Given the adult result, the extension would seem to follow naturally. University students are almost all adults. Those that are under eighteen are advanced to the point that, for free speech purposes, they ought to be treated as adults. While the dangers to free expression may be too great to allow the government to limit even hate speech for adults, the same need not be true of children. Society has stronger interests in protecting children from exposure to hate speech and those protections, as in other areas, pose less danger to the democratic vitality of our government and the adult interest in autonomy.

B. Shielding Children

As with other forms of speech that have a negative effect on children, a dual approach to the First Amendment would limit the rights of third parties to deliver their hate speech to other people's children. While there may be little that can be done about children's speech to one another on the street corner or at the mall, children in school should not have to hear hate speech, and those who would distribute hate speech commercially in the form of music like that from RaHoWa, for example, should be limited in their ability to pass the hate of one generation on to the next. The school issue has been presented recently in at least two circuits of the United States Court of Appeals,[33] with conflicting results.

The Tenth Circuit, in *West v. Derby United School District*,[34] examined a policy adopted by a school district for its middle and high school. The district had experienced racial tension between black and white students. White students, some wearing shirts with Confederate flags, and black students, some wearing "X" shirts referring to Malcolm X, had been involved in verbal confrontations. The Ku Klux Klan and the Aryan Nation, recognizing an opportunity, became active, and the verbal confrontations grew into racist graffiti on school walls and racial incidents on school buses and at athletic events, including at least one fight.

In response to these incidents, the district adopted a "Racial Harassment and Intimidation" policy that provided the following:

District employees and student(s) shall not racially harass or intimidate another student(s) by name calling, using racial or derogatory slurs, wearing or possession of items depicting or implying racial hatred or prejudice. District employees and *students shall not at school, on school property or at school activities wear or have in their possession any written material, either printed or in their own handwriting, that is racially divisive or creates ill will or hatred*. (*Examples:* clothing, articles, material, publications or *any item that denotes* Ku Klux Klan, Aryan Nation-White Supremacy, Black Power, *Confederate flags* or articles, Neo-Nazi or any other "hate" group. This list is not intended to be all inclusive).[35]

The result of the new policy was what was said to be a significant reduction in incidents of racial harassment and a demonstrated reduction in the number of disciplinary referrals.

The legal challenge grew out of the three-day suspension of a seventh-grader found to have violated the policy by drawing a Confederate flag on a piece of paper during class. While the district did not maintain that the student intended to harass or intimidate another student, it concluded that he knew of the rule and intentionally violated it by drawing the flag and handing it to another student. The court refused to rewrite the rule to require intent to harass or intimidate and held that lack of such a requirement was not a violation of constitutionally required due process.

The court then turned to the student's invocation of First Amendment protections. The court recognized that the student's drawing of the flag could reasonably be considered a form of political speech that would be protected by the First Amendment outside the school setting. The court also recognized the Supreme Court's statement that "students do not 'shed the constitutional rights to freedom of speech or expression at the schoolhouse gate.'"[36] But, the court also noted that the Supreme Court has recognized that students' free-expression rights in public schools are not coextensive with those of adults in other contexts. The First Amendment "'must be applied in light of the special characteristics of the school environment. A school need not tolerate student speech that is inconsistent with its basic educational mission even though the government could not censor similar speech outside the school.'"[37] The *West* court also quoted *Bethel School District v. Fraser*[38] to the effect that "[t]he determination of what manner of speech in the classroom . . . is inappropriate properly rests with the school board."[39] Schools have latitude to prevent disruption caused by speech that must be tolerated outside the schools.

While the court said that concerns over possible disturbance had to be based in reality rather than "undifferentiated fear or apprehension," here the school had a recent history of racial incidents and reason to believe that the display of a Confederate flag might cause disruption.

[S]chool officials in Derby had evidence from which they could reasonably conclude that possession and display of Confederate flag images, when unconnected with any legitimate educational purpose, would likely lead to a material and substantial disruption of school discipline. . . . The Racial Harassment policy . . . was clearly something more than a mere desire to avoid the discomfort and unpleasantness that always accompany an unpopular viewpoint. The history of racial tension in the district made administrators' and parents' concerns about future substantial disruptions from possession of Confederate flag symbols at school reasonable. The fact that a full-fledged brawl had not yet broken out over the Confederate flag does not mean that the district was required to sit and wait for one. . . . The district had the power to act to prevent problems before they occurred; it was not limited to prohibiting and punishing conduct only after it caused a disturbance.[40]

Finally, the court also determined that the policy was neither overly broad in that it did not reach material with a legitimate educational purpose nor unconstitutionally vague in that it provided students with adequate notice of what expression was addressed.

The Third Circuit reached a different result in *Saxe v. State College Area School District*.[41] The school district involved in *Saxe* also adopted an "Anti-Harassment Policy" but did so apparently without quite the same history of strife, and the policy it adopted was considerably broader than the policy at issue in *West*. The policy stated as its goal "'providing all students with a safe, secure, and nurturing school environment'" and noted that "'[d]isrespect among members of the school community is unacceptable behavior which threatens to disrupt the school environment and well being of the individual.'"[42] Prohibited was "'[a]ny harassment of a student by a member of the school community.'"[43]

The policy went on to define harassment as "ëverbal or physical conduct based on one's actual or perceived race, religion, color, national origin, gender, sexual orientation, disability, or other personal characteristics, and which has the purpose or effect of substantially interfering with a student's educational performance or creating an intimidating, hostile or offensive environment.'"[44] The policy also provided as examples of discrimination based on "other personal characteristics" discrimination based on "'clothing, physical appearance, social skills, peer group, intellect, educational program, hobbies or values, etc.'"[45]

Two students and their guardian, who was also a member of the Pennsylvania State Board of Education, challenged the policy. The plaintiffs alleged violations of First Amendment free speech rights. The assertions establishing standing to challenge the policy were interesting. They stated that they are Christians who believe that their religion teaches that homosexuality is a sin and that they have the right to speak out against the sinful nature of homosexuality and on a variety of other moral issues and that they feared punishment for speech or symbolic activities reflecting their beliefs.

The school district argued that its policy was constitutional, but the court was unconvinced. It refused to accept the contention that harassment, when it consists of speech, had been considered categorically unprotected by the First Amendment. Furthermore, the court noted that the reach of the policy was considerably broader than limitations under civil rights laws and seemed particularly troubled by the inclusion of "other personal characteristics," such as clothing, social skills and hobbies and values.

> [While] attempt[ing] to prevent students from making negative comments about each others' "appearance," "clothing," and "social skills" . . . may be brave, futile, or merely silly, . . . attempting to proscribe negative comments about "values," as that term is commonly used today, is something else altogether. By prohibiting disparaging speech directed at a person's "values," the Policy strikes at the heart of moral and political discourse—the lifeblood of constitutional self government (and democratic education) and the core concern of the First Amendment.[46]

Turning to First Amendment analysis independent of civil rights law, the court again found the policy lacking. The court's reading of *Tinker v. Des Moines Independent Community School District*[47] required that school speech restrictions be based on "a concrete threat of substantial disruption."[48] In fact, the court distinguished *West* based on the fact that the *West* court found such a concrete threat. The *Saxe* court did note the Supreme Court's recognition in *Bethel* that there is some in-school speech that may be limited without the substantial disruption envisioned in *Tinker*, but it considered *Bethel* to be limited to lewd, vulgar, indecent and plainly offensive speech, to speech that "offends for the same reasons that obscenity offends."

The court also concluded that the policy was unconstitutionally overly broad. In addition to including speech beyond the lewd and vulgar, it was not adequately limited in a geographic sense. It covered "[a]ny harassment of a student by a member of the school community," not only in an assembly, as in *Bethel*, but in classrooms, halls, athletic facilities and even private speech among students on school premises. It also punished speech intended to disrupt, even if it actually failed to do so. Even if it were accepted that the school district could limit speech that intrudes on the rights of others, the policy reached more.

> Because the Policy . . . does not, on its face, require any threshold showing of severity or pervasiveness, it could conceivably be applied to cover any speech about some enumerated personal characteristics the content of which offends someone. This could include much "core" political and religious speech: the Policy's "Definitions" section lists as examples of covered harassment "negative" or "derogatory" speech about such con-

tentious issues as "racial customs," "religious tradition," "language," "sexual orientation," and "values." Such speech, when it does not pose a realistic threat of substantial disruption, is within a student's First Amendment rights.[49]

Finally, any claim that the "hostile environment" provision was necessary for the school to maintain an acceptable educational environment was found inadequate. "Although [the district] correctly asserts that it has a compelling interest in promoting an educational environment that is safe and conducive to learning, it fails to provide any particularized reason as to why it anticipates substantial disruption from the broad swath of student speech prohibited under the Policy."[50]

The split between the circuits on middle and high school hate speech codes might be explained by noting that the provisions in *Saxe* really went beyond prohibiting hate speech.[51] The inclusion of disparagement based on values really did go to the heart of the First Amendment. The real issue raised, at least by that part of the rules, may have been the use of the schools to sway the debate in the adult, political community. Perhaps hurling gay-bashing epithets at homosexual students could have been barred, but debating the position that homosexual rights should not be recognized or that homosexuality is unnatural had to be protected.

If instead this really is a circuit split, it should be resolved in favor of protecting children from the pernicious effects of racial invective, as well as hate speech based on gender, and a variety of other immutable characteristics. The Tenth Circuit, in *West*, relied on the Supreme Court's decision in *Bethel School District v. Fraser*, and the Third Circuit, in *Saxe*, made the effort to distinguish the case. Thus, both courts, while disagreeing in the conclusions they drew, recognized the importance of *Bethel* to the issue. That case speaks strongly, by analogy, to the issue of hate speech and must be considered in some detail.

Bethel grew out of an election speech given at a high school assembly. The speech was characterized as lewd, rather than hate filled, but the language from the opinion is important.[52] The nominating speech was described by the Court as "an elaborate, graphic, and explicit sexual metaphor."[53] The assembly at which it was given was attended by approximately six hundred students, some as young as fourteen. The school considered the assembly part of its educational program as the teaching of self-government. Fraser had been warned by teachers who knew of the speech's content that it was inappropriate and in violation of a school rule against obscene or profane language and that delivering it might have severe consequences. He delivered it nonetheless, was met with reactions ranging from embarrassment to hooting and sexually suggestive gestures from his fellow students, and a three-day suspension and bar as a graduation speaker by the school.

The case eventually reached the Supreme Court, and the Court concluded that Fraser's First Amendment rights had not been violated. The language in which the Court explained its conclusion would seem to be of strong relevance to the issue of hate speech. It is true that the Court also pointed to its decisions that allowed greater restrictions on sexual material when the audience consisted of children, citing *Ginsberg v. New York*[54] and *Federal Communications Commission v. Pacifica Foundation*,[55] and thus might be read as limited to the sexual expression Fraser actually delivered, but the analysis it provided is far broader.

The Court began by stating: "The role and purpose of the American public school system were well described by two historians, who stated: '[P]ublic education must prepare pupils for citizenship in the Republic. . . . It must inculcate the habits and manners of civility as values in themselves conducive to happiness and as indispensable to the practice of self-government in the community and the nation.'"[56] The opinion goes on to quote an earlier decision in which the Court "echoed the essence of this statement of the objectives of public education as the 'inculcat[ion of] fundamental values necessary to the maintenance of a democratic political system.'"[57]

The Court went on to explain the nature of the fundamental values and "habits and manners of civility" the school system must inculcate.

> These fundamental values of "habits and manners of civility" essential to a democratic society must, of course, include tolerance of divergent political and religious views, even when the views expressed may be unpopular. But these "fundamental values" must also take into account consideration of the sensibilities of others, and, in the case of a school, the sensibilities of fellow students. The undoubted freedom to advocate unpopular and controversial views in schools and classrooms must be balanced against the society's countervailing interest in teaching students the boundaries of socially appropriate behavior.[58]

Recognizing that "[t]he First Amendment guarantees wide freedom in matters of adult public discourse,"[59] the Court said: "It does not follow, however, that simply because the use of an offensive form of expression may not be prohibited to adults making what the speaker considers a political point, the same latitude must be permitted to children in a public school."[60]

Children's rights of free expression, at least in the schools, do not enjoy the strength of the rights of adults. *Bethel* states:

> [T]he "fundamental values necessary to the maintenance of a democratic political system" disfavor the use of terms of debate highly offensive or highly threatening to others. Nothing in the Constitution prohibits the states from insisting that certain modes of expression are inappropriate and subject to sanctions. The inculcation of these values is truly the "work of the schools." . . . The determination of what manner of speech in the classroom or in school assembly is inappropriate properly rests with the school board.
>
> The process of educating our youth for citizenship in public schools is not confined to books, the curriculum, and the civics class; schools must teach by example the shared values of a civilized social order. Consciously or otherwise, teachers—and indeed the older students—demonstrate the appropriate form of civil discourse and political expression by their conduct and deportment in and out of class. Inescapably, like parents, they are role models. The schools, as instruments of the state, may determine that the essential lessons of civil, mature conduct cannot be conveyed in a school that tolerates lewd, indecent, or offensive speech and conduct such as that indulged in by this confused boy.[61]

The opinion directly addressed indecent speech, or at least indecent allusions, in school, but the analysis applies just as forcefully to hate speech. Uttering indecencies is nowhere near as threatening to the "fundamental values necessary to the maintenance of a democratic political system" as would be the toleration of hate speech. Indecency does not keep anyone from participating in democracy;[62] speech that demeans on the basis of race, ethnicity, gender, religion, sexual orientation, etc., may. While indecency and hate speech may both be seen as "highly offensive," hate speech is much more easily seen as "highly threatening." "[T]he shared values of a civilized social order" speak more strongly against hate speech than indecent speech, and, indeed, teachers as role models may be seen by students to say as much in one direction by tolerating such speech as they say in the other by prohibiting it. If the Constitution does not prevent the state from determining that Fraser's speech was inappropriate in the school, it ought not to prevent the state from coming to the same conclusion regarding hate speech. In both cases, values are being inculcated that are "truly the 'work of the schools.'"

It is true, once again, that Fraser's language was closer to the indecent language that *Pacifica* allows to be limited in the broadcast media in order to protect children and closer to, but still a long way from, the material that *Ginsberg* allows to be proscribed for children on the basis of a lower standard of obscenity. The rationale, however, remains the same. The schools may serve a role in the inculcation of values, and it is the school board's responsibility to identify those values that are inimicable to the school's mission and, so long as the decision is not based on religious or political bias,[63] prohibit that speech on campus.

There is another caveat in drawing a conclusion based on *Bethel*. The speech in that case was presented in a school assembly. Such an assembly is part of the educational program of the school. Furthermore, in a situation where the students are called together to hear a speaker in a formal setting, there is a greater likelihood that the speech given will be seen as endorsed by the school. That may give the schools a greater right to control the content of the speech than would otherwise be present. Indeed, Justice Brennan, in his *Bethel* concurrence, makes this point: "Respondent's speech may well have been protected had he given it in school but under different circumstances, where the school's legitimate interests in teaching and maintaining civil public discourse were less weighty."[64]

The possible limitation on *Bethel* should suggest some common sense in writing and enforcing hate speech rules. There does need to be some specificity in the sort of language addressed, although the *Bethel* Court said that a school disciplinary code need not have the specificity of a criminal code. Once the target expression is sufficiently spelled out, context and intent should be considered. Speech presented in an assembly by a person in the position of representing the school is the easiest case. Thus, a talent show rendition of RaHoWa's lyrics should be proscribable. But a student standing up in the cafeteria and letting loose a string of racial invective should also be an easy case. An easy nondisciplinary case is presented by two members of a minority group addressing each other in an overheard but private conversation using words that might be racist if addressed to the minority by a nonminority. There is a difference between self-naming and other-naming. There should also not be magic words that automatically incur discipline. Both the intent of the speaker and the likely reactions of hearers should be relevant. Zero tolerance has led to some absurd results in other areas and the importance of speech, even for children, and the less direct, physical harm that can flow from it make any absurd results that would flow from zero tolerance even more unacceptable.

The conclusion that schools should be allowed to restrict racist speech is a slightly longer jump from settled law than has been suggested in the analysis of the areas already discussed. Protecting children from sexual material that would come within the ambit of the First Amendment when distributed to adults is established in case law. The limitations on exposure of children to depictions of violence were argued on two bases. One was that violence comes within a properly understood obscenity exception, and thus children can be protected from exposure to images that would be appropriate for adults. The use of a two-tier First Amendment to address media violence was argued not to be necessary but to be a better approach that would prevent the harm such images may do for the young while allowing free expression for adults. Given the difficulties in limiting adult hate speech, the argument that such speech may be limited in schools requires the acceptance of the theory, argued for throughout the opening chapters, that the First Amendment simply should not apply to children with the strength with which it protects adults.

The jump to allowing limits on hate speech in schools is still minor compared to the next suggestion. Schools have had more latitude to limit speech than exists outside the schools. But if children are to be shielded from racist sentiments in order to reduce future racism in society, there must be limits outside the school as well as inside. Society has an interest in limiting the inculcation of racist, sexist and other hate-based values. Sometimes that interest is not strong enough to limit expression. If a child's parents are raising that child in a belief system that includes hate on the basis of race, ethnicity, sex, religion, sexual orientation, etc., the protected centrality of the role of parents in deciding how their children should be raised should protect those parents. This is not because they are right in their beliefs; indeed, the vast majority would agree that such hate is simply wrong. But there is sufficient concern over a state imposition of uniformity of thought in some areas that allowing parents their role as primary teachers of values should be allowed in all areas that fall short of teaching criminality.

Children should be protected from hate speech outside the schools when the expression is presented by third parties, that is, by individuals who are not the child's parents or guardians. The media should be restricted in their abilities to reach children with virulent hate speech. It is not the mainstream media that are the target here. Theoretically, a broadcast media outlet could air hate speech and be subject to regulation on the same basis as rules requiring sexually indecent material to be restricted to the hours of 10:00 P.M. to 6:00 A.M., when children are less likely to be in the audience. This has not, however, been a real-world issue. There may be some concern over representation of minorities, or with the lack of minority characters, but broadcast practices fall far short of the hate speech concerns raised by some members of the recording industry.

If the dual theory of the First Amendment is to have any effect, it should be with regard to a recording label like Resistance Records. Groups like Nordic Thunder, Angry Aryans, Blue-Eyed Devils and Ra-HoWa do not have a right to be heard by children. Society has a right to protect its children from listening to CDs such as *Racially Motivated Violence*, *Holocaust 2000*, *Retribution*, *Born to Hate* and *On the Attack*, and songs such as "Race Riot," "Third Reich" and "White Revolution." These groups have a right to believe as they do and a right to sing their songs, but they cannot demand access to the nation's children. They want this access, recognizing its effectiveness as a recruiting tool and its necessity to the fostering of hate in future generations, and this access must be denied. Once again, if a child's parents or guardians believe that such material is suitable for their child, the parent or guardian can buy it and make it available. But, there should be restrictions on direct sales to youths, and those restrictions should be recognized to be consistent with the First Amendment.

C. Inoculating Children against Hatred

In addition to the prevention of childhood exposure to hate speech, there are steps society may take to prevent the effects of the hate speech children may still hear and to which they are certainly likely to be exposed later in life. The communitarians stress teaching society's values to children, and even advocates of children's First Amendment rights such as Marjorie Heins suggest, instead of censorship, an emphasis on healthy influences and education in community values.[65] There is nothing in the thesis that expression rights, where children are involved, should have less strength that discounts the importance of teaching values, and such an approach should be a part of raising psychologically healthy children. Once again, it is the schools that can play a vital role. Just as the schools should protect children from hearing hate speech in that context, there are things the schools can do to provide the vaccine for protection against later adult exposure to this virus. There are educational activities that can help children develop attitudes that will make it more likely that they will be the sort of adults necessary to a civil society in which hatred based on race, ethnicity, sex, sexual orientation, etc. are nonexistent or at least minimalized.

An innovative program was developed by kindergarten teacher Vivian Gussin Paley and is described in her book *You Can't Say You Can't Play*.[66] The title of the book conveys the essence of her approach, a rule that children could not tell each other that they cannot play. She found that the rule was easily accepted by the kindergartners and that having a rule, like one against hitting, resolved incidents of rejection.

The kind of inclusion fostered by a program like Paley's should have an effect on hate speech. While special rules against rejection on the basis of race, gender or any other practice that presents itself could be adopted, the general rule may be the better approach. Rather than base a rule on the position that a minority in the particular school population needs some unique protection, it should be recognized that racial, gender and religious discrimination are merely specific forms of a practice that should be altogether barred. They are particularly invidious forms, since they are based on characteristics over which the victim has no control, but this is also true of many other bases for discrimination. Fostering general inclusion addresses the issues of racism, sexism and discrimination based on religions and sexual orientation, but it does so as specific instances of the general need to develop a sense of attachment and community.

A second program, implemented by third-grade teacher Jane Elliott, involved separating her class into blue-eyed and brown-eyed children.[67] She let each group experience discrimination based on her assertions that one eye color was better than the other and by implementing differential rules favoring one eye color. She later reversed the claims and rules. At the conclusion of the exercise, the children unanimously and enthusiastically agreed that eye color did not determine what sort of person one is. The teacher also asked the children to write compositions on discrimination and how they had felt on each of the two days of the experiment, with the expected result that they expressed their anger over their treatment on their inferior day, while enjoying their privileges on their superior day. On balance, having experienced it from both sides, they came out against discrimination.

The two approaches described above may have involved a greater commitment in time than most teachers are willing to make. They also involved a greater risk of negative reaction than many would be willing to face. Vivian Paley faced negative reaction from some of the children but probably little chance of a strong negative response from parents. Jane Elliott expected calls from parents about what she had put her students through and was surprised not to receive any complaints. Anyone replicating the experiment might not be so fortunate. While any complaint from a person objecting to teaching nondiscrimination might justifiably be ignored, even a parent sympathetic to the goal might object to the pain inflicted on his or her child.

There are, however, other less time-consuming, less risky alternative lessons that are directed toward the same goals of inclusion and nondiscrimination. If a teacher is not willing to impose a "You Can't Say You Can't Play" rule in his or her class, the teacher can still monitor play in class or on the playground. Even without direct observation, the students can be asked what happened on the playground, who played with whom and what the nature of the games were. Where a child has been excluded, steps can be taken to gain inclusion. If the teacher starts a game with the excluded child in an important role, the desire of the other children to be involved in the teacher's game is likely to lead to their acceptance of the formerly excluded child.

Some teachers, particularly at the beginning of a school year, have used a kind of bingo game to introduce students to one another. Bingo cards can have squares for children born in July or in a particular state, children with green eyes or taller than four feet, children who play the violin or soccer. In finding children to fill the squares, classmates must meet and talk with one another. Alternatively, a writing assignment or series of assignments that would be done and graded in any event can be based on interviews of classmates. Anything that gets the students to know one another is likely to foster inclusion, even if not to the degree of the "You Can't Say You Can't Play" approach.

An alternative to the brown eyes–blue eyes exercise can also take the form of a writing assignment. Students can be asked to write an essay on their own experience of discrimination. They can be asked to identify an instance in which they suffered discrimination because they were short, tall, thin, fat, pretty, unattractive, smart, less intelligent or having trouble reading, or on any other basis. They can be asked to go on to describe how the discrimination made them feel. What would it make them feel like if everyone acted toward them that way? What does it tell them about how they should react to others?

Any of these or a wide variety of other activities can help children learn inclusion and nondiscrimination. Just as Oscar Hammerstein said they can be taught to hate, children can be taught not to hate, and it is a lesson that can carry over to adult life and make for a less racist society in which all are treated with dignity.

10

The Coarsening of Society

Consider the case of a hypothetical disturbed individual who gains gratification from uttering profanity before an audience of children. The individual makes it a practice to dress as a clown and to frequent parks with children's playgrounds. He begins by juggling, making balloon animals and engaging in comic banter. As a crowd of children gathers around him, with parents in the background, he begins to add profane words to his running monologue. The frequency of profanity increases, at a low tone that he hopes will not be heard by the parents, until he notices looks of alarm beginning to occur in the back rows of parents. At that point he ends his performance.

Surely, society should be able to do something to prevent someone from giving such a speech to children. An individual, knowing his audience to be composed of children, should not have the free-expression right to utter profanities to them. Again, this is not a restriction on language parents can use with their children. Nor is it a claim that there should be a limitation on the rights of parents to take their children to hear speech others might think inappropriate for children. But third parties should not have the right to impose their profane speech on children, especially to an audience consisting totally or primarily of children and when the parents of those children do not realize that the speech will be profane. There is, however, case law that, at least at first blush, speaks against this conclusion and must be considered.

A. *Cohen v. California*

Cohen v. California grew out of an incident in the Los Angeles County Courthouse.[1] Cohen was observed in a hallway outside a courtroom, wearing a jacket bearing the legend "Fuck the Draft." Women and children were present in the corridor. He was arrested and charged with "maliciously and willfully disturb[ing] the peace or quiet of any neighborhood or person ... by ... offensive conduct."[2] Cohen testified that he knew the words were on his jacket and that he intended to convey a message of opposition to the draft and the Vietnam War. Cohen did not threaten violence, nor did anyone respond to his jacket by threatening violence against him. Nor did Cohen disturb the peace through any loud or unusual noises or, it appears, make any oral statement prior to his arrest. Cohen was sentenced to thirty days in jail.

Cohen sought review by the Supreme Court on the grounds that his freedom of expression, as guaranteed by the First Amendment, had been violated. The Court began its opinion by noting that the conviction was based on the offensiveness of the word Cohen had used in conveying his message; that is, his conviction was based on his speech and not on any "separately identified" conduct. Further, it is clear that Cohen could not be punished for the underlying sentiment he expressed regarding the draft, so the only basis for limiting his speech would have to be the manner in which he expressed himself.

The Court also took the time to explain what the case did not involve. First, the statute under which he was convicted applied throughout the state, so it was not a limited attempt to protect the decorum of courthouses. Second, the speech did not fit within any of the established exceptions to the First Amendment. It was not obscene, the Court said, since obscenity requires that the expression be erotic. Further, while the word involved is often used as a fighting word, in the context in which Cohen used it, it was not directed at any individual hearer and it was unlikely to be taken as a personal insult. Nor was it, according to the Court, an intentional provocation of a hostile audience.

Finally, the Court addressed the argument that Cohen's "distasteful mode of expression was thrust upon unwilling or unsuspecting viewers" and that the state could legitimately act to protect those sensitive to such language from exposure that would otherwise be unavoidable. In response, the Court said:

> While this Court has recognized that government may properly act in many situations to prohibit intrusion into the privacy of the home of unwelcome views and ideas which cannot be totally banned from the public dialogue, we have at the same time consistently stressed that "we are

often 'captives' outside the sanctuary of the home and subject to objectionable speech." The ability of government, consonant with the Constitution, to shut off discourse solely to protect others from hearing it is, in other words, dependent upon a showing that substantial privacy interests are being invaded in an essentially intolerable manner. Any broader view of this authority would effectively empower a majority to silence dissidents simply as a matter of personal predilections.[3]

In the Court's view, those who saw and would object to Cohen's jacket could avoid "further bombardment of their sensibilities" by not continuing to look.

The Court saw the issue as "whether California can excise, as 'offensive conduct,' one particular scurrilous epithet from the public discourse, either upon the theory of the court below that its use is inherently likely to cause violent reaction or upon a more general assertion that the States, acting as guardians of public morality, may properly remove this offensive word from the public vocabulary."[4] The answer to that question was a clear "No." The Court saw no likelihood that Cohen's language would cause disturbance. There was "no evidence that substantial numbers of citizens are standing ready to strike out physically at whoever may assault their sensibilities with execrations like that uttered by Cohen."[5] And, even if some might be so inclined, that would not be a sufficient basis to allow the state to force dissenters to use more generally acceptable language.

The Court also rejected the argument that states can prohibit profanity to maintain "what they regard as a suitable level of discourse within the body politic."[6]

> The constitutional right of free expression is powerful medicine in a society as diverse and populous as ours. It is designed and intended to remove governmental restraints from the arena of public discussion. . . . That the air may at times seem filled with verbal cacophony is, in this sense not a sign of weakness but of strength. We cannot lose sight of the fact that, in what otherwise might seem a trifling and annoying instance of individual distasteful abuse of a privilege, these fundamental societal values are truly implicated. That is why "[w]holly neutral futilities . . . come under the protection of free speech as fully as do Keats' poems or Donne's sermons."[7]

The Court saw the state's attempt to counter these general values as having no logical stopping point, as "inherently boundless." If Cohen's choice of word could be proscribed, it is unclear what other words might also be banned, and the Court would not countenance the state "cleans[ing] public debate to the point where it is grammatically palatable to the most squeamish among us."[8] While California was clearly addressing something more objectionable than a split infinitive, the Court's conclusion that the state could not cleanse all objectionable language was clear. While admitting that the particular four-letter word involved was more distasteful than many other offensive words, the Court said that it is nonetheless true that "one man's vulgarity is another's lyric."[9]

Finally, the Court noted that linguistic expression occurs on different levels. There is the proposition conveyed by the language, in this case a distaste for the draft. But there is also an emotional level that can be communicated by the language chosen to embody that proposition. It has long been clear that the Constitution protects the cognitive content of the message, and the Court could not accept a more limited view of the protection due the emotive content. Indeed, the level of emotion conveyed may be of equal or greater importance to the speaker than the proposition presented.

B. The Broadcast Cases

While the Court refused to allow bans on the use of profanity in public, it has been more willing to allow restrictions on the broadcast media. The major Supreme Court ruling in this area, *Federal Communications Commission v. Pacifica Foundation*,[10] was discussed in chapter 6. The case arose from the radio broadcast of George Carlin's "Filthy Words" monologue which took place in mid-afternoon. In considering the constitutionality of the FCC position restricting the broadcast of indecent material to hours when children were less likely to be in the audience, the Court first noted that the broadcast media enjoy lesser First Amendment protection than the other media.

The Court also showed that concerns over children were central to its decision. "[B]roadcasting is uniquely accessible to children, even those too young to read. Although Cohen's written message might have been incomprehensible to a first-grader, Pacifica's broadcast could have enlarged a child's vocabulary in an instant."[11] While the Court noted that other forms of indecent expression can be kept from children at the point of distribution, by requiring that children not be sold certain books or not be admitted to certain films, children could be protected from indecency in the broadcast media only by regulating it at the source.

Pacifica was not a singular case. The FCC's 1987 action *In re Infinity Broadcasting* involved the broadcast of Howard Stern's morning program.[12] The Commission recognized that the broadcast in *Pacifica* had involved repeated use of specific vulgarities, but said the holding was not limited to the seven words Carlin had employed. Nor did the fact that the Stern broadcast relied on double entendre or innuendo shield it from scrutiny. The broadcast was sanctionable if the language used could reasonably be taken as patently offensive uses or references to sexual or excretory organs and activities. While a double entendre may be sufficiently opaque as to be protected in one context, in another context, surrounded by other references that make the meaning clear, the same phrase may be indecent and unacceptable when it is broadcast at a time when children are likely to be in the audience.

The ruling was appealed within the FCC and was heard before the full commission as *In re Pacifica Foundation*.[13] The commissioners upheld the application of the indecency rules to the Stern broadcast. The commission also again said that the issue was channeling rather than an outright ban. Furthermore, the FCC addressed the role of serious literary, artistic, political or scientific value, noting that patent offensiveness requires a consideration of context, and the merit of the material broadcast may be one aspect of the examination of context. The FCC's decision was appealed to the United States Court of Appeals for the District of Columbia Circuit. The appellate process resulted in a series of three opinions by panels of the court, with the third eventually vacated and replaced by an *en banc* opinion by the entire court. The *en banc* decision, *Action for Children's Television v. Federal Communications Commission (ACT)*,[14] recognized the continuing, or even growing, importance of the FCC's indecency regulations, noting that as the scope of application of obscenity law decreases, the amount and explicitness of indecent material increases. The Court concluded that a 6:00 A.M. to 10:00 P.M. ban was justified. This more recent broadcast case demonstrates that *Pacifica* is not just an old case that may be disregarded because societal mores have passed it by. The courts are still willing to allow restrictions on indecent language for the protection of children, at least in the broadcast context.

C. *"The Cursing Canoeist"*

A recent interesting case that comes between the situation in *Cohen* and the hypothetical cursing clown arose recently in Michigan.[15] The Rifle River, about 130 mile north of Detroit, is a popular venue for float trips in canoes. It is a river that does not demand expertise in canoeing, and the atmosphere is more party than adventure. Activities on the river had caused those who lived on its banks and the operators of campgrounds similarly located to complain that boaters were drunk and unacceptably rowdy. In response, the local police began patrolling the river.

One Saturday in August, a twenty-five-year-old was floating the river with a group of friends. His canoe hit an underwater rock, and he ended up in the river. He waded after the other boats holding his friends, and whether in anger or in jest he indicated in strong terms his feelings regarding the river and the incident. There was some dispute over how long a string of obscenities resulted, with testimony that there may have been a couple of uses of "the f-word" to claims that the word was used between twenty-five and seventy times.

The wader and his friends were not the only people on that stretch of the river. Also present were a couple with their two- and five-year-old children. The mother covered the ears of her two-year-old daughter and told the five-year-old son not to listen. There were also two deputy sheriffs patrolling that portion of the river, and they too heard the outburst and ticketed the individual, who would quickly become known as "the cursing canoeist."

He was charged under an 1897 Michigan statute making it a crime for anyone to use "indecent, immoral, obscene, vulgar or insulting language in the presence or hearing of a woman or child." The defendant moved to have the charges dismissed but the trial judge denied the motion. He did decide that the Equal Protection Clause would not allow a conviction based on uttering the offensive language in the presence of a woman and limited the application of the statute to instances where children were exposed to the expletives at issue. The case went to trial and the defendant was convicted by the jury and sentenced to four days of community service and ordered to pay a seventy-five dollar fine or serve three days in jail.

The canoer-turned-wader appealed the case, and his conviction was reversed,[16] but the ground for the reversal was the vagueness of the statute. The Michigan Court of Appeals held that allowing a prosecution for the utterance of "insulting" language could place a large portion of the population in jeopardy of prosecution. The statute did not provide adequate notice as to the language addressed, and even reading a requirement into the statute that a reasonable person recognize the indecency, immorality, vulgarity or insulting nature of the language would not cure the vagueness. The holding seems to leave open the possibility that a more specific statute, spelling out the sort of language addressed, would survive the court's analysis.

Free speech advocates would still argue that even an improved statute would be a violation of expression rights under the First Amendment. Indeed, it might seem that *Cohen* would preclude a conviction, but that is actually less than clear. One possible basis for distinction is the fact that the language in *Cohen* was political speech, particularly colorful political speech but clearly expressing a political position in opposition to the draft. The language in the case of the cursing canoeist had no political content but merely expressed the speaker's displeasure with his situation. Political speech is at the core of the First Amendment, so it might be held that the political content of Cohen's message required that society tolerate the language used but that in a nonpolitical context, society's interest in civility and decorum may dominate. This argument is, however, unlikely to prevail. The Court has granted protection to more than political speech, including a great variety of forms of expression, and has declined to draw lines between political speech and entertainment, pointing to difficulties in determining where that line would be.[17] A line between political and nonpolitical speech would be just as difficult to draw regarding the use of offensive language.

A better distinction is found in a footnote to the *Cohen* opinion that seems to have been overlooked in most analyses of the case. It is regularly pointed out that the Court noted the general application of the statute and thus rejected any potential claim that it was intended to protect the dignity of the courthouse. There was, however, another sense in which the statute was general and in which the Michigan statute was not. The Court looked at the interests of members of society in being free from profane language and said:

> [I]f Cohen's "speech" was otherwise entitled to constitutional protection, we do not think the fact that some unwilling "listeners" in a public building may have been briefly exposed to it can serve to justify this breach of the peace conviction where, as here, there was no evidence

that persons powerless to avoid appellant's conduct did in fact object to it, and where that portion of the statute upon which Cohen's conviction rests evinces no concern . . . with the special plight of the captive auditor, but, instead, indiscriminately sweeps within its prohibitions all "offensive conduct" that disturbs "any neighborhood or person."[18]

It then added a footnote:

In fact, other portions of the same statute do make some such distinctions. For example, the statute also prohibits disturbing "the peace or quiet . . . by loud or unusual noise" and using "vulgar, profane, or indecent language within the presence or hearing of women or children, in a loud and boisterous manner." . . . This second quoted provision in particular serves to put the actor on much fairer notice as to what is prohibited. It also buttresses our view that the "offensive conduct" portion, as construed and applied in this case, cannot legitimately be justified in this Court as designed or intended to make fine distinctions between differently situated recipients.[19]

Thus, it would appear that the Court might have come to a different conclusion, had the California law been more limited. Like the Michigan trial court, the Court should find equal protection issues with the inclusion of woman as a class needing special protection from offensive language, but the footnote indicates that the Court might have allowed a proscription on the use of vulgar, profane or indecent language in the presence of children. The difficulty in this conclusion is the balance of protecting youth and the strong interest in allowing adult-to-adult communication, even in offensive terms.

D. Balancing Free Speech with the Protection of Children

However *Cohen* is interpreted, it is clear that the Court will allow the government to impose some regulations on expression to protect children from hearing indecent language. *Pacifica* and the *ACT* case demonstrate this strongly. The concerns expressed in those cases included the right of the individual to be free from offensive language within the confines of his or her own home, despite the indecency one may be forced to tolerate in public. The interest in protecting children, however, was more central.

The invasive character of radio and television were part of the rationale for affording the broadcast media lesser First Amendment protection, but that must be read in the context of the exposure of children. Channeling indecency into late-night hours leaves the broadcast media just as invasive in those hours and the exposure of the listening or viewing audience in that timespan to offensive material just as injurious—if this really qualifies as an injury for adults—as in earlier hours. The difference is that children are less likely to be in the audience in the late night hours. Since it is this difference that shaped the remedy, it certainly must be taken as having played a strong, or the strongest, role.

The government, even in the context of traditional First Amendment analysis, has the right to limit the access of children to indecent material. As the FCC pointed out, that interest has grown, as the scope of obscenity law has decreased. As less and less is considered legally obscene, the residuum of expression with a sexual or excretory theme that would be considered indecent or only obscene as to children has come to include material that would formerly have been considered generally obscene. The compelling interest in protecting children in their psychological development will justify regulations that are narrowly tailored to that end and do not unduly limit the rights of adults.

With a dual First Amendment, nonsexual uses of the offensive language, uses like that at issue in *Cohen*, could be limited in their dissemination to youth. A dual First Amendment can serve to justify the decisions in the *Pacifica* and *ACT* cases, but it can go beyond that as well. If *Pacifica* requires the repeated use for shock value and the *ACT* case requires a clearer sexual or excretory context, the dual First Amendment approach will reach additional material that includes the use of indecent language, even when not repetitive or highly sexual. If it is recognized that the communicative rights of children are not as important as those of adults, and the communicative rights of adults do not include the right to express themselves to other people's children, if it is recognized that society has an interest in raising children who are civil and not just psychologically healthy, society should be accorded the right to limit the language to which children are exposed, a right limited by the parents' decisions but not by the decisions of those with no such role in raising individual children.

The clearest application of this dual approach would be in limitations on sales to children of CDs with offensive or indecent language or the sale or rental of videos with similar content. As long as a statute specifies the language to be barred, such restrictions should be upheld under a dual approach to the First Amendment. To avoid limitations on serious material that employs a word or a number of words on the statutory list, there should be a savings clause similar to that in obscenity law. If material, taken as a whole, has serious literary, artistic, political, or scientific value for children, the distribution of the material to children should be protected. For material lacking such value, parents are still free to obtain it for their children, but strangers to that parent-child relationship could be prohibited from making it directly available to other people's children.

More difficult issues arise in any effort to restrict indecent expression that has an effect on the rights of adults to hear or see such material. The Court has made it clear in a series of cases that the interests in protecting children will not justify at least any unnecessary restrictions on adult-to-adult communication.[20] Even accepting restrictions on indecent language to an audience of children, the effect of such restrictions on adults must be minimized. The broadcast cases do recognize a government interest in protecting children that is at least strong enough to limit indecent language in the broadcast media in hours when children are likely to be in the audience. Such a limitation does also limit adult access, but the Court has seen the cost as worth bearing. Outside the arena of the broadcast media, the costs to adult expression may be less acceptable. The Court in *Cohen*, however, did suggest, if only in dictum, that a statute aimed at speech like Cohen's in the presence of children could have presented a different case. If the Court was serious in that distinction, the prosecution of another cursing canoeist, under a nonvague statute, may be constitutional, even though the statute would have an effect on the canoeist's expression to other adults, when children were present.

The hypothetical clown with which the chapter opened should be an easier case. The entire audience was composed of children. The clown made an effort to keep the adults present in the dark regarding the content of his speech. A prohibition that was limited to speech such as that in the clown's situation would not affect adult to adult communication, since there were no intended adult recipients. Thus, a regulation against indecent or profane speech in elementary or middle schools, or even in high schools, should be upheld under a dual approach to the First Amendment. Similarly, as long as there was sufficient specificity regarding the language and a savings clause for language with serious value for children, a statute prohibiting indecent or profane language that is limited to situations in which the audience consisted primarily of children should also be constitutional.

The most difficult case is one in which language is prohibited whenever a child can hear the profanity or indecent speech. Despite the *Cohen* Court's indication that a statute limited to prohibiting offensive language in the presence of children might be constitutional, Cohen's specific use of language should probably remain protected even in the presence of children. Cohen used one written offensive word and did so in a political context. His political speech deserved protection, and perhaps he should have been free to so express himself to other adults despite the fact that children may have been exposed.

The FCC cases may provide some guidance here. The *Pacifica* case and the FCC enforcement that followed the case centered on the repeated use, for shock value, of the words George Carlin had used. This was despite the fact that in Carlin's case his speech had value as social satire on society's concerns over language. If Cohen had repeated aloud his sentiments regarding the draft, using the same colorful language, and did so knowing himself to be in the presence of children, his speech might have been proscribable. If the *Cohen* dictum is to have any application, that would seem to come within it. Similarly, if speech as explicitly sexual as that in the FCC action against the broadcast of *The Howard Stern Show* is presented to an audience that the speaker knows includes children, that too should be proscribable.

11

Advertising

Imagine an advertising campaign in which flyers advertising cigarettes are passed out to children leaving Cub Scout or Brownie meetings. Given the illegality of sales of cigarettes or alcohol to children, the campaign seems almost unimaginable. But clearly ad campaigns for such products, while said to be aimed at adults, have an effect on children, and it seems hard to believe that they were not intended to have that impact.

In 1988, R. J. Reynolds changed its image and advertising campaign by introducing a more appealing version of its camel symbol. The camel that had long appeared on cigarette packs standing in front of pyramids became, in Camel's ads, Joe Camel. The Food and Drug Administration described Joe Camel as a "more hip . . . spokescamel," depicted as "a humorous figure in history, as an advisor to young adults with 'smooth moves' and eventually as one of a gang of hip camels ('the hard pack' band and the gang at the watering hole bar)."[1] Prior to the introduction of Joe Camel, Camel cigarettes sales constituted less than 3 percent of the national market for those under eighteen. Within a year, Camel's share of that market had increased to 8.1 percent, and within four years it had grown to between 13 and 16 percent of the youth market.[2] The ad campaign even developed brand awareness in young children. A study published in 1991 found that 30 percent of three-year-olds and 91 percent of six-year-olds recognized Joe Camel as a symbol for smoking, a recognition rate higher than that of Ronald McDonald.[3]

Of course, Joe Camel and other characters, such as the Budweiser frogs or the macho figure of the old Marlboro Man, do not appeal only to those too young to smoke or drink legally. Tobacco and alcohol companies can claim to be attempting to attract the younger end of the legal markets, even if an incidental effect on the youth market accompanies those attempts. Nonetheless, the FDA examined tobacco industry documents that indicated that the companies had done extensive research on the smoking behavior and attitudes of the young and how to make advertisements appeal to youth, including children as young as fourteen.[4]

The likelihood that these ads were directed toward those too young to smoke is increased by the results of studies of smoking habits. Again according to the FDA, if a person does not begin to smoke before the age of eighteen, he or she is unlikely ever to begin, with 82 percent of all adults who have ever smoked having begun prior to eighteen, half of them already having become heavy smokers by that age.[5] Furthermore, research indicates that brand loyalty is particularly strong among smokers, with most smokers continuing to smoke the brand they smoked at the time they became regular smokers.[6] Given this brand loyalty and the fact that smokers become regular smokers while they are minors, it is hard to believe that the industry's advertising efforts are directed solely toward adults.

As one last bit of evidence regarding the target, and certainly strong evidence of the effect of cigarette advertising, research shows that children smoke the brands that are advertised. Eighty-six percent of those under eighteen who purchase cigarettes bought Marlboro, Camel or Newport, the three most heavily advertised brands at the time of the research.[7] Those same three brands captured only 35 percent of the overall smoking market. Most popular among adults were generic, private label or plain-packaged cigarettes.[8] While adults seem more likely to make decisions based on price, children seem more affected by advertising campaigns, whoever the declared audience for those ads may be.

While the illegality of tobacco and alcohol sales to youth requires those industries to take the position that any effect on youth is a spillover from ads directed at legal audiences they have a right to attempt to reach, the entertainment industry can assert not only the spillover argument but also a right to direct ads to children, and it appears that they at least partially direct those ads to kids. The Federal Trade Commission, in its 2000 report *Marketing Violent Entertainment to Children*,[9] addressed two questions posed by the president: Do the movie, music recording and electronic games industries promote products that they themselves say warrant parental caution in contexts in which children will be a substantial percentage of the audience, and do the industries intend to attract children in so doing? The commission concluded that, for all three industries and for both questions, the answer was a clear "yes."

The FTC studied marketing plans for the various media and found clear statements of intent to reach children younger than the ratings for the particular items involved. They cited as an example a marketing plan for a film rated R for violence. The plan stated: "Our goal was to find the elusive teen target audience and make sure everyone between the ages 12–18 was exposed to the film."[10] That statement was not an isolated example. Of the forty-four films in the study that were rated R for violence, 80 percent were found to be targeted to children, with almost two-thirds stating explicitly in their marketing plans that the target audience included those under seventeen and the remainder adopting similar plans without the explicit statements.[11] Focus group research for eight of the R-rated films included twelve-year-olds, with one of the films including children as young as ten.[12] Similar arguably inappropriate marketing activities occurred with PG-13-rated films being marketed to younger children, including toys provided in children's meals by fast-food restaurants.

While the electronic games industry has been given credit for a stronger voluntary system of limiting exposure of children to advertising, both before the report and for changes it made after the report, it is also clear that members of the industry have targeted children that the industry's own ratings indicate are too young. The commission examined marketing plans for M-rated games, "M" meaning "mature," defined as seventeen and older. Seventy percent of the marketing plans for the 118 games studied included children under seventeen, 51 percent openly doing so and the remainder adopting similar plans. One plan said that the target audience was "Males 12–17—Primary[;] Males 18–34—Secondary," and another said "Males 17–34 due to M rating (the true target is males 12–34)."[13] A third listed the 17–34 target for an M-rated game but said "the true target is M9-34."[14] Some marketing plans for violent M-rated games targeted children as young as six years old.[15]

The music recording industry does not rate its recordings for age. Companies may choose to include a parental advisory label when the recordings contain strong language or include references to sex, drugs or violence. But the industry only provides the information to parents without recommending an age limitation. Thus, while the FTC did find marketing practices seemingly aimed at young teenagers and statements in marketing plans that identified that age group as a part of the target audience, there was no seeming contradiction in identifying an age at which the material became appropriate and then marketing below that age.

Advertising media, of course, do not split evenly along a line defined by the age of seventeen. As with alcohol and tobacco, ads aimed at a young adult audience will find an audience of minors. While the entertainment industries advertise in magazines that have an audience including those under seventeen and on television programs that also reach that audience, the magazines and television shows have readers and viewers who are proper targets under the industry ratings. The movie industry, however, also offers another justification for its advertising practices. While age limits on alcohol and tobacco are part of the law, movie ratings are only advisory. They are voluntarily adopted by the industry and impose no legal constraints but do provide warnings to parents. Thus, the industry can, and does, take the position that it is appropriate to target advertising for R-rated films to those under seventeen and for PG-13-rated films to those under thirteen. The FTC explained the industry view: "'Many socially and artistically important films have received PG-13 and R ratings . . . ' [T]hose film makers have the right to draw as much attention to their work as possible—'even the attention of persons under the age of 17, who are entitled to view such films with the permission and in the company of their parents.'"[16] However, while children may attend an R-rated film when accompanied by a parent, the claim that advertising is directed toward that result will ring hollow to the extent that theaters do not check identification when selling tickets to R-rated films, nor check to be sure that a ticket purchased for a PG-13-rated film is not used to gain admission to an R-rated film at the same multiplex.

A. Protection for Commercial Speech

Speech that proposes a commercial transaction enjoys some but not full First Amendment protection. *Virginia State Board of Pharmacy v. Virginia Citizens Consumer Council* explains the reason for protecting such speech.[17] The case concerned a ban on pharmacists advertising the prices of prescription drugs implemented because of state concern over the professional status of pharmacists. The Court recognized that the advertiser's motives may be purely economic, with no intent to influence political or social policy, but that does not mean that commercial speech is without import. In fact, the Court noted, the average person may be more interested in the free flow of commercial information than in political debate. Where pharmaceuticals are involved, there is also an interest in obtaining, at affordable prices, the goods necessary to a healthy life.

Another rationale for protecting commercial speech, and one that draws support from the role of speech in the political system, was found in the relationship between such information and the free-market economy. Where an economy is not price regulated, the prices of goods and services are set by the combined decisions of market suppliers and consumers. The true price of a commodity, the market price, depends on what each of these persons is willing to accept or pay for the good. These decisions must be informed for this approach to the market to work properly. Advertising of prices, then, is not only of interest to consumers, it is necessary to the economic approach the country has come to follow and is as important as speech aimed at political and social change.

It may be questioned how well this rationale applies to commercial speech directed to youth. It would seem to apply to the sort of goods purchased primarily by teenagers. If the market price for music on CDs were determined only by the combined decisions of adult consumers, the failure to include the decisions of a significant portion of that market would have a skewing effect. Since teenagers purchase a significant percentage of the CDs sold, advertising directed at that audience is important to determining the market price of the recordings. Advertising directed at younger children creates a demand to which their parents may respond. A rational decision, including the price to pay, is involved, and without the message the demand side of the equation would be reduced to the point where the result could again be skewed.

There is an important limitation here. Where the market is not a legitimate market, there is no, or at least less, reason to protect the free flow of commercial information necessary to reach a market price. Distributors of illegal products are unlikely to advertise their wares, since doing so would expose them to criminal investigation. They will at least thinly disguise their goods or services, as with escort services, in hopes of avoiding prosecution. Children complicate the matter, since there are goods and services that are legal for adult consumers but illegal where minors are the purchasers. Here, there is reason to protect the free flow of information to the legal consumer, but as long as that is done, there is no reason to allow additional communication to minors.

The current test for laws directed at commercial speech was established in *Central Hudson Gas & Elec. Corp. v. Public Service Comm'n.*[18] The facts of the case are unimportant here, but the four-part test that was set out is. Under that test, a court must first determine whether the commercial speech involved enjoys any First Amendment protection.

Commercial speech does enjoy such protection, as long as the product or service advertised is legal and the advertising is not false or misleading. Even concluding that the speech does come within the protections of the First Amendment, the protection given is not as strong as in other areas. Rather than demanding the compelling interest necessary to meet strict scrutiny where political speech is involved, the inquiry demands only a substantial governmental interest. The issues then become whether the regulation directly advances the interest and does so without being more extensive than necessary. With regard to these issues the Court has made clear in later cases that anecdotal evidence can meet the requirement that the regulation will further the interest and that the extensiveness issue does not require the least restrictive means but only a reasonable fit between the interest and the regulation.[19]

B. Children and Tobacco Advertising

The Supreme Court recently addressed the issue of advertising restrictions aimed at the protection of children. At least with regard to the regulations at issue in that case, the child protection interests came out on the short end. The case might have seemed the best possible for child advocates. The tobacco products involved cannot be sold to minors, and tobacco clearly presents a major threat to the health of children. Nonetheless, while not concluding that all attempts to shield children would be unconstitutional, the Court struck down the regulations.

The case, *Lorillard Tobacco Co. v. Reilly*,[20] grew out of an attempt by the attorney general of Massachusetts to limit the exposure of children to advertising for cigarettes, cigars and smokeless tobacco by declaring certain practices to be unfair or deceptive trade practices. Outdoor advertising was banned within 1,000 feet of a school or public playground, including advertising in stadia and ads inside retail establishments that were visible from outside the store. Advertising also included oral statements. There were additional regulations regarding tobacco advertising inside stores. Any ad in a store within the 1,000-foot radius, except in an adults-only establishment, had to be, in its entirety, at least five feet above the level of the floor.

The Court held the regulations regarding cigarette advertising to be preempted by federal law. The Federal Cigarette Labeling and Advertising Act already placed limitations on cigarette advertising, and the act specifically declared that any state regulations were preempted.[21] The Court went on to consider the effect of the First Amendment on the cigar and smokeless tobacco restrictions. The federal act did not address those commodities, so preemption could not be the basis for resolving that dispute. There the Court found a violation of the protections the First Amendment provides to commercial speech, and it seems clear that the violations noted would also have applied to the cigarette restrictions if the Court had been required to reach that issue.

The Court applied the *Central Hudson* test, but it found only the last two parts of that test to be at issue. The first, that the advertising be non-misleading and for a legal product, was satisfied for adult recipients of the speech. The state's interest in the protection of children is also at least substantial. With regard to the third step, that the advertising restriction directly advance the state's interest, the Court was also willing to side with the state, at least with regard to the restrictions on outdoor advertising. Under that step, the state must show a real harm and that the restrictions will materially alleviate that harm. The Court recognized not only that tobacco causes harm to children, calling its use by children and adolescents "'perhaps the single most significant threat to public health in the United states,'"[22] but that advertising tobacco contributes to that harm. The Court noted that advertising stimulates demand and cited a conclusion by the surgeon general and the Institute of Medicine that "'advertising and labeling play a significant and important contributory role in a young person's decision to use cigarettes or smokeless tobacco products.'"[23] While the evidence spoke more strongly to cigarettes and smokeless tobacco, the Court held that all the restrictions, including those on cigars, were based on more than simple speculation or conjecture that use by minors would be reduced.

It was the last step in the *Central Hudson* analysis—reasonable fit between the restrictions and the goal of the limitations—that doomed the state's advertising regulations. The Court noted that prohibiting outdoor ads within 1,000 feet of a school or playground would ban tobacco ads from roughly 90 percent of Boston, Worcester and Springfield, significantly cutting off the flow of truthful information to adult consumers. That, the Court said, did not demonstrate a careful analysis of the speech interests at issue. This lack of careful calculation was also seen in the application of the restrictions not just to billboards but also to smaller signs, including those inside stores but visible from the street, and in prohibiting oral communication outside the store and within the

1,000-foot zone. The outdoor bans were simply too injurious to adult interests in receiving communications regarding tobacco.

Turning to the indoor requirement that ads be five feet above the floor, the Court found the restriction lacking under both the third and fourth steps of the *Central Hudson* test but concentrated its analysis on the third step. The Court saw little fit between the regulations and their end in that children in the store would certainly be capable of seeing an ad placed at the five-foot limit. As the Court said, "[n]ot all children are less than 5 feet tall, and those who are certainly have the ability to look up and take in their surroundings."[24] While the restriction would seem to have had little effect on communication to adults, the bright-line five-foot rule, rather than a rule aimed at displays that would be particularly enticing to children, failed to reasonably fit the goal.

While the decision was a blow to those who would protect children from the effects of advertising products that do them harm, the Court did not foreclose all attempts at limiting ads. It was the broad effect of the Massachusetts regulations that constituted the constitutional violation. But if child advocates can identify practices that are particularly likely to lead to tobacco use by children, the Court indicated that those practices may be limited. The Court, in discussing the failure to tailor the outdoor regulations to the concern over children, said "[t]o the extent that studies have identified particular advertising and promotion practices that appeal to youth, tailoring would involve targeting those practices while permitting others."[25] That at least holds out the hope that restrictions on varieties of tobacco advertising that appeal most strongly to youth can be restricted. Presumably this result would apply to other products that cause harm to youth or at least those that cannot legally be sold to minors.

C. Restrictions to Protect Children

Several suggestion for limiting the effects of advertising on children will be offered. The possibilities addressed are by no means exhaustive. Neither is their constitutionality clear. The area of commercial speech is in flux. While the *Central Hudson* test still applies to commercial speech, if the Court were to follow the lead of those who would elevate the protection of commercial speech to the level of protection provided political speech, the actions proposed would have to meet a more stringent test than that which is discussed below.

1. Billboards

The attorney general of Massachusetts clearly thought that billboards presented a problem for the health of children. The ban on tobacco advertising in that medium within 1,000 feet of a school or public playground was intended to remove the sort of regular influence that such a semipermanent display provides. The attorney general was by no means the first government official or body to express that concern. The Food and Drug Administration, in its 1995 proposal and 1996 rule-making on the distribution and advertising of tobacco products to children and adolescents, also addressed billboards. Like Massachusetts, the FDA concluded that a 1,000-foot protective ring around schools and public playgrounds was a constitutional means to address its concerns. While the Supreme Court's decision in the Massachusetts case indicates that the FDA was wrong in that regard, there were other aspects of the FDA's rule-making that provide protection for children and would not necessarily be unconstitutional under the analysis provided in the *Lorillard* case.

It is, again, important to recognize that the Court in *Lorillard* did recognize that the government's interest in protecting children is at least substantial. The Court also concluded that the advertising limitations directly advanced that interest, because tobacco advertising contributes to use by minors and the resulting harm to their health. It was the requirement of a reasonable fit between the restrictions and the interest that led to the demise of the Massachusetts rules. But the Court was clear in its conclusion that more narrowly drawn rules, directed at advertising practices that particularly affect youth, could be constitutional.

The FDA, in its rule making, identified such an advertising practice. The research literature showed that advertisements using four-color printing increase attention and recall compared to black-and-white formats.[26] Furthermore, imagery or pictorial material was found to enhance an ad's ability to communicate quickly and to be remembered, and in particular provided a way to communicate with the functionally illiterate and the young.[27] Thus, this is a form of advertisement raising particular risks for minors. The fit the Court demanded in *Lorillard* may be accomplished by limiting color and imagery, while allowing other forms of advertising.

The FDA's analysis of color and imagery was the motivation for its approach to regulating print advertisements in magazines with a significant youth readership, an issue to be discussed in the next section. Cigarette ads in such magazines would be limited to black and white text. When it came to billboards, the FDA believed that the constant exposure to such ads within 1,000 feet of schools and public playgrounds warranted stronger action. Since the *Lorillard* Court threw out such a state-imposed ban, the FDA approach to print ads should be considered for billboards. Furthermore, it is not only billboards within 1,000 feet of a school or playground that contribute to smoking by minors. While a flat ban on tobacco ads may have required a geographical restriction to allow the manufacturers to reach an adult audience, a limitation on format might be justified without regard to boundaries.

The governmental interest recognized as adequate in *Lorillard* remains the same. The relationship between advertising and tobacco use also remains the same, and, in fact, the relationship is more finely focused by limiting regulation to restricting color and imagery. The studies that show the effectiveness of such advertising formats for youth also indicate that the restrictions are likely to have the effect of furthering the government's interest. The major difference in effect, and a difference that should lead to a different result than that handed down in *Lorillard*, is the effect on adult communication.

A restriction that requires tobacco billboards, or all tobacco advertising visible from the street, to be text only, with no use of color or imagery, still allows the passage of information to adults regarding a product that they may lawfully purchase. It does not prevent the retail establishment from letting passersby on the street know that cigarette and other tobacco products are available for sale inside the store and certainly does not reach the oral representations of concern to the Court in *Lorillard*. It allows manufacturers to offer information and make claims regarding their products that may be useful to their potential customers. There is no restriction on information; the only restrictions are on the noninformational, emotive aspects of advertising, aspects to which youth are particularly susceptible. While the tobacco industry will claim injury, the real portion of that injury is likely to be the loss of the illegitimate youth market. Given research that only 6.7 percent of adult smokers switch tobacco companies each year,[28] coupled with the adult trend toward unadvertised cheaper cigarettes, the lion's share of any decrease in the effectiveness of the vast sums of money the industry spends on advertising will be right where it ought to be: a reduction in the attraction of new underage smokers.

There is also no reason why this sort of restriction must be limited to tobacco products. The effect of color and imagery on the young is not restricted to cigarettes and smokeless tobacco. Assuming that the governmental interest in preventing youth consumption of alcohol is as substantial as that of preventing tobacco use and if the effect of advertising on consumption is found to be similar for such products, alcohol advertisements visible from the street might also be restricted to black and white text.

2. Magazine Advertising

The Food and Drug Administration's approach to tobacco advertising in magazines was to limit print ads to black and white text. The FDA did allow an exception for adult magazines. "Adult publication" was not meant as code for pornography but was defined as a magazine with fewer than 15 percent readership under age eighteen and fewer than 2 million readers in that age group.[29] When the rule was first proposed, it met with criticism from both sides. There was concern that the restrictions were inadequate and that ads should be limited to black and white text in all magazines or that magazine advertising not be allowed at all, but the FDA concluded that the adult exception to the text requirements was reasonable.[30] Industry advocates, on the other hand, questioned the 85 percent line.

If the 15 percent figure fails to have a reasonable fit, it is because the standard is not sufficiently restrictive. The FDA based the 15 percent limit on the fact that 15 percent of the population of the United States is between the ages of five and seventeen.[31] That decision falls far short of identifying adult publications. If the population between five and seventeen is 15 percent and adult publications are those with less than 15 percent youth readership, adult publications are simply general circulation magazines; that is, they are not aimed at adults but draw from the various age groups in the population relatively evenly.[32] Thus, what should be characterized as general circulation magazines may use color and imagery. The FDA approach should extend to general circulation magazines with the exemption limited to those publications that are "adult" in what had become the popular meaning of the word.

A step beyond the FDA's approach would provide greater protection for youth while still allowing for adult advertising. Various magazines publish versions intended for a youth audience, alongside their regular offerings for an older readership. *Sports Illustrated for Kids* and *Teen People* are aimed at younger audiences. Certainly there is nothing in the normal issue of *Sports Illustrated* or of *People* that is inappropriate for children, but a companion publication with a selection of material of particular interest for minors serves to increase the overall readership and profits of the magazines. Magazines also now regularly include ads aimed at particular geographical areas, so there is the capacity to vary the content of what is essentially the same magazine. This approach can be carried over to provide insulation for children from tobacco advertising as well as advertising for alcohol products and other negative influences for which government may see a need for protection.

Magazines could be made unavailable for purchase by children unless they were certified by the publishers as suitable for children. Magazines may already be found unsuitable for children based on their sexual content, and arguments have been offered herein for the extension of such an approach for violence or hate speech. The magazine vendor may be liable for the sale to a minor of a magazine whose sexual content is unsuitable for minors. That does not prevent the sale to adults but simply requires the vendor to check the age of the purchaser. The same approach could be applied to the advertising content of the magazine. A minor should not be sold a magazine containing advertising for tobacco or alcohol products. Presumably publishers that do not include such ads would indicate on the covers of their magazines that the publications are free of these ads in order to assure vendors that the issue can be sold to minors. Publishers may well decide, in order to maximize their ad revenue, to publish two versions of a magazine, one suitable for children and another limited to adults.

As with any regulation, there may be some chilling effect. A publisher may decide no longer to accept tobacco or alcohol advertising in order not to lose readership. But such a decision would be a sign that a significant portion of the readership was in fact composed of young people, and it is advertising in this sort of magazine that is of the greatest concern. A publisher may, alternatively, decide that it will continue to accept vice ads and not produce a child-friendly version but will instead make its publication unavailable to children. In that case, children will be deprived of the ability to purchase the magazine. But it will still only be the direct sale that is limited. If the child's parents believe that the magazine is important or even merely appropriate, despite its ad content, the parents can still purchase the magazine for the child or subscribe to the publication.

The greatest chilling effect of age limitations will be less for this restriction than for those limitations already accepted. If a young adult

wishes to purchase a sexually explicit publication, the vendor may demand identification to avoid the possibility of being charged with distributing to a minor material that is obscene as to children. A potential
purchaser who is reluctant to be seen buying the publication will be made
more so by the possibility of having to provide an identification that will
reveal not only age but also name, address and other information. This
would seem to be a real chilling effect on the First Amendment rights of
young adults stemming from the interest in protecting minors. Under the
proposal, however, the embarrassment that might be present for a magazine with sexual content will not be present in having one's identification
checked to be sure the advertising content is appropriate. Being identified
as one who reads sports magazines that happen to contain beer ads is not
the same as being identified as one who purchases sexually explicit material.

3. Broadcast Media and Film

The broadcast media and film present a problem not regularly present
in the print media. They also present a problem in common with print.
The common problem is advertising. While cigarettes are not advertised
on television, beer is, and there is no legal proscription against ads for
hard liquor. Indeed, it appeared for a period in 2002 that network television would see such ads. Where the broadcast media present the same
problem as print media, they should be subject to similar restrictions, particularly given the greater government right to regulate broadcasts. The
FDA did respond in its rule-making process to comments concerning
video and audio media.[33] The agency's approach was to adapt the black
and white, text-only approach. The video advertising equivalent was simply the same as for print: static black-and-white text only. The audio
equivalent was text with no music. This approach would again address
the characteristics of advertising that the FDA found to have a particular
effect on youth, while still allowing the informational aspects of advertising to be conveyed to adults.

There are additional possibilities for addressing advertising concerns
in the broadcast media that would further limit the exposure of youth to
advertisements for products that pose risks to children. The harm that advertising does children may provide a basis for barring commercials for
not only tobacco but for alcohol and similar products during hours when
children are likely to be in the audience. The same approach could even

apply to excessive and positive depictions of vice products in the entertainment portion of the broadcast media during those hours. To claim that the authority comes within the holding of *Federal Communications Commission v. Pacifica Foundation* that indecent material may be so restricted in the broadcast media may be a serious stretch.[34] The Court did conclude that material is indecent if it is contrary to public morality. That would not seem to mean that the acts depicted themselves must be immoral; an explicit depiction of marital procreative sex on television in the early evening could lead to FCC action, but the act itself is certainly not immoral. Thus, while smoking and drinking by adults may not be contrary to morality, such depictions during the family hour may be. On the other hand, if the indecency of *Pacifica* must be tied to the subject matter of obscenity, even if this subject matter is accepted as including violence, the extension of *Pacifica* to ads for products harmful to children would not be justified by that case.

Even if *Pacifica* cannot be expanded to include the ads and depictions at issue here, the limitations might still be justified. The Court has been willing to protect youth, but communication to adults must not be unnecessarily restricted. As with sexual material, the later hours would remain open for adult programming and advertising. Furthermore, while the ad restriction might be absolute, presumably any FCC rule on program content would not bar every reference or use of vice products. In the arena of sexual material, it is only rather flagrant uses of language or imagery that are subject to sanction. Howard Stern's programs have been the subject of action, but the sexual banter of situation comedies goes unsanctioned. If the FCC were to apply a similar approach to depictions of harmful vices in hours when children are in the audience, it would not be the occasional cigarette or drink that would be targeted but a focus, and particularly a positive focus, on such behavior.

Turning to film, advertising would seem not to be a concern. However, theaters do show what amounts to commercials prior to showing a film. The ratings for the film to be shown should limit the subject matter of any ads. If a theater is showing a PG-13 film, tobacco or alcohol ads should not precede that film. While there may also be adults in the audience for whom those products are legal, the target audience, or at least a large part of that audience as indicated by the rating, is of an age for which the products are illegal. There does not appear to be a widespread practice contrary to this suggestion, but there are other practices that do raise concerns.

Film, as with the broadcast media, presents images that children are likely to mimic. Where a film portrays vices, particularly in an excessive and positive manner, the film can affect the beliefs of children as to the prevalence and acceptability of such behavior. This is a message that society may not want conveyed to children, but again adult communication must remain open. The use of the ratings system is the key to limitations here. The use of illegal drugs is already a factor in determining the rating to be assigned to a film. The use of other drugs that are legal for adults but not for children should play a similar role. The assignment of a rating, even an R rating, does not limit adult exposure even if the ratings are to be legally enforced, but it does limit the exposure of children to these influences unless their parents allow such exposure.

The presence of these suggestions regarding program or film content and the channeling of broadcast images or applying increased ratings to film images in a chapter on advertising may seem out of place, but some use of products in film or television is the equivalent of advertisement. Companies pay for the placement of their products so that potential consumers see the product used by the actors. While the filmmaker's expression may be noncommercial, the product manufacturer's paying for placement is a form of commercial speech. It should be subject to limitations similar to those already suggested for other forms of advertisement. But if the use of products contributes to the rating of a film or the time at which a broadcast is appropriate, the goal may be accomplished without a ban on placement. Again, adult communication is unaffected, and the film production company can make its own decision on placements or other uses of vice products based on balancing its own interests in both story line and product placement income against a rating or time slot that would allow it to reach a young audience.

12

Speech in the Schools

Schools are central both to this effort and to the child's life. Once children begin school, they may spend more of their time on the average school day interacting with the school population than with their parents. Their experiences in school, both in the formal classroom setting and in informal settings such as the hallways, the cafeteria and the locker room, are important to their psychological development. Any reconception of the First Amendment intended to protect children from influences that negatively affect their safety and psychological development will necessarily have an impact on the speech rights of children in the schools.

At the same time, a number of writers have recognized the important role the schools must play in the development of children as participants in our political system. The schools are important to civic education in a broader sense than teaching how a bill becomes a law. Children must learn to engage in the sort of debate that sustains the political process. Thus, Amy Gutmann argues for a "principle of nonrepression" as a limitation on adult use of the state "to undermine the future deliberative freedom of children."[1]

> Children must learn not just to *behave* in accordance with authority but to *think* critically about authority if they are to live up to the democratic ideal of sharing political sovereignty as citizens. . . . [P]eople who possess sturdy moral character without a developed capacity for reasoning are ruled only by habit and authority, and are incapable of constituting a society of sovereign citizens.[2]

Bruce Hafen expresses similar sentiments: "The interest in self-governance . . . applies to students in a longer term sense. As holders of inchoate rights of democratic citizenship, students have a high stake in the development of their own critical powers to act in the future as sovereign citizens."[3]

That does not require adoption of a moral neutrality in the schools. Schools can teach values and prepare students for active citizenship. As Suzanna Sherry notes, there is no necessary conflict between value inculcation and critical thinking. The two tasks must be furthered concurrently. The child must develop the capacity "both to understand and internalize the norms of her society and to judge those norms against rational attack."[4] Not all restrictions on the short-term autonomy of children will thwart their civic development and, indeed, some restrictions can further the long-term autonomy necessary to their future role in the polity.[5] What restrictions will and will not negatively affect the future role of children as adult participants in the political system will be a major consideration in this chapter.

In addition to keeping in mind the implications of civic republicanism, it is necessary to examine the Supreme Court's rulings in the area of schools and expression, before turning to a theory of what speech should be free and what subject to control. Having discussed the cases, a line can then be drawn recognizing the need to educate children with the implication that schools may sometimes limit speech, while at the same time showing concern for the potential distorting effect controlling student speech can have on the political future of the community.

A. *The Supreme Court Cases*

1. Background

Several cases that may seem not directly on point as to the expression rights of children in schools do make points that are related to the issue and have been cited in the later Supreme Court cases that are more directly relevant. The first of them also provides a still current limitation on the inculcation of values. That case is *West Virginia State Board of Education v. Barnette*.[6] The issue there was a state statute requiring public school student participation in a flag salute. Refusal to so participate was grounds for expulsion. A group of Jehovah's Witnesses, whose religious beliefs forbid saluting the flag, challenged the requirement, and the statute was held to be a violation of the First Amendment.

The Court characterized the question raised as whether or not a cere-
mony "touching matters of opinion and political attitude" can be imposed on the individual.[7] Speaking of the role of public education, the
court said "[f]ree public education, if faithful to the ideal of secular instruction and political neutrality, will not be partisan or enemy of any
class, creed, party, or faction."[8] On the other hand, the Court said that
government may foster national unity, the goal of the flag salute requirement, by example and by persuasion. It was the coercive nature of the
statute that led to the conclusion of unconstitutionality. "If there is any
fixed star in our constitutional constellation, it is that no official, high or
petty, can prescribe what shall be orthodox in politics, nationalism, religion, or other matters of opinion or force citizens to confess by word or
act their faith therein."[9] But that should not be read to assert that school
boards do not have the authority to determine the explanation of history
to be taught or the values to be honored in the schools. The Court was
concerned with "a compulsion of students to declare a belief."[10] While
choosing the varieties of speech that are to be presented or tolerated in
the schools remain to be examined, it is clear that requiring students to
assert their agreement with official orthodoxy goes beyond the authority
the First Amendment permits the schools.

The second of these background cases is *Keyishian v. Board of Regents*.[11] The case arose when the formerly private University of Buffalo
became a part of the state university system. Employees were required to
sign certificates regarding affiliation with the Communist Party or membership in groups advocating the overthrow of the United States government by force or unlawful means. The plaintiffs refused to sign and sued
to enjoin the enforcement of the requirements. The Supreme Court found
the requirement unconstitutional and in so doing expressed its view of
academic freedom.

> Our Nation is deeply committed to safeguarding academic freedom,
> which is of transcendent value to all of us and not merely to the teachers
> concerned. That freedom is therefore a special concern of the First
> Amendment, which does not tolerate laws that cast a pall of orthodoxy
> over the classroom. "The vigilant protection of constitutional freedoms
> is nowhere more vital than in the community of American schools." The
> classroom is peculiarly the "marketplace of ideas." . . . Teachers and stu-
> dents must always remain free to inquire, to study and to evaluate, to

gain new maturity and understanding; otherwise our civilization will stagnate and die."[12]

It was the university that was at issue, but more generally the Court realized the importance of the classroom as a part of the marketplace of ideas. Justice Blackmun, in a partial concurrence in *Board of Education v. Pico*,[13] took this language, in conjunction with *Barnette*, as making it clear that "imposition of 'ideological discipline' [is] not a proper undertaking for school authorities."[14]

The third case is *Ambach v. Norwick*, which involved the issue of whether the state of New York could refuse to certify as elementary or secondary school teachers aliens who were eligible for citizenship but refused to seek naturalization.[15] Again, the issue was not limits on speech in the schools, but the Court's analysis touched on the importance and role of elementary and secondary education. The Court determined that such discrimination was allowable, and central to the decision was the role of the schools in fostering the values and attitudes that are considered important to the maintenance of our political culture. The teacher is central to that role. "Within the public schools system, teachers play a critical part in developing students' attitude toward government and understanding of the role of citizens in our society. . . . [A] state properly may regard all teachers as having an obligation to promote civic virtues and understanding in their classes."[16]

The background cases indicate competing concerns. There is a recognition that the schools, at least at the elementary and secondary levels, may and must play a role in teaching values to children. That role must allow the schools to speak to students in that regard, and it may also allow schools to restrict other in-school influences running contrary to the values the school is teaching. On the other hand, there is the recognition that the imposition of a political orthodoxy is dangerous and that this may limit the right of the schools to stifle debate. It is a tension that carries over to the cases more directly addressing the issues of speech rights in the schools.

2. *Tinker v. Des Moines*

Turning to the most relevant cases, the seminal case in the area of children's speech rights in school is *Tinker v. Des Moines Independent*

Community School District.[17] *Tinker* grew out of a protest over the involvement of the United States in the conflict in Vietnam. The district school principals learned of a planned demonstration, limited to wearing arm bands, and adopted a policy under which any student wearing an arm band in school would be asked to remove it. Students who refused to do so would be suspended. The plaintiff students and their parents went to federal court seeking an injunction against school officials barring discipline of the students for wearing black arm bands.

The case eventually reached the Supreme Court, and the Court began its analysis by noting that in considering First Amendment rights in the school context, the special characteristics of the school environment must be taken into account. Those rights do, nonetheless, exist. In the most quoted statement from this line of cases, the Court said: "It can hardly be argued that either students or teachers shed their constitutional rights to freedom of speech or expression at the schoolhouse gate."[18] That, the Court said, had been its "unmistakable holding" for almost fifty years. On the other hand, the Court also noted that it had repeatedly emphasized the authority of school officials to control the conduct of students, as long as they do so in a manner consistent with constitutional rights.

The Court noted that the activity motivating the suspensions was akin to pure speech, that it was silent and passive and that there was no evidence of interference "actual or nascent" with the rights of the school authorities to engage in the work of education or the rights of other students to be secure and to be left alone. Very few students in the system wore arm bands, and there was no evidence that their act disrupted any class or activity. While some students reacted with hostility outside the classroom, there were no threats of violence nor was there any violent response. While the District Court had found the school system's response reasonable, because of a fear of disturbance, the Supreme Court said that "in our system, undifferentiated fear or apprehension of disturbance is not enough to overcome the right to freedom of expression."[19]

As the Court noted, any disagreement with the majority view may, in a sense, cause trouble or raise fears. Any comment made, whether in the classroom or in the cafeteria can, if it is made to one who disagrees with the position espoused, lead to an argument and thus may cause a disturbance. But, under our Constitution, this is a risk we must take. It is a right that merits protection even in the schools. "In order for the State in the person of school officials to justify prohibition of a particular expression of opinion, it must be able to show that its action was caused by something more than a mere desire to avoid the discomfort and unpleasantness that always accompany an unpopular viewpoint."[20]

The Court said that the record contained no evidence even of antici- pation of disturbance arising from the wearing of the arm bands. In fact, the Court found a distinctly different motivation. "[T]he action of the school authorities appears to have been based upon an urgent wish to avoid the controversy which might result from the expression, even by the silent symbol of arm bands, of opposition to this Nation's part in the conflagration in Vietnam."[21] Of strong relevance was the fact that the school authorities had singled out this one symbol for prohibition. Even other symbols with political significance or likely to raise controversy were allowed. Students in the same schools wore political campaign but- tons and even the German Iron Cross. This prohibition on one particular point of view must raise a red flag and be permitted only when necessary to avoid material and substantial interference with the operation of the school. "[S]tudents may not be regarded as closed-circuit recipients of only that which the State chooses to communicate. They may not be confined to the expression of those sentiments that are officially ap- proved."[22]

3. *Island Trees v. Pico*

The second Supreme Court opinion of particular relevance here is *Is- land Trees Union Free School District v. Pico.*[23] As in *Tinker*, the free speech rights of students may be seen to have won out over the right of the school system to control expression. This time it was not expression offered by students but students' access to the expression of others in the context of books in the school library. While the case is sometimes seen as another strong holding for First Amendment rights in the school con- text, the lack of a majority opinion and the procedural context in which the case reached the Court limit the strength of the holding.

Several members of the Island Trees school board attended a confer- ence sponsored by a politically conservative parents' organization and came away with a list of objectionable books. Returning to their home school system, they determined that the high school library contained nine of the listed books, and the junior high library contained one. The members requested that the books be delivered to the board for review, and when asked about their interest, the Board characterized the books as "anti-American, anti-Christian, anti-Sem[i]tic, and just plain filthy."[24]

The books in the high school library were: Kurt Vonnegut Jr.'s *Slaughter House Five*; Desmond Morris's *The Naked Ape*; Piri Thomas's *Down These Mean Streets*; *Best Short Stories of Negro Writers*, edited by Langston Hughes; the anonymously authored *Go Ask Alice*; Oliver La-Farge's *Laughing Boy*; Richard Wright's *Black Boy*; Alice Childress's *A Hero Ain't Nothin' but a Sandwich*; and Eldridge Cleaver's *Soul on Ice*. The junior high library book was *A Reader for Writers*, edited by Jerome Archer, and another of the listed books, *The Fixer*, by Bernard Malamud, was used in a twelfth-grade literature course.

The Board appointed a committee of parents and school staff to review the books at issue. The committee was to recommend the action to be taken based on the books' "educational suitability," "good taste," "relevance," and "appropriateness to age and grade level." The committee recommended that *The Fixer*, *Laughing Boy*, *Black Boy*, *Go Ask Alice*, and *Best Short Stories by Negro Writers* be retained and that *The Naked Ape* and *Down These Mean Streets* be removed. It reached no agreement on *Soul on Ice* and *A Hero Ain't Nothin' but a Sandwich*, made no decision on *A Reader for Writers*, because not everyone had read the book, and recommended that *Slaughter House Five* be available only with parental approval. The Board largely rejected the committee's recommendation, determining that *Laughing Boy* should be returned to the high school library, that *Black Boy* be available with parental approval, and that all the remaining books be removed. A group of students then challenged the board's action, alleging a denial of their First Amendment rights.

The Supreme Court found the removal to at least raise a triable constitutional issue, but again there was no majority opinion, and the procedural context makes it difficult to extract clear, generalizable principles. The Board of Education had been granted summary judgment by the trial court. This judgment could be sustained only if there were no genuine issues of fact and if, even with the evidence construed most favorably to the original plaintiffs, the law made the Board entitled to judgment. First Amendment cases often turn on government intent, so any unresolved issues over the board's motives in removing the books would bar summary judgment.

The plurality, Justice Brennan, with only Justices Marshall and Stevens in complete support and with Justice Blackmun joining in part, began its analysis by recognizing the broad discretion school boards enjoy in managing the affairs of the schools and that it was "in full agreement" with the board's position that "local school boards must be permitted 'to establish and apply their curriculum in such a way as to transmit community values,' and that 'there is a legitimate and substantial community interest in promoting respect for authority and traditional values be they social, moral, or political.'"[25] Nonetheless, discretion must be exercised in harmony with the dictates of the First Amendment.

The plurality recognized that, as established by *Tinker*, students do have First Amendment rights, even if the special characteristics of the school environment affect the scope of those rights. Furthermore, the First Amendment protects not only the right to expression but also a right to receive information, and the government cannot contract the spectrum of knowledge. Meaningful exercise of expressive rights requires the receipt of the ideas necessary to form opinions, and this applies to students as well as to adults. While the school environment might limit those access rights in the classroom, the nature of the library, the plurality said, makes that environment particularly appropriate for the recognition of the rights the First Amendment provides students.

> Petitioners might well defend their claim of absolute discretion in matters of *curriculum* by reliance upon their duty to inculcate community values. But we think that petitioners' reliance upon that duty is misplaced where, as here, they attempt to extend their claim of absolute discretion beyond the compulsory environment of the classroom, into the school library and the regime of voluntary inquiry that there holds sway.[26]

Turning to the First Amendment limitations on the school board's control over the elimination of books from the library, the lessons the plurality drew from the case law focused on motives.

> [The Board] rightly possess[es] significant discretion to determine the content of their school libraries. But that discretion may not be exercised in a narrowly partisan or political manner. If a Democratic school board, motivated by party affiliation, ordered the removal of all books written by or in favor of Republicans, few would doubt that the order violated the constitutional rights of the students denied access to those books. The same conclusion would surely apply if an all-white school board, motivated by racial animus, decided to remove all books authored by blacks or advocating racial equality and integration. Our Constitution does not permit the official suppression of ideas.[27]

The plaintiffs had alleged that the decision was based on the board's belief that the books were "anti-American" and contrary to the "personal values, morals and tastes" of the members of the board. When asked about the "anti-American" nature of the books, two of the members had objected to a passage in *A Hero Ain't Nothin' but a Sandwich* that noted that George Washington was a slave holder, one of them stating, "I believe it is anti-American to present one of the nation's heroes, the first President, . . . in such a negative and obviously one-sided life."[28] Since this motivation would be violative of the First Amendment, there was a factual issue. Summary judgment had to be vacated and the case remanded for trial.

As indicated earlier, Justice Blackmun joined the plurality opinion only in part. He, too, recognized a tension between the role of the schools and the dictates of the First Amendment. He acknowledged the importance of schools in the preparation of students for participation as citizens and in preserving societal values. Schools may promote civic virtues and inculcate fundamental values. On the other hand, schools cannot impose political orthodoxy or ideological discipline. Justice Blackmun did not see the outcome of the case as resting on the peculiar nature or role of school libraries and found a general principle: "[T]he State may not act to deny access to an idea simply because state officials disapprove of that idea for partisan or political reasons."[29]

> In my view, we strike a proper balance here by holding that school officials may not remove books for the *purpose* of restricting access to the political ideas or social perspectives discussed in them. . . . [T]he school board must "be able to show that its action was caused by something more than a mere desire to avoid the discomfort and unpleasantness that always accompany an unpopular viewpoint," and that the board had something in mind in addition to the suppression of partisan or political views it did not share. . . . First Amendment principles would allow a school board to refuse to make a book available to students because it contains offensive language, . . . or because it is psychologically or intellectually inappropriate for the age group, or even, perhaps, because the ideas it advances are "manifestly inimical to the public welfare."[30]

Thus, Justice Blackmun stressed the suppression of ideas on political or partisan bases, and even there, he possibly allows the suppression of ideas if they are not just discomforting or unpleasant because of their conflict with the popular point of view but are inimical to the public welfare.

Even with Justice Blackmun's vote, this still only yields four votes for the judgment, so the opinion of Justice White, concurring in the judgment but not in the plurality opinion, is important. Justice White agreed that there was a factual dispute in the case that made summary judgment inappropriate. He chided the plurality, however, for going on to "issue a dissertation on the extent to which the First Amendment limits the discretion of the school board to remove books from the school library."[31] He saw no reason to do so, arguing that the time for that issue would be if or when the case returned after a trial.

Since Justice White refused to sign on to any part of the plurality opinion, this opinion, even limited in order to receive the support of Justice Blackmun, has no binding effect and really carries no more weight than the opinions of the four dissenters. Those dissenters saw no First Amendment problem, since the schools were not prohibiting reading the books at issue but simply choosing not to provide them, and the First Amendment does not require, the four dissenters said, the schools to become "a slavish courier of the material of third parties."[32]

Among the several dissenting opinions was one by Justice Rehnquist, joined by Chief Justice Burger and Justice Powell, discussing the role of elementary and secondary education and the need both to include and to exclude material. "Education consists of the selective presentation and explanation of ideas. . . . Determining what information *not* to present to the students is often as important as identifying relevant material."[33] In the dissenters' view, the library does not have special status.

[E]lementary and secondary schools are inculcative in nature. The libraries of such schools serve as supplements to this inculcative role. Unlike university or public libraries, elementary and secondary school libraries are not designed for freewheeling inquiry; they are tailored, as the public school curriculum is tailored, to the teaching of basic skills and ideas.[34]

Given the split in the Court, it is difficult to draw much guidance from *Pico*. It is clear that a majority would allow the school to remove a book on the basis of excessive vulgarity. It is also clear that decisions on what books to acquire, as opposed to which books may be removed, allow for more discretion on the part of school boards. In acquisition, the values that the books promote may be considered, since the books may supplement the school's general effort to impart values to the next generation. With regard to removal, value decisions that rest on political or partisan positions seem the most suspect, but even on this issue there was no majority. Other values, such as a belief that vulgarity is unsuitable in a school library, are acceptable bases for removal.

4. *Bethel School District v. Fraser*

Bethel School District v. Fraser grew out of what was described as a lewd speech given by a student at a high school assembly.[35] The speech by Fraser nominated a fellow student running for student government office. The assembly was attended by some six hundred students, some as young as fourteen. The Court described the assembly as "part of a school-sponsored educational program in self-government" and the speech as "an elaborate, graphic, and explicit sexual metaphor."[36] Fraser had been warned by two teachers, who knew of the content of the speech, that there might be severe consequences, but he delivered it nonetheless. The speech was met with hooting, yelling and some sexually suggestive gestures on the part of some students, bewilderment and embarrassment on the part of others. The administrative response was to find a violation of a school rule prohibiting conduct that "materially and substantially interferes with the educational process" and specifically including obscene or profane language or gestures. Fraser was suspended for three days, although he was allowed to return after two days, and his name was removed from the list of potential speakers at graduation.

Given the centrality of the speech, it is worth setting it out in the text. The Court's description, at various places in the opinion as "obscene," "vulgar," "lewd" and "offensively lewd," leaves one expecting something far more explicit than the actual language used.

> I know a man who is firm—he's firm in his pants, he's firm in his shirt, his character is firm—but most of all, his belief in you, the students of Bethel, is firm.
>
> Jeff Kuhlman is a man who takes his point and pounds it in. If necessary, he'll take an issue and nail it to the wall. He doesn't attack things in spurts—he drives hard, pushing and pushing until finally—he succeeds.
>
> Jeff is a man who will go to the very end—even the climax, for each and every one of you.

So vote for Jeff for A.S.B. vice-president—he'll never come between you and the best our high school can be.[37]

As Justice Brennan said in concurrence: "Having read the full text of respondent's remarks, I find it difficult to believe that it is the same speech the Court describes."[38]

The school's disciplinary action led to litigation, and when it reached the Supreme Court, the school district prevailed. The Court first determined that *Tinker* was not controlling. There was a "marked distinction between the political 'message' of the arm bands in *Tinker* and the sexual content of respondent's speech in this case."[39] *Tinker* had involved "a nondisruptive, passive expression of a political viewpoint" that had not intruded on the work of the schools or the rights of other students,[40] distinguishing it from the speech at issue.

The Court then noted the role of public education in preparing students for citizenship and inculcating the fundamental values and civility necessary to a democratic society.

These fundamental values of "habits and manners of civility" essential to a democratic society must, of course, include tolerance of divergent political and religious views, even when the views expressed may be unpopular. But these "fundamental values" must also take into account consideration of the sensibilities of others, and, in the case of a school, the sensibilities of fellow students. The undoubted freedom to advocate unpopular and controversial views in schools and classrooms must be balanced against the society's countervailing interest in teaching students the boundaries of socially appropriate behavior.[41]

Even in congressional debates, the Court noted, there are rules of civility that prohibit the use of offensive expression. The conclusion that the schools could not insist on similar restrictions seemed unreasonable.

The Court recognized that the First Amendment provides strong protection for "adult public discourse," even to the point of protecting the offensive expression regarding the draft on Cohen's jacket in *Cohen v. California*.[42] That did not mean that "simply because the use of an offensive form of expression may not be prohibited to adults making what the speaker considers a political point, the same latitude must be permitted to children in a public school."[43]

Surely it is a highly appropriate function of public school education to prohibit the use of vulgar and offensive terms in public discourse. Indeed, the "fundamental values necessary to the maintenance of a democratic political system" disfavor the use of terms of debate highly offensive or highly threatening to others. Nothing in the Constitution prohibits the states from insisting that certain modes of expression are inappropriate and subject to sanctions. The inculcation of these values is truly the "work of the schools." . . . The determination of what manner of speech in the classroom or in school assembly is inappropriate properly rests with the school board.[44]

Furthermore, the education of children for citizenship is not limited to the classroom. The examples provided by teachers and fellow students are also formative, and the schools "may determine that the essential lessons of civil, mature conduct cannot be conveyed in a school that tolerates lewd, indecent, or offensive speech and conduct."[45]

The Court summed up its analysis:

We hold that petitioner School District acted entirely within its permissible authority in imposing sanctions upon Fraser in response to his offensively lewd and indecent speech. Unlike the sanctions imposed on the students wearing arm bands in *Tinker, the penalties imposed in this case were unrelated to any political viewpoint.* . . . [I]t was perfectly appropriate for the school to disassociate itself to make the point to the pupils that vulgar speech and lewd conduct is wholly inconsistent with the "fundamental values" of public school education.[46]

The Court thus merged consideration of political content, lewdness and vulgarity and school disassociation with the behavior involved.

5. *Hazelwood School District v. Kuhlmeier*

The most recent relevant Supreme Court case is *Hazelwood School District v. Kuhlmeier*,[47] which involved the school newspaper at Hazelwood East High School in Missouri. The paper was produced by the school's Journalism II class, and each issue was submitted for review to the school principal prior to publication. The last edition for the school year was to contain two articles the principal found objectionable, one on the pregnancy experiences of three students from the school and the other on the impact of divorce on Hazelwood East students. The principal's objections to the pregnancy story were that, even though false names were used, the pregnant students might be identifiable and that the article's discussion of sexual activity and birth control were inappropriate for the school's younger students. The objection to the divorce story was that a student, who was identified in the story,[48] had complained that her father was not spending enough time with her family, was always out of town or playing cards with his friends and was constantly arguing with her mother. The principal believed that the parents should have been given the opportunity to respond or consent to the publication of their daughter's comments. Since the principal believed there was no time to rewrite the stories or recompose the pages on which the stories were to appear, he ordered that the two pages be deleted.

Three staff members of the school newspaper sued, alleging that their First Amendment rights had been violated. When the case reached the Supreme Court, the Court began with the *Tinker* conclusion that students do not give up all their expression rights at the schoolhouse gate and cannot be punished merely for expressing their personal views at school. On the other hand, those rights are not necessarily coextensive with the rights of adults in other settings, and "[a] school need not tolerate student speech that is inconsistent with its 'basic educational mission,' . . . even though the government could not censor similar speech outside the school."[49]

Turning from the recitation of general principles to the specific concerns raised, the Court first considered the nature of the school newspaper, determining that the paper was not a public forum where speech by all is tolerated absent a strong reason for suppression. The school's curriculum guide described the Journalism II course as a laboratory situation for applying the skills learned in Journalism I, including "development of journalistic skills under deadline pressure, 'the legal, moral, and ethical restrictions imposed upon journalists within the school community,' and 'responsibility and acceptance of criticism for articles of opinion.'"[50] The paper was seen as a supervised learning activity for the students enrolled in Journalism II, and the school was entitled to regulate it in any reasonable manner.

Turning to the reasonableness of the principal's action, the Court began by noting that there was a difference between the student speech of *Tinker* and "school-sponsored publications, theatrical productions, and other expressive activities that students, parents, and members of the public might reasonably perceive to bear the imprimatur of the school."[51] Where an activity is designed to teach, educators must have the right to exercise more control to "assure that participants learn whatever lessons the activity is designed to teach, that readers or listeners are not exposed to material that may be inappropriate for their level of maturity, and that the views of the individual speaker are not erroneously attributed to the school."[52] Citing *Fraser*, the Court said that the school, as publisher of a newspaper or producer of a school play, may disassociate itself from speech not only that interferes or impinges on the rights or other students, as in *Tinker*, but also from speech that is "ungrammatical, poorly written, inadequately researched, biased or prejudiced, vulgar or profane, or unsuitable for immature audiences."[53]

> A school must also retain the authority to refuse to sponsor student speech that might reasonably be perceived to advocate drug or alcohol use, irresponsible sex, or conduct otherwise inconsistent with "the shared values of a civilized social order," or to associate the school with any position other than neutrality on matters of political controversy. Otherwise, the schools would be unduly constrained from fulfilling their role as "a principal instrument in awakening the child to cultural values, in preparing him for later professional training, and in helping him to adjust normally to his environment."[54]

The principal's actions were reasonable, motivated as they were by concerns over issues of confidentiality and journalistic ethics and the belief that there was no way to protect those interests other than by removing the articles from the paper.

B. Reconciling the Cases

Any attempt to reconcile the cases must take into account two recurring themes. The Court has consistently recognized the interests of the school authorities, indeed of society in general, in furthering the educational mission of the schools. Certain restrictions on speech in the schools will be tolerated in order not to interrupt the education of the students. This most clearly applies to actual disruption through speech that is itself raucous or leads to such a reaction, but it may potentially apply to other disruptions as well. On the other hand, there is the countervailing concern over the classroom as the marketplace of ideas. This concern is strongest at the university level, since the role of the schools in the inculcation of society's values is clearly recognized at the elementary level. Nonetheless, the *Tinker* and *Pico* cases demonstrate that this interest is also of at least some concern at the secondary level as well.

Before turning to an attempt to reconcile the cases, several possible approaches should be examined and dismissed.[55] First, it might be argued that the distinctions drawn speak to the role of the school in the speech itself. There might, that is, be a line drawn between speech that is clearly that of the student alone and that which is sponsored by the school. This approach would draw its greatest strength from *Hazelwood*. The Court there clearly stated that the school was allowed to "disassociate itself" from speech on the grounds of bad writing, prejudice, vulgarity or profanity and could also decide not to disseminate speech on the basis of its inconsistency with society's shared values. There is also an additional slender reed of support for this position to be drawn from *Fraser*. There, the Court said that "it was perfectly appropriate for the school to disassociate itself [with Fraser's speech] to make the point to the pupils that vulgar speech and lewd conduct is wholly inconsistent with the 'fundamental values' of public school education."[56]

Disassociation, however, appears to be an inadequate basis on which to distinguish the cases. Furthermore, it does not adequately distinguish the elementary and secondary educational setting from others in which the government might be involved. Government generally can disassociate itself from the speech of others. In fact, such disassociation has been seen as vital in some situations.[57] But disassociation is not all that happened in *Fraser*. The school could have disassociated itself by making a statement prior to the speeches declaring that the speeches are by individual students and not on behalf of the school. Even lacking such foresight, the school could have disassociated itself after the speech by later disclaiming any connection to its content. The school authorities instead chose to punish Fraser, probably with the intent to deter similar speeches in the future. Such interest is suppression rather than disassociation.

A more convincing claim of disassociation can be made in the *Hazelwood* case. The paper was school sponsored, and an argument could be made that the only way to disassociate the school from the articles was to refuse to publish those articles. While the school might have included a disclaimer in each issue of the paper or made such a statement in response to the particular issue containing the objectionable articles, this solution

244 | *Speech in the Schools*

may reasonably have been seen as inadequate. While *Fraser* may have had a spontaneity, despite the foreknowledge of some teachers, that would allow the school to issue a later statement of disavowal or take that spontaneity into account in recognizing the prior need to make such a statement, the class context and review of the paper would make such a statement ring hollow. Furthermore, the school did not discipline the paper's writers or editors. Its response was disassociative and educational rather than punitive.

A further argument against disassociation as an explanatory principle is found in the *Pico* decision. If disassociation is the justification, a case could be made that it leads to the dissenting position in *Pico*. A school is associated with the material it conveys to its students. There is a strong association with the ideas and expression contained in the material that is a part of the formal curriculum, and the courts allow the school strong control over that material. But the school could also be seen as associated with the ideas and the language contained in the books it chooses to include in the school library. Perhaps the school could offer a disclamatory statement regarding the content of the library, but there is even less spontaneity in the library collection than there is in the school paper, and the disclaimer would ring even less true. In fact, the speech is, in a strong sense, the school's own, since it earlier included the material in its library, and the right to disassociate itself, to recognize the inclusion as a mistake, would seem stronger than in any of the other cases.

The case for disassociation seems stronger here than in *Fraser*, yet the plurality found a constitutional violation in excluding the books. It did, along with the dissenters, seem willing to allow the school to disassociate itself with books containing vulgarity, but not if the school system had certain other motives. It would seem, then, that disassociation is not a justification but a remedy. If the reason for objecting to the ideas is sufficient to allow the school to respond, it may do so through disassociation. But what motives are constitutionally adequate for any limiting response? And if a motive justifies disassociation, might it not also justify other responses?

It might also be argued that the distinctive characteristic among the cases is lewdness. Seeing the remarks in *Fraser* as lewd, vulgar or obscene may have motivated the majority. But, again, the comments in *Fraser* were far less offensive than some of the language in the books at issue in *Pico*. This fact may not refute the position that lewdness is central, since the *Pico* plurality, along with the dissenters, were willing to allow the exclusion of books from the library due to their excessive vulgarity. Still, the language in *Fraser* does seem fairly mild by our current cultural standards. It certainly does not reach the level that would justify regulation of language outside the schools, even with an audience of high school children. If the level of lewdness present in Fraser's speech is to play a role, it would have to be in conjunction with the right of the school to disassociate itself from the speech. But again, the school did more than disassociate itself.

It would seem that some other principles must be at work. The position to be taken here is that there are two principles. The first is the recognition of the role of the schools in educating the nation's youth and inculcating cultural values. That interest allows the schools to teach values and to limit certain speech for two reasons. The first reason is the disruptive effect the speech may cause, understood more expansively than *Tinker* might be read to include. The second is the development of practices that society may consider positive in the adult world but cannot be regulated there due to concerns over abuse. The interests are, however, limited by a need for political neutrality in the schools, so that the majority does not use schools to limit dissenting views in the next generation on issues of controversy in the political community.

1. Educational Function/Spring Training

Tinker recognized that school authorities can interfere with student speech, but only when they have reason to believe that the speech will "substantially interfere with the work of the school or impinge upon the rights of others."[58] Just how limiting this requirement is, of course, depends on what it means. If it reaches the point of requiring the elements of incitement to riot, speech rights in the schools would be coextensive with those in public. However, the Court in *Fraser* also stated that students' First Amendment rights inside schools "are not automatically coextensive with the rights of adults in other settings."[59]

Something less than a breach of the peace should suffice. In fact, the *Hazelwood* Court explained *Tinker* in response to an argument by the students that, under *Tinker*, "[o]nly speech that 'materially and substantially interferes with the requirements of appropriate discipline' can be found unacceptable and therefore be prohibited."[60] The Court reacted with a statement that this was not an accurate reflection of *Tinker*'s holding. Thus, it is not even a breach of discipline, far short of a breach of the peace, that is required. The First Amendment rights of students are limited by the fact that "[a] school need not tolerate student speech that is inconsistent with its 'basic educational mission.'"[61] Clearly, protection of the educational mission can go beyond avoiding excessive noise or other speech that would be considered disruptive outside the schools.

The school desegregation case *Brown v. Board of Education* offers insight into what may disrupt the educational process.[62] The Supreme Court concluded in the case that educational segregation, even if physical facilities are equal, deprives minority children of equal educational opportunities.[63] Justifying that conclusion, the Court said: "To separate [schoolchildren] . . . solely because of their race generates a feeling of inferiority as to their status in the community that may affect their hearts and minds in such a way unlikely ever to be undone."[64] The Court went on to adopt the view of the lower court that segregation, with the interpretation it carries of the inferiority of black students, affects the motivation of black students to learn and retards their educational and mental development. The Court found the psychological evidence convincing that segregation's stamp of inferiority had the effect of producing a sort of inferiority that made separate education inherently unequal.

The opinion did note that the segregation it was addressing had the sanction of law, but it did not offer any reason to believe that less formal racism, while perhaps not a constitutional violation, would not have a similar effect. Certainly the societal statement implicit in segregation might seem to have the strongest effect, but the effect on the individual child is more likely to be felt in the attitudes of age mates. That effect can come from comments on the playground as easily as from laws passed in the adult world. If a student is sufficiently sophisticated to recognize a difference between legally imposed segregation and the racism of individuals, the toleration of racist speech by the school may well erase that perception. If so, it would seem that hate speech would have a negative effect on the educational process; that is, such speech is inherently disruptive of the mission of the schools. If *Tinker* is not limited to the effects of noise but addresses anything that interferes, it would make a case for the schools protecting their students from hate speech.

This interest may be seen in *Fraser* where the Court noted that the speech at issue, "[b]y glorifying male sexuality . . . was acutely insulting to teenage girls."[65] While the speech may or may not have been more insulting than that which was commonly heard by those teenage girls, the Court does indicate that this is a real interest. It is an interest that mirrors the concerns of feminists over the effects of pornography and of hate speech in marginalizing women. Certainly, the marginalization of female students would impact their educational opportunities. Just as the reasoning that justified *Brown* provides a basis for the claim that racist speech "substantially interfere[s] with the work of the school," the same marginalization provides a basis for limits on in-school sexist speech. The same could be said for hate speech aimed at homosexuals or at people on the basis of handicap or religion.

Among our stronger societal values are commitments to equal treatment and dignity. If the inculcation of society's values is "truly the 'work of the schools,'"[66] then it should be just as "highly appropriate [a] function of public school education" to prohibit the use of these terms in discourse in public schools as it was to prohibit the "vulgar and offensive terms" in *Fraser*.[67] As *Fraser* recognized, "schools must teach by example the shared values of a civilized social order," and teachers and other students are role models in providing that example.[68] Just as "[t]he schools . . . may determine that the essential lessons of civil, mature conduct cannot be conveyed in a school that tolerates lewd, indecent, or offensive speech and conduct . . . ,"[69] the schools should also be allowed to determine that the essential lessons of civil conduct and the inculcation of the shared values of society cannot be conveyed in an atmosphere of hate speech.

The other basis under which school authorities may limit student speech is explained by the "spring training" metaphor provided by John Garvey. As Garvey says, "[c]hildren are not full-fledged First Amendment actors. . . . Freedom of speech for children is instrumentally important, not intrinsically so—it is a right we protect in order to help kids become real First Amendment players."[70] The fact that the real season has not yet begun for children allows differing treatment of their speech rights. Nonetheless, the government must exercise some restraint and recognize free speech rights that contribute to the child's development. Garvey, in an earlier article, offered several considerations in this regard. He discounts readings of *Tinker* that would give children free speech rights equal to those of adults, more limited only by the particular demands of nondisruption of the educational endeavor. Instead, he concludes that "the child's claim to recognition of such a right is valid only insofar as free speech is instrumental in the growth of his ability to participate in self-government."[71] He also recognizes an interest in the search for knowledge and truth, but it is characterized as a training interest; that is, there may be no immediate good, but children's debates on adult issues train them for their future active role in the political community.[72] The most significant restraint Garvey would place on the schools is that they not be allowed to subvert their own mission of teaching children to pursue knowledge.[73]

Betsy Levin makes a somewhat similar point regarding the training interest in arguing that schools should be subject to First Amendment restraints. She recognizes the role of the schools in inculcating values but would give greater recognition to the expression rights of students. Otherwise, she says, "students will not come to an understanding of the value of a democratic, participatory society, but instead will become a passive alienated citizenry that believes government is arbitrary."[74] Certainly, if the schools are too restrictive, this is a danger. While that justifies the imposition of some First Amendment restraints, it does not mean that they need have the same strength as in the adult world. While students must come to value democracy and participation, the extent of democracy and the nature of participation may differ in the two communities.

Fraser can certainly be seen as a spring training case. Student government elections are not the politics of the real season. They are the politics of the grapefruit league. It is not that they are not real but that they do not count in the world of real politics. The importance of elections for student leadership positions is not found in the issues of prom themes and the like that student government addresses. The importance is in the lessons provided in electoral politics. Student government leaders earn an item on their resumés that colleges, law schools and political organizations find valuable, but the value is not found in the fact that the prom was very popular and ran firmly in the black. Student government leaders do not rescue social security or reform health care. The value of the resumé item is the experience in getting elected, conducting meetings and working with others. It is the exercise, rather than any result obtained after election, that is important. For student leaders, school politics is spring training for later electoral campaigns or community leadership. For those not inclined toward leadership, school politics is still spring training for their role as voters in choosing leaders.

Since school politics is spring training, the rules may be different. They can be aimed at teaching lessons rather than solely at protecting the real political process. The government cannot insist on decorum in real-world politics; that would raise the specter of government suppression of positions with which it disagrees by finding the speech advocating the position uncivil. Schools should not face the same restrictions. The school may insist that candidates not campaign on the basis of how much homework should be assigned or the provision of free ice cream in the cafeteria. The school should be allowed to insist on campaigns addressing issues that student government is allowed to affect. Similarly, while the government cannot insist that real political campaigns restrict themselves to serious commentary on the issues and not use sensational speech, schools should be allowed more latitude. Spring training rules should allow the school to insist that nomination speeches present reasons why the candidate deserves support that are related to leadership qualities, rather than that the candidate is "firm in his shirt" and "firm in his pants."

Hazelwood can also be seen as a spring training case. The students in the Journalism II class were clearly in training, and school papers are to the outside world media what school politics are to real-world elections. Again, the major result of school newspaper work is a resumé item relevant to colleges and work on college newspapers as a step to professional journalism. Society cannot control the real-world press because of the danger of suppression of dissent. Indeed, society cannot even insist on evenhandedness in newspaper coverage.[75] Nonetheless, fairness and balance are ideals to which the press should aspire and to which the culture, without official sanction, should hold the media. The same can be said of other issues in journalistic ethics, such as protecting the privacy of individuals when not central to an issue of true public concern. Concerns over protecting the role of the real-world press do not necessarily translate to high school newspapers. They do not serve the same essential role in preventing governmental abuse.[76] They are training grounds for journalists and just as school elections can be idealized versions of real elections, school newspapers can be held to ethical standards one can only hope the real-world press will meet.

A word should be said here about the role of sponsorship that was seen as important in *Hazelwood* and of some importance in *Fraser*. There is a difference between a school newspaper and a paper produced outside the school by individuals who happen to be students. The same would be true of a school election compared to the selection of a leader by a group of students, again outside the school, to express their concerns to the school board or the city council. The difference, which would allow control of the school paper and election but not the outside activities, may be seen as one of a sponsor having the right to disassociate itself from expression.

But sponsorship also speaks to the spring training rationale for regulation. When the activity is sponsored, it is part of the educational mission of the schools. It is then subject to regulation to make the activity teach the lessons intended to be conveyed by the experience, even if the lessons are the idealization of real-world activities.

2. Neutrality in the Political Debate

The only one of the four Supreme Court cases clearly to find a First Amendment violation in the control of in-school expression was *Tinker*. If there is guidance to be found in the cases as to limitations on school authorities, it must be in that case. The second of the four cases, *Pico*, was a remand for consideration of the motives for the removal of the books at issue. The concerns expressed in that remand will provide additional insight. In fact, the principle to be drawn from *Tinker* and *Pico* also finds support in the background cases.

Barnette and *Keyishian* concerned the imposition of orthodoxy, but there are differences in orthodoxies. Teaching a heliocentric solar system, rather than a geocentric system, is the imposition of an orthodoxy. So are teaching Shakespeare as great writing while ignoring or criticizing the writing of lesser lights, and teaching about the Holocaust while refuting those who deny its occurrence. These orthodoxies may be imposed, at least in the sense of teaching their veracity and denying time to their opposing positions, though most likely, given *Barnette*, not in the sense of requiring that students profess belief in the positions in addition to having knowledge regarding the views.

Tinker demonstrates the real problem behind concerns over the imposition of orthodoxy found in the earlier cases. The real lesson of *Tinker* has to do with the school system's one-sidedness regarding a political or social issue in the adult world. The arm bands in *Tinker* were worn in protest of the actions of the United States in Vietnam. The issue was one debated widely in the political community, and the school authorities shut off expression taking one side in that debate. The Court found telling the fact that the school allowed other symbols. Campaign buttons and even an Iron Cross were tolerated. A wide variety of political sentiments were acceptable; only a symbol expressing disagreement with a particular, controversial national policy was suppressed.

Tinker may then be seen as limited to situations in which there is a political debate in the real world, and only one side of that debate is allowed in the schools.[77] The danger such one-sidedness presents is that those ad-hering to the majority position could use the schools to try to assure that their position carries the day with those soon to join, or perhaps already members of, the voting population. Certainly, some students will hear the other side from their parents or others, but the political process is skewed. Those students, whose parents are on the same side as the school's posi-tion, will have their beliefs reinforced. Those whose parents disagree will have their beliefs questioned. And those whose parents have expressed no belief will have their beliefs formed by the school. This is, admittedly, an oversimplification, since students are influenced by others besides parents and the schools, but the school's suppression of views with which the au-thorities disagree will have an unacceptable effect.

Language from *Pico* adds support for this understanding of *Tinker*. According to the *Pico* plurality, the school board did have discretion in determining what was in the school library, but there are limitations. The Court said that a Democratic school board could not remove books writ-ten by Republicans; nor could an all-white school board remove all books by blacks or those fostering racial equality.[78] Clearly, the reference to De-mocrats and Republicans invokes concern over domination of the schools by one side of a political division. The racial concern seems more tied to Equal Protection Clause issues but again shows that rights in the broader community are what limit the school authority to determine the content of the library.

The plurality, as well as the dissenters, would allow the school board to eliminate books based on vulgarity, irrelevance or educational unsuit-ability. It was the possibility that the decision had been based on a desire to eliminate books seen as anti-American or contrary to the values, morals or tastes of the board members that led to a remand to determine motive. Since vulgarity is a matter of values, morals or tastes, it is not all values, morals or tastes that are objectionable bases. It is the same vari-ety of personal conviction that is reflected in the "anti-American" label. There are differences in the political community as to what constitutes anti-Americanism, and for most, pointing out that the founders of the na-tion included slave holders is only a recognition of a sad era of our his-tory and not anti-Americanism. Learning about what we now recognize to be moral fault in the founders and the framers of the Constitution can shed light on that document and perhaps on how it should be seen in modern times. To ban a book on that basis is to take a narrow political view that requires the recognition of the sainthood of our founders and perhaps an unremitting adherence to their views, and the school board cannot be allowed to skew that debate by refusing to allow acknowledgment of our political history.

Justice Blackmun, in his concurrence, backs up this view. He would allow the schools to convey societal values and civic virtues but not to impose political orthodoxy. For him the limiting principle is that "school officials may not remove books for the *purpose* of restricting access to the political ideas or social perspectives discussed in them, when that action is motivated simply by the officials' disapproval of the ideas involved."[79] The dissenters, in seeming contrast, took the position that the First Amendment does not require that the schools become "a slavish courier of the material of third parties."[80] Schools have to be free, the dissenters said, to exclude as well as to include in compiling the body of material that makes up the educational experience.

These quoted portions of the *Pico* opinions are not really in as complete disagreement as they may at first appear. The school authorities cannot be allowed to interfere in the political debate. They cannot suppress political ideas or social perspectives because of disagreement with the positions taken. Neither, however, must they include in the library collection anything a writer wishes to donate. Material that is unsuitable for the student population, because of vulgarity or because it is historically or scientifically inaccurate, may be excluded. It is only finding a book unsuitable because of the political position taken that is an unacceptable basis for exclusion.

To take the baseball metaphor in a different direction, high school students, for the most part, are not involved in the major league of real politics. They are, however, playing Triple A ball and will soon be sent up to the majors. They need to know the game that is being played at that level. They need to be familiar with the issues on which they will soon play an equal role in addressing—and indeed that some already do. The school does them and the rest of society an injustice when it suppresses, and particularly when it skews, the debate on those issues.

This approach is sensitive to the concerns of civic republicanism and to the need to prepare children for participation in the political community. Issues that are actual subjects of political debate are protected under this interpretation. But there is a difference between discussions of affirmative action or race relations in general and the nonpolitical ascription of a racial epithet to a classmate. There is a difference between a discussion of limits on the exposure of children to violent or sexually indecent media and the use of vulgar language. Difficulties in making these distinctions may lead us to avoid them in the interest of not stifling political discussion in the adult world where the conversation has real and perhaps immediate political consequences. Where the interest in allowing political debate is a training interest, there is less need for concern over line drawing, so long as real debate in the political community is not skewed.

This difference is recognized by those concerned with civic education. Amy Gutmann would not deny school boards all authority to ban books. While concerned over the factors that have led to actual bannings, she says her principle of nonrepression only "prohibits educational authorities from shielding students from reasonable (not correct or uncontroversial) political views represented by the adult citizenry or from censoring challenges to those views."[81] Suzanna Sherry also recognizes a distinction between differing varieties of expression. In examining the school speech cases, she says:

> The cases usually pit student claims of independent, critical speech against the school's purported need to keep order and transmit values. But this is a false dichotomy. Most student speech, like the armbands . . . in *Tinker* . . . , is rational, civil, and a model for reasoned republican dialogue. Where the student speech is irrational or uncivil, . . . there is no harm in suppressing it. There may even be an educational benefit in doing so. Critical dialogue need not be uncivil; indeed, civility—especially in its concern for the sensibilities of others—is a moral value that is particularly useful in a diverse democracy.[82]

Educational value is different from the self-governing values behind protecting speech in the adult political community. Suzanna Sherry recognizes this and specifically concludes that hate speech regulations, while intolerable as a restriction on adult speech, may be appropriate tools to teach the young tolerance and sensitivity.[83]

C. Inculcation of Values in the Schools

It is clear that the schools can teach values. Time and again, the Supreme Court has recognized as an essential role of the schools the conveying of society's values to the next generation. The schools teach civic virtue and prepare children for their assumption of the role of active participant in the political society.[84] That is not to say that there are no constitutional limits on this part of the educational process. The First Amendment's Establishment Clause, which protects children as well as adults and in fact limits government more strongly when children are involved, provides one constraint. The teaching of values cannot be turned into the teaching of religion. The schools can certainly teach that it is wrong to steal or commit murder, but they cannot teach the Ten Commandments as God's law.

The second constraint is that the schools cannot insist that students profess their belief in the values taught. While there was a religious aspect to *Barnette*, the more general principle is that the state cannot impose an orthodoxy and require that students state their adherence to the positions taken. Schools can generally insist that student behavior adhere to imposed norms, but they cannot insist that students believe in conformance with the values the schools espouse. But the limitation that schools not be allowed to require the students' acceptance of beliefs does not mean that schools cannot attempt to convey those values.

The more difficult issue has been the need of the schools to insist that contrary beliefs not be advocated in the schools. There are certainly some rights on the part of the schools to limit expression. The most clearly established basis for limitation is vulgarity. Schools can also insist that certain other values not be furthered, but those disfavored values must run counter to the basic values of democracy, which should include society's commitment to equality and the dignity of all. Again, there can be no insistence that all students actually agree with those values. Nor can there be an insistence that students not espouse those negative values outside the schools. Indeed, even in the schools, it is difficult to justify the regulation of private conversations, at least when neither of the participants finds the language objectionable. The more public the speech or the direction toward a listener whose equality and dignity is attacked, the better the case for regulation. In the case of public speech, the appearance of sponsorship adds to the need for regulation; but even in the case of less public speech directed against an individual, there may be the appearance of official acceptance of the sentiment expressed in the fact that it is tolerated. Schools teach a rejection of bigotry by responding to bigoted speech and teach an acceptance of bigotry by tolerating such speech when it is openly made. Once again, there can be no limitation on politically debatable points, but racial and sexual superiority are no longer debatable in our society.

This distinction is brought to the fore by the decisions of the federal courts of appeals in *West v. Derby United School District*[85] and *Saxe v. State College Area School District*[86] discussed in chapter 9. The Tenth Circuit, in *West*, upheld a policy aimed with accuracy at racial harassment. On the other hand, the Third Circuit, in *Saxe*, found unconstitutional, as a violation of the First Amendment, a policy barring harassment "based on one's actual or perceived race, religion, color, national origin, gender, sexual orientation, disability, or other personal characteristics,"[87] and defining "other personal characteristics" to include discrimination based on "'clothing, physical appearance, social skills, peer group, intellect, educational program, hobbies or values, etc.'"[88]

There was a difference in that the school in the *West* case had had racial incidents, while no such history existed in *Saxe*. But the more important difference is that the rule at issue in *Saxe* included speech that touched on political debate, while the rule in *West* was limited to speech that violated core values. The complaint in *Saxe* was brought by individuals whose religious beliefs taught the sinfulness of homosexual practices, and they argued that they had the right to assert that belief and a variety of other moral positions. This was the crux of the violation. As the court said, "[b]y prohibiting disparaging speech directed at a person's 'values,' the Policy strikes at the heart of moral and political discourse—the lifeblood of constitutional self government (and democratic education) and the core concern of the First Amendment."[89]

The real flaw in the policy at issue in *Saxe* was that it could be seen as an attempt to use the schools to skew a real debate in the adult political community. The issues of the criminalization of homosexual activities and the rights of homosexuals to equal treatment or of the justice and constitutionality of affirmative action on the basis of race, color or gender are political issues. The schools cannot suppress either side in those debates. But those debates are a far cry from hurling racist, sexist or gay-bashing epithets at fellow students. The debate must be protected but so should the victims of the epithets, and the school should have the right to further inclusive values even through the suppression of this highly objectionable speech.

Conclusion

The entertainment industry is not likely to greet the arguments presented here with anything close to enthusiasm. There are certain to be invocations of the importance of the freedom of expression, not only for political advocates but for artists, writers, singers and filmmakers. Such freedom of expression is important. Indeed, it is vital in a democratic society, at least as far as political speech is concerned, and it is vital for a vibrant culture, even when the expression has no political content. The imposition of socialist-realist standards in the art of communist countries was as stifling, although in a different way, as the imposition of limitations on political speech. That being said, the freedom of expression does not include the right to whatever audience one may wish.

Admittedly, the freedom of expression may be an empty right, if one is denied an audience. A totalitarian government could well tolerate a right to express one's opinions, however contrary to those acceptable to the government, so long as they were expressed with no one else present. It might even be questioned whether such vocal activity can count as expression. Solitary vocalization amounts to nothing of consequence beyond thinking the politically disagreeable thoughts. A true freedom of expression includes the right to present that expression to an audience.

While the freedom of expression includes the right not to be interfered with in addressing a willing, and in some cases less than willing, audience, the audience to which one has that right does not include other people's children. Children are not full players in the political arena, and they do not enjoy the greater autonomy reserved for adults. They are protected by their parents and by the state. Their parents, and to a lesser degree the state, make the decisions for them as to the material that is appropriate for their age and stage of psychological development. Any claims by the media that they have constitutionally protected rights to access audiences of children are in conflict with the rights of parents and of the state and should give way to them. Any separate claims by children that they should have access to materials that their parents believe to be inappropriate are issues to be resolved by the parent and child. The recognized right of parents to make child-rearing decisions should not give way to childhood attractions to pornography, violence or hate-filled music. Children will soon be adults who are able to make their own decisions, and access to these negative influences can wait until after their parents and the schools have finished trying to instill the values they deem important in the next generation of adults.

Reasonable restrictions on the access of children to negative media influences should be recognized as constitutional. The government should be allowed to restrict the direct sale or rental of sexually indecent material to children, as it already can. The same sorts of restrictions should be allowed for violent materials and for materials that foster hatred on the basis of race, color, ethnicity, gender, sexual orientation, religion or handicap. While parents may choose to make such materials available to their own children, the children should not have a right to obtain the material contrary to their parents' wishes, and distributors should have no right to sell directly to other people's children.

Regulation may also address access other than through sales. Government should be allowed to impose restrictions, similar to those currently voluntarily in place, on the admission of minors to sexually indecent films. Further, similar restrictions based on violence or hate speech should be allowed. Restrictions should also be acceptable when applied to video games, with both sales and play in video arcades limited, if there is no parental permission. The broadcast media may face channeling requirements, limiting offensive material to hours when children are less likely to be in the audience.[1] Cable broadcasters might even be required to include signals that activate the v-chip contained in newer televisions, when they distribute material that would come within the scope of limits on admission to theaters.[2] Similarly, Internet software should be modified to allow people to conform to requirements that material not suitable for children include a signal that activates filtering software. Finally, reasonable restrictions on advertising to children should be allowed.

The word "reasonable" is important here. If the dual approach argued for here is to have any meaning, that meaning is that restrictions when children are involved need not meet the strict scrutiny tests required for most restrictions involving adults. The media influences addressed do have negative consequences for children, but those consequences may not provide an adequate basis for meeting the strict scrutiny test of being necessary to a compelling government interest. The interest in the safety and psychological health of children has been regularly recognized as compelling, but it has been difficult to demonstrate necessity. This difficulty may not be answered by increased social science research. Analysis of necessity under the First Amendment has always focused on the immediate result of the speech concerned. But the influences of concern here are not of that variety. No one suggests that a single exposure of a normal child to a film, video game or CD will lead to immediate criminal behavior or permanent psychological injury. It is the continued exposure over the child's formative years that does harm. First Amendment theory has been incapable of handling such influences, and strict scrutiny is unlikely to be met. But if access by, or distribution to, children is not as protected as it is when only adults are involved, strict scrutiny should not be required, and a rational basis for regulation should suffice. Limits need only be rationally related to the recognized legitimate interest in the safety and psychological health of children.

Limitations on government attempts to protect children should focus on the restrictions' effects on adults. The materials at issue are protected for adult consumption, and any limits should have no more impact on those rights than necessary. Restrictions on sales to minors or on admission to films or play in video arcades do not restrict adult access. Neither do v-chip or Internet filtering signal requirements, so long as they are not sufficiently onerous as to prevent broadcast or posting. Broadcast channeling does have some impact, but it is an impact that has been found acceptable in the context of sexual indecency, and this interpretation should carry over to other negative influences. The greatest difficulties raised by this concern are in the area of profane speech and advertising. Any restrictions must be narrowly drawn so as to allow such speech for audiences of adults.

Another requirement for any regulation imposed to protect children, indeed a requirement for all limitations on all expression, is that the rules or statutes involved make clear the material addressed. Distributors of media must be able to determine whether or not the material they sell or rent is restricted for children. This does not mean that there cannot be any jury issue as to suitability for minors. It does mean that statutes must clearly define the sorts of depictions addressed. In the harmful-to-minors statute at issue in *Ginsberg v. New York*,[3] these are nudity, sexual conduct, sexual excitement, or sadomasochistic abuse; in many obscenity statutes it is the depiction of actual or simulated ultimate sexual acts. Statutes in other areas should have to meet similar requirements. For example, in a violent depiction statute, the definitional section should list the sorts of acts that are of concern, such as murder, manslaughter, rape, mayhem, battery, or an attempt to commit any of these crimes. Such a statute should also require provisions, similar to obscenity statutes, that the material, taken as a whole, must appeal to a shameful or morbid interest in violence of minors; must be patently offensive to prevailing standards in the adult community as a whole with respect to what is suitable material for minors; and must, considered as a whole, lack serious literary, artistic, political and scientific value for minors. These later provisions need not be defined with the clarity that the list of acts addressed requires.

This does not mean that all media restrictions, so long as they only limit access by youth, should automatically be constitutional. Children do have other constitutional rights, even if those rights are weaker than adult rights. The savings clause in obscenity law and its argued-for extension to violence should have more general application. Material with serious literary, artistic, political or scientific value for minors should not be repressed. Thus, information on health or on developing sexual identity should be beyond the power of government prohibition.

In addition to restrictions on media access by and to children, the role of the schools in the preservation and inculcation of values should be recognized and protected. The schools should not only be allowed to teach values, restricted by the First Amendment's Establishment Clause and the approval of the political community, but the schools must also be allowed to place certain restrictions on the speech of members of the school community. Those restrictions must, however, not be attempts to limit or skew the debate in the adult community as it is experienced by the school community.

There may be an issue over the age employed in statutes restricting access by and to minors. The age of majority is eighteen, and since a variety of rights attach at that age, that may be the best line to draw here as well. It is also the line the U.S. Court of Appeals for the District of Columbia Circuit allowed in the *Action for Children's Television v. Federal Communications Commission* cases.[4] The court noted the increasing levels of explicitness necessary for material to be considered obscene and the resulting levels of explicitness in material that would then still only be considered indecent. That made it reasonable to restrict access to all minors. The court also found support for that position in the case law and societal consensus.[5] On the other hand, the *Reno v. American Civil Liberties Union* Court,[6] in striking down the Communications Decency Act's attempt to protect children under eighteen from Internet indecency, distinguished *Ginsberg* in part on the fact that the New York statute in *Ginsberg* addressed distribution to those under seventeen, while the CDA age limit was eighteen. While the factor was not dispositive, it may counsel caution in adopting statutes with an eighteen-year-old limit and favor a line at seventeen.

The choice of the age of seventeen would also address a concern raised by Judge Richard Posner in ordering an injunction against the enforcement of an ordinance limiting access by those under eighteen to violent video games.[7] He took the position that, with the eighteen-year-old vote, it is necessary for those approaching that age to develop their own ideas in order to be independent voters and that this required First Amendment rights. "Now that eighteen-year-olds have the right to vote, it is obvious that they must be allowed the freedom to form their political views on the basis of uncensored speech *before* they turn eighteen, so that their minds are not a blank when they first exercise the franchise."[8] While one may question whether playing violent video games is necessary to becoming an informed voter, Judge Posner's arguments do speak in favor of some greater expression rights as children approach majority.

It bears repeating that the arguments offered on each theory and topic presented are based both in law and in policy. The legal arguments were intended to show that there is an already recognized basis for the conclusions asserted; that is, the jump from the law as it exists to that suggested is not as great a leap as it might at first seem. The arguments based on the role of the First Amendment and the dangers behind free expression where children are concerned can also be taken if the courts were to reject the interpretation offered herein for the speech and press clauses, as policy arguments that the amendment, as interpreted, should be changed. If the courts reject attempts to protect children, believing that such efforts violate the First Amendment, the policy arguments would still support the proposition that the Constitution should be changed, that it should no longer be a societal suicide pact.

Any constitutional amendment limiting free expression properly raises concerns over the very nature of our political system. When an amendment allowing proscriptions against flag desecration was proposed, worries over a slippery slope were reasonable. If feelings regarding the flag were strong enough to amend the Constitution, feelings about other symbols or about prayer in schools might prove strong enough to have their own amendments. Having given in on one issue, Congress and the states might have found it difficult to take a stand against other demanded changes. The line drawn based on age is, however, different. An amendment to the point that nothing in the free-expression clauses shall be interpreted as denying the right of the state to protect its children from the dangers of free expression, while still allowing reasonable access for adults, does not present the same expansion problem. The age at which full First Amendment rights attach will not creep to twenty-five and then forty. While there may or may not be the tendency to include more material in the group believed to be dangerous for minors, this does not have the same effect on the nature of the political system that increasing limitations on adult communication would.

For those still not convinced by the arguments offered, one further attempt is warranted. There has been a great deal of concern recently over the harsh treatment given juveniles who find themselves at the hands of the criminal justice system. Children who in the past would have faced delinquency proceedings are now often confronted with a full-blown criminal prosecution. Indeed, trial as an adult can be mandated for certain crimes.

The issue is not one merely of the procedures afforded the juvenile. There are important consequences that attend the conviction of a crime instead of an adjudication of delinquency. The juvenile treated as a child faces a shorter period of confinement in a facility that has, or at least should have, a focus on reform. The child treated as an adult receives much harsher treatment. Trial as an adult, coupled with mandatory sentences for adult crimes, may lead to life imprisonment for an act done as a thirteen- or fourteen-year-old.

The argument for mitigating the harshness of penalties for juveniles, if it is to have any greater strength than general and likely unsuccessful arguments for more lenient sentencing, has to be based on the recognition that there are relevant differences between children and adults. The distinction cannot be based on the consequences of the actions of minors. Children have engaged in behavior with terrible results, including the loss of multiple lives. Looked at only on that dimension, the visceral response to impose strong punishment is understandable.

The position that children should not face the lengthy prison terms adults would face for the same acts can only be based on the recognition that children are different because they are incomplete. It be may rational to imprison an adult for an extended period on an assumption of incorrigibility. When a fully formed person has demonstrated a dangerousness to society, long-term incarceration may be necessary. The best argument that such harsh punishment for minors is unreasonable is that juveniles are not incorrigible. Children are still developing their judgment and moral sense. Even if we have largely given up on our belief that we can rehabilitate adults, most children are more malleable. Recognition that they can reform demands rehabilitation attempts and the possibility of release.

Certainly not all will agree with this seeming aside, but those who do are likely to be the same people who disagree with the arguments presented regarding free expression and children. But, the two arguments are the obverse of each other.[9] Recognizing the malleability of youth that demands more lenient treatment also argues for restrictions on the expression to which children are exposed. If good influences, through reform efforts, can have the effect necessary for the juvenile offender to be released eventually, it is clear that harmful influences can drive the juvenile in the opposite direction. If the nature of minors demands that they be treated differently in the one regard, it leads in the same direction for the other. Society should be allowed to protect its children from negative influences, even when those influences come in the form of expression.

Notes

1. Crawford v. Lundgren, 96 F.3d 380, 389 (9th Cir. 1996) (upholding a ban on selling sexually indecent material through unsupervised sidewalk vending machines), *cert. denied*, 520 U.S. 1117 (1997).

2. Terminiello v. Chicago, 337 U.S. 1, 37 (1949) (Jackson, J., dissenting).

3. Kennedy v. Mendoza-Martinez, 372 U.S. 144, 160 (1963).

4. *See, e.g.* , Haig v. Agee, 453 U.S. 280 (1981); Aptheker v. Secretary of State, 378 U.S. 500 (1964).

5. *See, e.g.* , Edmond v. Goldsmith, 183 F.3d 659 (7th Cir. 1999), *aff'd*, 531 U.S. 32 (2000).

6. *See* Deaths: Final Data for 1997, 47 National Vital Statistics Reports No. 19, 1, 8 (June 30, 1999) (available at www.cdc.gov/nchs/data/nvsr/nvsr47/nvs47 _19.pdf).

7. National Center for Health Statistics, Births: Final Data for 1998 (2000) (summary available at www.cdc.gov/nchs/releases/oonews/nrbrth98.htm).

8. Admittedly, the use of unadvertised illegal drugs indicates that there would be alcohol and tobacco use, even without advertising. It seems likely, however, that there would be less use.

9. For data and sources, see www.tobaccofreekids.org/research/factsheets/pdf /0002.pdf). These figures were reported as of February 2003. The site's data is updated regularly.

10. Campaign for Alcohol Free Kids, Facts You Should Know, www.alcohol-freekids.com/facts_you_ should_know.html. The Web page cites a March 1997 report by the American Council on Alcohol Problems.

11. 250 U.S. 616 (1919).

12. *Id..* at 630 (Holmes, J., dissenting).

13. Mill's argument will be discussed in slightly more detail in Chapter 1, as will its application to expression by, or aimed toward, children.

14. There should also be constitutional limitations on society's attempts to influence children. The Establishment Clause provides one such limitation in that schools cannot be used to further religion. Chapter 12 will discuss another limitation intended to prevent schools from barring one side of current political

debate in an attempt to assure that the next generation maintains the majority's view on that issue.

15. John Stuart Mill, On Liberty ch. 4 (London, 1859).

16. *Id.* at ch. 5.

17. The attempts to regulate minor access to the Internet will be discussed in Chapter 8.

18. *Violence Chip: Why Does the ACLU Oppose the V-Chip Legislation Currently Pending in Congress?* archive.aclu.org/library/aavchip.html.

19. *Id.*

20. *Popular Music under Siege*, archive.aclu.org/library/pbr3.html.

21. The legislation involved was the Children's Internet Protection Act, enacted as part of Pub.L. No. 106-554 (2000). The constitutional challenge to the act is discussed in Chapter 8.

22. *ALA Applauds Court Ruling on CIPA Decision* (July 27, 2001) (quoting Judith Krug, director of the ALA Office for Intellectual Freedom), www.ala.org/cipa/decision1.html.

23. Marjorie Heins, Not in Front of the Children: "Indecency," Censorship and the Innocence of Youth (New York: Hill and Wang, 2001).

24. *Id.* at 12.

25. *Id.* (footnote omitted) (emphasis in original).

26. These negative effects are discussed in Chapter 2.

27. 393 U.S. 503 (1969).

28. *Id.* at 506.

29. 422 U.S. 205 (1975).

30. *Id.* at 212–13 (citations omitted).

31. These cases, too, are discussed in Chapter 12.

32. 390 U.S. 629 (1968).

33. 422 U.S. at 213.

34. *Id.* at 213–14.

35. 244 F.3d 572 (7th Cir.), *cert. denied*, 122 S.Ct. 462 (2001).

36. *Id.* at 576–77 (emphasis in original).

37. 390 U.S. at 639.

38. *See* Winters v. New York, 333 U.S. 507 (1948).

39. *See, e.g.*, Video Software Dealers Ass'n v. Webster, 968 F.2d 684 (8th Cir. 1992).

NOTES TO CHAPTER I

1. *See, e.g.*, Chaplinsky v. New Hampshire, 315 U.S. 568, 572 (1942).

2. *See, e.g.*, Leonard Levy, Freedom of the Press from Zenger to Jefferson (New York: Bobbs-Merrill, 1996).

3. *Id.* at xxi–xxii.

4. *Id.* at xlix (quoting Sir William Blackstone, Commentaries on the Laws of England (Oxford, 1765–69)).

5. Alexander Meiklejohn, Free Expression and Its Relationship to Self-Government 25 (New York: Harper and Brothers, 1948).

6. *Id.* at 26–27 (emphasis added).

7. Vincent Blasi, *The Checking Value in First Amendment Theory*, 1977 Amer. Bar Found. Res. J. 521, 527.

8. *Id.* at 561–62.

9. Alexander Meiklejohn, *supra* note 5, at 26.

10. *See* John H. Garvey, What Are Freedoms For? 106–11 (Cambridge, MA: Harvard University Press, 1996).

11. Political speech and minors, in the school setting, will be discussed in Chapter 12.

12. *See generally* Franklin E. Zimring, The Changing Legal World of Adolescence (New York: Free Press, 1982).

13. John H. Garvey, *supra* note 10, at 106.

14. Amy Gutmann, Democratic Education (Princeton, NJ: Princeton University Press, 1987).

15. *Id.* at 51 (emphasis in original).

16. *Id.* at 51–53.

17. Suzanna Sherry, *Responsible Republicanism: Educating for Citizenship*, 62 U. Chi. L. Rev. 131, 157 (1995).

18. *Id.* at 190.

19. Stanley Ingber, *Liberty and Authority: Two Facets of the Inculcation of Virtue*, 69 St. John's L. Rev. 421, 440–41 (1995).

20. 333 U.S. 507 (1948).

21. *Id.* at 514.

22. *Id.* at 510.

23. *See* C. Edwin Baker, Human Liberty and Freedom of Speech (New York: Oxford University Press, 1989); C. Edwin Baker, *Scope of the First Amendment Freedom of Speech*, 25 UCLA L. Rev. 964 (1978). Martin Redish goes so far as to assert that this self-realization value is the only true value served by the freedom of expression. The values behind democracy itself are only an outgrowth of the value of self-realization. *See* Martin H. Redish, *The Value of Free Speech*, 130 U. Pa. L. Rev. 591 (1982).

24. C. Edwin Baker, *supra* note 23, at 54.

25. David A. J. Richards, *Free Speech and Obscenity Law: Toward a Moral Theory of the First Amendment*, 123 U. Pa. L. Rev. 45 (1974).

26. *See* John Rawls, A Theory of Justice (Cambridge, MA: Harvard-Belknap, 1971).

27. David A. J. Richards, *supra* note 25, at 62 (emphasis added).

28. John Stuart Mill, On Liberty ch. 4 (London, 1859).

29. *Id.*

30. *Id.* at ch. 5.

31. For example, legislation discussed in Chapter 7 would have prevented the rental of violent videos to minors. The restrictions were on third-party video stores, not on parents themselves renting such videos and allowing their children to view them.

32. David A. J. Richards, *supra* note 25, at 62 (emphasis added).

33. This issue will be discussed in Chapter 4.

34. 250 U.S. 616, 630 (1919) (Holmes, J., dissenting).

35. 274 U.S. 357, 377 (1927) (Brandeis, J., concurring).

36. *See* John Stuart Mill, *supra* note 28, at ch. 5.

37. Thomas I. Emerson, *Toward a General Theory of the First Amendment*, 72 Yale L.J. 877 (1963).

38. *Id.* at 884.

39. *Id.* at 886.

40. *Id.*

41. The issue of how adult speech, in areas touching on manners, may be limited in the presence of children will be discussed in Chapter 10.

42. This issue and limitations on school authority will be discussed in Chapter 12.

43. Lee Bollinger, The Tolerant Society 107 (New York: Oxford University Press, 1986).

44. 315 U.S. 568 (1942).

45. *Id.* at 572.

46. Lee Bollinger, *supra* note 43, at 187.

47. More will be said on this issue in Chapters 9 and 12.

48. Lee Bollinger, *supra* note 43, at 124.

49. *See* Pierce v. Society of Sisters, 268 U.S. 510 (1925); Meyer v. Nebraska, 262 U.S. 390 (1923). States may make school attendance compulsory, but even this has been limited in cases where the education of children has been seen as adequate without school attendance. *See* Yoder v. Wisconsin, 406 U.S. 205 (1972) (holding that the Amish need not send their children to school beyond an elementary education).

NOTES TO CHAPTER 2

1. A. P. Huston, E. Donnerstein, H. Fairchild, N. D. Feshbach, P. A. Katz, J. P. Murray, E. A. Rubinstein, B. Wilcox and D. Zuckerman, Big World, Small Screen: The Role of Television in American Society 53–54 (Lincoln: University of Nebraska Press, 1992).

2. *Id.* at 54.

3. A discussion of the studies on this subject can be found in Chapter 3 of

Kevin W. Saunders, Violence as Obscenity: Limiting the Media's First Amendment Protection (Durham, NC: Duke University Press, 1996).

4. *See* Albert Bandura, Dorothea Ross and Sheila Ross, *Imitation of Film-Mediated Aggressive Models*, 66 J. of Abnormal and Social Psychology 3 (1963).

5. Leonard Berkowitz and Joseph T. Alioto, *The Meaning of an Observed Event as a Determinant of Its Aggressive Consequences*, 28 J. of Personality and Social Psych. 206 (1973).

6. *See* Brandon S. Centerwall, *Television and Violence: The Scale of the Problem and Where to Go from Here*, 267 J. Am. Med. Ass'n 3059 (no. 22, June 10, 1992).

7. Monroe M. Lefkowitz, Leonard D. Eron, Leopold O. Walder and L. Rowell Huesmann, *Television Violence and Child Aggression: A Followup Study* in George Comstock and Eli Rubinstein, editors, Television and Social Behavior: Reports and Papers, Vol. 3: Television and Adolescent Aggressiveness 35 (Washington, DC: U.S. Government Printing Office, 1972).

8. *See, e.g.* , Marcia Pally, Sex and Sensibility: Reflections on Forbidden Mirrors and the Will to Censor (Hopewell, NJ: Ecco Press, 1994).

9. *Joint Statement on the Impact of Entertainment Violence on Children: Congressional Public Health Summit* 1 (2000), available at www.aap.org/advocacy/releases/jstmtevc.htm.

10. Committee on Communications, *Media Violence*, 95 Pediatrics 949 (1995).

11. *Id.*

12. *Testimony of American Association of Pediatrics President Dr. Donald E. Cook before the U.S. Senate Commerce Committee* 2–3 (September 13, 2000). Available at www.aap.org/advocacy/releases/medvioltest.htm.

13. Youth Violence: A Report to the Surgeon General (2001) at App. 4B, available at www.surgeongeneral.gov/library/youthviolence/chapter4/appendix4bsec3.html.

14. *Id.*

15. Brad J. Bushman and Craig A. Anderson, *Media Violence and the American Public: Scientific Fact versus Media Misinformation*, 56 American Psychologist 477, 485 (2001).

16. *Id.*

17. *See* Dave Grossman, On Killing: The Psychological Cost of Learning to Kill in War and Society (New York: Little, Brown and Co., 1995); Dave Grossman and Gloria DeGaetano, Stop Teaching Our Kids to Kill: A Call to Action against TV, Movie and Video Game Violence (New York: Crown Publishers, 1999).

18. Dave Grossman, *supra* note 17, at 251.

19. Dave Grossman and Gloria DeGaetano, *supra* note 17, at 72.

20. Grossman and DeGaetano say that the United States Army's simulator

Multipurpose Arcade Combat Simulator is a modification of the Super Nintendo game Duck Hunt and that the Fire Arms Training Simulator used by many law enforcement agencies is "more or less identical" to the video game Time Crisis. *See id.* at 74.

21. *Id.* at 75–76. It appears from other accounts that there may have been nine shots fired. *See, e.g.* , James Prichard, *Suit Blames Hollywood, Net for Heath Shootings*, Lexington Herald-Leader A1 (April 13, 1999).

22. Dave Grossman, *supra* note 17, at 254.

23. *See* Craig A. Anderson and Karen E. Dill, *Video Games and Aggressive Thoughts, Feelings, and Behavior in the Laboratory and in Life*, 78 J. of Personality and Social Psych. 772 (2000)).

24. *Id.* at 787.

25. *Id.* at 788 (citations omitted).

26. Craig A. Anderson and Brad J. Bushman, *Effects of Violent Video Games on Aggressive Behavior, Aggressive Cognition, Aggressive Affect, Psychological Arousal, and Prosocial Behavior: A Meta-Analytic Review of the Scientific Literature*, 12 Psychological Science 353 (2001).

27. *Id.* at 357.

28. *Id.* (emphasis added).

29. *Id.*

30. *See id.* at 358.

31. *See generally* David Hume, An Enquiry Concerning Human Understanding (London, 1748).

32. *See* Brad J. Bushman and Craig A. Anderson, *supra*, note 15, at 481.

33. Marjorie Heins, Not in Front of the Children: "Indecency," Censorship, and the Innocence of Youth 228 (New York: Hill and Wang, 2001).

34. *See id.* at 229.

35. Sissela Bok, Mayhem: Violence as Public Entertainment 43–44 (Reading, MA: Addison-Wesley, 1998).

36. *Id.* at 43.

37. Obscenity law, the obscenity exception to the First Amendment and arguments against the exception will be discussed in Chapter 6.

38. Catharine MacKinnon, *Pornography as Defamation and Discrimination*, 71 Boston Univ. L. Rev. 793 (1991).

39. *Id.* at 799. The 1986 Attorney General's Commission on Pornography, Attorney General's Commission on Pornography: Final Report 323 (1986), supports this claim. Frederick Schauer, a member of the commission sums up the evidence examined:

> [I]f . . . we are testing only for the relationship between sex and sexual violence, there is *no* causal relationship. . . . But if the sexualization (and not just the sexual explicitness) of the violence is eliminated, the evidence indicates that the strength of the causal relationship dimin-

ishes. Thus, although the studies indicate some relationship between non-sexualized violence and attitudes about sexual violence, or aggressive tendencies toward women, this relationship, in probabilistic terms, becomes stronger when the sexualization is added.

Frederick F. Schauer, *Causation Theory and the Causes of Sexual Violence*, 1987 Am. Bar Found. Res. J. 737, 765 (emphasis in original) (footnotes omitted).

40. Catharine A. MacKinnon, *Pornography, Civil Rights, and Speech*, 20 Harv. Civ. Rts.-Civ. Lib. L. Rev. 1, 18 (1985)).

41. The language, with emphasis added, is from the Indianapolis ordinance inspired by Catharine MacKinnon and Andrea Dworkin. The ordinance was declared unconstitutional in American Booksellers Ass'n v. Hudnut, 771 F.2d 323 (7th Cir. 1985), *aff'd*, 475 U.S. 1001 (1986). The full text of the ordinance can be found there.

42. Nadine Strossen, *A Feminist Critique of "The" Feminist Critique of Pornography*, 79 Va. L. Rev. 1099, 1111–12 (1993).

43. Strossen's views on the positive aspects of even obscene material are discussed in Chapter 6.

44. Nancy L. Buerkel-Rothfus and Jeremiah S. Strouse, *Media Exposure and Perceptions of Sexual Behaviors: The Cultivation Hypothesis Moves to the Bedroom* in Bradley S. Greenberg, Jane D. Brown and Nancy Buerkel-Rothfuss, editors, Media, Sex and the Adolescent 225, 243 (Cresskill, NJ: Hampton Press, 1993).

45. *Id.* at 245.

46. Jeremiah S. Strouse and Nancy L. Buerkel-Rothfus, *Media Exposure and the Sexual Attitudes and Behaviors of College Students* in Bradley S. Greenberg, Jane D. Brown and Nancy Buerkel-Rothfuss, *supra* note 44, at 277, 290.

47. Nancy L. Buerkel-Rothfus and Jeremiah S. Strouse, *supra* note 44, at 226.

48. *See* Lloyd D. Johnson, Patrick M. O'Malley and Jerald G. Bachman, National Survey Results on Drug Use from the Monitoring of the Future Study, 1975–2000, Vol. 1: Secondary School Students 22 (Bethesda, MD: National Institutes of Health, 2001).

49. *See id.*

50. *See* Elizabeth M. Ozer, Claire D. Brindis, Susan G. Millstein, David K. Knopf and Charles E. Irwin, Jr., America's Adolescents: Are They Healthy? 22 (San Francisco: National Adolescent Health Information Center, 1997).

51. Commercial speech and its legal treatment will be discussed in Chapter 11.

52. *See, e.g.* , T. N. Robinson, H. L. Chen and J. D. Killen, *Television and Music Video Exposure and Risk of Adolescent Alcohol Use*, 102 Pediatrics 1 (1998); R. G. Rychtarik, J. A. Fairbank, C. M. Allen, D. W. Fox and R. S. Drabman, *Alcohol Use in Television Programming: Effects on Children's Behavior,*

8(1) Addictive Behaviors 19 (1993); J. B. Kotch, M. L. Coulter and A. Lipsitz, *Does Televised Drinking Influence Children's Attitudes Toward Alcohol?* 11(1) Addictive Behaviors 67 (1986).

53. *See* Peter G. Christenson, Lisa Henriksen and Donald F. Roberts, Substance Use in Popular Prime Time Television (Washington, DC: Office of National Drug Control Policy, 2000); Donald F. Roberts, Lisa Henriksen and Peter G. Christenson, Substance Use in Popular Movies and Music (Washington, DC: Office of National Drug Control Policy, 1999).

54. Peter G. Christenson, Lisa Henriksen and Donald F. Roberts, *supra* note 53, at 17.

55. Donald F. Roberts, Lisa Henriksen and Peter G. Christenson, *supra* note 53, at 17.

56. *Id.* at 26.

57. Peter G. Christenson, Lisa Henriksen and Donald F. Roberts, *supra* note 53, at 19.

58. *Id.* at 28.

59. *Id.*

60. *Id.*

61. Donald F. Roberts, Lisa Henriksen and Peter G. Christenson, *supra* note 53, at 35.

62. *Id.*

63. *Id.* at 36 (only 13 percent of use by minors involved consequences).

64. *See* Allan Korn, *Leave Prescribing to the Doctors, Not Advertising,* Newsweek 65 (Nov. 15, 1999).

65. *Id.*

66. 403 U.S. 15 (1971).

67. *Id.* at 25.

68. 438 U.S. 726 (1978).

69. For discussions of the costs of hate speech, *see, e.g.* , Richard Delgado, *Words That Wound: A Tort Action for Racial Insults, Epithets, and Name-Calling,* 17 Harv. Civ. Rts.-Civ. Lib. L. Rev. 133 (1982); Patricia Williams, *Spirit-Murdering the Messenger: The Discourse of Fingerpointing as the Law's Response to Racism,* 42 U. Miami L. Rev. 127 (1987); Mari J. Matsuda, *Public Response to Racist Speech: Considering the Victim's Story,* 87 Mich. L. Rev. 2320 (1989); Charles R. Lawrence, III, *If He Hollers Let Him Go: Regulating Racist Speech on Campus,* 1990 Duke L.J. 431.

70. Richard Delgado, *Are Hate-Speech Rules Constitutional Heresy? A Reply to Steven Gey,* 146 U. Pa. L. Rev. 865, 869–70 (1998) (footnotes omitted).

71. Matsuda, *supra* note 69, at 2236–37 (footnotes omitted).

72. *See* Delgado, *supra* note 70, at 868.

73. *See* the Anti-Defamation League's website, www.adl.org.

74. *See id.*

75. *See id.*
76. *Id.*
77. *Id.*
78. *Id.*
79. 376 U.S. 254 (1964).
80. 388 U.S. 130 (1967).
81. 485 U.S. 46 (1988).
82. For a discussion of the case and the events leading to it, *see* Rodney A. Smolla, Jerry Falwell v. Larry Flynt (New York: St. Martin's Press, 1990).
83. 485 U.S. at 54.
84. *See* Delgado, *supra* note 70, at 874.
85. While there are experiments that indicate college-aged students become more aggressive after viewing violent materials, *see supra* note 5, it is children in their formative years that are the major concern.
86. 773 F.Supp. 1275 (W.D. Mo. 1991), *aff'd*, 968 F.2d 684 (8th Cir. 1992).

NOTES TO CHAPTER 3

1. Zechariah Chafee, Jr., Free Speech in the United States (Cambridge, MA: Harvard University Press, 1941).
2. *Id.* at 33.
3. *Id.*
4. Alexander Meiklejohn, Free Speech: and Its Relation to Self-Government (New York: Harper Brothers, 1948).
5. *Id.* at 62–63.
6. *Id.* at 63.
7. Zechariah Chafee, Jr., Book Review, 62 Harv. L. Rev. 891 (1949) (reviewing Alexander Meiklejohn, Free Speech: and Its Relation to Self-Government (1948)).
8. *Id.* at 900.
9. *See* Alexander Meiklejohn, *The First Amendment Is an Absolute*, 1961 Sup. Ct. Rev. 245, 255.
10. *Id.* at 256.
11. *Id.* at 263.
12. Whatever Meiklejohn may have intended or have come later to conclude, commentators have assigned that position to him. *See, e.g.* , Harry Kalven, *Metaphysics of the Law of Obscenity*, 1960 Sup. Ct. Rev. 1, 15–16.
13. The positions of Meiklejohn and Blasi on the purpose of the First Amendment are discussed in Chapter 1.
14. *See* Vincent Blasi, *The Pathological Perspective and the First Amendment*, 85 Colum. L. Rev. 449 (1985).
15. *Id.* at 456–57.

16. *Id.* at 463.

17. *Id.* at 467.

18. *Id.* at 477.

19. *Id.* at 478.

20. Obscenity is considered more fully in Chapter 6.

21. This issue will be discussed in Chapter 6.

22. *See* Consolidated Edison Co. v. Public Service Commission, 447 U.S. 530 (1980) (protecting the insertion of pro-nuclear power materials with electric bills).

23. Amitai Etzioni, The New Golden Rule: Community and Morality in a Democratic Society xviii (New York: Basic Books, 1996).

24. *Id.*

25. Mary Ann Glendon, Rights Talk: The Impoverishment of Political Discourse 14 (New York: Free Press, 1991).

26. Etzioni, *supra* note 23, at xix–xx (emphasis in original).

27. *Id.* at 13, 16.

28. *Id.* at 52.

29. *Id.* at 13 (emphasis in original).

30. *Id.* at 17.

31. Amitai Etzioni, The Spirit of Community: Rights, Responsibilities and the Communitarian Agenda 263 (New York: Crown Publishers, 1993) (emphasis in original).

32. Hate speech will be discussed in Chapter 11.

33. Richard Delgado, *Are Hate-Speech Rules Constitutional Heresy?* 146 U. Pa. L. Rev. 865, 878 (1998).

34. Richard Delgado and Jean Stefancic, *Hateful Speech, Loving Communities: Why Our Notion of "A Just Community" Changes So Slowly*, 82 Calif. L. Rev. 851, 856 (1994).

35. Mari J. Matsuda, *Public Response to Racist Speech: Considering the Victim's Story*, 87 Mich. L. Rev. 2320, 2357 (1989).

36. *Id.*

37. Other articles considered ground breaking in the area of racist speech include Richard Delgado, *Words That Wound: A Tort Action for Racial Insults, Epithets, and Name-Calling*, 17 Harv. Civ. Rts.-Civ. Lib. L. Rev. 133 (1982); Charles R. Lawrence III, *If He Hollers Let Him Go: Regulating Racist Speech on Campus*, 1990 Duke L.J. 431.

38. 771 F.2d 323 (7th Cir. 1985), *aff'd* 475 U.S. 1001 (1986).

39. The ordinance is most easily found in *Hudnut*, 771 F.2d at 324 (quoting Indianapolis Code sec. 16-3(q)).

40. *See* Caryn Jacobs, *Patterns of Violence: A Feminist Perspective on the Regulation of Pornography*, 7 Harv. Women's L.J. 5, 23 (1984). *See also* Andrea Dworkin, *Against the Male Flood: Censorship, Pornography, and Equal-*

ity, 8 Harv. Women's L.J. 1, 9 (1985) ("The insult pornography offers, invariably, to sex is accomplished in the active subordination of women: the creation of a sexual dynamic in which the putting down of women, the suppression of women, and ultimately the brutalization of women, *is* what sex is taken to be").

41. 771 F.2d at 325.

42. Catharine MacKinnon, *Pornography as Defamation and Discrimination*, 71 Boston Univ. L. Rev. 793, 802 (1991).

43. *Id.* at 800.

44. 771 F.2d at 329.

45. Robert P. George, Making Men Moral: Civil Liberties and Public Morality 1 (Oxford: Clarendon Press, 1993).

46. *Id.* at 1, 45.

47. *Id.* at 45.

48. *Id.* at 47.

49. *Id.* at 71.

50. *Id.* at 99.

51. *Id.*

52. *Id.* at 100 (emphasis in original).

53. John H. Garvey, What Are Freedoms For? 1–2 (Cambridge, MA: Harvard University Press, 1996).

54. *Id.* at 58.

55. 394 U.S. 557 (1969).

56. *Id.* at 565.

57. *Id.* at 566.

58. The issue of intergenerational value transmission will be discussed in Chapter 4.

NOTES TO CHAPTER 4

1. For a general discussion of the moral development of youth, *see, e.g.* , Danuta Bukatko and Marvin W. Daehler, Child Development: A Topical Approach 535–73 (Boston: Houghton Mifflin, 1992).

2. *Id.* at 536.

3. *Id.*

4. *Id.* at 537.

5. *Id.* at 537–38.

6. *Id.*

7. *Id.* at 539 (citing L. I. Rosenkoetter, *Resistance to Temptation: Inhibitory and Disinhibitory Effects of Models*, 8 Developmental Psychology 80 (1973).

8. *Id.* at 536.

9. *See* Jean Piaget, The Moral Judgment of the Child (London: Routledge

and Kegan Paul, 1932). Piaget's work is discussed in Danuta Bukatko and Marvin W. Daehler, *supra* note 1.

10. Danuta Butkatko and Marvin W. Daehler, *supra* note 1, at 541–42.

11. *Id.* at 542.

12. *See, e.g.* , Lawrence Kohlberg, *Stage and Sequence: The Cognitive-Developmental Approach to Socialization* in D. A. Goslin, editor, The Handbook of Socialization Theory and Research (Chicago: Rand McNally, 1969); Lawrence Kohlberg, *Moral Stages and Moralization: The Cognitive Developmental Approach* in T. Lickona, editor, Moral Development and Moral Behavior: Theory, Research, and Social Issues (New York: Holt, Rinehart and Winston, 1976); Lawrence Kohlberg, Essays on Moral Development, Vol. 2: The Psychology of Moral Development (San Francisco: Harper and Row, 1984).

13. A discussion of these stages may be found in Danuta Butkatko and Marvin W. Daehler, *supra* note 1, at 544–46.

14. *Id.* at 545.

15. Carol Gilligan criticizes Kohlberg for developing a male-centered theory and has offered her own examination of the differing stages of the moral development of girls. *See* Carol Gilligan, In a Different Voice: Psychological Theory and Women's Development (Cambridge, MA: Harvard University Press, 1982).

16. The primary sources on these changes consist of magnetic resonance imaging and positron emission tomography studies of the brains of children and young adults at various ages and seem largely incomprehensible to the lay person. Textbook secondary sources have yet to develop fully, but news accounts can be found in various places. *See, e.g.* , Sharon Begley, *Getting inside a Teen Brain*, Newsweek 58 (Feb. 28, 2000); Shankar Vedantarn, *Are Teens Just Wired That Way? Researchers Theorize Brain Changes Are Linked to Behavior*, Washington Post A01 (June 3, 2001); Mara Rose Williams, *Science Finds Neurological Clue to Teen Irresponsibility*, Philadelphia Inquirer A36 (Nov. 24, 2000).

17. 262 U.S. 390 (1923).

18. *Id.* at 400.

19. 268 U.S. 510 (1925).

20. *Id.* at 535.

21. 406 U.S. 205 (1972).

22. *Id.* at 232.

23. 390 U.S. 629 (1968).

24. The issues of variable obscenity and obscenity as to children, along with a more detailed discussion of *Ginsberg*, will be found in Chapter 6.

25. 390 U.S. at 629 n.7.

26. *Id.* (quoting Louis Henkin, *Morals and the Constitution: The Sin of Obscenity*, 63 Colum. L. Rev. 391, 413 n.68 (1963)).

27. 390 U.S. at 640 (quoting People v. Kahan, 206 N.E.2d 333, 334 (N.Y. 1965) (Fuld, J., concurring)).

28. The Communications Decency Act of 1996, Title V of the Telecommunications Act of 1996, Pub.L. No. 104-104, 110 Stat. 56.

29. 521 U.S. 844 (1997).

30. *Id.* at 865 (quoting *Ginsberg*, 390 U.S. at 639).

31. 268 U.S. at 535.

32. The quote may be found in various places, including www.rit.edu /~andpph/text_quotations.html.

33. This quote may be found at www.wandererforum.org/publications /focus034.html.

34. The quote may be found in a number of places, including www.nea.org /columns/BC970216.html.

35. Again, there are a number of sources for the quote, including www.geocities.com/notablequotables1/VIRGIL.html.

36. Amitai Etzioni, The New Golden Rule: Community and Morality in a Democratic Society 93 (New York: Basic Books, 1996).

37. *Id.* at 104–5.

38. *Id.* at 106.

39. *Id.* at 107.

40. The Establishment Clause of the First Amendment prohibits government actions that have the purpose or primary effect of advancing or inhibiting religion or endorse religion. Thus, teaching a particular religion is off limits.

41. Amy Gutmann, Democratic Education 53–54 (Princeton, NJ: Princeton University Press, 1987).

42. Etzioni, *supra* note 36, at 182–83.

43. *Id.* at 183.

44. *Id.* at 184 (footnote omitted). Susan Bitensky also examines the moral development of youth in considering the choice between values clarification and values inculcation in the schools. She too concludes that the schools may inculcate values, at least "if the values transmitted are those which will further the maintenance of a civilized social order and promote democracy . . . because such values transcend the status of debatable values and have effectively become 'ideational prerequisites' to collective human existence." Susan H. Bitensky, *A Contemporary Proposal for Reconciling the Free Speech Clause with Curricular Values Inculcation in the Public Schools*, 70 Notre Dame L. Rev. 769, 773 (1995).

45. Amitai Etzioni, The Spirit of Community: Rights, Responsibilities, and the Communitarian Agenda 91 (New York: Crown Publishers, 1993).

46. The issue of hate speech will be discussed in Chapter 9.

47. Amitai Etzioni, *supra* note 45, at 103.

48. *Id.*

49. Leslea Newman and Diana Souza, Heather Has Two Mommies (Boston: Alyson Wonderland, 1990).

50. *See, e.g.* , George Gerbner and Larry Gross, *Living with Television: The Violence Profile*, 26 J. of Communication 173 (1976); George Gerbner, Larry Gross, Michael Eleey, Marilyn Jackson-Beeck, Suzanne Jeffries-Fox and Nancy Signorielli, *Violence Profile No. 8: The Highlights*, 27 J. of Communication 171 (1977); George Gerbner, Larry Gross, Michael Eleey, Marilyn Jackson-Beeck, Suzanne Jeffries-Fox and Nancy Signorielli, *Cultural Indicators: Violence Profile No. 9*, 28 J. of Communication 176 (1978).

51. A 1982 meta-analysis of the research in the area reached the conclusion that the evidence provided support for the proposition that television influences some aspects of social reality, especially in areas related to violence; *see* R. P. Hawkins and S. Pingree, *Television's Influence on Social Reality* in D. Pearl, L. Bouthilet, and J. Lazar, editors, Television and Behavior: Ten Years of Scientific Progress and Implications for the Eighties 224 (Washington, DC: U.S. Government Printing Office, 1982), although the same meta-analysis also suggested that other variables may also play a role.

52. W. James Potter, *Perceived Reality and the Cultivation Hypothesis*, 30 J. of Broadcasting and Electronic Media 159, 168 (1986).

53. Ronald Slaby, *Combating Television Violence*, The Chronicle of Higher Education sec. 2, p. 1, 1 (Jan. 5, 1994). Dr. Slaby was a member of the American Psychological Association Commission on Youth and Violence.

54. *See* Elayne Rapping, *Make Room for Daddy*, 57 The Progressive no. 11, p. 1 (Nov. 1993).

NOTES TO CHAPTER 5

1. 410 U.S. 113 (1973).

2. 381 U.S. 479 (1965).

3. *See* Planned Parenthood v. Danforth, 428 U.S. 52 (1976). The Court also, in that case, struck down another provision of the same statute that required the written consent of a married woman's spouse for her to obtain an abortion.

4. *See* Planned Parenthood v. Casey, 505 U.S. 833 (1992); Planned Parenthood v. Ashcroft, 462 U.S. 476 (1983); Bellotti v. Baird, 443 U.S. 622 (1979).

5. *See supra* note 3.

6. 405 U.S. 438 (1972).

7. *Id.* at 453.

8. 381 U.S. at 486.

9. 431 U.S. 678 (1977).

10. *Id.* at 715 (Stevens, J., concurring).

11. The decision that changed the nature of the Free Exercise Clause was Employment Division v. Smith, 494 U.S. 872 (1990). The case concerned the denial of unemployment benefits to an individual fired for peyote use. Smith was a member of the Native American Church, which uses peyote as a part of its reli-

gious ceremonies, but the state law did not provide an exception in its criminal law for use within religious ritual. The Court found no violation of the Free Exercise Clause, holding that the clause is not violated by any generally applicable law but only by laws directed at practices because of their religious significance.

12. 321 U.S. 158 (1944).

13. *Id.* at 165.

14. 319 U.S. 624 (1943).

15. 268 U.S. 510 (1925).

16. 321 U.S. at 168.

17. *Id.* at 170.

18. For a discussion of religious-based refusal to accept medical treatment and the cases involving the failure to provide medical treatment for a child based on religious beliefs, *see, e.g.* , Elizabeth A. Lingle, *Treating Children by Faith: Colliding Constitutional Issues*, 17 J. Legal Med. 301 (1996); Anne D. Lederman, *Understanding Faith: When Religious Parents Decline Conventional Medical Treatment for Their Children*, 45 Case W. Res. L. Rev. 891 (1995).

19. 497 U.S. 261 (1990).

20. In John F. Kennedy Memorial Hospital v. Heston, 279 A.2d 670 (N.J. 1971), a twenty-two-year-old woman was severely injured in an automobile accident and needed a life-saving blood transfusion. The patient and her parents were Jehovah's Witnesses, and her mother refused permission. There was conflicting testimony with regard to statements by the patient. She later said that she, too, had refused transfusion, but medical testimony was that, when admitted, she was in shock, disoriented and incoherent. The hospital obtained a court order appointing a guardian, the transfusion was administered and the patient survived.

On appeal, the Supreme Court of New Jersey found no constitutional right to die and decided that such a right did not result from adding a claim of religious belief as motivating the decision to accept death. While stating its position in general terms, the question of the patient's mental state seemed to play a role. The court said, "Complicating the subject of suicide is the difficulty of knowing whether a decision to die is firmly held. . . . Then, too, there is the question whether . . . the person was and continues to be competent (a difficult concept in this area) to choose to die." 279 A.2d at 672.

A transfusion was also ordered in United States v. George, 239 F.Supp. 752 (D. Conn. 1965), involving a Jehovah's Witness patient at a Veterans Administration Hospital. Here, too, there was discussion of the patient's mental state. The court cited psychiatric reports showing "a lack of concern for life, and a somewhat fatalistic attitude about his condition [that] was described as 'a variant of suicide.'" 239 F.Supp. at 753. Most interestingly, the Court described its meeting with the patient, at the hospital, while considering the issuance of an order for a transfusion:

George's first remarks were that he would not agree to be transfused but would in no way resist a court order permitting it, because it would be the Court's will and not his own. His "conscience was clear," and the responsibility for the act was "upon the Court's conscience." . . . George stated he would "in no way" resist the doctors' actions once the court's order was signed.

Id. The patient's wife was portrayed as far more assertive, as being "adamant in her opposition to the transfusions." *Id.* The patient's mother, who was not a Jehovah's Witness, favored the transfusion and testified that the patient had been a member of the sect for only two years. It seemed from the description of the events that the patient would be relieved to have the transfusion ordered, despite his recently adopted beliefs, while his strongly believing wife resisted treatment.

In Application of the President & Directors of Georgetown College, Inc., 331 F.2d 1000 (D.C. Cir. 1964), *cert. denied sub nom* Jones v. President & Directors of Georgetown College, Inc., 377 U.S. 978 (1964), the patient also received a court-ordered transfusion, but it is important to note that she was the mother of minor children. Courts willing to honor a patient's refusal to accept treatment have distinguished *Georgetown* on that basis, arguing that "[t]he State might well have an overriding interest in the welfare of the mother in that situation, for if she expires, the children might become wards of the State." In re Estate Brooks v. Brooks, 205 N.E.2d 435, 440 (Ill. 1965). That also was an important factor in Raleigh Fitkin–Paul Morgan Memorial Hospital v. Anderson, 201 A.2d 537 (N.J. 1964), *cert. denied,* 377 U.S. 985, where the New Jersey Supreme Court ordered a transfusion for a pregnant Jehovah's Witness. The court argued it was necessary to save the life not only of the woman but of the quick fetus.

21. *See, e.g.*, In re Estate Brooks v. Brooks, 205 N.E.2d 435, 440 (Ill. 1965). Brooks, again a Jehovah's Witness needing a transfusion, was married and had two adult children. All were Jehovah's Witnesses. Noting that Mrs. Brooks was a competent adult, had steadfastly maintained her religious opposition to a transfusion and had so notified her physician and hospital and released them from liability, and had no minor children, the Illinois Supreme Court was willing to honor her decision. "Even though we may consider appellant's beliefs unwise, foolish or ridiculous, in the absence of an overriding danger to society we may not permit interference therewith in the form of a conservatorship established in the waning hours of her life for the sole purpose of compelling her to accept medical treatment forbidden by her religious principles." 205 N.E.2d at 442.

22. 321 U.S. at 166–67.

23. 104 N.E.2d 769 (Ill. 1952), *cert. denied,* 344 U.S. 824.

24. 497 A.2d 616 (Pa. Super. Ct. 1985), *cert. denied,* 488 U.S. 817 (1988).

25. *Id.* at 621–22 (footnote omitted).

26. 497 A.2d at 624–25.

27. 808 P.2d 1159 (Wash. App. 1991).

28. *Id.* at 1163.

29. For a discussion, *see* Joan-Margaret Kun, *Rejecting the Adage "Children Should Be Seen and Not Heard"—The Mature Minor Doctrine*, 16 Pace L. Rev. 423 (1996).

30. The strongest case cited, *see id.* , for the recognition of a mature minor rule is In re E.G., 549 N.E.2d 322 (Ill. 1989). A seventeen-year-old Jehovah's Witness with leukemia needed blood transfusions. Neither the patient nor her mother, also a Jehovah's Witness, would consent to the procedure. It appears that E.G. was mature beyond her seventeen and one-half years. The Supreme Court of Illinois recognized a common law right in Illinois law for adults to refuse medical treatment, even when necessary to protect one's life. While the court recognized differences in the legal treatment of adults and minors, it said that "age is not an impenetrable barrier that magically precludes a minor from possessing and exercising certain rights normally associated with adulthood." *Id.* at 324. In fact, the court pointed to several circumstances in which the state legislature had authorized minors to seek and receive medical treatment without the consent of their parents. Because the court resolved the dispute it faced under Illinois common law, it did not address the Free Exercise Clause issue, which of course makes the case less relevant to the issue under consideration here.

Other cases cited for the proposition that there is a mature minor exception are even less convincing. In re Swan, 569 A.2d 1202 (Me. 1990), involved an individual who was roughly seventeen years and four months old when an automobile accident left him in a persistent vegetative state. At the time of the decisions of both the lower and appellate courts, Swan was no longer a minor. The only relevance of Swan's past minority was in the analysis of what his wishes were. Swan's mother and brother both testified that Swan had told them that he did not want to be kept alive by artificial means, if he should ever suffer an injury that made him incapable of existing without such support. While the statements had been made when Swan was still a minor, the court concluded that that fact was "at most a factor to be considered by the fact finder in assessing the seriousness and deliberativeness with which the declarations were made." *Id.* at 1205. There would seem to be a gap between allowing statements made during late minority as to what the wishes of a vegetative adult would be and allowing a minor to make his or her own decisions as to medical treatment necessary to sustain life.

In re Rosebush, 491 N.W.2d 633 (Mich. App. 1992), did not involve a mature minor but a ten and one-half year-old in a persistent vegetative state. Her parents sought to discontinue life support, so the issue was one of parental rights to make the decision. The Michigan Court of Appeals decided that there was a right in Michigan to refuse medical treatment, including life support. That right was not lost because of incompetence or youth of the patient. However, the court said "because minors and other incompetent patients lack the legal capacity to make decisions concerning their medical treatment, someone acting as a surrogate must exercise the right to refuse treatment on their behalf." *Id.* at 636. Thus, the court concluded that the parents had the right to make the decision to withdraw life support for their daughter. The court, then, only weakly recognized a mature minor exception. The holding allowed the parents to make the decision, and the only difference discussed regarding mature minors was in how the parents should make the decision. For the mature minor, the parents should decide based on what they believe the patient would have decided had she been able. For the immature minor, the parents should decide what is in the best interests of the child. But, again, it must be recognized that this was not a choice between normal life and death but rather whether or not to prolong life in a persistent vegetative state.

Another case cited for the mature minor exception is Cardwell v. Bechtol, 724 S.W.2d 739 (Tenn. 1987). This case involved a seventeen-year, seven-month-old girl who visited a physician for treatment of back pain. The physician believed her to be an adult and did not inquire as to parental consent to treatment. When her condition worsened, she sued the physician for malpractice and added a count alleging a technical battery for manipulations performed without parental consent. The Tennessee Supreme Court decided that a mature minor exception to the general rule requiring parental consent for medical treatment to a minor existed as a part of state common law. While the court did recognize the exception, allowing a minor to seek treatment without the physician having to obtain parental consent seems a long way from a rule allowing minors to refuse medical treatment necessary to sustain life.

A last case suggested the wisdom of a mature minor exception but did not so hold and the suggestion was only in dictum. In the Matter of Long Island Jewish Medical Center, 557 N.Y.S. 2d 239 (N.Y. Sup. 1990), involved a minor just seven weeks short of his eighteenth birthday. He was suffering from cancer and had become anemic. His survival required a transfusion, but because the minor, his stepfather and his mother were all Jehovah's Witnesses, none would consent to the transfusion. The court recognized a common-law right for competent adults to refuse medical treatment but held that, when the patient is a minor, the court must act in *parens patriae*, because parents cannot throw away the lives of their children. The court did not recognize a mature minor exception, although the judge did recommend that the appellate courts or the legislature consider establishing such an exception. The court also saw the patient as simply not sufficiently mature for this to be the case for such a recognition.

31. 549 N.E. 2d 322 (Ill. 1989). The case is discussed *supra* note 30.
32. 319 U.S. 624 (1943).
33. 406 U.S. 205 (1972).
34. 403 U.S. 602 (1971).
35. *Id.* at 612–13.
36. *Id.* at 616.

37. 473 U.S. 373 (1985). The holding in this case was overruled but not in a way that distracts from the concern over impressionability of children. *See* Agostini v. Felton, 521 U.S. 203 (1997).

38. *Id.* at 383.

39. *Id.* at 385.

40. Justice O'Connor's test was presented in a concurring opinion in Lynch v. Donnelly, 465 U.S. 668, 688 (1984) (O'Connor, J., concurring).

41. 473 U.S. at 390. There is a lessening in reliance on age and impression in the equal access cases. In Widmar v. Vincent, 454 U.S. 263 (1981), a university policy excluded religious groups from using university facilities that were available to other student groups. The Supreme Court considered the university to have created an open forum for student groups and concluded that the exclusion of student religious groups was unconstitutional, content-based speech discrimination. The university argued that it had to discriminate to avoid problems under the Establishment Clause, but the Court responded that, while the open forum would be of some benefit to religion, it would not have the primary effect of furthering religion. There would be no imprimatur placed on religious practice found in allowing religious groups to participate, along with a variety of other student groups. At least some of this view that an endorsement would not be implied was based on age: "University students are, of course, young adults. They are less impressionable than younger students and should be able to appreciate that the University's policy is one of neutrality toward religion." 454 U.S. at 274 n.14.

This right of access extended to younger students in 1984, when Congress passed the Equal Access Act, requiring that schools that allow extracurricular clubs access to facilities not discriminate against students who wish to conduct meetings on the basis of the religious, political, philosophical speech at those meetings, 20 U.S.C. § 4071. The constitutionality of the act came before the Supreme Court in Board of Education of the Westside Community Schools v. Mergens, 496 U.S. 226 (1990). On the Establishment Clause issue there was no majority opinion. The plurality argued that the logic of *Widmar* applied equally to the Equal Access Act and that Congress had rejected the position that high school students would confuse the accommodation required by the act with state sponsorship of religion.

A concurring opinion expressed continuing concern over influence on school-children. The concurrence determined that the vigilance required in monitoring Establishment Clause compliance in elementary and secondary schools must extend to the effects of equal access. The nature of student clubs at a university, as in *Widmar*, differs from the role they play in a secondary school, and on that basis the concurrence saw a real danger that there could be a perception that the religious club would be seen as a school effort to inculcate religious values. This was seen as requiring that the high school redefine its relationship to the entire club program so as to more fully disassociate itself from the club's religious speech.

More recently, in Good News Club v. Milford Central School, 533 U.S. 98 (2001), the Court found no Establishment Clause problem in a public elementary school allowing a Christian organization to use school rooms for student meetings outside school hours. The meetings were not sponsored by the school. Despite their younger age, elementary-school children were seen as unlikely to assume state endorsement. Even here, however, the Court noted that the meetings would not take place in an elementary classroom.

42. 463 U.S. 783 (1983).

43. 505 U.S. 577 (1992).

44. *Id.* at 597.

45. *Id.* at 593.

46. 120 S.Ct. 2266 (2000).

47. 442 U.S. 584 (1979).

48. *Id.* at 627 (Brennan, J., dissenting).

49. *Id.*

50. *See* Matthews v. Eldridge, 424 U.S. 319, 335 (1976).

51. 442 U.S. at 600.

52. The law does not afford minors lesser procedural rights in all contexts. In cases adjudicating whether or not a minor is a juvenile delinquent, the Supreme Court has required levels of due process that are similar to those for adult criminal determinations. In re Gault, 387 U.S. 1 (1967), did not hold that precisely the same procedures were required but did hold that the essentials of due process and fairness must be provided. The minor must be notified of the charges he or she was facing, has the right to be represented, the right to confront and examine witnesses and must be afforded the privilege against self-incrimination. In re Winship, 397 U.S. 358 (1970), added that proof beyond a reasonable doubt, rather than by a preponderance, was also required in such proceedings. The lesson to be drawn from these cases is, however, not contrary to the position argued for here. Rather, the point is that, when society decides to treat the minor as an adult for purposes of punishment for acts that are considered crimes when committed by adults, society must provide procedural protections similar to those granted adults.

53. For a discussion of the varying positions, *see* Glenn Harlan Reynolds, *A Critical Guide to the Second Amendment*, 62 Tenn. L. Rev. 461 (1995); Don B. Kates, Jr., *Handgun Prohibition and the Original Meaning of the Second Amendment*, 82 Mich. L. Rev. 204 (1983).

54. Kates, *supra* note 53, at 209–10.

55. *See* Reynolds, *supra* note 53, at 478.

56. *Id.*

57. 469 U.S. 325 (1985).

58. *Id.* at 336–37.

59. *Id.* at 340.

60. *Id.* at 341–42 (footnotes omitted).

NOTES TO CHAPTER 6

1. 354 U.S. 476 (1957).

2. *See id.* at 482 n.12.

3. *See id.* at 483.

4. *Id.* at 487.

5. *Id.* at 487 n.20 (quoting Webster's New International Dictionary (Unabridged, 2d ed. 1949)).

6. *Id.* at 487 n.20 (quoting A.L.I. Model Penal Code, § 207.10(2) (Tent. Draft No. 6, 1957)).

7. 413 U.S. 15 (1973).

8. *Id.* at 24 (citations omitted).

9. *See* Jacobellis v. Ohio, 378 U.S. 184, 197 (1964).

10. *See, e.g.* , Hamling v. United States, 418 U.S. 87, 123–24 (1974).

11. 383 U.S. 502 (1966).

12. *Id.* at 505.

13. *Id.* at 508 (footnote omitted).

14. *Id.*

15. (1868) L.R. 3 Q.B. 360, *cited in* 383 U.S. 502, 509.

16. 383 U.S. at 509 (footnote omitted).

17. *Id.* at 509–10.

18. William Lockhart and Robert McClure, *Censorship of Obscenity: The Developing Constitutional Standards,* 45 Minn. L. Rev. 5 (1960).

19. 390 U.S. 629 (1968).

20. *See id.* at 647, app. A (quoting N.Y. Penal Law § 484–h(2)).

21. *See id.* at 646, app. A (quoting N.Y. Penal Law § 484–h(1) (f)).

22. *See id.* at 645, app. A (quoting N.Y. Penal Law § 484–h(1) (b)).

23. *See id.* at 646, app. A (quoting N.Y. Penal Law § 484–h(1) (c)).

24. *See id.* at 645, app. A (quoting N.Y. Penal Law § 484–h(1) (d) & (e)).

25. *See id.* at 647 (app. B).

26. *Id.* at 633.

27. *Id.* at 636 n.4 (quoting Lockhart and McClure, *supra* note 18, at 85).

28. *Id.* at 636.

29. *Id.* at 637. The Court noted a number of judicial opinions and academic articles arguing for laws aimed specifically at protecting minors from pornographic material. *See id.* at 637 n.5 (citing Jacobellis v. State of Ohio, 378 U.S. 184, 195 (1964) (opinion of Brennan and Goldberg, JJ.); *id.* at 201 (Burger, C.J., dissenting); Ginzberg v. United States, 383 U.S. 463, 498, n. 1 (1966) (Stewart,

J., dissenting); Interstate Circuit, Inc. v. City of Dallas, 366 F.2d 590, 593 (5th Cir. 1966); In re Louisiana News Co. v. Dayries, D.C., 187 F. Supp. 241, 247 (E.D. La. 1960); United States v. Levine, 83 F.2d 156 (2d Cir. 1936); United States v. Dennett, 39 F.2d 564 (2d Cir. 1930), 76 A.L.R. 1092; Richard H. Kuh, *Foolish Figleaves?* 258–60 (New York: Macmillan, 1967); Thomas I. Emerson, *Toward a General Theory of the First Amendment*, 72 Yale L.J. 877, 939 (1963); Albert B. Gerber, *A Suggested Solution to the Riddle of Obscenity*, 112 U. Pa. L. Rev. 834, 848 (1964); Louis Henkin, *Morals and the Constitution: The Sin of Obscenity*, 63 Colum. L. Rev. 391, 413, n.68 (1963); Harry Kalven, Jr., *The Metaphysics of the Law of Obscenity*, 1960 Sup. Ct. Rev. 1, 7; C. Peter Magrath, *The Obscenity Cases: Grapes of Rosh*, 1966 Sup. Ct. Rev. 7, 75).

30. *Id.* at 639 n.6 (quoting Thomas I. Emerson, *supra* note 29, at 938–39).

31. *Id.* at 639 n.7 (quoting Louis Henkin, *supra* note 29, at 413 n.68).

32. *Id.* at 640 (quoting People v. Kahan, 206 N.E. 2d 333, 334 (N.Y. 1965) (Fuld, J., concurring)).

33. *Id.* at 641 (quoting N.Y. Penal Law § 484-e).

34. *See id.* at 642–43.

35. 438 U.S. 726 (1978).

36. *See* Butler v. Michigan, 352 U.S. 380 (1957).

37. 438 U.S. at 750 n.28.

38. 529 U.S. 803 (2000). This case is also discussed in Chapters 8 and 11.

39. Cass Sunstein, Democracy and the Problem of Free Speech 210 (New York: Free Press, 1993).

40. 413 U.S. at 32.

41. Edward de Grazia, Girls Lean Back Everywhere: The Law of Obscenity and the Assault on Genius (New York: Vintage, 1992).

42. *Id.* at 6–7. De Grazia also notes a factor in common between the English and American prosecutions in that both were against the works of foreigners.

43. *Id.* at 40–53.

44. *Id.* at 7–39.

45. *See* United States v. One Book Entitled Ulysses by James Joyce, 72 F.2d 705 (2d Cir. 1934).

46. Edward de Grazia, *supra* note 41, at 30.

47. *See* Southeastern Productions v. Atlanta, 334 F. Supp. 634 (N.D. Ga. 1971); Southeastern Productions v. Charlotte, 333 F. Supp. 345 (W.D. N.C. 1971).

48. *See* Southeastern Productions v. Conrad, 341 F. Supp. 465 (E.D. Tenn. 1972), *rev'd*, 420 U.S. 546 (1975).

49. Southeastern Productions v. Conrad, 420 U.S. 546 (1975).

50. *See* Rex v. Wilkes, 4 Burr. 2527 (K.B. 1770).

51. *See, e.g.* , Leo M. Alpert, *Judicial Censorship of Obscene Literature*, 52 Harv. L. Rev. 40, 44 (1938).

52. The description of events is drawn from a series of newspaper articles in the Cincinnati Post, *see* Jerry Stein, *Community Is Still Divided on Mapplethorpe Issues*, Cincinnati Post 6B (April 16, 1991); *Arts Debate Picks Up Steam: "Free Expression" Argued beyond CAC*, Cincinnati Post 1A (Oct. 12, 1990); Lisa Popyk, *CAC Verdict Won't Stop "Anti-Porn Force*, Cincinnati Post 4A (Oct. 9, 1990).

53. H. Montgomery Hyde, A History of Pornography 65 (New York: Farrar, Straus and Giroux, 1964).

54. *See id.* at 71, 153.

55. *See id. See also* David Loth, The Erotic in Literature 65–66 (New York: Julian Messner, 1961).

56. Lynn Hunt, editor, The Invention of Pornography: Obscenity and the Origins of Modernity, 1500–1800 (New York: Zone Books, 1993).

57. *Id.* at 31.

58. *Id.* at 35.

59. 485 U.S. 46 (1988). For a description of the case and the incidents leading to it, see Rodney Smolla, Jerry Falwell v. Larry Flynt: The First Amendment on Trial (New York: St. Martin's Press, 1990).

60. Nadine Strossen, Defending Pornography: Free Speech, Sex, and the Fight for Women's Rights 163 (New York: Scribner, 1995).

61. *Id.* at 164–65 (emphasis added).

62. *See, e.g.*, Frederick A. Schauer, Free Speech: A Philosophical Inquiry 181 (New York: Cambridge University Press, 1982). Schauer's discussion is of very hard-core material.

63. Edward de Grazia, *supra* note 41, at 138 (quoting the District Attorney) (emphasis in de Grazia).

64. *Id.* (quoting the Supreme Judicial Court of Massachusetts).

65. It should be remembered that the statute in *Ginsberg* did not prohibit the parental provision of sexually explicit material and that such a prohibition is not the position taken here. The parental decision is protected by laws that prevent others from directly providing such material to children while not prohibiting parents from taking a more open view than may be present in the majority of the population.

66. *Paris Adult Theater I v. Slaton*, 413 U.S. at 47–48 (Brennan, J., dissenting).

67. Thomas G. Krattenmaker and L. A. Powe, Jr., *Televised Violence: First Amendment Principles and Social Science Theory*, 64 Va. L. Rev. 1123 (1978).

68. It is possible that an extreme case of exposing one's own children to sexual images—presumable images that would currently be obscene for adult use—could play a role in determining that parents are unfit, if it would do so under current law. That does not speak against the changes argued for here, since adult rights, including those of parents, would be stronger or just as strong as they are now.

NOTES TO CHAPTER 7

1. Descriptions of the events at Heath High School are available from a wide variety of news sources. *See, e.g.* , James Prichard, *Suit Blames Hollywood, Net for Heath Shootings*, Lexington Herald-Leader A1 (April 13, 1999).

2. Another source states that only eight shots were fired. *See* Dave Grossman and Gloria DeGaetano, Stop Teaching Our Kids to Kill: A Call to Action against TV, Movie and Video Game Violence 76 (New York: Crown Publishers, 1999).

3. The Colombine events were widely covered in the news. *See, e.g.* , Kevin Simpson, *Slain Teacher's Family Sues to Limit Media Violence: "Doom" Video Game Spurs Separate Warning from Injured Teen's Dad*, Denver Post B 05 (April 22, 2001).

4. H. Rep. No. 186, 106th Cong., 1st Sess. 62–63 (1999).

5. *Id.* at 63.

6. 390 U.S. 629 (1966).

7. 413 U.S. 15 (1973).

8. 481 U.S. 497 (1987).

9. 145 Cong. Rec. H4401 (1999).

10. *Id.* at H4403.

11. *Id.* at H4404.

12. *See, e.g., id.* at H4404 (comments of Representative Berman); H4410 (comments of Representative Barr).

13. *Id.* at H4414.

14. 968 F.2d 684 (8th Cir. 1992).

15. 773 F. Supp. 1275 (W.D. Mo. 1991), *aff'd*, 968 F.2d 684 (8th Cir. 1992).

16. The distinction between violent material and obscenity was also drawn in a recent Seventh Circuit case, American Amusement Machines Ass'n v. Kendrick, 244 F.3d 572 (7th Cir.), *cert. denied*, 122 S. Ct. 462 (2001). The federal district court had refused to enjoin the enforcement of an ordinance limiting violent video game play by minors without parental permission and came to its conclusion based on a belief that the games were obscene as to children. The Seventh Circuit rejected that position and ordered an injunction.

17. *See* Kevin W. Saunders, Violence as Obscenity: Limiting the Media's First Amendment Protection (Durham, NC: Duke University Press, 1996).

18. 333 U.S. 507 (1948).

19. *Id.* at 520.

20. 403 U.S. 15 (1971).

21. Joel Feinberg, The Moral Limits of the Criminal Law (New York: Oxford University Press, 1985).

22. *Id.* at 115.

23. Harry Clor, Obscenity and Public Morality 225 (Chicago: University of Chicago Press, 1969).

24. *Id.* at 234.

25. *Id.* at 225–26.

26. For a more extensive discussion of the treatment of sex and violence in drama, *see* Kevin W. Saunders, *supra* note 17, at 70–80.

27. *See* Cynthia A. Freeland, The Naked and the Undead: Evil and the Appeal of Horror 5, 183 (Boulder, CO: Westview Press, 2000). Catharsis and the issue of whether the theory is relevant to modern depictions of violence are discussed in Chapter 2.

28. *See* Richard C. Beacham, The Roman Theatre and Its Audience 136 (Cambridge, MA: Harvard University Press, 1991).

29. *See* Sheldon Cheney, The Theatre: Three Thousand Years of Drama, Acting and Stagecraft 103–4 (4th ed.) (New York: McKay, 1972).

30. In *Titus Andronicus* the worst of the violence is off stage. Lavinia is raped, and her hands are cut off and her tongue is cut out. The violence against her is described, and she appears on stage with bleeding mouth and bloody stumps where her hands were, but Shakespeare chose not to show the violence.

31. Jonas Baras, *Shakespearean Violence: A Preliminary Study* in James Redmond, editor, Violence in Drama 101, 102 (New York: Cambridge University Press, 1991). There are, however, Shakespearean killings where this equality and flavor of trial by combat are lacking. The smothering of Desdemona by Othello and the blinding of Gloucester in *King Lear* provide such examples.

32. *See* Eberhard and Phyllis Kronhausen, Pornography and the Law 66–67 (New York: Ballantine Books, 1964).

33. *See id.*

34. 354 U.S. 476 (1957).

35. *Id.* at 483.

36. The cases and statutes are discussed in Kevin W. Saunders, *supra* note 17, at 98–104.

37. Frederick F. Schauer, The Law of Obscenity 7 (Washington, DC: Bureau of National Affairs, 1976).

38. 161 U.S. 446 (1896).

39. Frederick F. Schauer, *supra* note 37, at 19.

40. 1884 N.Y. Laws 464–65.

41. *See* Kevin W. Saunders, *supra* note 17, at 114–17.

42. The statutes are discussed *id.* at 111–19.

43. Vincent Blasi, *The Checking Value in First Amendment Theory*, 1977 Am. Bar Found. Res. J., 521, 527.

44. *See* Alexander Meiklejohn, Free Speech and Its Relation to Self-Government (New York: Harper and Brothers, 1948).

45. Frederick F. Schauer, Free Speech: A Philosophical Inquiry 181 (New York: Cambridge University Press, 1982).

46. For a consideration of other justifications for the obscenity exception and

the extension of those justifications, see Kevin W. Saunders, *supra* note 17, at 135–60.

47. 438 U.S. 726 (1978).

48. *See* Thomas G. Krattenmaker and L. A. Powe, Jr., *Televised Violence: First Amendment Principles and Social Science Theory*, 64 Va. L. Rev. 1123 (1978).

49. *Pope* considered the standard for judging the "serious literary, artistic, political or scientific value" prong of the *Miller* test. The Court held that the test was not one of community standards but instead asked "whether a reasonable person would find such value in the material, taken as a whole." 481 U.S. at 501.

50. For a suggested violent obscenity statute, see Kevin W. Saunders, *supra* note 17, at 185–90.

51. 773 F. Supp. 1275 (W.D. Mo. 1991), *aff'd*, 968 F.2d 684 (8th Cir. 1992).

52. 390 U.S. at 641 (quoting N.Y. Penal Law sec. 484-e).

53. *Id.* at 641.

54. *Id.* at 643 (quoting Noble State Bank v. Haskell, 219 U.S. 104, 110 (1911)).

NOTES TO CHAPTER 8

1. *See* Shea v. Reno, 930 F.Supp. 916, 931 (S.D.N.Y. 1996), *aff'd*, 521 U.S. 1113 (1997).

2. 930 F. Supp. at 931.

3. *See id.* at 932.

4. *See* American Civil Liberties Union v. Reno, 929 F. Supp. 824, 842 (E.D. Pa. 1996), *aff'd*, 521 U.S. 844 (1997).

5. Some programs may, at some point, have the ability to examine combinations of skin tones in graphic files to make artificial intelligence guesses as to the sexual content of the picture involved, but an effective program would appear to be in the somewhat distant future. Furthermore, such programs would not be able to make the offensiveness, prurience or value judgments required in determining whether or not material is harmful to minors.

6. 352 U.S. 380 (1957).

7. *Id.* at 381 (quoting Michigan Penal Code, Comp.Laws Supp.1954, § 750.343 (1954)).

8. 390 U.S. 629 (1968).

9. 352 U.S. at 383.

10. *Id.*

11. Pub.L. No. 104-104, 110 Stat. 56. The Communications Decency Act is Title V of the Telecommunications Act. It is found at section 502, 110 Stat. at 133–35.

12. *Id.*

13. *Id.*

14. 929 F. Supp. at 829–30 (quoting 47 U.S.C. § 223(e)).

15. 521 U.S. 844 (1997).

16. 438 U.S. 726 (1978).

17. 475 U.S. 41 (1986) (allowing zoning of adult entertainment to alleviate concerns over crime that may be more prevalent in an adult entertainment district).

18. 521 U.S. at 886 (O'Connor, J., concurring in part and dissenting in part).

19. *See* American Civil Liberties Union v. Reno, 31 F. Supp. 2d 473, 477 (E.D. Pa. 1999), *aff'd,* 217 F.3d 162 (2000), *rev'd,* 535 U.S. 564 (2002). The language quoted was to be codified as 47 U.S.C. § 231.

20. 47 U.S.C. § 231(e) (2).

21. 47 U.S.C. § 231(e) (6).

22. 47 U.S.C. § 231(c) (1).

23. 31 F. Supp. 2d 473 (E.D. Pa. 1999), *aff'd,* 217 F.3d 162 (2000), *rev'd,* 535 U.S. 564 (2002).

24. The first decision is American Civil Liberties Union v. Reno, 217 F.3d 162 (3d Cir. 2000), *rev'd,* 535 U.S. 564 (2002). After remand the case was heard as American Civil Liberties Union v. Ashcroft 322 F.3d 240 (3d Cir. 2003).

25. Ashcroft v. American Civil Liberties Union, 535 U.S. 564, 122 S.Ct. 1700 (2002).

26. 122 S.Ct. at 1712.

27. Pub. L. 106–554 (2000).

28. American Library Ass'n, Inc. v. United States, 201 F. Supp. 2d 401 (E.D. Pa.). The decision was recently reversed by the Supreme Court on June 23, 2003, as case no. 02-361.

29. Pub. L. 107–317 (2002).

30. Alternatively, Congress could decide to require only that software used to publish or post contain the requirements suggested herein and allow parents to decide whether or not to purchase and use software designed to screen out material containing the PICS signal.

31. This is, of course, technically connecting through a link, since the list that results from a search is a list of links. It would seem to be unreasonable, however, to require that those constructing search engines and providing browser services have examined every page to which they provide a link.

32. *See* Miller v. California, 413 U.S. 15, 31 (1973).

NOTES TO CHAPTER 9

1. Richard Rodgers and Oscar Hammerstein, *You Have to Be Careful Taught,* South Pacific (1949).

2. Declaration of War (Resistance Records 1992). The lyrics can be found on the group's Website, www.RaHoWa.com/rahowa/rahowa.

3. 343 U.S. 250 (1952).

4. *Id.* at 251 (quoting § 224a of Division 1 of the Illinois Criminal Code, Ill.Rev.Stat.1949, c. 38, § 471).

5. *Id.* at 252.

6. *Id.* at 258.

7. *Id.* at 259.

8. *Id.* at 261.

9. *Id.* at 257 (quoting Cantwell v. Connecticut, 310 U.S. 296, 309–10 (1940)).

10. 505 U.S. 377 (1992).

11. *Id.* at 380 (quoting St. Paul Bias-Motivated Crime Ordinance, St. Paul, Minn., Legis.Code § 292.02 (1990))

12. *Id.* at 380 (quoting In re Welfare of R.A.V., 464 N.W.2d 507, 510 (Minn. 1991)).

13. Chaplinsky v. New Hampshire, 315 U.S. 568, 573 (1942) (quoting State v. Brown, 38 A. 731 (N.H. 1895); State v. McConnell, 47 A. 267 (N.H. 1900)).

14. 505 U.S. at 381 (quoting 464 N.W.2d at 511).

15. *Id.* at 381.

16. *Id.* at 383–84 (emphasis omitted).

17. *Id.* at 391.

18. *Id.* at 391–92.

19. *Id.* at 389.

20. *Id.* at 394.

21. *Id.* at 395.

22. *Id.* at 392 (quoting Brief for Respondent 25).

23. 721 F. Supp. 852 (E.D. Mich. 1989).

24. *Id.* at 856.

25. *Id.* at 862.

26. *Id.* at 863.

27. 774 F. Supp. 1163 (E.D. Wis. 1991).

28. *Id.* at 1165 (quoting UWS 17.06).

29. *Id.* at 1166–67 (quoting Discriminatory Harassment: Prohibited Conduct under Chapter UWS 17 Revisions).

30. *Id.* at 1173.

31. *Id.* at 1181.

32. The Supreme Court recently upheld a Virginia statute against cross burning but only when there is an intent to intimidate. The Court threw out a statutory presumption that anyone burning a cross does so with such an intent. *See* Virginia v. Black, case number 01-1107, decided April 7, 2003.

33. The Tenth Circuit opinion in West v. Derby Unified School District, 206

F.3d 1358 (10th Cir. 2000), cited two other circuit court decisions addressing the issue of the Confederate flag in schools:

> At least two other circuits have addressed student suspensions based upon display of the Confederate flag. In *Melton v. Young*, 465 F.2d 1332 (6th Cir. 1972), a divided panel of the Sixth Circuit held that a student's suspension for refusal to stop wearing a Confederate flag patch did not violate his First Amendment rights where substantial racial disorder had occurred at the racially integrated school and school officials had every right to anticipate that a tense racial situation continued to exist. Just last summer in *Denno v. School Bd. of Volusia County, Fla.* , 182 F.3d 780 (11th Cir.), *vacated* 193 F.3d 1178 (11th Cir. 1999) a panel of the Eleventh Circuit reversed the district court's dismissal of a student's complaint alleging a violation of his First Amendment rights when school officials suspended him for displaying a picture of the Confederate flag. Accepting the complaint's allegations as true, the court stated that a student had a right to display the flag which gave rise to nothing greater than an undifferentiated fear or apprehension of disturbance. Interestingly, three months later, the panel vacated its opinion and ordered rehearing before the panel. As of today, the case remains pending.

206 F.3d at 1365 n.4. The Eleventh Circuit case, on rehearing, upheld the dismissal of the student's suit. *See* Denno v. School Board of Volusia County, 218 F.3d 1267 (11th Cir.), *cert. denied*, 532 U.S. 958 (2000). The court, using language supportive of the position to be taken here, held that the vice principal defendants enjoyed qualified immunity, because the state of the law as to schools and this sort of symbolic speech was not clear. The school system was also not liable in a federal civil rights suit because the assistant principals had not acted pursuant to school system policy prohibiting Confederate symbols.

34. 206 F.3d 1358 (10th Cir. 2000).

35. *Id.* at 1361 (emphasis added by the court).

36. *Id.* at 1365 (quoting Tinker v. Des Moines Independent Community School District, 393 U.S. 503, 506 (1969)).

37. *Id.* at 1366 (quoting Hazelwood School District v. Kuhlmeier, 484 U.S. 260, 266 (1988)).

38. 478 U.S. 675 (1986).

39. 206 F.3d at 1366 (quoting Bethel School District v. Fraser, 478 U.S. at 683).

40. *Id.* at 1366–67 (quoting and adopting the findings of the district court judge in West v. Derby Unified School District, 23 F. Supp. 2d 1223, 1223 (D. Kan. 1998)).

41. 240 F.3d 200 (3d Cir. 2001).

42. *Id.* at 202 (quoting the school system's Anti-Harassment Policy).

43. *Id.* at 203 (quoting the school system's Anti-Harassment Policy).

44. *Id.* at 202 (quoting the school system's Anti-Harassment Policy).

45. *Id.* at 203 (quoting the school system's Anti-Harassment Policy).

46. *Id.* at 210.

47. 393 U.S. 503 (1969).

48. 240 F.3d at 212.

49. *Id.* at 217.

50. *Id.*

51. The Third Circuit recently enjoined the enforcement of another school system harassment policy. *See* Sypniewski v. Warren Hills Regional Board of Education, 307 F.3d 243 (3d Cir. 2002). There had been racial incidents involving a group of white students calling themselves "The Hicks," and a student was suspended for wearing a T-shirt bearing a comedic "Redneck Sports Fan" message. The court rejected the claim that "redneck" was sufficiently related to "hick" to allow its suppression. The court also rejected a part of the policy addressing material that "creates ill will," concluding that such material may be at the core of the First Amendment. The court did, however, note that school systems may have more latitude than government generally or than universities.

52. The case and its relationship to political speech in the schools will be further discussed in Chapter 12.

53. 478 U.S. at 678.

54. 390 U.S. 629 (1968).

55. 438 U.S. 726 (1978).

56. 478 U.S. at 681 (quoting C. Beard and M. Beard, New Basic History of the United States 228 (1968)).

57. *Id.* at 681 (quoting Ambach v. Norwick, 441 U.S. 68, 76–77 (1979)).

58. *Id.* at 681.

59. *Id.* at 682.

60. *Id.*

61. *Id.* at 683.

62. Indecency that reaches a level that can be seen as demeaning women may have that effect, but such speech could be considered sexist speech, as well as indecent speech, and because of its sexism could be analyzed in the same way as racist speech.

63. The issue of political speech in the schools will be discussed in Chapter 12. Suffice it to say here that the sort of bias that should be seen as a constitutional violation does not include a bias in favor of the position that individuals should not be attacked on the basis of their race, ethnicity, gender, etc.

64. 478 U.S. at 689 (Brennan, J., concurring).

65. *See* Marjorie Heins, Not in Front of the Children 12 (New York: Hill and Wang, 2001).

66. Vivian Gussin Paley, You Can't Say You Can't Play (Cambridge, MA: Harvard University Press, 1992).

67. The experience is recounted in William Peters, A Class Divided: Then and Now (New Haven: Yale University Press, 1987). There was an earlier version, published without the "Then and Now" subtitle in 1971. The 1987 book includes a discussion of a later reunion of the students in the class.

NOTES TO CHAPTER 10

1. 403 U.S. 15 (1971).

2. *Id.* at 16 (quoting California Penal Code § 415).

3. *Id.* at 21 (quoting Rowan v. United States Post Office Dept., 397 U.S. 728, 738 (1970)) (citations omitted).

4. *Id.* at 22–23.

5. *Id.* at 23.

6. *Id.* 23 (footnote omitted).

7. *Id.* at 24–25 (quoting Winters v. New York, 333 U.S. 507, 528 (1948) (Frankfurter, J., dissenting)) (citations omitted).

8. *Id.* at 25.

9. *Id.*

10. 438 U.S. 726 (1978).

11. *Id.* at 749.

12. 2 FCC Rcd. 2705 (1987).

13. 64 Rad. Reg.2d (P & F) 211, 3 FCC Rcd. 930 (1987).

14. 58 F.3d 654 (D.C. Cir. 1994) *(en banc)*.

15. The facts of the case may be found in a number of newspaper articles. *See, e.g.*, James J. Kilpatrick, Examining the Case of the Cursing Canoeist, Augusta Chronicle A4 (Feb. 13, 2000); *"Cursing Canoeist" Sentenced*, The Washington Post A5 (Aug. 24, 1999); *Court Convicts Cursing Canoeist under Century-Old Michigan Law*, St. Louis Post Dispatch 29 (June 12, 1999).

16. *See* People v. Boomer, 653 N.W. 2d 406 (Mich. Ct. App.), *appeal denied*, 655 N.W. 2d 255 (Mich. 2002).

17. *See, e.g.* , Winter v. New York, 333 U.S. 507 (1948).

18. 403 U.S. at 22 (citation omitted).

19. *Id.* at 22 n.4.

20. *See* United States v. Playboy Entertainment Group, Inc., 529 U.S. 803 (2000); Reno v. American Civil Liberties Union, 521 U.S. 844 (1997); Denver Area Educational Telecommunications Consortium v. Federal Communications Commission, 518 U.S. 727 (1996); Sable Communications v. Federal Communications Commission, 492 U.S. 115 (1989); Bolger v. Youngs Drug Products Corp., 463 U.S. 60 (1983); Butler v. Michigan, 352 U.S. 380 (1957).

NOTES TO CHAPTER 11

1. Regulations Restricting the Sale and Distribution of Cigarettes and Smokeless Tobacco Products to Protect Children and Adolescents, FDA Proposed Rule, 60 Fed. Reg. 41314, 41333 (1995).

2. *Id.*

3. *Id.* (citing P. M. Fischer et al., *Brand Logo Recognition by Children Aged 3 to 6 Years: Mickey Mouse and Old Joe the Camel*, 266 J. Amer. Med. Ass'n 3145 (1991); R. Mizerski, *The Relationship between Cartoon Trade Character Recognition and Product Category Attitude in Young Children*, presented at "Marketing and Public Policy Conference" (May 13–14, 1994).

4. *Id.* at 41330.

5. *Id.* at 41314.

6. *Id.* at 41330.

7. *Id.* at 41332.

8. *Id.*

9. Federal Trade Commission, Marketing Violent Entertainment to Children: A Review of Self-Regulation and Industry Practices in the Motion Picture, Music Recording and Electronic Game Industries (2000).

10. *Id.* at iii.

11. *Id.*

12. *Id.* at 14.

13. *Id.* at iv.

14. *Id.* at 46.

15. *Id.* at iv, 45.

16. *Id.* at 12 (quoting Walter E. Dellinger and Charles Fried, *First Amendment Implications of the Federal Trade Commission's Inquiry into the Marketing to Minors of Motion Pictures That Depict Violence* 3–4, paper presented to the Federal Trade Commission on behalf of Sony Pictures Entertainment Inc., Metro-Goldwyn-Mayer Studios, Inc., Miramax Films, Paramount Pictures Corp., Twentieth Century Fox Film Corp, Universal City Studios, Inc., Warner Bros., and Walt Disney Pictures and Television).

17. 425 U.S. 748 (1976).

18. 447 U.S. 557 (1980).

19. *See* Greater New Orleans Broadcasting Ass'n, Inc. v. United States, 527 U.S. 173, 188 (1999).

20. 533 U.S. 525 (2001).

21. 15 U.S.C. § 1333.

22. 533 U.S. 570 (quoting Food and Drug Administration v. Brown and Williamson Tobacco Corp., 529 U.S. 120, 161 (2000)).

23. *Id.* at 558 (quoting Regulations Restricting the Sale and Distribution of

Cigarettes and Smokeless Tobacco Products to Protect Children and Adolescents, FDA Proposed Rule, 60 Fed. Reg. 41314, 41332 (1995)).

24. *Id.* at 566.

25. *Id.* at 563.

26. Food and Drug Administration, Regulations Restricting the Sale and Distribution of Cigarettes and Smokeless Tobacco Products to Protect Children and Adolescents, 61 Fed. Reg. 44396, 44467 (1996).

27. *Id.*

28. *See id.* at 44495.

29. *See id.* at 44513.

30. *Id.* at 44514.

31. *See id.* at 44516.

32. It is true that a sampling of readership for a magazine evenly attractive to the general population would produce a youth readership somewhat less than 15 percent, since the youngest group are not readers, but the basic point that the magazine is one of general circulation is still the same.

33. *See* Food and Drug Administration, *supra* note 26, at 44512.

34. 438 U.S. 726 (1978).

NOTES TO CHAPTER 12

1. Amy Gutmann, Democratic Education 44–45 (Princeton, NJ: Princeton University Press, 1987).

2. *Id.* at 51.

3. Brice C. Hafen, *Developing Student Expression through Institutional Authority; Public Schools as Mediating Structures*, 48 Ohio St. L.J. 663, 707 (1987).

4. Suzanna Sherry, *Responsible Republicanism: Educating for Citizenship*, 62 U. Chi. L. Rev. 131, 188 (1995).

5. *See* Bruce C. Hafen and Jonathan O. Hafen, *The* Hazelwood *Progeny: Autonomy and Student Expression in the 1990's*, 69 St. John's L. Rev. 379, 379 (1995).

6. 319 U.S. 624 (1943).

7. *Id.* at 636.

8. *Id.* at 637.

9. *Id.* at 642.

10. *Id.* at 631.

11. 385 U.S. 589 (1967).

12. *Id.* at 603 (quoting Shelton v. Tucker, supra, 364 U.S. 479, 487 (1960); United States v. Associated Press, 52 F. Supp. 362, 372 (S.D.N.Y. 1943); and Sweezy v. State of New Hampshire, 354 U.S. 234, 250 (1957)).

13. 457 U.S. 853 (1982).

14. *Id.* at 877 (Blackmun, J., concurring in part and concurring in the judgment).

15. 441 U.S. 68 (1979).

16. *Id.* at 78–80.

17. 393 U.S. 503 (1969).

18. *Id.* at 506.

19. *Id.* at 508.

20. *Id.* at 509.

21. *Id.* at 510.

22. *Id.* at 511.

23. 457 U.S. 853 (1982).

24. *Id.* at 857 (correction in Court's opinion).

25. *Id.* at 864 (quoting Brief for Petitioners 10).

26. *Id.* at 869.

27. *Id.* at 870–71.

28. *Id.* at 873 n.25 (quoting Deposition of Petitioner Frank Martin 22).

29. *Id.* at 879 (Blackmun, J., concurring in part and in the judgment).

30. *Id.* at 879–80 (quoting Tinker v. Des Moines School Dist., 393 U.S. 503, 509 (1969); and Pierce v. Society of Sisters, 268 U.S. 510, 534 (1925)) (other citations omitted) (emphasis in original).

31. *Id.* at 883 (White, J., concurring in the judgment).

32. *Id.* at 889 (dissenting opinion of Chief Justice Burger, joined by Powell, Rehnquist and O'Connor, JJ.)

33. *Id.* at 914 (dissenting opinion of Rehnquist, J., joined by Burger, C.J., and Powell, J.) (emphasis in original).

34. *Id.* at 915 (dissenting opinion of Rehnquist, J., joined by Burger, C.J., and Powell, J.).

35. 478 U.S. 675 (1986).

36. *Id.* at 677–78.

37. *Id.* at 687 (Brennan, J., concurring) (quoting App. 47).

38. *Id.* (Brennan, J., concurring).

39. *Id.* at 680.

40. *Id.*

41. *Id.* at 681.

42. 403 U.S. 15 (1971).

43. 478 U.S. at 682.

44. *Id.* at 683 (citations omitted).

45. *Id.*

46. *Id.* at 685–86 (emphasis added).

47. 484 U.S. 260 (1988).

48. The name had actually been omitted from the final version of the story, but not from the proofs examined by the principal.

49. 484 U.S. at 266.

50. *Id.* at 268 (quoting the Hazelwood East Curriculum Guide).

51. *Id.* at 271.

52. *Id.*

53. *Id.*

54. *Id.* at 272–73 (quoting *Fraser*, 478 U.S. at 683; and Brown v. Board of Education, 347 U.S. 483, 493 (1954)).

55. Mark Yudof notes that *Tinker* was one of the Warren Court's last cases and that it has caused considerable "gnashing of teeth" by the Burger and Rehnquist Courts. *See* Mark Yudof, Tinker *Tailored: Good Faith, Civility, and Student Expression*, 69 St. John's L. Rev. 365, 365–66 (1995). The view expressed there is that, while not overruling *Tinker*, later Courts have not been sympathetic to its holding and have limited the application of the case. *See id.* at 366. The attempt here will be to reconcile *Tinker* and those later cases rather than to discount *Tinker*.

56. 478 U.S. at 685–86.

57. In Rosenberger v. Rectors and Visitors of University of Virginia, 515 U.S. 819 (1995), where the Court found no Establishment Clause problem in the university paying the printing costs of a publication with a Christian perspective, the conclusion was at least in part because the university had required disclaimers that the views of the publication were not those of the university and, thus, "ha[d] taken pains to disassociate itself from the private speech involved." *Id.* at 821.

58. 393 U.S. at 509.

59. 478 U.S. at 675.

60. 484 U.S. at 269 n.2 (quoting *Spectrum*'s Statement of Policy).

61. *Id.* at 266 (quoting *Fraser*, 478 U.S. at 685).

62. 347 U.S. 483 (1954).

63. *Id.* at 493.

64. *Id.* at 494.

65. 478 U.S. at 683.

66. *Id.* (quoting *Tinker*, 393 U.S. at 508).

67. The quoted phrases are drawn from *Fraser*, 478 U.S. at 683.

68. 478 U.S. at 683.

69. *Id.*

70. John H. Garvey, What Are Freedoms For? 106 (Cambridge, MA: Harvard University Press, 1996).

71. John H. Garvey, *Children and the First Amendment*, 57 Tex. L. Rev. 321, 338 (1979).

72. *See id.* at 344. Garvey also discusses the autonomy interest behind some adult theories of free expression and concludes that a child's development needs more guidance than is envisioned under an autonomy-based approach. He does,

however, see instrumental roles for free speech in that development. *See id.* at 346–50.

73. John H. Garvey, *supra* note 70, at 108.

74. Betsy Levin, *Educating Youth for Citizenship: The Conflict between Authority and Individual Rights in the Public School*, 95 Yale L.J. 1647, 1654 (1986).

75. *See* Miami Herald v. Tornillo, 418 U.S. 241 (1974).

76. There can, of course, be abuse by school authorities that the press could serve a vital role in exposing. While students might sometimes be in the best position to recognize that abuse, exposure in the school newspaper is not vital. It reaches a primary readership of students, rather than the adults who can take action against the school authorities. There is also nothing preventing the students alleging abuse from going to the local press with the story or even writing the story for the local press.

77. This limitation seems similar to what has been called a "Political Establishment Clause." *See* Robert D. Kamenshine, *The First Amendment's Political Establishment Clause*, 67 Calif. L. Rev. 1104 (1979). While Kamenshine's principle might be read not to allow any inculcation of values, as a parallel to the religious Establishment Clause, he does say that a violation occurs when the public schools advocate one political viewpoint "to the exclusion of others." *Id.* at 1133.

78. 457 U.S. at 870–71.

79. *Id.* at 879 (emphasis in original).

80. *Id.* at 889 (dissenting opinion of Chief Justice Burger, joined by Powell, Rehnquist and O'Connor, JJ.).

81. Amy Gutmann, *supra* note 1, at 98.

82. Suzanna Sherry, *supra* note 4, at 189–90.

83. *Id.* at 190.

84. Susan Bitensky suggests that the values to be inculcated in the public schools be found in the developing principles of international human rights law. *See* Susan H. Bitensky, *A Contemporary Proposal for Reconciling the Free Speech Clause with Curricular Values Inculcation in the Public Schools*, 70 Notre Dame L. Rev. 769 (1995). Certainly these values should be taught, but values inculcation should not be limited to those so accepted. The reliance on international human rights may make its greater contribution in finding values that the schools may protect by limiting contrary speech. That is, schools may more broadly teach values, but suppression should be based on a firmer ground such as that suggested.

85. 206 F.3d 1358 (10th Cir. 2000). The case is more fully discussed in Chapter 9.

86. 240 F.3d 200 (3d Cir. 2001). The case is more fully discussed in Chapter 9.

87. *Id.* at 202.
88. *Id.* at 203 (quoting the school system's Anti-Harassment Policy).
89. *Id.* at 210.

NOTES TO THE CONCLUSION

1. This is, of course, already the case for sexually indecent material. *See* Federal Communications Commission v. Pacifica Foundation, 438 U.S. 726 (1978).

2. For an argument to this end, *see* Kevin W. Saunders, *Electronic Indecency; Protecting Children in the Wake of the Cable and Internet Cases*, 46 Drake L. Rev. 1, 38–42 (1997).

3. 390 U.S. 629 (1968).

4. 852 F.2d 1332 (D.C. Cir. 1988); 932 F.2d 1504 (D.C. Cir. 1991), *cert. denied*, 503 U.S. 913 (1992); 58 F.3d 654 (D.C. Cir. 1994) (*en banc*).

5. *See* 58 F.3d at 664 ("In light of Supreme Court precedent and the broad national consensus that children under the age of 18 need to be protected from exposure to sexually explicit materials, the Commission was fully justified in concluding that the Government interest extends to minors of all ages.")

6. 521 U.S. 844 (1997).

7. *See* American Amusement Machines Ass'n v. Kendrick, 244 F.3d 572 (7th Cir. 2001).

8. 244 F.3d at 577 (emphasis in original).

9. Professor Franklin Zimring has recognized the two sides of this coin. He argued that adolescent offenders should be treated more leniently than adults because they had yet to outgrow a developmental stage in which such criminal conduct was more likely. *See* Franklin E. Zimring, *Pursuing Criminal Justice: Comments on Some Recent Reform Proposals*, 55 U. Detroit J. Urban L. 631 (1978). He later argued for differences in liberty, also recognizing the need to help adolescents in their developing psychological maturity. *See* Franklin E. Zimring, The Changing Legal World of Adolescence (New York: Free Press, 1982).

Index

Abortion rights of minors, 104–5
Abrams v. United States, 4, 30
Action for Children's Television v. Federal Communications Commission, 206, 210, 259–60
Adults: enhancing adult rights by limiting children, 143–44; need to allow access by regulating children, 166, 168, 177, 212, 222–25, 258
Advertising, 53–56, 213–27; effects on children, 1, 3, 54–55, 219–23; and free market, 217; of films, R- and PG-13 rated, aimed at children, 214–16; of tobacco aimed at children, 213–14; of violent entertainment aimed at children, 214–16. *See also* Commercial speech, protection for
Age for full rights, 14–15, 65, 252, 259–60
Alcohol: portrayal in the media, 53–55; use by children, 1, 53
Alternative, less restrictive. *See* Narrow tailoring; Strict scrutiny
Ambach v. Norwick, 231
Amendment to the Constitution to protect children, 17, 260–61
American Academy of Child and Adolescent Psychology, joint statement on media violence, 45
American Academy of Family Physicians, joint statement on media violence, 45
American Academy of Pediatrics, joint statement on media violence, 45
American Amusement Machines Association v. Kendrick, 13–15
American Booksellers Association v. Hudnut, 78–79
American Civil Liberties Union, 10–12
American Library Association, 11

American Library Association v. United States, 289n. 28
American Medical Association, joint statement on media violence, 45
American Psychiatric Association, joint statement on media violence, 45
American Psychological Association: joint statement on media violence, 45; Task Force on Television and Society, 43–44
Anderson, Craig, 47–48
Anti-Defamation League, 59–60
Aristotle, 50, 152
Autonomy as a First Amendment interest, 27–29, 38–40, 42, 265n. 23, 297–98n. 72

Baker, Edwin, 27–28
Bandura, Albert, 44
Beauharnais v. Illinois, 180–81
Belief, requiring declaration of, 229–30, 250, 254
Benefits of free expression, 4–7, 19–42
Bethel School District v. Fraser, 190, 192–97, 238–40, 243–49
Bigotry. *See* Hate speech
Bitensky, Susan, 275n. 44, 298n. 84
Blackstone, William, 19
Blasi, William, 21, 70–72, 155
Board of Education, Island Trees Union Free School District v. Pico, 231, 233–38, 243–44, 250–52
Bok, Sissela, 50
Bollinger, Lee, 35–37
Brandeis, Louis (Justice), 30
Brennan, William (Justice), 143–44
Brown v. Board of Education, 246–47
Bushman, Brad, 48
Butler v. Michigan, 166

About the Author

Kevin W. Saunders is Professor of Law at Michigan State University-DCL College of Law and author of *Violence as Obscenity: Limiting the Media's First Amendment Protections*.

DATE DUE

MAR 1 4 2005	
MAR 1 7 2006	
APR 2 3 2006	APR 1 5 2015
MAR 2 1 2007	
APR 0 7 2008	
ILL 5-1-10 (Iup)	

DEMCO, INC. 38-2931

THE TRUTH ABOUT ENVIRONMENTAL HAZARDS

Robert N. Golden, M.D.
University of Wisconsin–Madison
General Editor

Fred L. Peterson, Ph.D.
University of Texas–Austin
General Editor

John V. Perritano
Principal Author

Facts On File
An imprint of Infobase Publishing

The Truth About Environmental Hazards

Copyright © 2010 by DWJ BOOKS LLC

Facts On File, Inc.
An imprint of Infobase Publishing
132 West 31st Street
New York, NY 10001

Library of Congress Cataloging-in-Publication Data

Perritano, John.
    The truth about environmental hazards / John Perritano, principal author; Robert N. Golden, general editor, Fred L. Peterson, general editor.
        p. cm.
    Includes index.
    ISBN-13: 978-0-8160-7646-8 (hardcover: alk. paper)
    ISBN-10: 0-8160-7646-4 (hardcover: alk. paper) 1. Natural disasters—Popular works. 2. Environmental disasters—Popular works. 3. Environmental health—Popular works. I. Golden, Robert N. II. Peterson, Fred (Fred L.) III. Title.
    GB5018.P47 2010
    363.7—dc22   2009022200

Facts On File books are available at special discounts when purchased in bulk quantities for businesses, associations, institutions or sales promotions. Please call our Special Sales Department in New York at (212) 967-8800 or (800) 322-8755.

You can find Facts On File on the World Wide Web at http://www.factsonfile.com

Text design by David Strelecky
Composition by Mary Susan Ryan-Flynn
Cover printed by Art Print, Taylor, PA
Book printed and bound by Maple Press, York, PA
Date printed: May 2010
Printed in the United States of America

10 9 8 7 6 5 4 3 2 1

CONTENTS

LIST OF ILLUSTRATIONS

PREFACE

The Truth About series—updated and expanded to include 20 volumes—seeks to identify the most pressing health issues and social challenges confronting our nation's youth. Adolescence is the period between the onset of puberty and the attainment of adult roles and responsibilities. Adolescence is also a time of storm, stress, and risk-taking for many young people. During adolescence, a person's health is influenced by biological, psychological, and social factors, all of which interact with one's environment—family, peers, school, and community. It is a time when teenagers experience profound changes.

With the latest available statistics and new insights that have emerged from ongoing research, the Truth About series seeks to help young people build a foundation of information as they face some of the challenges that will affect their health and well-being. These challenges include high-risk behaviors, such as alcohol, tobacco, and other drug use; sexual behaviors that can lead to adolescent pregnancy and sexually transmitted diseases (STDs), such as HIV/AIDS; mental health concerns, such as depression and suicide; learning disorders and disabilities, which are often associated with failure at school and dropping out of school; serious family problems, including domestic violence and abuse; and lifestyle choices, which can increase adolescents' risk for noncommunicable diseases, such as diabetes and cardiovascular disease.

Broader underlying factors also influence adolescent health. These include socioeconomic circumstances, such as poverty, available health care, and the political and social situations in which young people live. Although these factors can negatively affect adolescent health and well-being, as well as school performance, many of these negative health outcomes are preventable with the proper knowledge and information.

With prevention in mind, the writers and editors of each topical volume in the Truth About series have tried to provide cutting-edge information that is supported by research and scientific evidence. Vital facts are presented that inform youth about the challenges experienced during adolescence, while special features seek to dispel common myths and misconceptions. Some of the main topics explored include abuse, alcohol, death and dying, divorce, drugs, eating disorders, family life, fear and depression, rape, sexual behavior and unplanned pregnancy, smoking, and violence. All volumes discuss risk-taking behaviors and their consequences, healthy choices, prevention, available treatments, and where to get help.

In this new edition of the series, we also have added eight new titles in areas of increasing significance to today's youth. ADHD, or attention-deficit/hyperactivity disorder, and learning disorders are diagnosed with increasing frequency, and many students have observed or know of classmates receiving treatment for these conditions, even if they have not themselves received this diagnosis. Gambling is gaining currency in our culture, as casinos open and expand in many parts of the country, and the Internet offers easy access for this addictive behavior. Another consequence of our increasingly "online" society, unfortunately, is the presence of online predators. Environmental hazards represent yet another danger, and it is important to provide unbiased information about this topic to our youth. Suicide, which for many years has been a "silent epidemic," is now gaining recognition as a major public health problem throughout the life span, including the teenage and young adult years. We now also offer an overview of illness and disease in a volume that includes the major conditions of particular interest and concern to youth. In addition to illness, however, it is essential to emphasize health and its promotion, and this is especially apparent in the volumes on physical fitness and stress management.

It is our intent that each book serve as an accessible, authoritative resource to which young people can turn for accurate and meaningful answers to their specific questions. The series can help them research particular problems and provide an up-to-date evidence base. It is also designed with parents, teachers, and counselors in mind so that they have a reliable resource that they can share with youth who seek their guidance.

Finally, we have tried to provide unbiased facts rather than subjective opinions. Our goal is to help elevate the health of the public with an emphasis on its most precious component—our youth. As young people face the challenges of an increasingly complex world, we as educators want them to be armed with the most powerful weapon available—knowledge.

Robert N. Golden, M.D.
Fred L. Peterson, Ph.D.
General Editors

HOW TO USE THIS BOOK

NOTE TO STUDENTS

Knowledge is power. By possessing knowledge you have the ability to make decisions, ask follow-up questions, and know where to go to obtain more information. In the world of health, that is power! That is the purpose of this book—to provide you the power you need to obtain unbiased, accurate information and *The Truth About Environmental Hazards*.

Topics in each volume of the Truth About are arranged in alphabetical order, from A to Z. Each of these entries defines its topic and explains in detail the particular issue. At the end of most entries are cross-references to related topics. A list of all topics by letter can be found in the table of contents or at the back of the book in the index.

How have these books been compiled? First, the publisher worked with me to identify some of the country's leading authorities on key issues in health education. These individuals were asked to identify some of the major concerns that young people have about such topics. The writers read the literature, spoke with health experts, and incorporated their own life and professional experiences to pull together the most up-to-date information on health issues, particularly those of interest to adolescents and of concern in Healthy People 2010.

Throughout the alphabetical entries, the reader will find sidebars that separate Fact from Fiction. There are Question-and-Answer boxes that attempt to address the most common questions that youth ask about sensitive topics. In addition, readers will find a special feature called "Teens Speak"—case studies of teens with personal stories related to the topic in hand.

This may be one of the most important books you will ever read. Please share it with your friends, families, teachers, and classmates. Remember, you possess the power to control your future. One way to affect your course is through the acquisition of knowledge. Good luck and keep healthy.

NOTE TO LIBRARIANS

This book, along with the rest of the series the Truth About, serves as a wonderful resource for young researchers. It contains a variety of facts, case studies, and further readings that the reader can use to help answer questions, formulate new questions, or determine where to go to find more information. Even though the topics may be considered delicate by some, don't be afraid to ask patrons if they have questions. Feel free to direct them to the appropriate sources, but do not press them if you encounter reluctance. The best we can do as educators is to let young people know that we are there when they need us.

Mark J. Kittleson, Ph.D.
Adviser

ENVIRONMENTAL HAZARDS: A PART OF DAILY LIFE

Most people live on the edge of an environmental hazard—whether they know it or not. Whether someone resides in Southern California where earthquakes are common, or near an abandoned copper mine that leaks dangerous **arsenic** into the groundwater, environmental dangers are part of our daily lives.

Some environmental hazards, such as a rising flood or a smoking volcano, are easy to spot. Others are not as easy to detect. A nearby factory might be secretly dumping hazardous chemicals into a lake. Asbestos fibers might be floating in the air of a local construction site. Whereas some environmental threats, such as earthquakes, can occur quickly, with little notice, other environmental hazards might take years to become known, such as the influence of the pesticide DDT on wildlife and human tissue.

The Truth About Environmental Hazards takes a close look at the various environmental dangers the planet faces and how those hazards impact our lives. As the world's population continues to grow, so do the risks associated with our environmental health. The World Health Organization (WHO) defines environmental health as "those aspects of human health, including quality of life, that are determined by physical, chemical, biologic, social, and psychosocial factors in the environment."

Anything that affects the environmental health of humans, plants, and animals in a negative way is an environmental hazard. Air pollution, contaminated food, and water pollution are all examples of the environmental hazards Earth's population faces.

Sometimes environmental hazards are minor, such as a wastewater treatment plant's accidentally dumping raw sewage into a river after a summer downpour. Other environmental hazards are more profound, like Hurricane Katrina, which ravaged the Gulf Coast of the United States in 2005.

Most environmental hazards are generally associated with human activities and seem to make headlines on an almost daily basis. A recent example occurred in January 2009, when health officials found that peanut butter from a processing plant in Georgia had become contaminated with the bacteria *Salmonella,* which causes food poisoning. As a result, more than 500 people in 43 states became ill by eating crackers and other products made with the tainted peanut butter. Eight people died, and more than 100 children under the age of five become sick. The Georgia food plant, owned by the Peanut Corporation of America, had sold contaminated peanut paste to some of the nation's largest food producers, including Kellogg's and McKee Foods. Human error played a key role in this environmental hazard. Apparently, the company knowingly sold the contaminated product and did not take any steps to clean its plant after its own tests confirmed that some of the peanut butter paste was contaminated with the salmonella bacteria.

As you investigate the topics in this volume, it is a good idea to keep several questions in mind. Is our planet becoming more vulnerable to environmental hazards? If so, which environmental hazards will become major problems in the future? What are the consequences of the environmental hazards outlined in this book? How do communities try to stop the risks of environmental hazards and prepare for natural disasters?

ENVIRONMENTAL HAZARDS EXPLAINED

When is something an environmental hazard? Some hazards are obvious, such as earthquakes, tornadoes, oil spills, and floods. There is no doubt that these hazards impact people, animals, plants, and the rest of the natural environment. Other situations may seem hazardous to some, but not to others. Using an electric stove to boil water, for example, might seem harmless; however, the energy that creates the electricity that heats the water emits harmful gases into the air. Driving to work in an SUV that wastefully burns gasoline is hazardous to the environment. Even fertilizers that farmers use to grow crops can impact the environment in a harmful way.

Indeed, one person's environmental hazard is not necessarily an environmental hazard for someone else. A blizzard might pound an area with more than a foot of snow causing power outages in neighborhoods and the evacuation of elderly and sick people to shelters. However, that same blizzard keeps thousands of children at home and not at school. For these students, the blizzard is not a hazard at all, but a day off. Wildfires might char thousands of acres, but the fires also spur new growth in the forest. In that respect, are wildfires always hazardous?

Perceptions of what constitutes an environmental hazard may vary. While we would like to take into account those various perceptions, we need to be able to measure and quantify what an environmental hazard actually is. For the purposes of this volume then, we will use the generic definition of environmental hazards: *natural or human-made forces that pose a threat to the environment.*

The language of environmental hazards is very specific. A *hazard* is the most general term and underscores the impact of an event on humans, society, and the environment. Hazards threaten people and the things they value. On the other hand, *risk* refers to the likelihood of an event occurring. *Disasters* are one-time only events, like volcanic eruptions and earthquakes. *Vulnerability,* or the potential to be harmed, applies to everyone and the environment.

TYPES OF ENVIRONMENTAL HAZARDS

Natural disasters constitute one type of environmental hazard. They include earthquakes, floods, hurricanes, blizzards, tornadoes, and volcanic eruptions. These natural environmental hazards often spur other types of environmental hazards, such as devastating tsunamis propelled by volcanic or **tectonic activity.** Tsunamis could ravage seacoasts, killing thousands as did the 2004 Indonesian tsunami. The resulting flood from a tsunami can spur an epidemic of waterborne diseases and other biological hazards. Flooding was so bad during Hurricane Katrina, for example, that when the water receded, it left many homes and buildings uninhabitable. Not only did the water destroy many buildings, but it also fostered the growth of harmful mold spores on walls, ceilings, floors, and furniture in those homes that were not destroyed. Breathing in mold spores can harm a person's health.

Droughts, hail storms, heat waves, and erosion can also endanger the environment and human health. Extreme heat conditions push the body beyond its limits. Older adults and younger children are most likely to become sick during intense summer heat waves.

Biological hazards make up another type of environmental hazard. Sources of biological hazards include bacteria, viruses, insects, plants, birds, animals, and humans. Some biological hazards take the form of disease epidemics, such as cholera, **Ebola**, and **influenza**. One biological hazard is **anthrax**, an infectious disease that can harm the skin, the lungs, as well as the throat and the **gastrointestinal** tract. A bacterium called *Bacillus anthracis* causes anthrax.

Other biological hazards include infestation of termites, locusts, rats, bees, and invasive species of plants. Animals and plants that appear in a place that is not their natural **habitat** can be environmental hazards. For example, a few years ago a tiny tree frog called the coquí angered many people in Hawaii. The frog is noisy and a pest. Although it weighs less than a grape, the tiny frog has a shrill cry. The coquí was accidentally brought to Hawaii from Puerto Rico, probably in a houseplant. In Puerto Rico the frogs are common. In Hawaii they are not. They do not have any natural predators in Hawaii. Because they have no natural enemies, the frogs continued to lay eggs, creating many more noisy coquís.

Technology can also create untold hazards for the environment. Technological hazards include nuclear accidents, industrial accidents, hazardous material spills, power failures, and oil spills. Usually, technological hazards include incidents involving hazardous materials. Often there is little or no warning that precedes these incidents. In many cases, victims might not know they have been impacted until many years later.

One of the most devastating technological environmental hazards occurred in 1986, when a nuclear reactor in Ukraine, which at the time was part of the former Soviet Union, exploded. The explosion sent a huge cloud of **radioactive particles** into the air. The cloud drifted over much of Europe, contaminating millions of acres in Ukraine, Belarus, and Russia. Hundreds of thousands of people had to leave their homes. Many people suffered various illnesses because of their exposure to the radiation.

Sometimes humans create technological environmental hazards on purpose. A case in point is the construction of the Three Gorges Dam in China. The Chinese government wanted to build the dam to create economic development using the vast hydroelectric resources of the Yangtze River, the third largest river in the world.

Despite the positive aspects of the project, the Three Gorges Dam brought several environmental and social pitfalls. The Chinese government forced almost 2 million people, mostly peasants, to leave their homes. Many villages and forests had to be ripped apart during construction of the dam. The loss of forests and farms led to erosion problems and the buildup of sediment at the base of the river and the reservoir created by the dam. That meant that the nutrients in the sediment would not reach farmland downstream of the dam.

Moreover, the Yangtze River is already polluted because many of China's industrial areas are along the river. Pollutants from towns and factories washed into the river, creating a toxic nightmare for many people. The problem got worse when rising water flooded the region. In addition, many environmentalists say the dam is harming many species of animals, including the Chinese tiger, the Siberian crane, and the giant panda. The dam is also affecting the water quality above and below the dam.

While all the environmental hazards mentioned above significantly impact our world, they are chiefly confined to limited areas. Perhaps no category is as threatening as the impact of *global catastrophic hazards* created by human activity. Pollution, environmental degradation, global warming, and **famine** are global in scope and the most pressing environmental issues facing us all. No corner of the world is spared from these environmental hazards. Furthermore, these hazards are caused only by human activities.

For centuries, humans have been polluting the air, the soil, and the water. When humans first appeared on the planet, the pollution they caused was generally cleansed by the environment, which always renewed itself. In fact, it was not until fairly recently that human activities have begun to seriously jeopardize life on Earth.

The Industrial Revolution in the mid-18th century impacted the environment in ways we still do not fully understand. Many species of animals are dying off because of human activity. People are cutting down huge forests to make way for farms and pasture land. Humans use dangerous chemicals in the manufacturing process, dumping those harmful contaminants into the air, the ground, and the water. The planet is failing to renew itself as it once did because the amount of pollution is too great. The oceans used to cleanse the air of **carbon dioxide**, a harmful gas. That is no longer the case. Oceans are losing their ability to absorb any excess carbon dioxide.

Why have humans allowed such degradation to take place? In short, humans have done everything possible to meet the needs of a growing population. Thus, people have cut down forests to build homes and to cultivate land for food. Those forests inhale carbon dioxide and exhale oxygen, which animals, plants, and humans need to live. People have mined Earth for precious metals and for coal to use as fuel and have built power plants that spew harmful chemicals into the air. Some of those chemicals come back to Earth as acid rain. Men and women drive automobiles that emit dangerous chemicals that everyone breathes.

Perhaps the most telling way humans have damaged the environment is through their impact they have on global warming. Global warming is the gradual increase in Earth's temperature. The burning of **fossil fuels**, such as coal, natural gas, and oil, spurs global warming.

Factories burn fossil fuels to run their machines. People burn fossil fuels every time they drive cars or heat their homes. The gases emitted by the burning of fossil fuels trap the heat from the Sun close to Earth's surface, warming the planet.

The problems caused by global warming seem endless, creating a bounty of environmental hazards. For example, in the western United States, wildfires are on the rise. In fall 2008, for example, record heat dried out vegetation near Los Angeles. Dried vegetation, coupled with strong winds gusting up to 75 miles an hour, fueled several wildfires. The fires charred thousands of acres and destroyed almost 1,000 homes. Nearly 4,000 firefighters battled the blazes.

Climate change also causes glaciers to melt and the sea level to rise. Moreover, as the Earth warms, disease-carrying insects, germs, and viruses increase. Many germs and viruses find it difficult to survive when it is cold. Warmer temperatures have already increased the number of disease-carrying insects, such as mosquitoes. Near the equator, many countries are facing epidemics of **malaria, cholera,** and **dengue fever** because of the increased heat.

FACING THE RISKS

The various environmental hazards caused by natural or by human activity have put the environment in a very precarious state. The risks facing humanity are great.

Environmental hazards are not just the work of natural events or the failure of human beings. Instead, environmental hazards are the result of a complex web of interaction between humans and nature. In fact, we can no longer separate the impacts of specific disasters or hazards from more encompassing social and environmental issues.

What does this have to do with you? A person need not live in Tornado Alley or next door to a toxic waste site to be impacted by environmental hazards. Every time you draw a breath or sip a drink, you can put yourself at risk. This book outlines the hazards people face on a daily basis and also describes various ways people have tried to mitigate the impact of environmental hazards.

RISKY BUSINESS SELF-TEST

The environmental hazards described in this book should give you a clear understanding of your risk level, no matter where you live. By understanding the risks you face, you can be aware of the challenges that might come your way. You also should determine how to best deal with those risks.

A. Community-Wide Risks

The following self-test is designed to let you determine the risks you face as they relate to environmental hazards. To identify whether or not you might be at risk, record your answers to these short true-or-false questions on a separate sheet of paper.

_____ I live in an area where tornadoes are common.

_____ I live in an area where hurricanes have come ashore.

_____ There is a nuclear power plant within 20 miles of my town.

_____ My neighborhood is next to a mine, such as a coal mine.

_____ There is a Superfund site in my community.

_____ There are chemical factories in my community.

_____ Smog is a problem in my town.

_____ I have experienced an earthquake.

_____ I live in an area that is prone to wildfires.

_____ I live by a river that often floods.

_____ I live next to a farm that uses chemical fertilizers.

_____ There are oil refineries near my house.

_____ I live in an area where supertankers or railroad cars laden with hazardous materials pass by.

Scoring

Part A

Answering "true" to any of these questions means that your town or neighborhood might be at risk for some type of environmental disaster, such as a hazardous chemical spill or flood. However, that does not mean that your house will be flooded or a cloud of noxious gas will waft through your neighborhood. Every community is at risk for some type of disaster to occur. For example, New York City rarely gets hit by a tornado, but in 2007, one ripped through a neighborhood in Brooklyn. The key is to be mindful of what might happen. You do not have to be frightened, but educating yourself about the impacts of specific environmental hazards cannot hurt.

B. Household/Lifestyle Risks
True or False
Record your answers to the following true/false questions on a separate sheet of paper.

_____ I live in a house that does not contain lead paint.

_____ My parents do not use chemical fertilizers to make our lawn green.

_____ We never use herbicides to kill weeds or unwanted plants in our backyard.

_____ We have a radon detector in our house.

_____ We have a carbon monoxide detector in our house.

_____ We have had our house tested for radon gas.

_____ Our water comes from a municipal water supply that treats the water to make sure it is clean to use and drink.

_____ There are smoke detectors in our house.

_____ The children in my family do not play with toys that contain lead.

_____ We rarely use insecticides in our house to kill bugs.

Scoring
Part B
Answering "true" to any of the above statements means that you and your family have taken steps to minimize the risks of some environmental hazards in your house. Deciding not to use chemical fertilizers, herbicides, and insecticides is very important to maintaining a healthy environment. It is important to know that some substances, such as lead and radon, could cause serious health problems.

Minimizing exposure to these and other substances will make you a healthier person.

C. Environmental Awareness

On a separate piece of paper, record your answers to the following true/false questions.

____ Deforestation adds to the problem of global warming.

____ Burning greenhouse gases harms the environment.

____ It is important to protect sources of groundwater.

____ Cleaning lakes and rivers can help the ecosystem.

____ By recycling glass and other products, we help land-fills last longer.

____ The Superfund law is important to cleaning up toxic waste sites.

____ Enforcing environmental laws is important in stopping pollution.

____ I should turn off my computer when I am not using it.

____ I should never throw out household batteries with the regular garbage.

____ Reducing emissions of greenhouse gases will help slow global warming.

Scoring
Part C

Now total your score and compare your score to the maximum score of 10. Give yourself one point for each "true" answer and zero points for each "false" answer. A score between 8 and 10 is excellent. That means you have a keen awareness of some of the environmental problems facing the planet. If you scored between 6 and 8, you have a good understanding of the issues. A score of 5 or lower means that you do not have a good grasp of the problems facing Earth and will want to do further research.

A-TO-Z ENTRIES

■ AIR POLLUTION

The results of harmful airborne substances, such as smoke, automobile emissions, and chemical effluents that can damage the environment and the health, safety, and comfort of humans and animals. Air pollution can also harm plants and wreak havoc on building materials. Air pollution is caused by pollutants, which come in two main forms: **gases** and **particulates**. Gases are created when we burn **fossil fuels**, such as oil, natural gas, and coal. Particulates are tiny solid particles that automobiles pump into the atmosphere.

Earth's atmosphere is essential for all living things. The atmosphere covers the planet like an invisible blanket. While Earth's atmosphere protects living things from the Sun's harmful rays, it is also made up of several gases, including oxygen. Humans and animals need oxygen to survive. While some things in the atmosphere are good for us, air pollution is not. It is blamed for global warming and myriad health problems, such as the lung ailment called **asthma**.

HUMAN ACTIVITIES

While nature causes some air pollution, human activities are mainly to blame for this contamination of the atmosphere. Factories, power plants, trains, airplanes, and automobiles produce most of the world's air pollution.

Air pollution has been a problem since the Industrial Revolution of the 1700s. At that time, humans began building factories to produce manufactured goods. The factories burned fossil fuels to run their machines. As society grew, industrialization expanded. As workers built more factories, the amount of pollution in the environment increased.

Air pollution spiked in the 20th century with the increased burning of **gasoline** and **diesel** fuels by cars, trucks, planes, and ships. When vehicles burn gasoline, they give off poisonous gases, including **carbon dioxide** and **nitrous oxide**.

Q & A

Question: If solving the air pollution problem is such a big job, how can I reduce air pollution?

Answer: There are several ways you can help. First, you can turn off the lights, computer, and television when you are not using them.

You can also ride a bike or walk instead of riding in a car. Take public transportation. Recycle cans, bottles, newspapers, and plastic bags. By recycling, you are cutting down on the amount of trash, which reduces pollution of the environment.

DID YOU KNOW?

Air Quality Index

Levels of Health Concern	Numerical Value	Meaning
Good	0–50	Air quality is considered satisfactory, and air pollution poses little or no risk.
Moderate	51–100	Air quality is acceptable; however, for some pollutants there may be a moderate health concern for a very small number of people who are unusually sensitive to air pollution.
Unhealthy for Sensitive Groups	101–150	Members of sensitive groups may experience health effects. The general public is not likely to be affected.
Unhealthy	151–200	Everyone may begin to experience health effects; members of sensitive groups may experience more serious health effects.
Very Unhealthy	201–300	Health alert: everyone may experience more serious health effects.
Hazardous	>300	Health warnings of emergency conditions. The entire population is more likely to be affected.

Green   Yellow   Orange

Red   Fuschia   Maroon

So that people can tell when air pollution is reaching unhealthy levels, the EPA has divided the Air Quality Index into six sections, each with a specific color and a numeric value (go to http://airnow.gov/index.cfm?action=static.aqi#good). For example, red means that conditions are "unhealthy for everyone." Values below 100 are satisfactory. When values are above 100, air quality is considered to be unhealthy, first for sensitive groups of people and, then, as values get higher, for everyone else as well.

Source: U.S. Environmental Protection Agency, 2007.

SMOG

Air pollution levels are the highest in the cities where large amounts of people live. Smog, a poisonous fog, often hangs over major metropolitan areas. **Smog** forms when the pollutants of burned gasoline, also known as **hydrocarbons**, react with sunlight and water vapor. That reaction produces a dangerous gas called **ozone**.

Earth's atmosphere has an ozone layer that protects the planet from the Sun's rays; however, when ozone is too close to the ground, it produces an unhealthy haze. Cities, such as Los Angeles, that are located in valleys, trap the dirty air creating a major smog problem.

ACID RAIN

Air pollution does not only harm urban areas. When factories burn fossil fuels, especially coal, they release gases, such as sulfur dioxide and nitrous oxide. A weak sulfuric acid forms when these gases combine with water vapor in the air. When it rains, snows, or hails, the sulfuric acid falls to the ground as acid rain.

Acid rain harms everything it touches, including plants, animals, humans, and buildings. The wind carries clouds of sulfur emissions far from the source of pollution. Factories in the Midwest, for example, are responsible for poisoning forests hundreds of miles away in Canada and the Northeastern United States.

Q & A

Question: How does acid rain affect lakes and streams?

Answer: When acid rain falls into a lake, stream, or river, it increases the acidity in that body of water. Higher acidity can impact the growth and reproduction of fish and plants. Many rivers and lakes in the Adirondack Mountains of New York, for example, have lost entire populations of fish.

GLOBAL WARMING

Many scientists say air pollution causes global warming, the gradual increase of Earth's temperature. As humans burn fossil fuels, they release heat-trapping **greenhouse gases** such as carbon dioxide. People add about 4.4 billion tons (4 billion metric tons) of carbon dioxide into the atmosphere each year. Over the last century, the increase in greenhouse gases has caused temperatures across the planet to increase nearly 1°F (0.6°C).

As Earth warms, the polar ice caps melt, causing sea levels to rise. If global warming continues, many coastal areas such as Florida and the Gulf Coast might one day be underwater.

POOR HEALTH

Health officials cite air pollution as the cause of a variety of human ailments. Smog will often make a person's eyes water and throat itchy. Some people may have an allergic reaction to these airborne pollutants. Doctors also say young people and the elderly might develop asthma by breathing polluted air.

Petroleum companies once added lead to gasoline to make car engines run smoother. Lead is a highly toxic, or poisonous, material. Scientists found that lead can harm a person's kidneys, brain, and nervous system. Many countries have since banned lead from gasoline.

Fact Or Fiction?

Planting trees will reduce the amount of air pollution in the atmosphere.

The Facts: Planting trees can help the quality of the air we breathe. Trees clean the atmosphere by soaking up carbon dioxide. When trees take in carbon dioxide, they release oxygen, which humans and animals need to live. When loggers cut down huge swaths of forests and burn those trees, they are increasing the amount of carbon dioxide in the environment, which is what is happening to the rainforests. Every second of every day, a slice of rainforest about the size of a football field is mowed down.

See also: Allergies; Chemical Pollution; Global Warming; Ozone Layer; Water Pollution

FURTHER READING

Green, Jen. *Improving Our Environment, Reducing Air Pollution.* Chappaqua, N.Y.: Gareth Stevens, 2005.

Tyson, Peter. *Acid Rain.* New York: Chelsea House Publishers, 2002.

Sechrist, Darren. *Air Pollution.* Tarrytown, N.Y.: Marshal Cavendish, 2008.

■ ALLERGIES

Abnormal, defensive reactions by the body's immune system to foreign substances known as **allergens**. Although allergies can develop at any age, most begin in childhood. Many times, allergies are **genetic** in nature, passed from one generation to another. Health officials estimate that 50 million people in the United States have some type of allergy.

People may be allergic to many different things. Some are allergic to inhaled substances including pollen, the fine dust produced by plants and trees. Other people are allergic to foods, such as shellfish, peanuts, and milk from cows. Others suffer from allergic skin reactions brought on by touching or coming into contact with poison ivy, poison oak, and other plants, as well as fabrics and substances. Some people are allergic to over-the-counter medications or prescription drugs.

CAUSES

Allergies develop when the body's immune system, which battles foreign **microorganisms** such as bacteria and viruses, mistakes a generally safe substance for a substance that is harmful to the body. That misidentification causes the body to produce a special **antibody** called immunoglobulin E (IgE). IgE protects humans from **parasites**, but not from allergens. The IgE antibodies link with the body's **mast cells**. When a person comes in contact with that seemingly harmless substance again, the antibody signals the mast cells to release special chemicals called **histamines**, which will battle the intruding allergen. Histamines, however, cause allergic reactions, such as sneezing, itching, and watery eyes.

COMMON ALLERGIES

People can be allergic to just about anything. The most common allergic condition is hay fever (*allergic rhinitis*). Up to 30 percent of all Americans suffer from hay fever. Ten thousand American children miss school every day because of this allergy. Treating hay fever, which has nothing to do with hay or fever, costs more than $1 billion a year in the United States.

The symptoms of hay fever include itchy, watery eyes, nasal congestion, and postnasal drip. Dust mites, animal dander, mold spores, pollen, and fabric fibers can cause hay fever.

Common Allergies and Allergic Reactions

Drug Allergies	Skin Allergies	Food Allergies	Allergic Rhinitis	Sinusitis
Allergic reactions to the antibiotic penicillin cause 400 deaths per year.	About 27 percent of children who have a food allergy also have a skin allergy.	In 2007, an estimated 3 million children under the age of 18 were reported to have a food or digestive allergy in the previous 12 months.	In 2006, doctors diagnosed 8 percent of adults and more than 9 percent of children with hay fever.	About 40,000 people have sinus surgery every year.
Between six and 10 percent of all bad drug reactions are allergic or relate to the body's immune system.	Inflammation of the skin, which causes itching, leads to approximately 5.7 million doctor visits each year.	Children suffering from a food allergy are two to four times more likely to have conditions such as asthma and other allergies.	Allergic rhinitis accounted for more than 12 million doctor visits in 2006.	Chronic sinusitis affects 12 percent of Americans under the age of 45.
When it comes to drug allergies, the most common is an allergic reaction to penicillin.	Scientists have found more than 3,700 substances that are contact allergens.	More than 3 million people in the United States say they are allergic to peanuts, tree nuts, or both.	Between 10 percent and 30 percent of all adults and as many as 40 percent of children suffer from nasal allergic reactions.	There are an estimated 18 million cases of sinusitis each year.

More than half of all Americans—54.6 percent—test positive for one or more allergens. Moreover, allergic diseases affect 40 to 50 million Americans.

Source: The American Academy of Allergy Asthma and Immunology, 2009.

Asthma is another allergic reaction. People who suffer from asthma have chronic, or long-term, trouble breathing because their bronchial tubes, or air passages leading to and from the lungs, spasm or becoming inflamed. Symptoms include wheezing, shortness of breath, coughing, and watery eyes.

Some people are allergic to food, such as peanuts and fish. Peanut allergies are on the rise, especially in children. Some scientists believe that children are eating peanut butter at an earlier age, increasing their risks of a peanut allergy.

Fact Or Fiction?

There is no cure for a peanut allergy.

The Facts: Currently, there is no cure for peanut allergies. The only way to prevent a reaction is to stay away from peanuts, peanut butter, or any food with peanuts as an ingredient. Many people outgrow their allergies, but food allergies seem to be different. Food allergies often persist for life.

Roughly 12 million people in the United States suffer from food allergies, and 3.3 million are allergic to peanuts. Other people are allergic to different types of drugs, chemicals, cosmetics, soaps, and plants.

DIAGNOSIS AND TREATMENT

Doctors use a skin or blood test called a radioallergosorbent test, or RAST, to determine the substances to which a person is allergic. The skin test involves the doctor injecting or lightly scratching an allergen under the skin of a patient. After a few moments, the doctor will check the patient's reaction to the test. The doctor can also administer a blood test to measure the amount of IgE antibodies.

Fact Or Fiction?

If I move to another location, I'll get away from my allergies.

The Facts: Because most allergies are generally inherited, a person has the genetic tendency to produce the IgE antibodies for many different substances. The chances of making your allergies going away simply by moving to another area are slim. If you move from one location to another, you will just be substituting one set of allergens and symptoms for another set. Sometimes, though, a change could prove beneficial. Before moving, talk with your allergist. In some cases, people who suffer from seasonal allergies, such as pollen, might find it prudent to go on vacation to a pollen-free environment.

Unfortunately, allergies cannot be cured. They, however, can be controlled. The most obvious way is to keep away from the allergen. If that is impractical, drugs may reduce or eliminate allergic symptoms. Some of those drugs include **antihistamines**, which prevent watery eyes, coughing, and runny noses.

In severe cases, a patient might receive allergy shots. Doctors will inject a patient with small amounts of an allergen that, over time, causes the body's immune system to produce less of the antibodies that trigger the allergic reactions.

Sometimes allergic reactions are life threatening. When that happens, a person or doctor must administer a shot of **epinephrine**. The drug relaxes the muscles in a person's airway, making it easier to breathe.

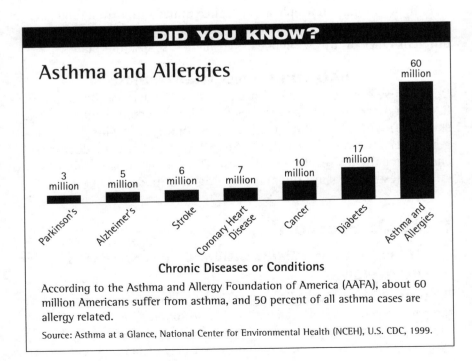

DID YOU KNOW?

Asthma and Allergies

Chronic Diseases or Conditions

According to the Asthma and Allergy Foundation of America (AAFA), about 60 million Americans suffer from asthma, and 50 percent of all asthma cases are allergy related.

Source: Asthma at a Glance, National Center for Environmental Health (NCEH), U.S. CDC, 1999.

TEENS SPEAK

Living with Allergies

If you did not know me, you would think that I am a normal girl. I love to play basketball, dance, and go to the mall with my friends. However, if you hang out with me for a week or two, you will notice that my eyes water, and that my nose is always runny. I sneeze and cough, especially when I first wake up. I suffer from allergies.

I am allergic to a lot of things. Penicillin makes my face swell up like a balloon. I am also allergic to dust mites, cat dander, and pollen. My allergies started early. I have been seeing an allergist since I was six years old. I go every two weeks to get an allergy shot. The shot doesn't bother me too much, because I know the shots allow me to be active.

Winter and spring are the worst times of the year for me. In the winter, it is cold outside and I'm cooped up in the house. All the dust in the house makes me sneeze a lot. They are not just the usual *achoo!* sneezes, but hard sneezes that come one right after the other. I always have a box of tissues near me. Allergies run in the family. My dad always sneezes when he cuts the lawn and he'll break out in a severe rash if he touches poison ivy.

I try not to let my allergies hold me back. All in all, my health condition is not as bad as some other people's. I can travel with my class on field trips. I can swim in my cousin's pool and hang out with my neighbor outside. The allergy shots help me immensely. I wish I could get a dog, though, or at least a cat. Maybe I can when my allergies get better.

See also: Bacteria; Lead Poisoning

FURTHER READING

Bowers, Elizabeth Shimer, and Paul M. Ehrlich. *Living with Allergies.* New York: Facts On File, 2008.

Ford, Jean. *Breathe Easy! A Teen's Guide to Allergies and Asthma.* Broomall, Penn.: Mason Crest Publishers, 2005.

Pescatore, Fred, M.D. *The Allergy and Asthma Cure: A Complete 8-Step Nutritional Program.* Hoboken, N.J.: John Wiley and Sons, 2008.

■ ASBESTOS, USES AND HEALTH RISKS OF

A common name given to a number of fire-resistant materials formed out of soft, flexible, threadlike fibers known for their high strength and **thermal** insulating capabilities. The use of building materials made from asbestos was widespread for decades, until scientists in the 1960s discovered that inhaling the fibers over long periods can cause severe lung ailments including **asbestosis**, lung cancer, and **mesothelioma**, a rare form of lung cancer.

The government now strictly regulates the production and use of asbestos. Products such as roofing shingles, floor and ceiling tiles, automobile brake linings, and textiles might contain asbestos.

ORIGINS

Asbestos occurs naturally in the environment and is mined from the ground like coal. The largest asbestos deposits are in Canada, the Russian Federation, and South Africa. There are two main forms of asbestos. Most asbestos is *chrysotile,* or "white" asbestos. Chrysotile comes from the mineral serpentine. Its fibers are curly and flexible. The other form is *amphibole,* or "blue" asbestos. Amphibole comes from iron silicate. Its fibers are straight. Both forms developed over millions of years when water filled Earth's rocks. Heat and geological pressure caused the water to evaporate, leaving behind the fibers of asbestos.

USES

The ancient Greeks and Romans were the first to use asbestos. They stitched the fibers into burial cloths and tablecloths. They also formed the fibers into lamp wicks that burned for a long time.

By the 1900s, asbestos use was common. Asbestos neither burns nor melts. Engineers used the fibers as a fireproofing material in roofing shingles and insulating products, especially for hot water pipes and furnace ducts. Construction workers used asbestos to reinforce floor tiles and wall shingles. They also added asbestos to strengthen plaster and give it texture. Companies also fashioned firefighting suits, furnace linings, and automobile brake and clutch linings out of the substance.

HEALTH RISKS

Almost everyone has been exposed to asbestos in varying degrees at one time or another. Air, drinking water, and a variety of consumer products contain small traces of asbestos.

Those who came in direct contact with asbestos mostly worked in asbestos mines or in the many industries that used the fibrous substance in the manufacturing process. In the 1960s, scientists discovered that airborne asbestos posed a serious health risk for those who inhale the fibers. The government began strictly regulating the use of asbestos in the 1970s. Many people who suffer from asbestos-related diseases came in contact with the substance before that time.

Q & A

Question: Is there a test that can determine whether my family or I have been exposed to asbestos?

Answer: There are no tests that will show whether you have asbestos fibers in your lungs. However, a lung X-ray could identify early stages of lung disease relating to asbestos exposure. Doctors also have a number of ways to tell if your lungs are functioning properly. If someone you know thinks they have been exposed to asbestos fibers on the job, through the environment, or at home, they should contact their doctor.

Asbestos only becomes dangerous when fibers are airborne. The danger comes from long-term exposure and the size and type of asbestos fibers in the air. A 2007 report by *The American Council on Science and Health* concluded that the most severe asbestos cases occur when humans inhale long, thin amphibole fibers. Exposure to asbestos is one of the chief causes of mesothelioma, a rare form of cancer that attacks the lining of the lungs, chest, and abdomen. Smokers are about 90 times more likely to develop lung cancer than someone who does not smoke, but has been exposed to asbestos.

Q & A

Question: Where might I find asbestos in my house?

Answer: The basement is a good place to start. Older heating systems might have furnace ducts wrapped in asbestos insulating tape.

Workers might have also wrapped older pipes in asbestos insulation. Older roofing shingles, as well as the siding on the house, might contain asbestos. Remember, asbestos is dangerous when it becomes airborne. Trained professionals must handle its removal.

Asbestosis

Asbestosis is a breathing disorder caused by long-term exposure to asbestos. Once inside the lungs, the asbestos fibers scar lung tissue, creating shortness of breath. Some cases of asbestosis are mild, while other cases are severe.

Lung cancer causes the largest number of asbestos-related deaths. The most common symptoms of lung cancer are coughing and a change in breathing.

Fact Or Fiction?

The government will pay for treatment for asbestos exposure.

The Facts: In general, those suffering from asbestos-related diseases must pay for their own health care, either through private or government insurance, or out of their own funds. The government will pay health costs for only certain groups of eligible individuals. Those with asbestos-related diseases might qualify for financial help under

DID YOU KNOW?

Mesothelioma Deaths

Year	Deaths
1999	2,484
2000	2,531
2001	2,509
2002	2,573
2003	2,625
2004	2,657
1999–2004:	15,379 total deaths

Source: U.S. Department of Health and Human Service, 2004.

state-worker compensation laws. Some people might be able to pursue legal options.

See also: Carcinogens

FURTHER READING
Albarado, Rebecca. *A Story Worth Telling.* Bloomington, Ind.: Author House, 2005.
Craighead, John E., ed. *Asbestos and Its Diseases.* New York: Oxford University Press, 2008.
Taylor, Rod. *Facts on Radon and Asbestos.* New York: Franklin Watts, 1990.

■ BACTERIA, TYPES AND IMPORTANCE OF

Microscopic, single-celled organisms that lack a **nucleus** and live both inside and outside the body. Bacteria are everywhere. You can find them on your body, in the air, in the soil, and in the water. Some bacteria are **parasites.** They live on, or in, other living things. Some parasitic bacteria can cause disease, while others are harmless. Some bacteria are helpful to their hosts. They aid in the digestion of food.

Bacteria generally reproduce by a process called **binary fission.** In other words, the cells divide into two equal parts. Scientists classify bacteria by the way they are shaped: **cocci,** or round; **bacilli,** rod shaped; **spirilla,** or spiral; and **vibrios,** which are shaped like commas.

FUNCTION

Bacteria have been around a long time—at least 3.5 million years. During that time, the organisms have adapted to their changing environments. Scientists have found bacteria in hot springs, on the tops of mountains, in the Arctic region, and even six miles (10 kilometers) under the ocean.

Although bacteria are simple, microscopic organisms, they perform the same functions as higher life forms. Like humans, bacteria use energy. They also grow, reproduce, and make waste. Scientists place most bacteria in three groups based on what they need to live. **Aerobic bacteria** need oxygen to survive. **Anaerobic bacteria** cannot survive in an oxygen-rich environment. Instead, they thrive in sediments located under the sea. **Facultative anaerobes** can live in environments where oxygen is or is not present.

Scientists also group bacteria by the way in which they create their food and sustain energy. **Heterotrophs** are bacteria that break down organic compounds. Heterotrophs are nature's recyclers. When an animal or plant dies, heterotrophic bacteria will break down the organic matter into simple substances that other organisms will use to sustain their life. **Autotrophs** need light or chemical energy to create food.

Some bacteria do not move, while others move quickly. Those that do move use tiny hairlike structures called **flagella** that move rapidly in a circular motion. Although bacteria do not have brains, they can sense when food is nearby and move toward it. They can also scamper away when they sense that a toxic chemical is near.

How long does it take bacteria to reproduce? It depends on the organism. Various types of bacteria will reproduce, or divide, in two or three hours. Some take as long as 16 hours. Others reproduce every 15 minutes.

BACTERIA AT WORK

All living things will die. They then decompose, or rot, over time. When organisms die, other living things cannot use the carbon contained in the dead organism's tissue. Bacteria help in the **decomposition** process, by returning carbon dioxide to the environment. Without carbon dioxide, there would be no **photosynthesis** in plants, and therefore no food for humans and animals to consume.

Fact Or Fiction?

Antibacterial soaps are better than regular soaps in killing germs.

The Facts: Many antibacterial soaps claim to kill much more bacteria than traditional soaps, yet most disease-causing bacteria are not killed by antibacterial products. For antibacterial soaps to work, scientists say, the soap must be left on a surface, such as your hand or face, for at least two minutes. Most people quickly rinse the soap off their bodies long before two minutes is up. Some scientists also believe that antibacterial soaps may cause some bacteria to develop a resistance to antibacterial agents over time.

Bacteria are also important in breaking down waste products. Sewage treatment plants and household septic systems use bacteria to break down waste humans generate. In 1989, scientists used bacteria to help clean up a massive oil spill off the coast of Alaska. The bacteria ate the oil.

Without bacteria, dairy farms in Vermont and Wisconsin could not make a block of cheese. Farmers could not produce buttermilk or yogurt. Microbes also help break down the hard shell of coffee beans. Without bacteria, people would not have pickles, sauerkraut, or olives to snack on. Humans also have bacteria in their intestines that help digest food.

DISEASES

While most bacteria sustain a healthy world, some bacteria can make people sick and some can be deadly. Since human history began, great epidemics have devastated towns and cities. Diseases such as **tuberculosis, cholera, diphtheria, smallpox,** and **bubonic plague** devastated whole populations at one time. No one understood what was causing these diseases. Thus, there were no effective treatments, and many people blamed these diseases on evil spirits.

Fact Or Fiction?

I heard the term *super bug.* Do super bugs exist?

The Facts: Super bugs are germs that have become resistant to antibiotics. More than 60 years ago, Alexander Fleming discovered penicillin, the first antibiotic. Ever since then, doctors have been prescribing antibiotics for a whole host of illnesses. Now, some bacteria are becoming stronger against antibiotics, including one "super bug" called MRSA. MRSA is a bacterial infection that is so powerful it can kill a person within days.

Then in the 1860s, two scientists, Louis Pasteur and Robert Koch, formulated the germ theory. They came up with evidence that suggested that microorganisms, not evil spirits, caused infectious diseases. These tiny organisms escaped the body's defense system, making people sick.

TREATMENT

Since the mid-1800s, scientists have developed various drugs to kill disease-spreading bacteria. Scientists call these drugs **antibiotics.**

Originally, the term *antibiotic* was used to describe organic compounds that were deadly to microorganisms. These compounds were made up of bacteria or molds.

The idea of using organic compounds to fight infection has been around since ancient times. It was not until the 20th century, however, that scientists began to understand how some organic substances work to kill infections. For example, penicillin was one of the first antibiotics. In 1928, British scientist Alexander Fleming accidentally discovered penicillin when he saw mold destroy bacteria in the laboratory.

Scientists also developed vaccines to prevent infection from some bacteria. One of the first vaccines was for **anthrax**. In 1881, the bacterium that causes anthrax infected and killed thousands of cattle and sheep in France. Pasteur isolated the bacterium and grew anthrax bacteria. Eventually, Pasteur developed a vaccine that made the livestock immune to the disease.

Q & A

Question: How do vaccines work?

Answer: Vaccines contain a killed or weakened part of the germ responsible for an infection. Because the germ in the vaccine is either dead or weakened, it cannot hurt you once it is inside your body.

When someone is vaccinated, the body reacts by making **antibodies**, which protect us. Antibodies will kill the germs when people come in contact with them; therefore, a vaccinated person will not get sick. Vaccines are currently available for the control of salmonella, but those vaccines differ in their effectiveness. A vaccine for *Escherichia coli,* also known as E. coli, is not currently available. Scientists need to study how these organisms grow and cause disease to develop successful vaccines.

Q & A

Question: My dad came back from a restaurant once and got sick. The doctor said he had something called salmonella, which mom told me is the bacteria that cause food poisoning. How did my dad get this bacterium inside him?

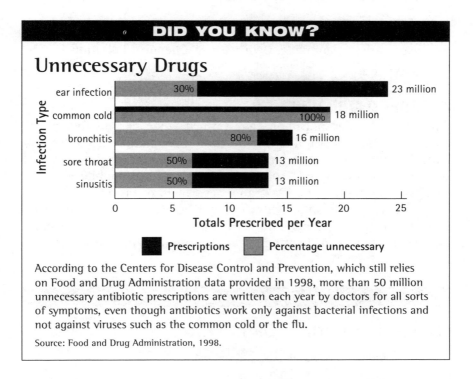

DID YOU KNOW?

Unnecessary Drugs

Infection Type

Infection	Percentage unnecessary	Prescriptions
ear infection	30%	23 million
common cold	100%	18 million
bronchitis	80%	16 million
sore throat	50%	13 million
sinusitis	50%	13 million

Totals Prescribed per Year

0   5   10   15   20   25

■ Prescriptions   ■ Percentage unnecessary

According to the Centers for Disease Control and Prevention, which still relies on Food and Drug Administration data provided in 1998, more than 50 million unnecessary antibiotic prescriptions are written each year by doctors for all sorts of symptoms, even though antibiotics work only against bacterial infections and not against viruses such as the common cold or the flu.

Source: Food and Drug Administration, 1998.

Answer: A variety of bacteria cause food poisoning. The most common are *Salmonella Staphylococcus aureus* and *Escherichia coli.* Raw meats and raw vegetables might contain these bacteria. Your dad may have eaten a piece of meat that was not cooked well enough to kill the bacteria, or he may have had a salad with contaminated lettuce or other vegetables.

Every year, millions of people get sick because of food poisoning. The Centers for Disease Control and Prevention (CDC) estimates that there are 6 to 33 million cases of food poisoning each year.

See also: Allergies; Clean water; Groundwater

FURTHER READING

Brunelle, Lynn, and Barbara Ravage, eds. *Bacteria.* Pleasantville, N.Y.: Gareth Stevens Publishing, 2003.

Thomas, Peggy. *Bacteria and Viruses.* Farmington Hills, Mich.: Lucent, 2004.

■ CAR EMISSIONS
See also: Carbon Monoxide, Ozone Layer, Chemical Pollution

■ CARBON MONOXIDE
Colorless, odorless, poisonous gas formed when carbon fuel is not completely burned. High levels of carbon monoxide are extremely lethal. Carbon monoxide **emissions** can come from a variety of sources, including faulty heating systems and automobile exhaust. Victims of carbon monoxide cannot see, smell, or taste the gas.

People who are subjected to low levels of carbon monoxide exposure can experience flulike symptoms, dizziness, headaches, nausea, fatigue, and disorientation. The impact of carbon monox-

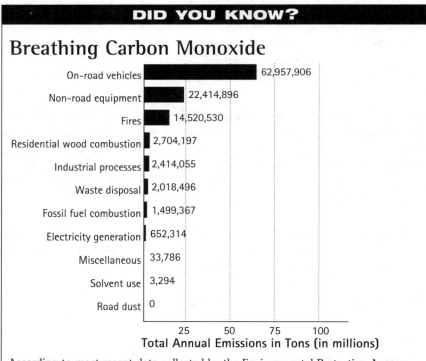

DID YOU KNOW?

Breathing Carbon Monoxide

	Total Annual Emissions in Tons (in millions)
On-road vehicles	62,957,906
Non-road equipment	22,414,896
Fires	14,520,530
Residential wood combustion	2,704,197
Industrial processes	2,414,055
Waste disposal	2,018,496
Fossil fuel combustion	1,499,367
Electricity generation	652,314
Miscellaneous	33,786
Solvent use	3,294
Road dust	0

Total Annual Emissions in Tons (in millions)

According to most recent data collected by the Environmental Protection Agency, carbon monoxide is spewed into the air from a variety of sources.

Source: Environmental Protection Agency, 2002.

ide poisoning varies from person to person depending on their age and size.

SOURCES

Carbon monoxide is one of the most dangerous gases in existence. It can be found in enclosed, unvented areas, such as a house or a garage. Some sources of carbon monoxide gas include: unvented kerosene and gas space heaters; wood stoves; gas water heaters; fireplaces; any gasoline-powered equipment, such as chain saws, leaf blowers, and lawn mowers; tobacco smoke; and gas-burning ovens.

Carbon monoxide is also a component of motor vehicle exhaust, contributing about 56 percent of all carbon monoxide emissions in the United States, according to the Environmental Protection Agency (EPA). Carbon monoxide is a major problem in many cities where traffic congestion is widespread. Factories, especially those in the metal processing and chemical industries, also emit carbon monoxide, spewing tons of the gas into the air each year.

The burning of wood, either in wood stoves or by forest fires, contributes to carbon monoxide emissions. Scientists have found that high levels of carbon monoxide occur more frequently in the open air in the winter months, when **inversion** conditions are more frequent as air pollution becomes trapped near the ground beneath a layer of warm air.

Fact Or Fiction?

It is okay to light a charcoal or a gas grill indoors.

The Facts: It is never okay to light a barbecue grill inside a house, garage, tent, or any enclosed space. The grill will emit carbon monoxide. In an enclosed area, carbon monoxide can be fatal. Just as lighting a barbecue grill indoors, heating a room by a gas oven is also extremely dangerous.

Carbon monoxide emissions vary from state to state depending on a variety of factors, including the number of automobiles and factories that pump the gas into the air. In New York, for example, motor vehicles, factories, and other sources emit about 3.7 million tons of carbon monoxide each year. In a state such as Oklahoma, with a smaller population, emissions were slightly more than 1 million tons a year.

EFFECTS ON HEALTH

Carbon monoxide can cause a wide range of health problems. The gas reduces the delivery of oxygen to the body's organs and tissues when the carbon forms a stable **compound** with **hemoglobin** in the blood. Hemoglobin transports oxygen throughout the body. When the body's organs do not receive enough oxygen, they can malfunction.

Those who suffer from heart disease are at a substantial risk even from low levels of the gas. Limited exposure to carbon monoxide emissions might result in chest pain and breathing problems. The gas also affects the central nervous system of healthy people. A person who has inhaled a high level of carbon monoxide can develop vision problems. They might also exhibit learning difficulties. Carbon monoxide poisoning also limits a person's ability to move and pick up objects and accomplish complex tasks. Extremely high levels of carbon monoxide can cause death.

Carbon monoxide also contributes to the formation of **smog**, or ground level **ozone**, which forms by the interaction between sunlight and air pollution. Smog triggers breathing problems in some people.

REDUCING CARBON MONOXIDE

Beginning in the 1970s, the federal government set national standards to regulate and reduce carbon monoxide emissions from motor vehicles. In 1970, the U.S. Congress passed the Clean Air Act, which established the first auto emission standards. Four years later, the EPA set the country's first fuel economy standards for automobiles, reducing carbon monoxide even further by mandating that motor vehicle engines burn gas more efficiently.

In 1975, the government mandated that automakers begin installing catalytic converters on cars and trucks to decrease carbon monoxide and **hydrocarbon** pollution. Also in 1975, the government banned the use of **lead** in gasoline, greatly reducing the amount of that toxin in the environment. In 30 years, these and other regulations have reduced carbon monoxide emissions from cars, motorcycles, and trucks by more than 40 percent.

The government now requires large factories and other commercial buildings to obtain an EPA permit before construction, ensuring that these factories comply with all government environmental standards.

Q & A

Question: How many people are unintentionally poisoned by carbon monoxide?

Answer: On average, 170 people die from carbon monoxide poisoning each year. Most of those are poisoned because of a malfunctioning appliance in their home, such as a furnace, water heater, or room heater. The Centers for Disease Control and Prevention (CDC) estimates that several thousand people are rushed to the emergency room each year for treatment of carbon monoxide poisoning.

There are several ways that families can prevent exposure to carbon monoxide. Make sure a professional installs all appliances according to all rules and regulations. A qualified heating specialist should inspect and service your family's furnace each year. Also, make sure your chimney is inspected for flue blockages, corrosion, and any other problems. Never service a fuel-burning appliance without the proper tools and training.

In addition, never use a portable generator or other gasoline-powered tool in an enclosed space such as a house or a garage. Even if you keep the doors open, you risk exposure to the gas. Never run a car in a garage, even with the door open. Finally, install a carbon monoxide detector to alert you in case of a gas leak.

Q & A

Question: What should I do if I have symptoms of carbon monoxide poisoning?

Answer: Immediately go outside into the fresh air if you exhibit any of the symptoms related to carbon monoxide poisoning. Leave your home immediately and call the fire department from a neighbor's phone. You could pass out and die if you stay inside your house. Once you are safe, go to the hospital or see a doctor.

It is very important to have carbon monoxide detectors in various places in a home. They will warn the family before they are exposed to potentially life-threatening levels of carbon monoxide. The alarm manufacturers are always improving the devices. These devices have helped save lives.

See also: Air Pollution; Global Warming; Volcanic Activity; Chemical Pollution; Lead Poisoning

FURTHER READING
Tocci, Salvatore. *Carbon.* True Books. New York: Children's Press, 2005.
West, Krista. *Carbon Chemistry.* Essential Chemistry. New York: Chelsea House Publications, 2008.

■ CARCINOGENS, SOURCES AND DANGERS OF

Substances that increases the chance of a cell becoming cancerous. Some carcinogens include chemical compounds, viruses, X-rays, and other forms of **radiation**. Generally, health officials and scientists use the term to mean only chemical agents that cause cancer.

Mutations, or changes, in a cell's DNA cause cancer. DNA is the abbreviation for **deoxyribonucleic acid**, a **genetic material**. Genes determine inherited characteristics, such as eye and hair color. Exposure to a wide variety of things in our environment could cause a cell to mutate. People can get cancer from exposure to ultraviolet rays from the Sun; from certain medical treatments; or from lifestyle factors, such as poor nutrition.

Carcinogens do not always cause cancer. Some substances that scientists label as a carcinogen have different cancer-causing levels. The risk of someone developing cancer depends on many factors, including the intensity and duration of the exposure and how the person came in contact with the carcinogen.

LAB STUDIES

Over the years, scientists have labeled hundreds of substances as carcinogens. They range from **asbestos** to tobacco smoking to long-term X-ray and **gamma ray** exposure. Some infections, such as hepatitis C, may also cause cancer.

How do scientists know whether a substance is a carcinogen? Scientists get much of the information about carcinogens from conducting studies in the laboratory. Scientists study the chemical makeup of a substance and compare it to similar substances that they have already studied. Using that information, scientists can determine whether something can cause cancer.

Before labeling a substance a carcinogen, scientists usually test that substance on animals. In many cases, scientists have found that substances that cause cancer in laboratory animals also cause cancer in humans.

Fact Or Fiction?

Can radiation emitted by a cell phone can give you brain cancer?

The Facts: For years, rumors have persisted that handheld cell phones can give people brain cancer. In 2008, an official at the National Cancer Institute told a congressional panel that cell phones are safe. Others disagree. Cell phones use a form of radiation to send and receive radio signals. That radiation is not like the radiation you might find in X-rays and other radioactive materials, which are known carcinogens. The radiation given off by cell phones is the same as radiation given off by a microwave oven. Cell phones do not release enough radiation or energy to damage brain cells, which can lead to brain cancer. Three studies suggest that short-term exposure is harmless, but long-term exposure is a different story. Some say that long-term and frequent use of cell phones is associated with an increased risk of brain tumors.

In addition to lab studies, scientists use **epidemiologic** studies. They study different populations of humans to determine what factors might link them to cancer. For example, all people are exposed to many substances at work, in school, or at home, and on the playground. They are also exposed to many substances in the food they eat, the water they drink, and the air they breathe. Scientists study these various populations and factors in an attempt to pinpoint possible carcinogens.

However, epidemiologic studies might not always give scientists the correct answers. Laboratory experiments are conducted in a controlled environment but people are exposed to many things during the course of a day. In addition, people generally do not know everything they have touched, drunk, eaten, or come into contact with from the moment

Common Types of Childhood Cancer

Central Nervous System	Lymphoma	Leukemia	Melanoma
Cancer of the central nervous system begins when cells in the brain or spinal cord start to grow, ultimately forming a mass. Sometimes these tumors are noncancerous. Others are very aggressive or malignant.	Lymphoma is a cancer of the body's lymph system. The body uses the lymph system to fight infection and disease. The lymph system carries a colorless fluid containing white blood cells which helps the body fight off infection and disease. When lymphatic cells mutate, or change, they can grow into cancerous tumors. There are several different types of lymphoma	Leukemia, a cancer of the blood, is the most common type of childhood cancer. One type of leukemia known as acute lymphocytic leukemia, or ALL, destroys the normal cells in a child's bone marrow, replacing them with abnormal white blood cells. Normal white blood cells, also known as lymphocytes, fight infections in the body. If the abnormal lymphocytes overwhelm the normal red cells, the body is prevented from making red cells and other types of normal white blood cells.	Melanoma, cancer of the skin, begins when cells called melanocytes grow abnormally, forming a tumor. Melanoma can occur anywhere on a person's body. People who are constantly exposed to the Sun's ultraviolet radiation, or who are fair skinned, can develop melanoma more readily than others. Severe sunburn can also be a factor in developing the disease.

Central Nervous System	Lymphoma	Leukemia	Melanoma
Symptoms include: seizures or convulsions; nausea and vomiting; weakness; vision problems; headaches.	Symptoms include: swelling or lumps in the lymph nodes in the abdomen, groin, underarm or neck; fever not associated with a sickness; sweating; chills; fatigue	Symptoms include anemia and the easy bruising or bleeding of the body from minor injuries.	Symptoms include: large dark spots on the skin; a mole that changes color; firm, dome-shaped bumps anywhere on a person's body.
Doctors are always improving ways to pinpoint a tumor's location through imaging technology, such as an MRI.	An estimated 800 children were diagnosed in the United States with a type of lymphoma known as non-Hodgkin's lymphoma. This type of lymphoma accounts for about 4 percent of all childhood cancer.	ALL is the most common form of childhood cancer. In 2008, more than 2,600 children under the age of 20 in the United States were diagnosed with the disease.	In 2009, more than 62,480 men and women in the United States will be diagnosed with melanoma.

Cancer in children is very rare. While only about one of every 330 people under the age of 20 will suffer from cancer, one out of six adults over the age of 20 will develop cancer in their lifetime.

American Society of Clinical Oncology, 2009.

they wake up to the moment they go to bed. As a result, there remain huge gaps in the research, making it hard for researchers to pinpoint one particular substance common to a number of individuals.

Still, epidemiologic studies are important. Scientists use data from laboratory studies and epidemiologic studies together to make educated guesses about a substance's cancer-causing abilities.

CLASSIFICATION

The World Health Organization (WHO) has developed a system for classifying carcinogens. Since the 1970s, the International Agency for Research on Cancer (IARC), which is part of the WHO, has studied 900 possible carcinogens. The agency has placed these substances in four groups. They include:

- Group 1: Substances that cause cancer in humans
- Group 2A: Substances *probably* carcinogenic to humans
- Group 2B: Substances *possibly* carcinogenic to humans
- Group 3: Substances that *are* "unclassifiable" as carcinogenic to humans
- Group 4: Substances *not* carcinogenic to humans.

The agency has listed only 100 substances as "carcinogenic to humans."

EFFECTS ON HEALTH

There are many well-known substances that cause cancer in humans. For example, inhaling asbestos fibers over a long period can cause lung cancer. Exposure to **arsenic**, a semi-metallic element that is present in the soil, the water, and the human body can cause skin and lung cancer. A person can contract leukemia, a type of cancer of the blood cells, from exposure to toxins such as benzene, among other things.

TEENS SPEAK

Am I Drinking Poison?

My name is Jeremy and I live in Arizona. One day a reporter from the local newspaper came to my house. She was looking for my mom and dad. She told my parents that the local health district had found high traces of arsenic in groundwater just above our house.

We get our water from a well in our backyard. The well goes deep into the ground and taps the underground water supply. We drink and cook with well water. Mom and dad were shocked to find out that our groundwater might be contaminated with arsenic. I wasn't too concerned as the reporter talked to my parents, until I heard the reporter utter the words "cancer-causing."

I know what cancer is. My grandma died of lung cancer when I was small. Uncle Tom had skin cancer. What I didn't know was that arsenic is a carcinogen, a substance that causes cancer. The reporter told my parents that the arsenic might have come from the two copper mines near our house.

I did not know much about arsenic. I went online to look it up. I found that arsenic is odorless and tasteless. Some arsenic occurs naturally in the rocks and soil. Sometimes though, factories and mines dump waste into the environment. Some of that industrial waste has arsenic in it. Like I said, we live downhill from a couple of copper mining operations, and some people think the mines contaminated the groundwater above us.

We can all get arsenic by breathing in contaminated dust or drinking contaminated water. The town is trying to find out for certain the source of the arsenic contamination and whether our drinking water is polluted. The reporter said the town was supplying everyone with bottled water to drink and cook with. We should get ours in a few days.

The chances of my family developing cancer because of arsenic are very slim. You have to be exposed to it for a very long time, I learned. We just moved to town three months ago. I think we'll be okay.

Chewing or smoking tobacco products can cause various types of cancer, including lung cancer, throat cancer, cancer of the mouth, and cancer of the nasal passages. Tobacco is responsible for 87 percent of all lung cancer deaths and 30 percent of all cancer deaths.

DID YOU KNOW?

Childhood Cancer Deaths

	Number of deaths in millions	
Characteristic	1990	2004
Total	2,457	2,223
Sex		
Male	1,390	1,256
Female	1,067	967
Age Group		
0–14	1,698	1,492
15–19	759	731
Race		
White	1,987	1,748
Black	375	368
American Indian/Alaska Native	24	18
Asian/Pacific Islander	71	89
Region		
Northeast	415	366
Midwest	636	499
South	844	795
West	562	563
Primary Cancers		
Leukemia	738	566
Brain/Other Nervous System	568	555
Other	1,151	1,102

From 1999 to 2004, the number of childhood cancer deaths—especially from the leading killers in children, leukemia and brain cancer—has decreased. The chart above looks at the decline based on sex, age, race, ethnicity, and region of the country.

Source: Centers for Disease Control (2004)

See also: Asbestos; Chemical Pollution; Clean Water; Groundwater; Radiation; Radon

FURTHER READING
Mareck, Amy M. *Fighting for My Life; Growing Up with Cancer.* Minneapolis, Minn.: Fairview Press, 2007.
Wyborny, Shelia. *Science on the Edge, Cancer Treatments.* Farmington Hills, Mich.: Blackbirch Press, 2005.

■ CHEMICAL POLLUTION, CAUSES AND HAZARDS OF

The harmful effect on the environment by the release of chemical contaminants, principally from industrial and agricultural processes. Chemical pollution, chiefly caused by human activities, can poison air, soil, and water. In addition to impacting the health of humans, chemical pollution has had many adverse affects on wildlife and plant life.

Pollution in one form or another has been around since prehistoric times. However, the type of pollution changed drastically during the mid-20th century when industries began using a variety of chemicals in the manufacturing process. Factories used these chemicals to fashion products from **synthetic** materials, which include plastics, **polychlorinated biphenyls** (PCBs), and pesticides. These and other materials are not **biodegradable** and build up in the environment.

In addition to making people sick, chemical pollution impacts the **ecosystem**, leading to the extinction of many animal and plant species. The difficulty of disposing of chemicals and illegal dumping has generated many toxic, or poisonous, waste sites all over the world. In addition, farmers use chemical fertilizers and pesticides to grow and process food. These chemicals often find their way into lakes, rivers, streams, and groundwater. The sale of chemicals is a big business in the United States. Chemical sales total about $112 million each year, with more than 70,000 chemical substances on the market.

INDUSTRIAL CHEMICALS

The U.S. Environmental Protection Agency (EPA) estimates that American industry creates 50 percent of all pollution in the United States. After World War II (1939–1945), America's factories and those of other developed nations, began using a variety of chemicals to make many products.

One product that highlights the risks associated with chemical pollution is the pesticide *dichlorodiphenyl trichloroethane* (DDT). DDT saved millions of lives during World War II by reducing the number of cases of **typhus** and **malaria** on the battlefield. Many people used DDT after the war. The chemical found its way into water and soil. As the poison made its way through the **food chain**, many species of animals, including the bald eagle, began showing the harmful effects of ingesting it.

Eventually, the benefits of DDT did not outweigh the environmental hazards posed by the chemical. Most countries now ban the use of DDT, but many Latin American countries still use the pesticide.

Most of the chemical pollution in the world comes from companies that illegally discharged toxic chemicals into the environment. Many companies also buried chemicals in the ground. Often, these chemicals would leach into the groundwater from dumping sites. The release of these toxic chemicals caused massive wildlife kills and an increase in cancer and birth defects in people who lived near the water polluted by these factories. Industrial accidents, such as oil spills, are also a prime source of chemical pollution.

THE STORY OF LOVE CANAL

One story that underscores the dangers of chemical pollution is the tale of Love Canal, a community in Niagara Falls, New York. Love Canal remains one of the most severe chemical pollution cases in American history.

In the early part of the 20th century, William T. Love wanted to build a model community on the eastern edge of Niagara Falls. He dug a canal to generate power, but that is as far as Love got. Because of economic problems, he abandoned the project not long after he finished digging the canal.

In the 1920s, various companies and municipalities in the area turned Love Canal into a chemical waste dump. Dumping continued for years. In the late 1950s, developers built 100 homes and a school on land near the canal.

By 1978, health officials found that more than 80 chemical compounds, of which 11 were carcinogens, were bubbling up through the soil, contaminating backyards and basements. In several instances, rusted waste-disposal drums broke through the ground. Trees and gardens turned black and died. Even the foundation of a swimming pool broke free and began floating on a sea of chemicals. After playing in the area, children returned home with chemical burns on their hands and faces.

Even before the chemical leaks were discovered, Love Canal had a high rate of miscarriages and children born with birth defects caused by exposure to these chemicals. Moreover, a large percentage of Love Canal residents had high white-blood-cell counts, which could have led to leukemia, a cancer of the blood cells. The citizens of Love Canal left their homes, never to return.

INTO THE AIR

Chemical pollution does not just impact the soil and water. Chemicals also foul the air. Factories, automobiles, and other sources spew a number of harmful chemicals into the atmosphere. These include: sulfur oxides, produced by the burning coal and petroleum; nitrogen oxide, a reddish-brown toxic gas; carbon monoxide, a colorless odorless gas formed by the incomplete burning of natural gas, coal, or wood; and **chlorofluoro-carbons**. All of these chemicals are harmful to Earth's **ozone layer**, the part of the atmosphere that protects us from the Sun's harmful rays.

One of the most devastating types of chemical pollution is acid rain. When factories burn fossil fuels, especially coal, they release gases such as sulfur dioxide and nitrous oxide. Sulfuric acid forms when these gases combine with water vapor. The sulfuric acid falls to the ground as acid rain.

Acid rain harms plants, animals, humans, and buildings. The wind carries clouds of sulfur emissions far from the source of pollution. Factories in the Midwest, for example, are responsible for poisoning the Adirondack Mountains in upstate New York, hundreds of miles away.

Factories are not the only things which emit harmful chemicals into the atmosphere. About 44 percent of all nitrogen oxide emissions come from motor vehicles.

Q & A

Question: How does farming contribute to chemical pollution?

Answer: Farms use a variety of chemicals in growing and processing of food. Farmers use chemicals to fertilize their crops and pesticides to kill insects that can damage plants.

The chemicals released by pesticides include nitrates, ammonium salts, chlorine, sulphates, heavy metals, and other chemicals. Often these chemicals will find their way into a lake, river, or stream. Erosion of contaminated soil can damage wetlands and fish habitats by increasing water temperature and decreasing oxygen.

Q & A

Question: Can a chemical factory dump hazardous waste in a local landfill?

Answer: Some waste is too hazardous for companies to dump at an ordinary landfill. Waste from chemical factories needs to be disposed of in special treatment plants or incinerators. Some chemical companies still illegally dump into rivers or the oceans.

According to some estimates, factories release more than 4 billion pounds of toxic chemicals into the nation's environment each year. Seventy-two million pounds of those chemicals are known carcinogens.

Chemicals can provide some benefits too. Some chemicals preserve food. Other chemicals kill unwanted pests, like ants and termites. We use chemicals every day. We use them to clean our homes and we ingest chemicals when we are sick. However, chemicals must be used safely and wisely.

See also: Air Pollution; Carcinogens; Clean Water; Superfund Sites; Water Pollution

FURTHER READING

Fullick, Ann. *Chemicals in Action.* Chicago: Heinemann Library, 2000.
Owens, Peter. *Oil and Chemical Spills.* Farmington Hills, Mich.: Lucent Books, 2004.
Roleff, Tamara L., ed. *Pollution: Opposing Viewpoints.* Farmington Hills, Mich.: Greenhaven Press, 2000.

■ CLEAN WATER, SOURCES AND USES OF

Water of such high quality that humans can consume, or use it, without risking short-term or long-term harm. Clean water, suitable for drinking,

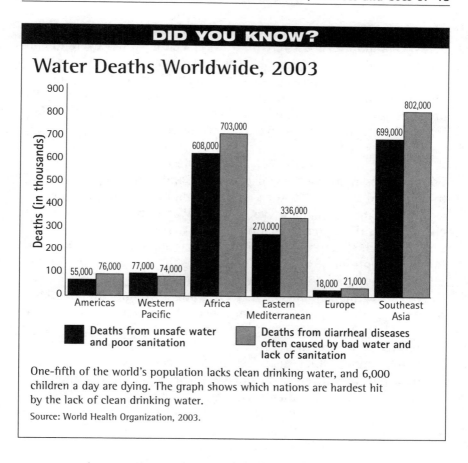

DID YOU KNOW?

Water Deaths Worldwide, 2003

One-fifth of the world's population lacks clean drinking water, and 6,000 children a day are dying. The graph shows which nations are hardest hit by the lack of clean drinking water.

Source: World Health Organization, 2003.

is usually defined as potable water and is generally supplied to households and industries. Developed countries, such as the United States and Canada, have set high standards on the quality of potable water.

In many nations, however, humans use and drink water that is contaminated with bacteria and unacceptable levels of dissolved contaminates or solids. Drinking or cooking with such water is often harmful and can cause a variety of chronic illnesses and even death.

WATER SUPPLY

Towns and cities generally provide residents with clean drinking water from nearby rivers, lakes, or underground water sources. The water supply is the difference between the amount of water a community collects and the amount of water it distributes.

Because towns and cities are always distributing water to its residents, communities must rely on a never-ending water cycle to continually refill the water supply. The water cycle begins when water rises from the oceans as vapor. The vapor collects in the clouds, and falls as precipitation. Precipitation includes hail, snow, and rain. The precipitation seeps into and runs over the ground, eventually returning to the ocean. Then the cycle begins again.

WATER TREATMENT

Communities treat water with chemicals and filters to make it safe to drink and use. The water you drink might have been cleaned at a water treatment plant in your town. Water treatment plants add chemicals in the water so that bits of soil and debris bind together in a process called **coagulation**. Through coagulation, clumps of debris fall to the bottom of a settling tank. Once the debris settles, workers mechanically remove the chunks as sludge.

Water treatment plants then pass water through filters to clean out any remaining impurities. They also add **chlorine** to kill disease-carrying bacteria that might be in the water. This process is known as **disinfection**. Some water treatment plants also pass water through **ultraviolet light**, which also destroys disease-carrying bacteria.

Some people, however, do not get their water from a municipal water supply; instead, they buy water from private water companies. Still others get their water from underground wells in their backyards.

CLEAN WATER STANDARDS

Clean water is so important to the health of individuals that most countries have developed clean water standards for lakes, rivers, streams, watersheds, and other waterways. The United States has one of the most sweeping set of standards.

By the 1960s, many lakes and rivers in the United States were nothing more than open sewers. Many cities discharged raw, untreated sewage, including human waste, directly into the water. Moreover, there were no standards on the discharge of toxic chemicals and other industrial pollutants. According to the Sierra Club, an environmental group, 70 percent of the all the water in the United States was unsafe for drinking.

In 1972, Congress passed the Clean Water Act. The legislation set a goal of eliminating pollution from the nation's waterways, lakes, rivers, and streams. The law gave money to local communities to build thousands of new sewage treatment plants and it established guidelines to reduce the destruction of wetlands.

By 2003, 61 percent of all rivers in the United States, along with 55 percent of all lakes and 40 percent of all estuaries, met federal safety standards.

DIRTY WATER

Many nations, especially those in developing countries, still do not have many sources of clean water to drink. These countries lack proper water treatment facilities and sewage treatment plants. Human waste and animal waste, both of which contain disease-carrying organisms, contaminate much of the water in these underdeveloped nations. Waterborne diseases cause four-fifths of all the illnesses in developing countries.

Scientists estimate that 1.1 billion people around the world lack access to clean drinking water. Waterborne diseases, such as malaria, typhus, and cholera, infect millions each year.

TEENS SPEAK

Little Clean Water to Drink

My name is Annan and I live in Candele, a village in the mountains of western Angola. Angola is a country in south-western Africa. It is very beautiful here, but not everything is as nice as it seems. Many of the people who live here cannot get enough to eat. They often get sick.

We do not have good water to drink. Oftentimes I become ill after drinking from the local well. There are no markets to buy bottled water. It takes me three hours each day to fetch water from a stream. My mother, my sisters, my brothers, and I must bring back water every day. Sometimes I get tired. Soon, though, things will get better. Workers are building a large reservoir to provide clean water for everyone. Once the reservoir is complete, we will not have to travel to bring back water from the river. We will be able to drink the water, and use it to cook and clean. We will also be able to safely grow vegetables that we can eat.

According to the United Nations Children's Fund (UNICEF), polluted water and the lack of basic sanitation claim the lives of 1.5 million children each year. Most die of waterborne illnesses. Diarrhea is responsible for 90 percent of all deaths of children under five years old in developing countries.

Q & A

Question: My mom says our drinking water has fluoride in it. What is fluoride?

Answer: Fluoride is a chemical used to fight tooth decay. The chemical hardens the enamel of growing teeth and helps prevent decay on the smooth surface of a tooth. Some people believe adding fluoride to drinking water is dangerous because high levels of the substance are toxic.

See also: Groundwater, Water Pollution

FURTHER READING

Warhol, Tom. *Water.* Tarrytown, N.Y.: Marshall Cavendish Benchmark, 2006.

Fredericks, Carrie, ed. *Water.* Fueling the Future. Farmington, Mich.: Greenhaven Press, 2006.

Tesar, Jenny E. *Food and Water: Threats, Shortages, and Solutions.* New York: Facts On File, 1992.

■ CONSERVATION

See also: Groundwater; Water Pollution

■ DESERTIFICATION, CAUSES AND EFFECTS OF

The process by which human activities and changes in climate turn productive land into desert. The desertification process involves multiple causes and impacts climates at different rates. During desertification in arid and semi-arid environments, sudden downpours and lashing wind can erode the land's fragile topsoil.

No matter the region of the world, poor farming practices, overgrazing of grassland by livestock, the destruction of forests by humans, and the intensive cultivation of soil contribute to desertification.

Land is not the only thing in danger. Desertification impacts the lives of some 200 million people living mostly in Africa, India, and South America. Desertification disrupts a person's livelihood. It also impacts a region's **ecosystem**.

CAUSES

In short, desertification throws a region's ecosystem into disarray. A healthy arid or semi-arid environment is generally populated by only a few animals and people. Each tries to survive on the area's scarce resources. Dry environments lack water, fertile soil, and vegetation.

Desertification knows no boundaries. It was a problem in the 1930s when parts of the Great Plains in the United States turned into what became known as the dust bowl. Poor farming practices, coupled with a severe **drought**, turned the region into a vast, dry wasteland. High winds turned states like Oklahoma into regions of blowing dust and dirt. Crops died. Rivers ran dry. Millions of people had to leave their homes and abandon their livelihoods. Since then, better methods of farming, along with better **irrigation** practices, have prevented the disaster from occurring again.

Nevertheless, desertification still affects millions of people on almost every continent, including North America. The root causes of desertification in most cases are poverty and overpopulation. Poverty forces poor people to overexploit the land for food, energy, houses, and income. The problem becomes worse as the population grows. In the 1990s, the driest and poorest regions of the world saw a jump in population of 18.5 percent. This population explosion puts an undue strain on the environments' scarce resources.

Developing nations increasingly used poor soil conservation and farming practices. As the population grew, people needed more living space, farmland, food, and building materials. People destroyed vegetation and plowed fields to grow food. They clear-cut vast areas to provide grazing land for cattle and other livestock.

Moreover, poor farmers did not cultivate fields with enough organic matter rich in nutrients. They overused fertilizers, did not rotate crops, and did not **irrigate**. When farmers and ranchers allow livestock to graze recklessly, the animals remove all the native grasses, which helps hold the soil in place. The topsoil is then wiped away by wind erosion and sudden downpours of rain. Drought conditions also contribute to desertification, as the desert expands.

THE PROBLEM WORSENS

According to a 2007 United Nations (UN) report, desertification could drive tens of millions of people, mostly living in sub-Saharan Africa and Central Asia, from their homes. The report calls desertification "the greatest environmental challenge of our time."

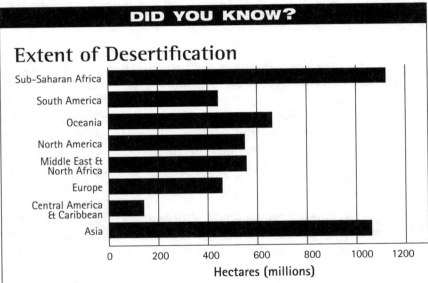

DID YOU KNOW?

Extent of Desertification

According to the United Nations Environment Programme, desertification—the drying up of land that was not previously desert—affects an estimated 25 to 30 percent of the world's land surface. This chart shows the extent of desertification in various regions. For example, Northern Africa and the Middle East have almost 600 million hectares (1.5 billion acres) of dryland, while Central America and the Caribbean have slightly more than 150 million hectares (371 billion acres) of dryland. One hectare is equal to 2.47 acres. According to the United Nations, desertification will become worse if proper farming practices and other steps are not adopted.

Source: United Nations Environment Programme, 2007.

The report warns that if governments do not take action immediately, about 50 million people will lose their homes within the next 10 years. While bad farming practices and the overexploitation of land are chiefly to blame for the calamity, the UN says that climate change is also a major factor in soil degradation.

The loss of land makes poverty worse in countries where desertification is a problem. It forces farmers to seek a living somewhere else, such as the cities. The UN says that 135 million people are at risk of losing their homes because of desertification. About 60 million people will move from sub-Saharan Africa to northern Africa and Europe within 20 years. In Mexico, between 700,000 to 900,000 people might leave their dry rural homeland to make a living as migrant workers in the United States.

MOVING FORWARD

Experts say that we can stop desertification. Scientists recommend that teaching farmers new methods of growing food will help improve soil conditions and that farmers need to learn about crop rotation, irrigation, and ways to put nutrients back in the soil.

Q & A

Question: Is desertification only a problem in Africa?

Answer: No. Desertification is a worldwide problem. Although two-thirds of Africa is desert or dry land, more than 30 percent of the land in the United States is affected by desertification. Desertification is a problem in one-quarter of Latin America, in one-fifth of Spain, and in China. Since the 1950s, expanding deserts have eaten away at 700,000 hectares of cultivated land in China, along with 2.35 million hectares of rangeland, and 6.4 million hectares of forests.

Planting millions of trees could also halt the expansion of several deserts, experts say. In China, for example, the government is planting a 3,000 mile–long (4,828 kilometer–long) stand of trees along the edge of the Gobi desert. On a long-term basis, governments have to make sure that their citizens do not have to rely solely on farming to eke out a living.

TEENS SPEAK

Living in a Dry Climate

My name is Degu, and I live in a small village in southern Ethiopia. Ethiopia is a country in Africa. My father is a farmer. He lost his last harvest because it does not rain much where I live. The soil is hard and dry. There is not enough food to eat. To make sure that we have enough food, my father has to work on the farms of other people and they do not pay him a lot. He can only buy half of a kilogram of maize with a day's salary.

Sometimes there is no food at home. My mother just heats water and puts salt in it. She then gives it to us to drink.

My little sister had to be taken to a feeding center in Danama a few weeks ago. While at the center, she had to stay a week for a checkup. She needed medicine and some *Plumpy'nut,* a type of peanut butter that is very nutritious and good for you.

My village is brown from the drought. My friends and I cannot play that much because we get tired. Once a month or so, aid workers bring us food and clean bottled water. It is never enough.

Teaching poor farmers how to better tend their fields and livestock is a start to stopping desertification, but because poverty forces people to depend on the land to survive, any effective strategy must address the plight of the poor and the specific needs of the areas affected.

See also: Environmental Conservation; Global Warming

FURTHER READING

Allan, Tony, and Andrew Warren, eds. *Deserts: The Encroaching Wilderness: A World Atlas.* New York: Oxford University Press, 1993.

Middleton, Nicholas, J. *Desertification.* New York: Oxford University Press, 1991.

Brezina, Corona. *Disappearing Forests: Deforestation, Desertification, and Drought.* New York: Rosen Publishing Group, 2009.

■ EARTHQUAKES AND TSUNAMIS, DANGERS OF

Geological events caused by the release of massive amounts of energy under Earth's crust. Earthquakes occur when the planet's tectonic plates, large regions of Earth's rocky outer shell, slide past each other, are pulled apart, or collide with one another. Tsunamis are giant sea waves caused by an underwater earthquake or volcanic eruption.

Earthquakes and tsunamis can be devastating natural events. In 2008, a massive earthquake in China killed more than 65,000 people. One of the worst tsunamis on record struck the Indian Ocean on December 26, 2004, killing nearly 300,000 people. An earthquake below the ocean floor triggered the massive wave that devastated many areas in South Asia, including Thailand, Sri Lanka, Indonesia, and India.

EARTHQUAKES

Earth is broken into tectonic plates that are always on the move. Most earthquakes occur at the boundaries of these huge slabs of Earth. When two plates move past each other, they become jammed and misshapen. When the plates free themselves, there is a rapid release of energy along the boundaries of the plates. That energy produces vibrations in the ground, also known as **seismic waves**. Those seismic waves can vibrate for hundreds, even thousands, of miles, shaking cities and causing massive amounts of damage.

Earthquakes occur along geologic **fault lines**. Fault lines are fractures in Earth's crust where the ground on one or both sides has moved. Most fault lines are below the surface. Some geologic faults, such as the San Andreas Fault in California, are clearly visible.

Faults come in several types. *Dip-slip* faults move vertically. One side moves up while the other side moves down. *Strike-slip* faults move horizontally. In a *lateral fault,* both sides of rock move past each other horizontally. In *oblique-slip faults,* the walls of rock move in the direction of a strike-slip fault and a lateral fault at once.

Seismologists, scientists who study earthquakes, estimate that 9,000 earthquakes strike each day around the world. Most of those earthquakes are minor, and cause no damage.

MEASURING EARTHQUAKES

Scientists measure the force, or magnitude, of an earthquake using the **Richter scale**. Scientists also measure the effect, or intensity, of a quake using the **Mercalli scale**.

In 1935, Charles Richter, a scientist at the California Institute of Technology, was the first to introduce the concept of earthquake magnitude. Magnitude is the total amount of energy released during an earthquake. Richter based his scale on the measurement of seismic waves.

Richter marked his scale with the numbers one (lowest) to nine (highest). He used those numbers to measure the amount of energy an earthquake releases. Each point on the Richter scale represents a thirtyfold increase in energy over the previous point. Major earthquakes measure five and above on the Richter scale.

When an earthquake rumbles, vibrations travel through Earth. A device called a **seismograph** measures and records these vibrations, no matter where they occur on the planet.

Tsunamis

Many people incorrectly call tsunamis tidal waves. Tsunamis are monster ocean waves caused by violent earthquakes, volcanic eruptions,

DID YOU KNOW?

Deadly Waves

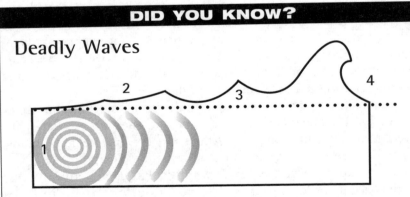

1. Seismic event sends shock wave outward.
2. Initial waves travel very fast but are only a few feet high.
3. As they approach the coastline, where the ocean floor becomes shallow, the waves decrease in speed while increasing in height.
4. Tsunami waves hit shores with deadly force, depositing water and debris.

Tsunamis form when a seismic event, such as an earthquake, strikes below the ocean floor. Their destructive power comes from the towering heights they attain as they approach the coast.

Source: United States Geological Survey.

and landslides that occur hundreds of feet below the ocean floor. The energy created by such geological disturbances radiates outward from the epicenter. Large volumes of water, known as swells, also move outward from the center.

At first, a person might not be able to tell a tsunami is occurring. The swell travels about 600 miles (965 km) an hour across the ocean. The swells become high waves as they bunch up in shallow water near the shore. By that time the monster wave strikes land, it might have grown as high as 50 feet (15 meters) or more.

Fact Or Fiction?

A boat way out at sea will sink as it rides over a tsunami.

The Facts: Out at sea, boaters will notice nothing more than a gentle rise and fall of the ocean surface as a tsunami passes underneath. A tsunami that struck Japan in 1896 went unnoticed by fishermen 20 miles (32.1 km) out to sea. Back on land, however, the giant wave killed 28,000 people.

Most tsunamis occur in the Pacific Ocean. The Pacific Ocean is encircled by what is known as the Ring of Fire, a band of volcanoes, mountains, and earthquake zones. The western United States, Japan, Korea, and Indonesia, border the Ring of Fire and are prone to tsunamis.

In 1946, an earthquake in Alaska generated the most devastating tsunami in the United States. The giant wave traveled 2,300 miles (3,700 km) in five hours, killing 159 people in Hawaii. Tsunamis are also a danger in California, Oregon, and Washington. In 1964, another Alaskan quake sent a 20-foot-high (six-meter-high) wall of water slamming into the west coast of the United States. The wave killed 123 people and caused more than $100 million in damage.

Q & A

Question: Can scientists predict an earthquake?

Answer: No, scientists have not been able to predict a major earthquake and will not be able to in the future. However, using various forms of scientific data, geologists can calculate the potential for future earthquakes. They speculate that California's San Francisco Bay area, which is a center of seismic activity, has a 67 percent chance of being struck by major earthquake in the next 30 years. Los Angeles has a 67 percent chance as well.

Humans cannot control earthquakes. Earthquakes are part of the planet's tectonic process. The focal point of most earthquakes is miles underground and the force of the quakes is just too much for humans to control. However, people can build buildings that lessen the impact of powerful earthquakes.

Fact Or Fiction?

California will eventually fall into the ocean.

The Facts: No. California is home to the San Andreas Fault System. The fault is the boundary between the Pacific Plate and the North American Plate. The Pacific Plate is currently moving northwest at an estimated 1.8 inches (46 mm) a year. California cannot fall into the ocean because the plates are moving horizontally. Still, Los Angeles will one day in the very distant future be near San Francisco.

See also: Volcanoes

FURTHER READING

Fradin, Dennis, and Julie Fradin. *Witness to Disaster: Earthquakes.* Washington, D.C.: National Geographic Children's Books, 2008.

Kusky, Timothy, Ph.D. *Earthquakes: Plate Tectonics and Earthquake Hazards.* New York: Facts On File, 2008.

——. *Tsunamis: Giant Waves from the Sea.* New York: Facts On File, 2008.

■ ENVIRONMENTAL CONSERVATION, HISTORY AND BENEFITS OF

A broad philosophy centered on the improvement, management and protection of Earth's **natural resources**. Environmental conservation comes in many forms: political, social, and scientific. At its core, environmental conservation is about finding ways for humans to use Earth's resources at a rate in which they can be replenished. That process is called *sustainability*.

Early conservation efforts began with a movement to protect fish and wildlife. Conservationists then began seeking ways to protect water, soil, and the forests. Since then, environmental conservation has broadened to include the protection of all life in a given **ecosystem**. That ecosystem could be as small as a lake or pond or as large as the entire planet.

LIMITED NATURAL RESOURCES

The environment is important to us all and its state of health helps determine whether people and animals have enough food to eat, enough water to drink, and whether all living things, no matter how small, will live long enough to reproduce.

Over the centuries, humans have impacted the environment in countless ways. They have hunted many animals to extinction. They have polluted the air, water, and soil with chemicals. They have cut down massive amounts of forests and destroyed the **habitats** of many plants and animals.

Between 1950 and 1990, Earth's population more than doubled, from 2.5 billion people to more than 5 billion. As Earth's population grows, so do the needs of its people. People will need more land to build homes, more food to eat, more clean water to drink. They will need more electricity to run appliances and more gasoline to power their cars.

THE BEGINNINGS OF CONSERVATION

Environmentalists are people who are concerned about the impact of human activity on Earth. They formulate ways for humans to live without further damaging the planet. As the world population grows, however, that task, though, is getting harder every day.

The relationship between people and the environment has always been complex. On one hand, humans have overexploited the world's natural resources, damming rivers, killing wildlife, and polluting the air, water, and soil. On the other hand, many have fought to protect the environment.

Throughout history, people have been concerned about the dangers of harming the environment. The modern environmental conservation movement began at the dawn of the industrial age in the late 1700 and early 1800s. At that time, great factories emerged in the world's cities, consuming large quantities of **fossil fuels** such as coal. These fuels powered the factories and created products that people bought. But the Industrial Age produced immense air pollution and the dumping of toxic chemicals. People began to realize that damaging the environment was not good. Because of this, nations began passing laws to protect the planet.

In the United States, historians trace the beginnings of the environmental movement back to 1739, when Philadelphia residents urged the Pennsylvania Assembly to stop tanneries in Philadelphia from dumping their wastes. In the 1800s, as Americans moved west, people began worrying that the nation would run out of many natural resources, including wood. These early conservationists also argued that great tracts of wilderness should be protected by law.

Individuals such as naturalist John Muir and philosopher Henry David Thoreau became interested in the relationship between people and the environment. Muir lobbied Congress to form Yosemite National Park. He also founded the Sierra Club, now one of the major environmental groups in the world. Thoreau wrote about how humans can live in harmony with Earth. In 1964, President Lyndon Johnson solidified this relationship by signing into law the Wilderness Preservation Act. This law not only protects 9 million acres (3,642,170.78 hectares) of wilderness in the United States, but it also legally defines a wilderness as "an area where the earth and its community of life are untrammeled by man, where man himself is a visitor who does not remain."

TODAY'S ENVIRONMENTALIST

As the environmental movement grew, the world's governments began passing legislation aimed at protecting the planet. Most developed nations now ban lead, a toxic substance, from all sorts of manufactured products, including gasoline and paint.

In 1962, Rachel Carson wrote *Silent Spring,* a book about the dangers of the pesticide DDT. In 1972, the United States Environmental Protection Agency (EPA) banned the use of the pesticide. In 1973, the U.S. Congress passed the Endangered Species Act to protect many animal **species**.

Today, environmentalists advocate the protection and restoration of the environment not only through legislation but through changes in individual behavior. Environmental conservation now involves simple tasks, such as turning off lights and not using plastic shopping bags, and more ambitious ones, such as taking court action to protect wolves, polar bears, and other animals.

TEENS SPEAK

I'm a Conservationist

My name is Jenna, I'm in the seventh grade, and I'm an environmental conservationist. Whenever I get the chance, I do things that will help Earth. Sometimes they are small things. Other times, they are big things.

Last year, my friends Sarah, Claire, and Karen, went to a creek near where we live. We bought garbage bags, gloves, and a picnic lunch. For three hours we went up and down the creek picking up garbage and putting it in the bags. When we were done, we went for a swim and had a good time. My dad took the bags of garbage and went to the local landfill to properly dispose of them.

That was one of the big things I've done. I always recycle cans and bottles. I also try to save energy. I turn off my computer when I'm not using it. I also turn off the lights when I leave a room. I tell my mom to open the blinds on the windows during a cool winter day. The Sun will heat the house right up. I save water by taking short showers and no baths.

I also planted a tree last year. That helps the environment. Being an environmental conservationist is fun. It is also hard work, but I know I'm helping to save the planet.

See also: Air Pollution; Chemical Pollution; Depletion of the Rainforests; Desertification; Global Warming; Ground Water; Hazardous Waste Disposal; Landfills and Superfund Sites; Recycling; Water Pollution

FURTHER READING

Dolan, Edward, F. *The American Wilderness and Its Future: Conservation Versus Use.* New York: Franklin Watts, 1992.

Libal, Angela, and Ida Walker. *Rural Teens and Nature: Conservation and Wildlife Rehabilitation.* New York: Mason Crest Publishers, 2007.

■ FIRES, CAUSES AND ENVIRONMENTAL DANGERS OF

Rapid and persistent chemical changes that release heat and light and are accompanied by flame. Fires kill more people each year than any other disaster. Fires are also the fifth-leading cause of unintentional death in the United States.

Numerous causes can spark a fire, and many hazards are associated with them. Leaking gas, an industrial accident, and even an explosion of gas in an underground coal mine are just a few of the ways fires can get started.

HOUSEHOLD FIRES

One of the most common forms of fires is household fires. Household fires can begin in a variety of ways, including faulty electrical wires, unsafe space heaters, and children playing with matches.

Not only does the house itself burn, but so does almost everything in it. And unlike the homes of 60 or 70 years ago, today's homes have a variety of materials that become toxic when burned. If you have ever seen a house fire, you might have noticed thick black smoke rising from the burning building.

The smoke billowing from a burning house includes at least 17 different gases that are deadly in small amounts. Many household items, including some dishes and furniture, are made of **plastic**. When some plastic burns it produces **phosgene** gas, which if inhaled is toxic, or poisonous, and can be deadly. Even the bedroom mattress, or the living room sofa, emits a harmful gas called **hydrogen cyanide**.

Burning wood also can be deadly. Wood products are often treated with a variety of chemicals. Today's wood products often include plastics, glue, laminates (which give wood its shine) and other substances. When the wood is set ablaze, these materials make it burn faster and hotter. When burned, particle board emits arsenic and formaldehyde.

Even the substances that are supposed to protect you from fire could cause health problems. A study by the Environmental Working Group found high traces of toxic chemicals in fire retardants in the home. These fire retardants, known as PBDEs (polybrominated diphenyl ethers) can build up in one's body during a lifetime of exposure. The study found that even common household dust contained these chemicals.

INDUSTRIAL FIRES

Fires in factories, mines, warehouses, chemical plants, and other industrial sites also pose a major environmental hazard, not only for workers, but for those living in the surrounding area. In 2005, a major fire engulfed a tire recycling plant in Watertown, Wisconsin. Plumes of noxious black smoke billowed from the area as nearly 1 million tires burned. The acrid smoke stretched more than 637 square miles (1,025 sq. km). The fire began when a piece of equipment that moved tires around the plant malfunctioned. The smoke from the burning rubber was so toxic that officials advised people in town to keep their windows and doors closed. The fire burned for several days.

Chemical plant fires are also very dangerous. In 2006, police in Great Britain declared an emergency when a chemical plant burned. The explosion from the fire involved the mixing of several gases, including oxygen, hydrogen, nitrogen, and ammonia.

The deadliest industrial accident in the United States occurred in Texas City, Texas, on April 16, 1947. A French freighter caught fire as workers loaded 2,300 tons of ammonium nitrate fertilizer. The area around the freighter contained other ships laden with the same materials. There were also a number of petrochemical plants nearby. The accident killed more than 500 people. The explosion injured 5,000 people and destroyed 3,000 homes.

FOREST FIRES

Forest fires have a dual personality. On one hand, they pose a serious environmental hazard. On the other hand, forest fires are beneficial to the environment. Most forest fires are influenced in some way by humans. Humans can either start forest fires or create an environment where the fires can burn out of control. A forest fire becomes problematic when it burns in areas where people live, causing devastation to homes and communities. The economic impact felt by homeowners and businesses, not to mention local governments who fight the blazes, is often staggering.

People burn forests on purpose. In Brazil and elsewhere, ranchers and farmers burn trees to clear land for crops and pasture. Such fires ruin the **biodiversity** of the area. Forest fires also spew huge amounts of carbon dioxide which scientists blame for global warming into the atmosphere.

Studies show that forest fires are releasing the chemical mercury in the Northern wetlands of the United States and Canada. Mercury is a highly toxic substance that can contaminate the **food chain** and cause kidney damage, brain damage, and birth defects in humans. Factories that burn **fossil fuels** released mercury into the atmosphere; the mercury fell back to Earth and accumulated in the water and soil; and, researchers at Michigan State University found, wildfires are releasing the long-hidden mercury.

Forest fires also flare up naturally by lightning strikes. Many species of trees take advantage of forest fires. Fires clear dead wood from the forest floor, sparking **regeneration**. The fires create ideal growing conditions for vegetation. After a forest fire burns through an area, quick-growing grasses and weeds spring up, followed by slower-growing trees.

TEENS SPEAK

Eyewitness to an Industrial Fire

My name is Keith and I live in Apex, North Carolina. When I was 11, there was a fire at a company that handled hazardous waste. When the fire started, the police came by and told us that we had to leave our home. I was scared at the time. My mom, dad, sister, and brother, and our dog, Sophie, got into our car and left for grandma's house in Durham.

The plant was only a few miles away from us. Apparently, the plant had leaked chlorine gas into the air around 9 P.M.

that Thursday. The plant also handled sulfur and pesticides, which is used to kill insects.

Anyway, Dad said it was not healthy to breathe in chlorine gas, and since he did not know what else was burning, we got out of there. When I went on the Internet, I found that chlorine gas can make you very sick. My mom uses small amounts of chlorine bleach to wash our clothes, but I learned that large amounts of chlorine can hurt your lungs. It can also hurt your skin.

Before we left, I remember that the fire smelled like burned rubber. The smoke from the blaze spread across town in a few hours.

On Friday it began to rain, and I read in the paper that the rain would help clean the air of any contaminates. I also read that 17,000 people had to leave their homes and spend the night elsewhere. I would not want to go through that experience again.

See also: Chemical Pollution; Hazardous Waste Disposal; Oil Spills

FURTHER READING

Beil, Karen Magnuson. *Fire in Their Eyes: Wildfires and the People Who Fight Them.* New York: Harcourt Children's Books, 1999.
Vogt, Gregory. *Forests on Fire: The Fight to Save Our Lives.* New York: Franklin Watts, 1990.

■ GLOBAL WARMING

An overall increase in Earth's temperature brought on by human activities, such as the burning of **fossil fuels**, which releases heat-trapping gases into the atmosphere. These gases hold in heat from the sun, warming Earth's surface.

During the past 100 years, the world's temperature has risen between 0.5 and 1.5°F (0.3 and 0.8°C). Some scientists predict that if global warming continues at its current rate the landscape of the planet will drastically change. Others believe climate change is due to natural climate patterns. They say Earth has undergone huge fluctuations in temperature in the past.

Q & A

Question: Does global warming increase the likelihood of disease?

Answer: Yes. Germs and viruses are less threatening when nights and winters are cold. Insects that carry viruses and germs are showing up in areas where they have never been before. As the climate warms, scientists say the populations of disease-carrying insects, such as the mosquito, are growing. For example, the West Nile virus used to be confined to a small part of the United States. That disease has now spread across the country.

With time, global warming will contribute to the flooding of coastlines. Extreme weather conditions will prevail and many species of animals and plants will become extinct.

GREENHOUSE EFFECT

Global warming occurs when Earth's atmosphere absorbs solar radiation from the Sun. Earth's surface reflects some of that radiation back into outer space. However, some of Earth's gases trap that radiation close to the planet's surface. Those gases act like the glass of a greenhouse. Greenhouses take in heat from the Sun and keep it inside.

Scientists call those gases **greenhouse gases**. Some greenhouse gases, such as **carbon dioxide** and **methane**, occur naturally. Humans produce other greenhouse gases, such as **chlorofluorocarbons (CFCs)**. Humans use CFCs in aerosol spray cans.

The burning of fossil fuels, such as coal, oil, and natural gas, are a major source of greenhouse gas **emissions**. Fossil fuels are the remains of plants and animals that lived hundreds of millions of years ago. Over the centuries, layers of rock covered this **organic matter**, compressing it into fuel. Fossil fuels power machines, factories, and automobiles.

The greenhouse effect is not all that bad. Without it, Earth would be a frozen planet. Without greenhouse gases, the average global temperature would sink to a bone-numbing 0 degrees Fahrenheit (-18 degrees Celsius).

Greenhouse Gas Emissions, Per Person

Annual Greenhouse Gas Emissions Per Person, in Tons

Every person in the United States emits 25 tons of greenhouse gases into the atmosphere each year, second only to Australia. The chart shows the average amount of carbon monoxide in tons released by each person in select countries in 1998.

Source: Environmental Protection Agency, 2008.

ICE AGES

Some scientists say that Earth is warming as part of a natural cycle of heating and cooling. The first **ice age** froze the planet 2.4 billion years ago. At the time, temperatures dipped below -90 degrees F (-68 degrees C). Then a period of warming began. Earth has undergone five ice ages since the planet was formed. A period of warming followed each ice age.

The last ice age occurred 18,000 years ago. Vast ice sheets covered the planet. About 7,000 years ago, Earth began to warm again. Ice from **glaciers** melted, causing the Earth's oceans to rise to their present level.

While scientists agree that Earth has gone through periods of natural cooling and warming, they are alarmed at the rate of warming that has occurred in the last 50 years. Earth is warming at a faster rate than anytime before. Scientists blame humans for the warming. Human activities add about 4.4 billion tons (4 billion metric tons) of carbon dioxide into the atmosphere each year.

GLOBAL WARMING'S IMPACT

The planet has undergone many changes since Earth has started to warm. Glaciers are melting. As a result, sea levels are rising in measurable amounts. The rate of glacial ice melt in Greenland has doubled in five years. Vast sheets of ice in Antarctica are breaking away.

Moreover, according to the United Nations, animal species, including the polar bear, the walrus, and emperor penguin, are disappearing as global warming causes the destruction of their **habitat**. There are about 200,000 pairs of emperor penguins in Antarctica, half the number of 50 years ago. Warmer temperatures are killing off the penguin's main food source, a tiny shrimplike creature called **krill**.

Q & A

Question: Will any part of the globe be spared the impact of global warming?

Answer: Global warming affects every corner of the planet. For example, rising sea levels are drowning the tiny Pacific Ocean island of Tuvalu. Scientists predict in 50 years the ocean will completely swallow the island. Many of the 11,000 residents who live on Tuvalu have left for other countries. In Alaska, the region's sheet ice is melting. The lack of sea ice is causing massive storm surges to strike the

DID YOU KNOW?

International Views on Global Warming

Cause	Human Activity *Is* a Significant Cause	Human Activity *Is Not* a Significant Cause	Did Not Know
USA	71%	24%	5%
Canada	77%	21%	2%
Mexico	94%	4%	2%
Brazil	88%	8%	4%
Chile	85%	9%	6%
Spain	93%	5%	2%
Italy	92%	7%	1%
France	89%	8%	2%
Germany	87%	11%	2%
Russia	79%	12%	9%
Great Britain	78%	17%	5%
Turkey	70%	14%	16%
Egypt	66%	33%	1%
Kenya	72%	20%	8%
Nigeria	72%	18%	10%
South Korea	91%	7%	2%
China	87%	11%	2%
Australia	81%	16%	3%
Philippines	76%	20%	4%
Indonesia	71%	17%	12%
India	47%	21%	32%

According to a 2007 poll of 22,000 people in 21 countries, most people believe that human activities, such as the burning of fossil fuels, are to blame for global warming. According to the BBC poll, 79 percent believe that human activity causes global warming and that strong action is needed. The table shows the percentage of those in each country who thought human activity *is a* significant cause of global warming, who thought *is not a* significant cause, or who did not know.

Source: British Broadcasting Corporation, 2007.

shore, thawing the once permanently frozen ground. The residents of Shishmaref, Alaska, voted to leave their home because their community is slowly being destroyed.

In the Arctic, warmer temperatures are melting sea ice. Polar bears need sea ice to hunt their prey. Melting sea ice means the bears must swim longer distances for their food. As a result, polar bears are drowning. Today, scientists estimate that there are only 25,000 polar bears left in the wild, far fewer than previous years. Because scientists only began counting the polar bear population in recent years, they are not sure of the exact number lost. However, they say that factors such as overhunting and global warming have been major factors in the decline in the polar bear population in the last 50 years.

Some scientists believe that as Earth warms, the planet will experience more droughts, more rainfall, and more powerful hurricanes. Flooding will be commonplace, as will heat waves and blizzards. In 2003, for example, a blistering heat wave in Europe killed 30,000 people. Temperatures in Paris reached a staggering 104°F (40°C).

Q & A

Question: If global warming continues at its current pace, what will the world look like?

Answer: No one knows for sure what will happen if global warming goes unchecked. However, some people speculate that rising oceans will sink most of the world's coastal areas, including Florida and New York City. Some areas that are now in colder climates, might turn tropical. In addition to changing the physical makeup of Earth, global warming will destroy crops all over the world, causing millions to starve. Still, there is time to reverse the effects of global warming. Scientists, politicians, and people all over the world are looking for solutions.

STOPPING GLOBAL WARMING

Many countries are trying to stop global warming. In 1987, 17 countries agreed to stop making chlorofluorocarbons, which were destroying Earth's **ozone layer**. The ozone layer of the atmosphere protects the planet from the Sun's harmful rays.

Ten years later, 150 countries authored the Kyoto Protocol. The treaty, named for the city in Japan where officials from each country met, sought to reduce the amount of greenhouse gas emissions. However, not every country signed the treaty or is abiding by its limits; the United States is one of the countries that did not sign it.

Fact Or Fiction?

The United States is a major source of carbon dioxide emissions.

The Facts: The United States and Australia are two of the largest sources of carbon dioxide pollution. The U.S. releases between 16 to 36 billion tons of the deadly gas into the atmosphere each year.

To stop the effects of global warming, some industries have begun experimenting with alternative fuels to replace fossil fuels. Alternative fuels including wind, solar, and **geothermal** power. Solar and wind power are sources of **renewable energy**. Car companies are experimenting with hydrogen-powered and electric-powered cars to replace gasoline as a source of fuel.

See also: Air Pollution; Clean Water; Depletion of the Rainforests; Desertification; Ozone Layer; Recycling; Water Pollution

FURTHER READING
Gore, Al. *An Inconvenient Truth: The Crisis of Global Warming, Adapted for a New Generation.* New York: Viking, 2007.
Perritano, John. *Earth in Danger.* New York: Scholastic, 2008.
Williams, Mary E., ed. *Is Global Warming a Threat?* Farmington Hills, Mich.: Greenhaven Press, 2002.

■ GROUNDWATER, SOURCES AND USE OF

Water below the earth's surface found in porous rock. Groundwater is found beneath hills, mountains, plains, and deserts. It can also be found in **aquifers** that are sandwiched between waterproof layers of rock called **aquicludes**. Aquicludes stop water from moving.

Groundwater may also appear close to the surface in marshes or wetlands, where space between rock particles allows water to move up from beneath the ground. Groundwater sources are also hundreds of feet below the ground.

HOW GROUNDWATER TRAVELS

Groundwater's journey begins in the clouds through a process known as the water cycle, also known as the **hydrologic cycle.** The world's oceans, rivers, lakes, and streams are full of water. When the Sun beats down on water **evaporation** occurs, turning water into water vapor. Water vapor travels up into the atmosphere. While in the atmosphere, water vapor condenses and forms clouds. That process is called **condensation.**

Water vapor continues to condense, eventually forming water droplets. These droplets become heavy and fall to the ground as rain, sleet, hail, or snow, all of which are also known as **precipitation.** Once the precipitation reaches the ground, some water will flow over Earth's surface as runoff. Some water will soak into the ground. Groundwater moves through the spaces between the rocks, settling in aquifers. Eventually, groundwater will find its way into an ocean, a lake, a stream or a river, where the cycle begins again.

GRAVITY IN CHARGE

Gravity, the force of attraction between two objects, moves groundwater down; it pulls water into the ground. Despite the power of gravity, water has a hard time moving through **bedrock** made of granite and other hard rock. However, in many places, the bedrock is made up of softer rock, such as sandstone, that is more porous. Water can move freely in porous rock.

USING GROUNDWATER

People use wells to pump water from the ground. Pipes then deliver the water to cities, towns, and even individual houses. Generally, most groundwater is clean to use and drink. The underground rocks scrub the water clean.

People use groundwater for drinking, cooking, and watering fields of crops. In fact, half of the people living in the United States drink groundwater. Industries also use groundwater in when making products such as steel, tires, and automobiles.

GROUNDWATER POLLUTION

The pollution of underground water is a major problem, not just in the United States, but all across the world. A groundwater pollutant is any substance that contaminates an aquifer and makes the water unsafe to use and drink. Surface water will mix with these contaminants as the ground soaks up the water. The moving water picks up chemicals, bacteria, and other pollutants and carries them into the groundwater.

Q & A

Question: Why is water conservation important?

Answer: There's only so much water to go around. In some places, water is hard to find. Conserving water will help the environment. For example, do not let water run when you are brushing your teeth. Take shorter showers. Fix leaking faucets. Do not let the garden hose run when washing the family car.

Naturally occurring minerals can also contaminate groundwater. It is difficult to clean polluted groundwater. Once groundwater is polluted, people might not be able to use it for many years.

Mostly, humans are to blame for groundwater pollution. Industrial waste sites, accidental oil spills, leaking gasoline storage tanks, chemicals used in fertilization, and the spraying of **pesticides** and **herbicides**, are just some of the ways that water becomes polluted. Gasoline and diesel fuel are also major contaminants.

Q & A

Question: What can I do at home to protect groundwater?

Answer: Everyone can do something to prevent groundwater from becoming contaminated. Do not pour chemicals, paints, or cleaners down the drain, or on the ground outside. Use environmentally friendly products, such as homemade cleaners. Recycle containers and other trash.

Natural pollutants, such as **arsenic** and **radon,** also find their way into underground water sources. Groundwater pollution often goes undetected for years and can spread over a wide area.

Federal, state, and local governments enforce strict water quality laws and regulations. Governments can force individuals and companies to cleanup contamination and to fix any other problems.

One way to clean up groundwater contamination is to contain, or stop, pollution from entering the water supply. To do this, workers will often build underground barriers of clay, cement, or steel. Cleanup crews can also use chemicals, such as **chlorine,** to reduce bacteria.

Another way to clean contamination is to use microorganisms to break down contamination into less toxic substances. For example, some bacteria will devour oil and other pollutants. If groundwater cannot be cleaned at its source, a water treatment plant might have to be built. Treatment plants use various methods, including special filters, to reduce water pollution.

See also: Clean Water; Herbicides; Landfills and Superfund Sites; Radon; Water Pollution

FURTHER READING

Hoff, Mary King, and Mary M. Rodgers. *Our Endangered Planet: Groundwater.* Minneapolis, Minn.: Lerner Publishing Group, 1991.

Nadeau, Issac. *Water Underground.* New York: PowerKids Press, 2003.

Rosenberg, Pam. *Watershed Conservation.* New York: Cherry Lake Publishing, 2008.

■ HAZARDOUS WASTE DISPOSAL

Discarding of unwanted substances, usually generated by industry, that represents a danger to people or to the environment. Hazardous wastes are the unwanted toxic by-products of different manufacturing processes. In making these products, factories produce tremendous quantities of toxic, or poisonous, wastes, roughly 150 million metric tons a year.

Some hazardous wastes can catch on fire, while others are poisonous or **corrosive.** Some hazardous wastes are **radioactive.** These materials can leak out of buried containers, contaminating soil and water.

Industrial accidents also release hazardous substances into the environment. Moreover, many companies and individuals illegally dump chemicals and other toxic materials. Factories that make plastics, pesticides, herbicides, drugs, and paints are among the biggest sources of hazardous waste. Toxic chemicals, radioactive materials, and biological wastes are all classified as hazardous materials. In other words, they can harm people at work, in the home, and in the community.

The most notorious hazardous waste is dioxin. Dioxin is a toxic chemical that is the by-product of **chlorinated phenols**, a group of organic compounds used to make a number of products, including pesticides, plastics, and wood preservatives. A small dose of dioxin can cause cancer, liver damage, and birth defects.

Hazardous waste can be found in a number of places, including factories, homes, automobile repair shops, photo labs, and in hospitals. Many individuals use hazardous materials on a daily basis. Exterminators use pesticides and insecticides to get rid of unwanted pests. Photo labs use hazardous chemicals in processing photos. Paint is a hazardous material, as is car oil and gasoline. In many countries, people and companies must follow a series of laws and regulations to safely discard hazardous material.

HOUSEHOLD HAZARDOUS WASTE

Believe it or not, the home is a storage shed for a variety of household hazardous wastes. Paint, bug spray, computers, batteries, and even radioactive material from some smoke detectors are all located in the house.

However, a person just cannot throw household hazardous waste into the garbage bin. Instead, people must comply with a series of rules to make sure the waste is disposed of safely. Modern landfills, the place where trash ends up after the garbage truck leaves the house, are not designed to hold hazardous materials. Most landfills will not accept many of the items from the home, including batteries, computer terminals, television sets, and mercury thermometers. All contain toxic materials.

In the United States, each community and state sets their own regulations on how to best dispose of hazardous household waste. For example, in California, the County of Los Angeles has set up various places for residents to bring discarded household batteries. It is possible your community has a hazardous-waste collection area. Some towns and cities ban together and specify a day or two each year to collect hazardous waste.

Tossing expired or unused medications down the drain is also illegal in many places. The chemicals in these drugs might find their way into the water supply or soil. The same holds true for car oil, antifreeze, and oil filters.

DISCARDING RADIOACTIVE WASTE

Discarding radioactive waste is a complicated process. Anything that produces or uses radioactive materials generates radioactive waste. Many industries, such as mining, nuclear power, and scientific research, as well as entities such as hospitals, produce hazardous radioactive waste.

In the United States, there are six categories of radioactive waste. They are:

- spent fuel from nuclear reactors
- nuclear fuel used in scientific research
- waste from nuclear weapon production
- tailings from the mining and milling of uranium ore
- low-level waste, such as paper, rags, protective clothing, cardboard, packing materials
- naturally occurring radioactive materials produced in medical research.

Finding a place to safely discard or render harmless radioactive waste depends on how long the waste needs to be contained. Some waste remains radioactive for only a few moments, while other waste remains radioactive for hundreds of thousands of years.

METHODS OF DISPOSAL

Several methods for disposing hazardous waste exist, regardless of what they might be. The cheapest way to dispose of some toxic material is to bury the waste in a secure landfill. Secure landfills have a thick seal of clay that water cannot penetrate. However, many experts believe even the best-built landfills will eventually leak.

Incinerating, or burning, waste at high temperatures is also another method. Incineration breaks down the toxic waste into harmless substances. However, incinerators might produce dangerous gases, such

DID YOU KNOW?

What Happens to E-Waste?

According to the U.S. Environmental Protection Agency, electronic waste, or e-waste, is growing fast. E-waste consists of computers and other electronic devices. In 2005, more than 87 percent of e-waste ended up in the landfill.

Source: Environmental Protection Agency, 2005.

as **sulfur dioxide** and **hydrogen chloride**. These incinerators must be fitted with special equipment to remove the harmful gases.

Recycling is another method of hazardous waste disposal. Recycling can recover some of the **heavy metals** used in electronic circuit boards, computer monitors, and cell phones.

Bioremediation, in which scientists use bacteria and plants, can also be used to clean up toxic chemicals. Some bacteria, for example, produce **enzymes** that will break down chemicals into harmless substances. Cleanup crews often use a special type of bacteria to "eat" oil after a spill. Scientists have also used plants to soak up contaminated water and filter out toxic chemicals.

See also: Air Pollution; Bacteria; Carbon Monoxide; Carcinogens; Chemical Pollution; Insecticide; Landfills and Superfund Sites; Radiation; Recycling; Water Pollution

FURTHER READING

Orr, Tamra B., and Peggy J. Parks. *Our Environment—Toxic Waste.* New York: KidHaven Press, 2006.

Stenstrup, Allen. *Hazardous Waste*. New York: Children's Press; 1991.
Wilcox, Charlotte. *Earth-Friendly Waste Management*. Minneapolis, Minn.: Lerner Publishing Group, 2008.

■ HERBICIDES, TYPES, USES, AND DANGERS OF

A chemical that kills some or all plants, such as weeds and other unwanted vegetation. Farmers, homeowners, city workers, and others use herbicides for a number of reasons. Farmers that grow crops such as wheat, cotton, and soybeans depend on herbicides to kill the many plants that can reduce the yield of their crops.

In addition, many homeowners use herbicides to destroy weeds and other undesirable plants. During the Vietnam War (1964–1973), the U.S. military also applied a herbicide called **Agent Orange**, this use was controversial. The military used Agent Orange to defoliate, or destroy, the jungles of Southeast Asia. Many soldiers who handled the herbicide returned home after the war with a variety of illnesses, including various forms of cancer, such as cancers of the brain and kidneys. Many died. In addition, the children of some Vietnam War veterans suffered birth defects, which several studies have linked to exposure to Agent Orange.

People also use herbicides to control plants, such as Eurasian milfoil, that grow in lakes and rivers. Although herbicides provide many benefits, the chemicals can be harmful to people and animals. Herbicides also pollute the environment; they find their way into soil, groundwater, rivers, lakes, and streams. Further, after long-term use, some weeds become resistant to some herbicides.

USES AND TYPES

No one likes a weed. They are unsightly and grow where they are not wanted. They grow between cracks in sidewalks, and along the foundations of buildings. Gardeners are constantly pulling weeds and landscapers are constantly whacking weeds.

In addition to being ugly, weeds and other unwanted plants harm the growth of farmers' crops. That is why people have been using various forms of herbicides since ancient times. Some of the first herbicides were ashes and salts. The Greek Theophrastus (372–287 B.C.E.) discovered that he could kill trees by pouring olive oil on the roots. Cato (234–149 B.C.E.), a Roman, also experimented with olive oil. He found that if he poured the watery residue of crushed olives over a plant's roots, the plant would die.

In 1896, scientists found that a fungicide made from copper sulfate, lime, and water controlled the growth of certain weeds. In the early 1900s, people began using solutions of sulfuric acid, iron sulfate, copper nitrate, and other compounds to control unwanted plants. More recently, people have used sulfuric acid, among other substances, to kill plants. A French scientist developed the first synthetic, or human-made, herbicide in 1932 to control weeds in bean production. In 1941, scientists developed the first widely used herbicide 2,4-D. The chemical was very good at killing many unwanted plants while not harming native grass.

Because people use billions of pounds of herbicides each year, herbicides are big business. In 1997, Americans used 2.2 billion pounds of herbicides. Farmers used 470 million pounds to treat large fields of soy, cotton, corn, and canola. Homeowners and other residential property owners used 49 million pounds of the plant killers.

HOW HERBICIDES WORK

Some herbicides destroy the tissue of a plant on contact. These so-called *contact* herbicides work very fast. Other herbicides destroy a plant from the inside out. If sprayed on leaves, the chemical will migrate, or move down, to the roots, destroying the plant as it travels. If the chemical is applied to the soil, the plant will ingest the herbicide through the root system. These systemic herbicides do not act as fast as contact herbicides, but they generally work better.

Applying herbicides to the soil will allow the plant's root system to absorb the chemicals. Some herbicides work best when people apply them to the ground before planting. Other herbicides, called pre-emergent herbicides, are applied to the soil before plants begin to sprout, preventing the germination, or early growth, of weeds.

Q & A

Question: Why are weeds bad for farming?

Answer: Weeds are invasive in farming. They compete with crops for moisture, nutrients, growing space, and sunlight. If farmers allowed weeds were to grow unchecked, they would lose roughly 65 percent of their corn crop, 74 percent of their soybean crop, and 94 percent of their cotton crop. Weeds account for a loss of $4 billion in crop production every year. Farmers spend about $8 billion a year to control weeds. Each year, cotton producers spend roughly $200 million on weed control, yet they still see a loss of about $600 million in crop production.

Soil-applied herbicides block the division of a plant's cells. The growth of the plant's root is slowed, which leads to stunted growth of the entire plant. Stems and leaves will turn purple because the plant lacks **phosphorus.**

Other soil-applied herbicides, such as 2,4-D, will affect the growth of new stems and leaves by harming cell division in plants. These herbicides will cause the plant to become deformed. The growth of new plants will be stunted, and seedlings will be malformed. In older plants, the herbicides will twist the stem in unnatural positions. **Calluses** may form on the stem. The plant might become brittle. Some herbicides will destroy **chlorophyll,** thus affecting the plant's tissue. These herbicides will turn the plant white or very light green in color.

Other herbicides will block **photosynthesis** in the plant. Photosynthesis is the process by which green plants trap light and energy to form carbohydrates. For photosynthesis to take place in a plant, the plant must contain chlorophyll and have a supply of carbon dioxide and water. Some herbicides block the captured light, preventing photosynthesis from taking place. Generally, the best way to apply most herbicides is to combine the chemical in a water-based spray.

Like bacteria that can become resistant to some forms of **antibiotics,** some weeds will become resistant to herbicides. When a weed becomes resistant to a killer chemical, it becomes more difficult to control that weed. In 1960, scientists discovered the first weeds that were becoming resistant to herbicides. Within 10 years, more than 30 weed species had become resistant to 15 different classes of herbicides. Thirty-five years later, that number had increased to more than 100.

Q & A

Question: Are there any other ways for farmers to control weeds?

Answer: Farmers will often cultivate, rotate, or cover crops to keep weeds at bay. Some farmers try to plant their crops early to give the plants a growing edge over the weeds.

EFFECTS ON HEALTH

If ingested or inhaled, herbicides pose a major health risk for humans. The problems could be as minor as skin rashes or as major as death. People have blamed exposure to herbicides for chest pain, headaches, nausea, and tiredness. Some herbicides can cause cancer.

People are exposed to herbicides in several ways. The chemicals can get on their skin. People can also inhale the herbicides, or swallow contaminated food or water. While some herbicides decompose quickly in the soil, other types linger in the environment for months or even years.

Perhaps the most infamous of all the herbicides is Agent Orange. Between 1962 and 1971, the U.S. military used about 20 million gallons of herbicide in Vietnam to remove tree and plant life that could shield the enemy. Three of the most common mixtures were Agent Orange, Agent White, and Agent Blue. The soldiers gave each chemical a name based on the colored stripe on the 55-gallon drums in which the military stored the substances.

Soldiers sprayed many areas in the war zone, including the forests in South Vietnam that border the countries of Laos and Cambodia. They also sprayed near Saigon, the capital of South Vietnam, and in mangrove forests southeast of the city. Most of the spraying was done with airplanes and helicopters. Some herbicides were also sprayed from boats and trucks and with soldiers using backpack spray systems.

In the 1970s, many Vietnam veterans returning from the war zone became sick with a variety of illnesses, including various cancers and respiratory problems. Their children were born with birth defects. The veterans blamed their bad health and the maladies of their children on exposure to Agent Orange. They later learned that the herbicide contained **dioxin**, a known **carcinogen**. In 1978, the U.S. Department of Veterans Affairs, known at the time as the Veterans Administration, began examining veterans who believed they had become sick because of exposure to Agent Orange.

Since that time, the National Academy of Sciences has linked Agent Orange with chronic leukemia, a cancer of the blood; various lung cancers; prostate cancer; and other illnesses. They also linked Agent Orange's use to **spina bifida** in the children of Vietnam veterans. Other studies suggest that Agent Orange caused other illnesses, such as brain, liver, kidney, and bone cancers. Some veterans sued the makers of the herbicide in 1979. The case was settled in 1987 for $180 million.

Agent Orange is not the only herbicide that affected the people's health. Other herbicides are also dangerous. Many people blame the herbicide atrazine for a variety of illnesses. The substance is most often used to spray farms and forests. Workers spray atrazine on crops, including corn, sorghum, wheat, and even Christmas trees. The health risks associated with atrazine include heart problems, kidney and liver damage, birth defects, and cancer.

Alachlor, an herbicide that kills mainly grassy weeds, can lead to eye, liver, and kidney problems. Endothall, which has been used since 1995 to control unwanted plants in fields of beets, spinach, and potatoes, can cause stomach and intestinal problems.

Some herbicides cause birth defects by harming the body's endocrine system. The endocrine system consists of many reproductive organs, including the ovaries in women and the testes in men, along with the adrenal, thyroid, and pituitary glands. These glands release the hormones needed for reproduction, including estrogen and testosterone. These hormones deliver chemical messages to the cells that regulate the reproductive process. If any chemical interferes with the function of natural hormones in the body, it could lead to various health problems, including the disruption of ovary function in women and sperm production in men. Babies could be born with low birth weight and birth defects.

Today, Americans release about 60 million pounds of herbicide annually into the environment. Some of these chemicals include herbicides, such as 2,4-D, 2,4,5-T, alachlor, and atrazine. Many people believe these herbicides cause birth defects in babies and infertility in men and women.

See also: Chemical Pollution; Insecticides; Water Pollution

FURTHER READING
Church, Wendy, Benjamin Wheeler, and Gilda Wheeler. *It's All Connected: A Comprehensive Guide to Global Issues and Sustainable Solutions*. Seattle, Wash.: Facing the Future: People and the Planet, 2005.
Sivertsen, Linda, and Tosh Siversten. *Generation Green: The Ultimate Teen Guide to Living an Eco-Friendly Life*. New York: Simon Pulse, 2005.

■ HURRICANES AND TORNADOES

Spinning atmospheric storms marked by high speed and violent winds. Hurricanes and tornadoes are the most dangerous of all climate phenomena. During a hurricane, sustained wind speeds can reach up to more than 156 miles (252 km) per hour. During a tornado, winds can reach up to 300 miles (482 km) per hour in a short time.

A hurricane is a tropical storm that often develops over Africa and moves westward over the warm waters of the Atlantic Ocean. It is there, in the warm water, where a hurricane gains its strength. Tornadoes are swirling, funnel-shaped clouds caused by a rising column of warm air propelled by strong winds. Tornados can reach up to 2,000 feet (609 m) in height and generate winds of between 100–300 miles per hour (160–180 km per hour). Tornadoes can travel hundreds of miles before they die out and can leave entire towns devastated.

HURRICANES

When Hurricane Katrina smacked into the U.S. Gulf Coast in August 2005, the nation witnessed one of the most destructive hurricanes on record. High winds tore the roofs off buildings, including the Super Dome in New Orleans. Katrina flung trucks, cars, and boats around like toys. A devastating **storm surge** caused massive flooding in many communities, especially New Orleans, which sits below sea level.

Why was this storm so violent? A hurricane, known as a *typhoon* in the Pacific Ocean, forms over tropical seas when a **low-pressure** [disturbance] slams into a wall of warm, moist air. Earth's strong rotational movement near the **equator** causes the air to twist and spiral upward.

As the moist air rises, it cools and **condenses**. Rain begins to fall. When the air condenses, it creates large amounts of energy. The result is a hurricane, a spinning rainstorm with destructive high winds and waves. Scientists classify hurricanes based on their wind speed. A storm's wind speed has to reach at least 74 miles (119 km) per hour before scientists call it a hurricane.

Q & A

Question: Why is the eye of a hurricane calm?

Answer: The eye is the calmest part of the hurricane. In fact, it might even be sunny inside the storm. The eye is calm because the wind cannot blow into the center of the storm. Think of it this way. If you tied a rope to a bucket full of water and spun it around very fast, what happens? The water does not fall out of the bucket. The force that keeps the water from spilling out is the same force that keeps the winds and rain out of the hurricane's eye.

Katrina first started out as a moderate tropical storm near the Bahamas. The storm grew in intensity as it picked up energy from the warm water of the Atlantic Ocean. By the time it hit Florida on August 23, 2005, Katrina had grown into a Category 1 hurricane. Category 1 hurricanes have wind speeds of between 74 and 95 miles (119–153 km) per hour.

As it crossed the Gulf of Mexico, Katrina picked up even more energy, developing into a Category 3 hurricane. Category 3 hurricanes have wind speeds of 131–155 miles (210–249 km) per hour. On August 29, 2005, Katrina slammed into southeast Louisiana. The storm passed just east of New Orleans, but its high winds and massive storm surge caused more than $81.2 billion in damage along the Gulf Coast. The storm killed more than 1,830 people. Katrina was the second costliest hurricane ever recorded, and the sixth strongest, although it pales in comparison to the power of Hurricane Andrew.

Q & A

Question: When did scientists begin giving hurricanes names?

Answer: Scientists did not begin naming hurricanes until 1950. Beginning in 1953, the National Hurricane Center began giving names to tropical storms in the Atlantic Ocean. That list of names is now maintained and updated by an international committee of the World Meteorological Organization. The list featured only women's names until 1979, when men's and women's names began to be alternated. Six lists are used in the rotation. Names are retired when storms are especially devastating.

Hurricane Andrew was also one of the strongest hurricanes on record, a Category 5 storm. In 1992, Andrew hit South Florida with

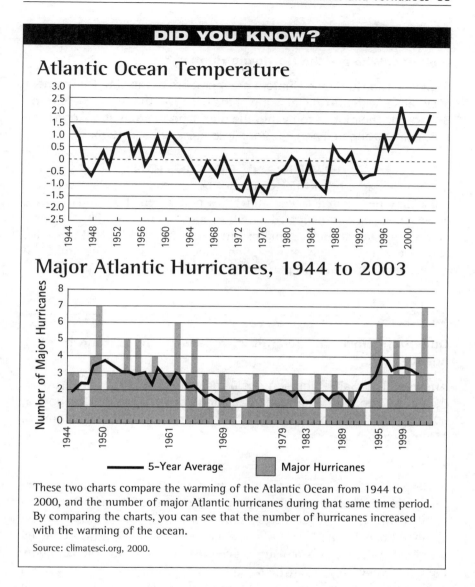

DID YOU KNOW?

Atlantic Ocean Temperature

Major Atlantic Hurricanes, 1944 to 2003

— 5-Year Average   ▨ Major Hurricanes

These two charts compare the warming of the Atlantic Ocean from 1944 to 2000, and the number of major Atlantic hurricanes during that same time period. By comparing the charts, you can see that the number of hurricanes increased with the warming of the ocean.

Source: climatesci.org, 2000.

sustained winds of 165 miles per hour (265.5 kilometers per hour), and wind gusts topping 200 miles per hour (321.8 kilometers per hour). At the time, Andrew caused $41 billion in damage. Andrew destroyed more than 25,000 homes and killed 65 people.

Q & A

Question: Who are the Hurricane Hunters?

Answer: The Hurricane Hunters are members of the U.S. Department of Defense, with the official name of the 53rd Weather Reconnaissance Squadron. Their job is to fly into the hurricane to study the storm. The U.S. military began flying missions into hurricanes in 1944.

HURRICANE PREDICTION

Many years ago, hurricanes could not be forecast with any accuracy; thus, they devastated towns and cities and killed thousands. Today, however, using sophisticated satellites and radar, scientists can predict when a hurricane is going to form, how powerful it will likely be, and where it will likely strike. Such forecasts allow people and local governments to make preparations, such as ordering evacuations.

Q & A

Question: How do scientists measure the strength of a hurricane?

Answer: The Saffir-Simpson scale measures the strength of a hurricane. A Category 1 hurricane has winds of 74–95 mph; Category 2, 96–110 mph; Category 3, 111–130; Category 4, 131–155; Category 5, 156 mph and higher.

Despite such accurate science, trying to stop a hurricane is currently impossible, although some people have ideas on how to kill a hurricane in its tracks. Researchers working for the Dyn-O-Mat company believe they have found a way to slow down a hurricane by soaking up the storm's moisture. Scientists working for the company have developed a fine powder. Each grain in the powder can absorb 2,000 times its weight in moisture. Without moisture, the storm would die out.

To test the powder, scientists flew an airplane into a storm cloud off the coast of Florida. While in the storm cloud, they released thousands of pounds of Dyn-O-Gel, the fine-grained powder. What happened? The storm disappeared. Would it work in a hurricane? Some scientists say it would be tough to stop a hurricane with the powder because the storms are so big.

TORNADOES

If you live in the Midwest or the Great Plains, you know where Tornado Alley is. Tornado Alley is an area of central North America that gets more tornadoes than anywhere else in the world. Although tornado season runs from March to August, the storms can form any time of the year. While scientists do a good job of predicting when and where a hurricane will strike, they have less luck predicting tornadoes.

A tornado begins its brief but damaging life as a severe thunderstorm, also known as a supercell, or mesocyclone. Supercells last longer than average thunderstorms. Severe thunderstorms form when cold air meets warm air. The wind that fuels the storm starts to swirl, eventually producing a funnel. Inside the funnel, the air is spinning faster and faster, creating a low pressure area that sucks more air, and anything else, into it. Scientists are not sure why that happens. Most tornadoes spin cyclonically, or counterclockwise.

Fact Or Fiction?

During a tornado, we should keep the windows and doors open to minimize damage.

The Facts: Someone came up with the myth of keeping the doors and windows open to equalize the air pressure between the inside of a building and the tornado. When there is a warning of a tornado, do not waste valuable time opening doors and windows. Seek an interior room or a room below ground level, such as the basement.

Tornadoes are like snowflakes—no two are alike. They can be thin clouds of turning air, or thick bowls that can destroy entire neighborhoods in a flash. Some twisters will move along a straight path, while others will bob, weave, and jump. Tornadoes can last for a few seconds or for several hours. A tornado might rip through one house, and leave the garage standing. Another tornado might devastate only one side of the street.

TEENS SPEAK

I Lived Through a Tornado

I don't know when I became afraid of thunderstorms. It might have been when I was young. The thunder and the lightning kept me up at night. I used to hide under my blanket and hope that the storm would pass. I never went into my parents' bedroom because I did not want them to see that I was afraid.

Anyway, all the fear must have bottled up inside of me. Because when the tornado siren sounded last year, I was scared out of my pajamas. I live in Kansas, where there are no mountains. When the alarm sounded, I raced down into the kitchen, where my mom, my dad, and my two baby brothers were already sitting. Mom had her portable battery-powered radio on the table. We followed the progress of the tornado as it roared closer. It was not too long before dad told everyone to get into the basement.

I grabbed my kitten, Freckles, and wrapped her in a towel. Josh, my brother, put a leash on Sam, our beagle. Mom grabbed some pillows and blankets. We could hear the strong storm outside.

The electricity went off. Mom led us down into the basement. Fortunately, we didn't have to use the outside door because there was a door to the basement in the kitchen. I followed my mom, and my brothers followed me. Dad was the last one out of the kitchen. He shut the door and locked it tight.

It was dark in the basement, except for the two flashlights we had. I held Freckles tight and put my head on my mother's shoulder as the storm whipped around us. When people tell you it was like a freight train, they are right. I could hear the doors to the barn smack open and shut.

My ears were popping and Sam was barking. I held on to Freckles as tight as I could. I felt the wind coming in through the outside door. I heard windows smashing upstairs, and chairs banging against the table.

Finally, everything was quiet. The tornado had passed. Dad opened the outside door. Trees were down, half of the barn's roof was torn off and its doors were gone. We went into the house. A few windows were broken and some of the furniture was on the ground, but the damage was not too bad. We survived, and that was all that mattered.

F-SCALE

Measuring a tornado is a difficult task. Not only are the winds moving at a rapid rate, but the storm also destroys on-site measuring equipment. In 1971, Dr. Theodore Fujita figured out a way to measure the wind speed of a tornado by looking at how much damage the twisters caused. Scientists call this system the F-Scale, or Fujita Scale.

About 70 percent of all tornadoes that hit the United States fall between the F-0 to F-1 categories on the F-Scale. About 30 percent fall between F-2 and F-3.

The strongest of all tornadoes is an F-5. F-5 tornadoes have wind speeds that blow between 261–318 miles per hour (420–511 kilometers per hour). One of those tornadoes ripped through Tornado Alley on May 3, 1999. On that day, a strong supercell spawned one twister after another in Oklahoma. One of the strongest was an F-5 tornado that touched down in Oklahoma City. Some 78 twisters popped up in Oklahoma and in Kansas that day, causing $1 billion in damage and killing 48 people.

Fact Or Fiction?

Tornadoes only occur during the day.

The Facts: Tornadoes can also occur at night. Usually, late afternoon is the prime time for the thunderstorms that trigger tornadoes to strike. Tornadoes can last into the evening.

See also: Global Warming

FURTHER READING
Challoner, Jack. *Hurricane & Tornado.* New York: DK Children. 2004.
Strain Trueit, Judy. *Storm Chasers.* New York: Franklin Watts, 2002.
Graf, Mike. *Tornado! The Strongest Winds on Earth.* Logan, Iowa: Perfection Learning, 1998.

■ INSECTICIDES, TYPES, USES, AND DANGERS OF

Any chemical, inorganic, or organic **compound** used to kill or control insects. Insecticides are routinely used in agriculture, in workplaces, and around the home. Many insecticides control insect population, not by killing the pests, but by stopping them from reproducing.

Because insecticides are designed chiefly to kill, these substances can harm humans, animals, and the environment. However, insecticides are helpful in killing potential disease-carrying insects, such as mosquitoes, which cause a variety of illnesses such as **malaria** and West Nile virus.

FIGHT AGAINST INSECTS

For ages, humans have been fighting a never-ending battle with insects. While some insects, such as the honey bee, are beneficial, many insects need to be controlled. Some insects, such as locusts, eat vast fields of crops. Others, such as mosquitoes and ticks, carry diseases that can kill humans and animals. Still other insects, like termites, can damage buildings and homes.

One way humans have learned to control these pests is through the use of insecticides. There are two types of insecticides: inorganic and organic.

Inorganic insecticides do not contain carbon atoms. They are mostly made from compounds containing **heavy metals** and **arsenic**. Some of these insecticides are **synthetic**, or human-made.

Organic pesticides are made from plants and other natural sources. Organic insecticides prepared from plants are becoming more popular to use because they are safer than synthetic insecticides. Microbial insecticides are organic pesticides that use naturally occurring bacteria to eliminate the pests.

HOW INSECTICIDES WORK

Insecticides control and kill pests in a number of ways. Some produce a toxin, or poison, that is specific to the pest. Other insecticides cause disease. Many insecticides work in more than one way.

Some insecticides are stomach poisons that are swallowed by an insect. This type of insecticide is generally applied to the leaves of plants. Once an insect eats the leaves, the poison will settle in the insect's stomach and kill it.

Other insecticides are contact poisons. Contact poisons work on insects that eat their food by piercing a plant with their **proboscis** and withdrawing liquid from the plant.

Insects can also come in contact with insecticides simply by touching them. Other insecticides can be placed on animals, such as a dog or cat. The animals absorb the insecticide. Once an insect, such as a tick or flea, feeds on that animal, the bug will receive a deadly dose of the toxin. Still other insecticides can by sprayed as a gas, affecting the insect's respiratory system.

Q & A

Question: What's the difference between an insecticide and a pesticide?

Answer: Many people use pesticides to describe insecticides. Insecticides are chemicals that kill and control insects. Pesticides are chemicals that kill and control insects, and other pests, such as rodents, and plants.

Some insecticides also work by attacking the nervous system of the insect. The compounds in the insecticide interrupt the signals in the insect's brain. One of the insecticides that wages war inside the nervous system of a bug is organophosphorus insecticide. Organophosphates are chemicals widely used in products that kill stinging insects and beetles. These insecticides can be found in any garden store.

The effects of organophosphorus were first discovered before World War II (1939–1945). The military of several governments used the substance to make nerve gas, which could be used in battle.

How do organophosphorus insecticides work? Insects produce a chemical called acetylcholine. Acetylcholine is a **neurotransmitter**. An insect's body uses the chemical to send information through the synapses, which are the junctions between a nerve cell and a muscle. In a healthy insect, an **enzyme** called cholinesterase combines with acetylcholine keeping the chemical at an acceptable level. That allows an insect's muscles to rest.

When the insect comes in contact with a lethal dose of organophosphorus insecticide, the killer attacks the cholinesterase, keeping the enzyme from fastening itself to the acetylcholine. Almost immediately, the insect's muscles become over-stimulated. Eventually, the insect becomes paralyzed and dies.

Q & A

Question: Is DEET an insecticide?

Answer: DEET is not an insecticide. It is the active ingredient in many insect repellents. Insect repellants are used to keep mosquitoes, ticks, and other biting insects off of human skin. Many of these insects can transmit diseases such as Lyme disease and Rocky Mountain spotted fever.

One of the big problems with exposing insects to insecticides is that they will most likely eventually become resistant to the chemicals. When that happens, newer, more powerful insecticides have to be produced, increasing the risks to humans. That is one reason why scientists study **genetic** differences in insects to determine their resistance to an insecticide.

Researchers in the Great Britain, for example, have identified several genetic factors in mosquitoes that carry malaria, which they said, might reveal the insect's level of resistance to certain insecticides. A team of scientists found two genes in one type of African mosquito that causes the resistance to the insecticide most commonly used to kill the insect.

Malaria is caused by a **parasite** carried by mosquitoes. The mosquitoes pass on the parasite to humans by feeding on blood. However, the constant spraying of certain insecticides designed to kill the mosquitoes has given the insects a resistance to the chemicals. By finding the genes that make the mosquito invulnerable to the insecticide, researchers can develop new ways to kill the pests. Malaria kills more than a million people each year.

Q & A

Question: Does the U.S. government regulate insecticides?

Answer: Yes. Before any company can sell an insecticide, or any pesticide for that matter, the Environmental Protection Agency (EPA) must examine the ingredients of the substance. The EPA tries to make sure that the risks to humans, the environment, and to animals are minimal.

HARMFUL EFFECTS

The use of insecticides is widespread. They are used on farms, in homes, in lakes, and even along the side of the road. As such, they contaminate soil, water, and air. Once in the environment, insecticides and other pesticides can be harmful to plants, birds, fish, humans and other wildlife. The poisons make their way into the food we eat and the water we drink. Depending on the type and level of insecticide contamination, people can become sick with a variety of illnesses, including rashes, weight loss, weakness, nervousness, and uncontrollable shaking.

A study by the National Cancer Institute concluded that some pesticides were responsible for causing cancer in farmers. In addition, several scientific studies note that infants and children are more susceptible to the effects of pesticides than adults.

Perhaps the most infamous insecticide that damaged the environment is DDT. DDT is the abbreviation for dichlorodiphenyltrichloroethane, an insecticide discovered in 1939 by Swiss chemist Paul Muller. DDT was used with much success during World War II to kill insect-borne diseases such as malaria and typhus.

Hailed as a "miracle" pesticide, DDT worked so well that in was used widely after the war. From 1942 to 1972, an estimated 675,000 tons (612 metric tons) of the insecticide was used in the United States.

While DDT worked well, its use had severe consequences for the environment. Many insect species developed a resistance to DDT. In addition, DDT was highly toxic and did not break down in the environment for a long time. The substance was not rapidly metabolized by many animals. Instead, the animals stored the toxin in their fatty tissues, where the toxin built up over time. DDT proved highly toxic to fish. The poison got into the food chain as those high on the food chain ate those on the lower end of the chain.

The effects of DDT were exposed by Rachael Carson in her book *Silent Spring.* In 1972, the United States banned DDT's use. Most developing nations followed suit, although many countries, especially in Latin America, still use the insecticide.

See also: Carcinogens; Chemical Pollution; Herbicide; Water Pollution

FURTHER READING

Glausiusz, Josie. *Buzz: The Intimate Bond Between Humans and Insects.* San Francisco, Calif.: Chronicle Books, 2004.

Lee, Sally. *Pesticides.* New York: Franklin Watts, 1991.

Macfarlane, Katherine. *Pesticides.* Chicago, Ill.: KidHaven Press, 2007.

■ LANDFILLS AND SUPERFUND SITES

Disposal sites where workers legally bury non-hazardous solid waste under layers of earth; also known as dumps or sanitary landfills. Such landfills are generally run by towns and cities, although some companies have landfills on their property. Superfund sites are toxic waste dumps in the United States that are selected for cleanup by the federal government, specifically the Environmental Protection Agency (EPA). Those sites, generally abandoned hazardous waste sites, became polluted because companies or individuals had illegally dumped or buried toxic waste at these locations.

Properly disposing of non-hazardous trash and cleaning up toxic waste sites are important ways to maintain the long-term health of the environment and the public.

DISPOSING OF GARBAGE

Without landfills, the world would be a much filthier place. According to the EPA, Americans generate 4.6 pounds (2.1 kilograms) of trash each day, twice as much per person as any other country. Each year, Americans throw away 254 million tons (230 million metric tons) of trash.

Most household trash consists of paper products, plastic, and food waste. What happens to all this garbage? About 81.8 million tons (74.2 million metric tons) gets **recycled** or **composted**. About 12.5 percent is burned in an incinerator. About 55 percent is buried in landfills. That figure has doubled since 1960. The United Kingdom in Europe buries the most trash in the world—roughly 90 percent.

Landfills are nothing new to society. One of the first landfills was in Athens, the ancient Greek city-state. About 2,500 years ago, the Athenians opened a municipal landfill. Athenian officials ordered that those living in Athens move their household waste at least one mile from the city's limits.

MODERN LANDFILLS

Today's landfills are modern facilities designed to protect the environment and the public's health from the various hazardous materials found in trash. Communities build landfills away from environmentally sensitive areas, such as streams, rivers, **aquifers**, lakes, and geological fault lines. When building landfills, engineers also minimize the impact on the local community and wildlife. Because contaminants from garbage can migrate, or move, from a landfill into groundwater, officials closely monitor each landfill for any sign of contamination.

Most municipal landfills are limited. Many types of household trash cannot be buried in solid waste landfills. Why? They are too hazardous. Such household hazardous waste includes paints, chemicals, motor oil, household batteries, pesticides, and e-Waste, including computer keyboards and monitors. People must dispose of all household hazardous waste in an environmentally safe way.

PARTS OF A LANDFILL

A landfill is engineered with different parts to protect the environment. The main parts include:

- **Liner.** Engineers install a liner at the bottom of the landfill to keep trash separated from the soil and the groundwater. The makers of these bottom liners usually fashion them out of a tough, puncture-resistant plastic. People operating the landfill also may decide to use a liner compacted out of hard clay.

- **Leachate collection system.** No matter how well engineers design a landfill, water will always find a way to move through it. As water moves, it picks up various contaminates from the garbage. These contaminates include metals and biological waste. Every landfill has a system to collect water, including rain water, and move it away from the landfill into a leachate pond. Contaminated water collects in the leachate. Workers then treat that water with chemicals until it is safe to release into the environment.

- **Cap.** Every day, workers cap each cell with six inches of soil, preventing air and animals from getting into the trash. Some landfills also have other types of coverings,

such as tarps. When a section of the landfill is full,
workers cover it with a **polyethylene** cap. They then
dump several feet of soil over the cap and later plant
grass and other plants to prevent erosion.

Once a landfill is full, it sits. Landfills bury waste, not get rid of it. The trash in the landfill, therefore, sits for years. Because the landfill allows in very little oxygen and moisture, the garbage does not break down rapidly.

SUPERFUND SITES

Before the 1980s, some companies in the United States disposed of their industrial wastes improperly. Many businesses and individuals buried hazardous materials wherever they could find a field. Others buried these toxins in unsafe landfills, or simply abandoned drums of chemicals in open areas. Moreover, many factories that used hazardous substances did not correctly store them.

Then, in the 1970s, two environmental disasters forced the United States to adopt tough laws to address abandoned hazardous waste sites. The first disaster occurred in upstate New York, near Niagara Falls in a place called Love Canal.

For many years, municipalities and various companies had dumped industrial chemicals in Love Canal. In the late 1950s, developers built 100 homes and a school in the neighborhood, not knowing the site was polluted by a variety of chemicals. By 1978, health officials found that more than 80 chemical compounds were leaching through the soil. Backyards and homes had become contaminated with chemical sludge. Residents of Love Canal had many health problems that they blamed on the dumping. They left their homes, never to return.

The second toxic-waste disaster occurred in Times Beach, Missouri. The entire town had to be evacuated after health officials found high levels of a cancer-causing substance called **dioxin**. The chemical came from a plant that made **Agent Orange**. Agent Orange was an herbicide that the U.S. military used during the Vietnam War to destroy the jungle in Southeast Asia.

To make matters worse, a local man sprayed waste oil from the plant to control dust on the town's roads. The waste oil contained levels of dioxin 2,000 times higher than the dioxin found in Agent Orange.

DID YOU KNOW?

Top States with Superfund Sites

New Jersey	140
Pennsylvania	122
New York	110
California	107
Michigan	84
Florida	71
Washington	65
Texas	54
Illinois	51
Minnesota	46

There are approximately 1,255 sites on the EPA's Superfund National Priority List. The chart lists the states with the most toxic sites. To see what Superfund sites are located in your state go to http://www.epa.gov/superfund/sites/npl/index.htm.

U.S. News and World Report, 2007.

In 1980, to address the cleanup of these and other toxic waste sites, Congress passed the Comprehensive Environmental Response, Compensation, and Liability Act, or CERCLA. Today, the law is known as the Superfund. The Superfund law provides for the cleanup of toxic waste sites that could harm the public's health or the environment. The EPA says that half of all Americans live within 10 miles of a Superfund site.

COMPLEX PROCESS

Cleaning up a Superfund site is a long and complex process. Since the Superfund law was enacted, the government has located and tested tens of thousands of hazardous waste sites. The law gives the government the power to force those responsible for the contamination to clean up the site. About 70 percent of the cleanup of Superfund sites has been paid for by the responsible party.

However, in recent years, Congress has underfunded the Superfund. The Center for Public Integrity, a government watchdog group, found that fewer than 20 percent of the toxic waste sites in the United States have been cleaned up enough to be removed from the Superfund list.

One of the worst Superfund sites is known as Tar Creek, a 40-square mile mine in Oklahoma. The government has spent 20 years and more than $100 million on the cleanup, yet it remains shrouded in white, mining waste containing lead and zinc. The water of nearby creeks and streams runs orange from the metals and acids in the mine. Local health officials discovered high traces of lead in the blood of area children. Among other things, chronic lead exposure can affect the body's nervous system, stunt the growth of children, and cause brain damage.

Environmental officials had hoped to turn the site into vast wetlands. Yet cleaning up Tar Creek has failed. Officials estimate it will cost around $250 million to finish the cleanup.

Why is Tar Creek so toxic that even the U.S. government is having problems cleaning up the site? Mining destroyed the land. During the mining process, workers dumped leftover tailings, or waste products, near homes and schools. These so-called chat piles include 74 million tons (67.1 metric tons) of debris taken from the mines over eight decades. The mined metal was used during World War II (1939–1945). Eventually, the mining companies went out of business, abandoning the mines 30 years ago and leaving behind a toxic legacy that seems to have no end.

One chat pile is more than 100 feet high. Children often play on these piles of heavy metal. Those living around Tar Creek are exposed to large amounts of lead, zinc, and **cadmium**. There are no longer any fish in the creek. Hundreds of miles of underground tunnels have filled with tainted water. Sinkholes have swallowed up homes. In addition, more than 400 open mine shafts still exist, causing another dangerous environmental hazard.

See also: Air Pollution; Chemical Pollution; Water Pollution

FURTHER READING
Reed, Jennifer Bond. *Love Canal.* New York: Chelsea House, 2002.
Crampton, Norm. *Green House: Eco-Friendly Disposal and Recycling at Home.* New York: M. Evans and Company, Inc., 2008.
Inskipp, Carol. *Reducing and Recycling Waste.* Pleasantville, N.Y.: Gareth Stevens, 2005.

■ LEAD POISONING

A result of exposure to lead, a highly toxic metal often found in construction materials, toys, computers, and batteries. Long-term exposure can cause nerve damage, **birth defects, learning disabilities,** coma, convulsions, and even death. The National Academy of Sciences reports that even low levels of lead in a child can reduce intelligence, impair hearing, and cause growth problems.

Although lead poisoning remains a major public health issue in the United States, the level of lead found in the blood of children has steadily decreased since the mid-1970s. That is when the government banned lead from gasoline, food, beverage cans, house paint, and industrial **emissions.**

According to the Centers for Disease Control and Prevention (CDC), 310,000 children between the ages of one and five suffer from high levels of lead poisoning. Many of these children are from low-income families living in older homes contaminated with lead-based paint.

LEAD IMPACT

The use of lead in various products is not uncommon. About 1,000 years ago, potters used lead to mold bowls, jars, and cups. The use of

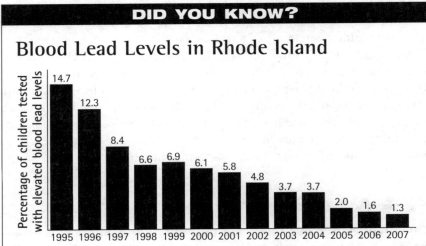

DID YOU KNOW?

Blood Lead Levels in Rhode Island

Percentage of children tested with elevated blood lead levels

Year	Value
1995	14.7
1996	12.3
1997	8.4
1998	6.6
1999	6.9
2000	6.1
2001	5.8
2002	4.8
2003	3.7
2004	3.7
2005	2.0
2006	1.6
2007	1.3

In the United States, the amount of lead in the blood systems of people has been substantially reduced after the government banned leaded gasoline and leaded paint in the 1970's. For example, in Rhode Island, the percentage of children with elevated blood lead levels decreased dramatically since 1995.

Source: Rhode Island Department of Health, 2007.

lead continued for centuries. It was used in water pipes, coins, knives, forks, spoons, and other items. Paint manufacturers added lead to household paint to make it more durable.

Despite the widespread use of lead, no one recognized how dangerous lead could be if ingested. The metal builds up in an individual's organs and blood. In the bloodstream, lead damages red blood cells by limiting their ability to feed the body's organs and tissues with oxygen. Lead can also affect the body's ability to absorb calcium, which bones need to grow. Calcium also helps nerve and blood vessels function properly.

Children are often the victims of lead poisoning. Many times they will accidentally poison themselves by eating toxic lead-paint chips. More likely, children will get sick after inhaling or swallowing lead dust that has flaked off the paint. Lead-contaminated dust accumulates on all surfaces including countertops, toys, tables, and the floor. Children can easily ingest the dust by touching these surfaces and later putting their hands in their mouths. The lead eventually makes its way into the bloodstream. Lead is most dangerous to children under the age of six.

FREQUENCY

Lead poisoning became a national health issue in the mid- to-late 20th century. At least 90 percent of all private homes built before 1940 contained some lead paint, according to the United States Department of Housing and Urban Development (HUD). African-American children were among the most at risk, because many of them lived in homes where lead contamination was a problem. Before 1946, more than 20 percent of African-American children and 15 percent of all children from low-income families suffered from lead poisoning. Often, people of low income live in older houses that have not been updated or cleaned of lead contaminants.

Q & A

Question: How can I tell if my four-year-old brother and three-year-old sister are suffering from lead poisoning? What are the symptoms?

Answer: Many children do not show any symptoms of lead poisoning, so it's important to have your brother and sister tested by a doctor.

However, some of the warning signs or symptoms of lead poisoning include: irritability or behavioral problems; the eating of items such as dirt and paint chips, a condition called pica; loss of appetite; weight loss; vomiting or nausea; constipation; stomach pain; a metallic taste in the mouth. Talk to a doctor about potential lead sources in the home and what people can do to protect children from danger.

By the 1970s, the number of children in the United States poisoned by lead had climbed to 14.8 million. The government's ban of lead-based paint in 1978 proved effective. By the early 1990s, the number of children suffering from lead poisoning had decreased to 890,000.

OTHER SOURCES OF DANGER

The government also sought regulations to decrease the amount of lead in soil and water. To that end, the government in the 1970s banned lead from gasoline. This sharply reduced the number of children with elevated levels of lead in their bloodstream.

In the 1980s, Congress focused its attention on lead in water. Congress passed the Safe Drinking Water Act, which restricted the use of lead in water pipes, solder, and other building materials.

In 1995, the government outlawed lead solder used in sealing metal food cans. Twelve years later, the federal Consumer Product Safety Commission began taking steps to prohibit lead in all children's toys.

In 2008, the Environmental Protection Agency (EPA) cut the limit on airborne lead by 90 percent. Although the government outlawed lead in gasoline in the 1970s, 16,000 other sources, including metal mines, trash incinerators, and aviation fuel, pumped out 1,300 tons of lead each year. Airborne lead eventually falls to the ground and mixes with indoor dust and outside dirt. Overall, the government's goal is to eliminate lead poisoning in children by 2010.

PREVENTIVE MEASURES

The presence of lead in a home does not always mean that those living in it will have an elevated level of the toxin in their bloodstream. Homeowners, however, can take steps to reduce the problem.

Although home lead tests are available, the Environmental Protection Agency recommends that a professional conduct a more

DID YOU KNOW?

Lead Poisoning in Children

Total	Population of children younger than 72 months	Number of children tested	Total children with elevated levels of lead in their blood
1997	23,345,397	1,611,569	122,641
1998	23,143,133	1,761,674	114,571
1999	23,023,683	1,875,500	94,292
2000	23,304,631	2,216,700	87,782
2001	23,380,551	2,538,008	76,992
2002	23,380,855	2,652,964	67,914
2003	23,380,859	2,989,517	59,759
2004	23,385,778	2,994,677	52,682
2005	23,390,107	2,975,794	47,147
2006	23,485,435	3,262,866	39,526

According to data compiled by the CDC of children younger than 72 months, there has been a steady decline since 1997 of children who show signs of elevated lead in their blood streams. This decline represents the U.S. government's goal to eliminate lead poisoning in children.

Centers for Disease Control and Prevention, 2007.

comprehensive inspection to determine if a house contains dangerous sources of lead. In addition, regular household cleaning and making sure children wash their hands can help prevent lead poisoning. Experts also recommend running the cold-water tap for a minute or two to flush out any lead that might have settled in the water. Running the water will also remove calcium and iron deposits. While these minerals are good for you, they can be harmful in large amounts.

If there is a major contamination problem, more drastic steps, such as the removal of all lead-based paint or renovating the plumbing system, may need to be taken.

Q & A

Question: Can doctors treat lead poisoning?

Answer: Yes, doctors can treat those poisoned by lead. Treatments vary, however, depending on how much lead is in the blood. Although doctors can easily treat small amounts of lead, treatment is most effective if further exposure to lead is minimized. The body will naturally eliminate lead, causing the levels of the toxin in the blood to fall. Doctors treat severe cases of lead poisoning using a chelating agent. Chelating agents are drugs that chemically bind with the lead in the body's tissues and blood stream. The chelating agents help the body naturally expel the lead through urine. In addition, nutritional meals with iron and calcium can help reduce the amount of lead absorbed by the body.

Fact Or Fiction?

Is it true that only children who live in the inner city are in danger of becoming poisoned by lead?

The Facts: Lead poisoning crosses all racial, economic, and geographical boundaries. Lead paint, a major source of lead poisoning, can be found in any home built before 1978. And just because a person has no symptoms does not mean that he or she is not affected. Lead can build up in the body over time. Many people are not aware they have been poisoned.

See also: Air Pollution; Chemical Pollution; Water Pollution

FURTHER READING

English, Peter C. *Old Paint: A Medical History of Childhood Lead-Paint Poisoning in the United States to 1980.* Piscataway, N.J.: Rutgers University Press, 2001.

Kessel, Irene. *Getting the Lead Out: The Complete Resource Preventing and Coping with Lead Poisoning.* New York: Perseus Books Group, 2001.

■ NUCLEAR ENERGY

Energy contained in the **nucleus**, or center, of an atom. The nucleus is the source of the most powerful energy in the universe. In the 1930s, scientists began figuring out how to release the awesome power of the atom. Atoms are the tiny particles that make up everything in the universe.

On December 2, 1942, a team of scientists led by Italian physicist Enrico Fermi demonstrated the first controlled nuclear reaction. It occurred in a nuclear reactor they built on a squash court at the University of Chicago in Illinois. That experiment opened the nuclear floodgates. Soon, scientists were harnessing the power of the atom, not only to generate power, but also to destroy.

In 1945, towards the end of World War II (1939–1945), scientists got their first glimpse of nuclear energy when they exploded the first atomic bomb in the New Mexico desert. Scientists were amazed at the power of the atom. J. Robert Oppenheimer, known as the "Father of the Atomic Bomb," knew that nuclear energy would change the world. "When you see something that is technically sweet, you go ahead and do it and you argue about what to do about it only after you have had your technical success," he said later. "That is the way it was with the atomic bomb."

The United States then dropped two atom bombs on Japan in August 1945. The devastation caused by the blasts forced Japan to surrender—and, thus, many argue, it spared countless lives.

Since then, scientists have found different uses for nuclear energy. Many scientists use the power of the atom in medical and scientific research. They also use nuclear energy to power seagoing ships and submarines. Nuclear power also fuels the spaceships that travel to distant planets. Scientists have also fashioned more powerful nuclear bombs that can destroy entire populations in a matter of seconds. While nuclear energy has many benefits, it also poses many risks to the health of individuals and to the environment.

UNDERSTANDING ATOMS

Every object in the universe, whether it is a book or a planet, is made up of atoms. Atoms that make up one element are different than the atoms that make up another element. Until 100 years ago, scientists were pretty sure that atoms were the tiniest particles in the universe and that they were indestructible. Atoms, they thought, could be simply rearranged to build many things, much like a child playing with building blocks.

That theory was disproved when British **physicist** Joseph John Thomson showed that atoms could be broken down into smaller particles. No matter what atom they came from, those particles were equal in weight and carried the same negative electrical charges. He called those fragments **electrons**. Atoms, however, could not exist with just negatively charged particles. Something else had to be inside that atom. Thomason's work gave rise to the theory of **subatomic particles.**

Subatomic particles not only included electrons, but also **protons** and **neutrons**. Protons carry a positive electrical charge. Neutrons do not have any charge at all. Neutrons and protons are bound close together. Because electrons carry a negative electrical charge, and protons carry a positive charge, they attract one another. That attraction holds the atom together.

Atoms of various elements can bind together to form **molecules.** For example, water contains one atom of **hydrogen** and two atoms of oxygen. The atoms join together by sharing electrons.

FISSION

One way to produce nuclear energy is through a nuclear reaction called fission. Fission is the splitting of atoms. Nuclear power plants use nuclear fission to generate electricity. Reactors use uranium-235, a powerful form of the radioactive element uranium, to generate energy. Other elements that can generate nuclear fission include plutonium or thorium.

Fission occurs when a neutron from one atom slams into the nucleus of another atom. When a uranium atom undergoes fission, it releases more neutrons. A chain reaction occurs when the released neutrons begin slamming other uranium atoms. That causes those atoms to split. As the atoms split, they change. When atoms change, they release huge amounts of energy called **radiation**. Nuclear radiation can take the form of **gamma rays**, which are similar to X-rays. Radiation can also take the form of alpha particles, which are positively charged, or beta particles, which are negatively charged.

Fact Or Fiction?

Fission powers the Sun.

The Facts: Actually, the Sun generates its massive amount of energy through the fusion of hydrogen atoms.

Scientists can control chain reactions in nuclear reactors. On the other hand, the powerful punch of a nuclear bomb is an example of an uncontrolled nuclear reaction.

When conventional power plants generate electricity they burn **fossil fuels,** such as oil or coal, to heat water. The steam from the boiling water turns huge fanlike machines called turbines. The turbines drive generators that produce electricity. Nuclear power plants use the energy generated by a nuclear reaction to boil the water.

FUSION

Another way to generate nuclear energy is through fusion. Instead of splitting atoms, fusion joins, or fuses, the nuclei of light elements together, creating a heavy element. For example, fusing **deuterium** nuclei produces **helium** and massive amounts of energy.

Unlike fission, fusion is difficult to duplicate in a controlled environment. Why is that? Because each nucleus has a positive charge, they are not attracted to one another. In fact, they repel each other. It takes massive amounts of energy, known as **thermonuclear energy,** to push the two nuclei together. A thermonuclear atomic bomb is an example of fusion at work.

DANGERS OF NUCLEAR ENERGY

Nuclear power accounts for about 19 percent of all the electricity generated in the United States. As of 2007, the U.S. Nuclear Regulatory Commission had licensed 104 commercial nuclear reactors.

To produce the energy needed to generate nuclear power, nuclear reactions have to be carefully controlled. If workers allow fission to subside, the nuclear reaction will eventually die down. If workers allow too much fission to take place, the nuclear reaction might run out of control. Nuclear reactors are designed for maximum safety. The nuclear material is housed in the protective core of the reactor. If the reactor begins to overheat, workers could flood the core with cold water.

Although it is very unlikely that a nuclear reactor could explode like a nuclear bomb, many dangers exist. If a reactor fails, it could release high doses of radioactive material. Radiation harms people and animals, poisons food, and contaminates a wide area of land.

Yet, sometimes accidents occur that can scar the environment for many years. In 1986, the world's worst nuclear accident occurred, at the Chernobyl nuclear reactor in the former Soviet Union. On April 26, 1986, the reactor exploded, tearing the top off the reactor, and sending a huge cloud of radioactivity into the atmosphere. The cloud drifted over much of Europe. The radioactivity badly contaminated a large part of the Ukraine, Belarus, and Russia. Hundreds of thousands of people had to leave their homes.

On March 28, 1979, an accident occurred at the Three Mile Island nuclear power plant near Middletown, Pennsylvania; it was the worst nuclear disaster in the United States. A cooling malfunction caused part of the reactor's core to melt. Although some radioactive gas was released, it was not significant. The accident caused no loss of life or adverse health effects. Yet, Three Mile Island showed just how dangerous nuclear power reactors could be. The reactor was permanently shut down.

Japan had its own nuclear accident in 1999. Workers mixing liquid uranium at the Tokaimura nuclear plant made a mistake that triggered a chain reaction. Workers at the plant were making fuel for the plant's nuclear reactor. There were working with uranium-235. At room temperature, uranium-235 is solid. However, if the temperature is allowed to rise about 260°F (126°C), it turns into a dangerous gas. To keep the element from turning into a gas, nuclear processing plants turn uranium-235 into pellets. To make those pellets, workers mix uranium with **nitric acid**.

That is what Japanese workers were doing on September 30, 1999, at the Tokaimura nuclear plant. They mishandled the mixing process, dumping too much uranium into the acid. With so much uranium concentrated in as small space in the mixing tank, the mixture reached **critical mass**. Critical mass is the smallest amount of uranium needed to cause a chain reaction. Water surrounding the mixing tank sped up the reaction, because water makes it easier for uranium atoms to split. The government ordered 310,000 people living near the plant to stay inside their homes. Radiation levels spiked to 20,000 times the normal level. Workers were able to stop the chain reaction before it caused too much damage.

Fact Or Fiction?

Nuclear power plants produce more energy than the burning of fossil fuels.

The Facts: The energy from one atom of uranium produces 10 million times the energy from an atom of carbon found in coal. One ton of uranium produces more energy than several million tons of coal or millions of barrels of oil. As such, nuclear power plants need less fuel than fossil-fuel power plants.

DISPOSAL OF NUCLEAR WASTE

Nuclear fuel and waste disposal is a hazard to the environment. After several years, the uranium fuel rods used in nuclear reactors are spent. However, they still contain highly radioactive materials. Because there is no one place to store radioactive materials, the spent rods have to be stored in pools of water at the site of the nuclear reactor.

Because these wasted fuel rods will remain radioactive for thousands of years, many people want a permanent place to store the fuel. It is one of the greatest challenges facing the nuclear industry. Most countries prefer to bury their spent nuclear fuel away from humans. To that end, the U.S. Department of Energy has developed a plan to store these fuel rods inside Yucca Mountain in Nevada. The government would store the materials deep underground.

Problems abound at Yucca Mountain, however. Many believe the mountain is not geologically stable enough for the disposal of spent nuclear fuel. Earthquakes have rumbled through the area in the past, making the danger of radioactivity leaking into the environment that much greater. Although it is in the desert, there is evidence that groundwater has welled up in the past. This is extremely important. If contaminated by radiation, water could easily find its way into the environment.

In addition, transporting spent nuclear rods to any disposal site is also a concern. Most likely, trucks carrying such hazardous materials would be traveling through major cities. Many people are concerned that these trucks could be targeted by terrorists or involved in highway crashes, either of which scenario would unleash a nuclear disaster that no community is prepared to handle.

Health conditions are also of concern for those working with radioactive materials. For example, if people come in contact with uranium-238, they would have an increased risk of lung cancer and bone cancer. At high concentrations, uranium is highly toxic and could cause damage to the body's internal organs. Exposure to uranium might affect a person's ability to reproduce. Developing fetuses are also in danger.

See also: Hazardous Waste Disposal; Radiation

FURTHER READING

Burgan, Michael, et al. *Nuclear Energy.* Pleasantville, N.Y.: Gareth Stevens, 2002.

McLeish, Ewan. *The Pros and Cons of Nuclear Power.* New York: Rosen, 2007.

Wheeler, Jill C. *Nuclear Power.* Edina, Minn.: Checkerboard Books, 2007.

■ OIL SPILLS

The release into the environment of liquid petroleum **hydrocarbons,** such as crude oil, gasoline, or diesel fuel. Oil spills can occur on land, in the ocean, and along shorelines. Most marine oil spills generally follow some sort of accident aboard an oil tanker or oil platform out in the ocean.

An oil spill can be toxic to the environment. On land, oil from a spill can contaminate soil, lakes, rivers, streams, and groundwater. Marine oil spills can damage shorelines and kill marine life, seabirds and other forms of wildlife. Toxins from the oil will find their way below the water, poisoning sea life there as well. Large oil spills are rather rare, but the devastation they cause can be catastrophic. Oil spills don't wreak only environmental havoc in an area; they also cause economic devastation, especially in areas that survive on money generated by the tourism and fishing industries.

Oil spills are almost always accidents resulting from human error. Equipment can break down and ships can get stuck on a shallow spit of land. When the ship's captain tries to pull the vessel loose, he can rip a hole in the side of the ship, causing massive amounts of oil to pour out.

Cleaning up oil spills is a time-consuming and difficult job. The environmental impact from oil pollution is often felt years after the spill.

A CASE STUDY

One of the worst oil spills in history provides a classic case study of how dangerous oil spills are and what factors influence their cleanup. The accident occurred on March 24, 1989, in Alaska. At the time, the *Exxon Valdez,* an oil tanker owned by the Exxon Oil Corporation, was traveling from Valdez, Alaska, to Los Angeles, California, with 53 million gallons of crude oil from Prudhoe Bay, Alaska. The 986-foot vessel left Valdez at 9:12 P.M., on March 23, 1989.

As the *Exxon Valdez* traveled away from its starting point at the Trans Alaska Pipeline, the ship's captain, Joseph Hazelwood, who was in charge of the ship's wheelhouse at the time, ordered his helmsman to steer clear of the icebergs out at sea. The ship maneuvered away from the normal shipping lanes to go around the floating ice.

Once the ship was out of its normal lane of travel and out of the way of the floating icebergs, Hazelwood ordered the ship's third mate to turn back into the correct shipping lane when the tanker reached a certain point. For some reason, the ship never returned to the shipping lane. Instead, the tanker ran aground on Bligh Reef while Hazelwood was in his cabin.

The *Exxon Valdez* spilled roughly 10.9 million gallons of oil into Prince William Sound within six hours of the accident. Images from the accident seen on television and in newspapers shocked the world. Thousands of people traveled to Alaska to help in the cleanup. The spreading oil would eventually cover 1,100 miles (1,770 km) of Alaskan coastline.

CLEANUP

Cleaning up the spill was a mammoth undertaking. It presented countless problems that cleanup crews often face when trying to contain an oil spill close to a coastline. Once the oil poured out of the tanker, it traveled south and west. Initially, the oil had concentrated near the location of the accident. However, on March 25, a storm with winds topping 70 miles (112 km) per hour blew through the region. The wind pushed the oil over an even larger area of Prince William Sound.

Four days later, the spill had moved 90 miles (144.8 km) from the accident site. Eventually, the oil wrapped around the Kenai Peninsula and into Cook Inlet. The **tide** also played a role moving the spill over a wider area. At nearly 18 feet (5.48 m), Alaska's spring tide deposited oil on shore way beyond the usual tidal boundary.

Fifty-six days after the accident, the oil had moved 470 miles (756 km) away from the accident site, contaminating some of the shoreline around Kodiak Island. The spill would eventually cover 1,100 square miles (1,770 square km). Cleanup crews used various methods to contain the oil, including laying down a large boom around the vessel. But the storm made containing the oil a difficult task.

Q & A

Question: Was the Exxon Valdez oil spill the largest oil spill in history?

Answer: No. The largest oil spill occurred in February 1991, during the Persian Gulf War. During the war, Iraqi soldiers opened the valves at an offshore oil terminal and dumped the contents of several oil tankers in the Persian Gulf. The oil polluted 420 miles (675 km) of Saudi coastline, and covered 4,000 square miles.

The *Exxon Valdez* oil spill created an economic and environmental disaster. Alaska's sport fishing industry lost at least $580 million in 1989 and an additional $50 million in 1990. Thousands upon thousands of animals died. The oil covered the feathers of birds. Birds use their feathers as an insulating blanket; many died of **hypothermia** because they lost the ability to keep warm. Others drowned or ingested the toxic hydrocarbons. Scientists estimate that 1,000 to 2,800 sea otters died, along with 302 harbor seals and at least 250,000 sea birds.

Q & A

Question: During an oil spill, does the oil spread quickly?

Answer: Yes, oil spreads very rapidly, traveling on top of the water. How fast oil spreads also depends on what type of fuel it is. Gasoline will spread more quickly than certain types of thick, black fuel oil. Oil that is less dense will spread out in a shiny, thin sheen. In addition, wave action and temperature also play a role in how quickly an oil spill moves. Obviously, faster currents will make oil spread more rapidly. Cold temperatures will slow down the oil's movement.

The environmental effects of the *Exxon Valdez* were still felt years after the disaster. Marsh and sediments in Prince William Sound retained oil, affecting fish **embryos**. Even after a decade, oil still remained. Mussels, clams, ducks, and sea otters still showed health problems long after the cleanup crews went away. Other animals, such as loons, killer whales, and harbor seals have yet to recover from the disaster. Some animals, such as the bald eagle and river otter, are successfully recovering.

Q & A

Question: How long does it take for spilled oil to make its way into the ground?

Answer: It depends on the type of soil. Oil will move through fine soil such as sand faster than it will through more compact soil such as clay.

The lingering oil toxicity came as no surprise to scientists. A small oil spill off Falmouth, Massachusetts, in the late 1960s caused problems for a decade afterward. Fiddler crabs were especially sensitive seven years later. The oil affected how the crabs burrowed. Usually the burrows of fiddler crabs go straight down. After the spill, the crabs did not burrow as they normally did. When winter came, the crabs' burrows leveled off after a time. Crabs that did not burrow below the freeze line froze to death.

Q & A

Question: How does salt water affect an oil spill?

Answer: Oil floats very easily in salt water. Salt water also affects some of the chemicals that workers use to treat an oil slick.

Oil spills are also dangerous to whales. Whales may eat fish contaminated by oil, and the oily sludge could block the blow hole that the whale uses to breathe. Moreover, tiny plankton, the food source for many undersea creatures, can die off in an oil spill, thus disrupting the ocean's food chain.

The *Exxon Valdez* was later repaired and sent out to sea again. Captain Hazelwood was tried for several criminal counts. Although he admitted drinking alcohol before boarding the ship, he said he was not drunk. An Alaska jury agreed. He was found guilty of negligent discharge of oil and fined $50,000 and given 1,000 hours of community service.

Q & A

Question: Does most of the oil spilled into the water come from major oil spills?

Answer: No. According to the National Aeronautics and Space Administration (NASA) and the Smithsonian Institution, only 5 percent of the oil that spills into the water comes from major oil spills. Most of the oil in water comes from small amounts of leakage, such as oil that leaks from automobiles. The National Academy of Sciences reports that nearly 85 percent of the 29 million gallons of petroleum that enter the oceans of North America come from land-based runoff, polluted rivers, airplanes, and small boats and watercraft.

CLEANUP METHODS

Whether an oil spill happens on the coast of Alaska or in the Persian Gulf, workers use several methods to clean up the spill. Some include:

- **Booms and skimmers.** Once oil is spilled in the water, crews will work quickly to surround the spill with booms and try to recover much of the oil by using skimmers that separate oil from the water.

- **Conveyor belt.** Workers will often try to lift the oil out of the water using a conveyor belt.

- **Sorbents.** Sorbents soak oil up like a sponge. Some sorbents are made from substances similar to those in baby diapers.

- **Dispersants.** Workers will spray chemicals to break down the oil in tiny droplets that naturally occurring bacteria can digest.

- **Burning.** Oftentimes, cleanup crews will burn the oil off the top of the water. While this method works very well, it creates thick black smoke that pollutes the air with harmful and toxic gases.

- **Bioremediation.** Workers will introduce oil-ingesting bacteria to destroy the oil. The procedure involves promoting the growth of bacteria.

- **High-pressure hoses.** Workers will wash the oil on the shoreline back into the ocean with high-pressure hoses. This procedure, however, can cause more problems by driving oil deep into the beach.

See also: Air Pollution; Chemical Pollution, causes and effects of; Water Pollution

FURTHER READING

Leacock, Elspeth. *The* Exxon Valdez *Oil Spill.* New York: Facts On File, 2005.

Nardo, Don. *Oil Spill.* Chicago: Lucent Books, 1991.

Walker, Jane, ed. *Oil Spills.* New York: Franklin Watts, 2003.

■ OZONE LAYER

Layer of the earth's upper atmosphere within the **stratosphere**, which absorbs harmful **ultraviolet radiation** from the Sun and keeps it from reaching the planet's surface. In recent years, a hole in this layer of colorless, odorless gas has formed over the Southern Hemisphere. The hole, centered over Antarctica, generally lasts from September through December. Due to the thinning atmosphere, scientists have linked exposure from ultraviolet radiation to **cataracts** and some forms of cancer.

OZONE DESCRIBED

Earth's ozone layer is like an invisible blanket that covers the planet. If not for the ozone layer, the Sun's radiation would fall with such intensity on Earth's surface that it would destroy all animal and plant life.

Earth's atmosphere is a complex mixture of gases that are kept in place by gravity, the force of attraction between two objects. Most of Earth's atmosphere is made up of nitrogen and oxygen. Humans need oxygen to live.

Billions of years ago, there was virtually no oxygen in the atmosphere. Ozone is made from oxygen. Because there was no ozone, the planet was constantly bombarded by the Sun's harmful rays. Those rays stopped complex life from forming on land.

However, in the oceans something entirely different was happening. The water blocked the oceans' depths from the Sun's ultraviolet radiation. It was deep below the sea that primitive life began. Eventually, Earth's early environment changed to the point where more complex life began to emerge on land. Eventually, a life-sustaining atmosphere formed. Ozone played a vital role in the emergence of life on Earth.

Ozone is a form of oxygen that contains three atoms of oxygen, rather than the two atoms that make up the oxygen we breathe. Ozone has a sharp, pungent odor. German chemist Christian Fredrick Schonbein first observed ozone during experiments with electricity.

He noticed that when there was an electrical discharge, the electricity produced ozone. The gas had a distinctive smell.

The interaction of oxygen **molecules** with ultraviolet light causes the two atoms of the oxygen to separate into separate atoms. Ozone forms when these atoms combine with two other oxygen molecules. The same process that turns oxygen into ozone is also powerful enough to turn ozone back into oxygen.

HARMING THE ATMOSPHERE

The ozone layer is located in the stratosphere, 31 miles to 50 miles (50 to 80 kilometers) above the planet's surface. The ozone layer absorbs nearly 99 percent of the Sun's radiation. For millions of years, there has been a delicate balance between ozone and oxygen. For a long time, no one thought anyone or anything could disrupt the awesome power of Earth's climatic and atmosphere conditions. No one realized, until fairly recently, that humans were destroying the ozone layer.

Q & A

Question: Has there been ozone loss other than in the Arctic and Antarctica?

Answer: Ozone loss has been reported in the mid to high latitudes in both the Northern and Southern Hemisphere. In Australia, for example, recent studies show that ozone depletion has been measured at 8 percent, while in New Zealand, it has reached about 10 to 15 percent.

Humans have been polluting the air since prehistoric times. However, pollution began getting worse during the Industrial Revolution, which began in the late 1700s. Factories began springing up in Europe and North America. The factories burned **fossil fuels** to run their machines, and the burning of fossil fuels created air pollution.

No one knew what this air pollution was doing to the ozone layer. In 1966, however, a Canadian scientist named Dr. John Hampson published a report that shook up the scientific community. At that time, the Soviet Union, the United States, Great Britain, and France all wanted to build a fleet of supersonic jets that could fly faster than the speed of sound. Sound travels roughly 1,087 feet (331 meters) per second.

These supersonic jets, including the famous Concorde, would fly through the lower part of the atmosphere in the ozone layer. When these planes flew through the ozone layer, their exhaust would contain water vapor. Water vapor is relatively harmless. However, Hampson said water vapor would react with the ozone, turning the gas back into oxygen. Then Hampson asked a question: If that were to happen, would the Sun's harmful ultraviolet radiation reach Earth's surface?

Suddenly, scientists began working to determine what would happen to the ozone layer if the supersonic plane programs were allowed to continue. At a congressional hearing in the United States, the scientist James McDonald told lawmakers that the ozone layer would be depleted by several percentage points if the world's nations allowed their supersonic programs to continue. What did that mean? McDonald said that even a depletion of 1 percent would cause 5,000 to 10,000 new cases of skin cancer in the United States.

Q & A

Question: Can the ozone layer repair itself?

Answer: Some scientists think so. They say the hole in the ozone layer over Antarctica will shrink and close by 2050. They claim that the ban on CFCs is working and they believe that as long as countries continue to ban the chemicals, the ozone layer should repair itself.

Another scientist had even more grim figures. Harold Johnson said that a full fleet of supersonic aircraft would cause the ozone layer to deplete by 10 percent in only two years. The companies that were hoping to build the planes said ozone depletion was just a theory. In the United States, Congress shut funding down for the planes because they said the government could not afford to spend money on the research.

Still, people began to understand that humans were harming the atmosphere and the planet. The debate over the supersonic planes prompted scientists to begin studying the ozone layer with renewed interest.

THE BIRTH OF CFCS

Part of the blame for the hole in the Earth's ozone layer lies in the seemingly harmless aerosol spray cans and the gases inside those cans, known as *chlorofluorocarbons,* or CFCs. Before 1972, only a few people had heard of CFCs.

CFCs were first discovered by Thomas Midgley in 1928. Working as a chemist at General Motors, Midgley was trying to find nontoxic compounds that would not burn and could be used as coolants in refrigerators. Midgley developed several compounds of CFCs.

The chemicals that make up CFCs are mainly chlorine and fluorine. CFCs were perfect for cooling refrigerators and air conditioners. People also used CFCs in other ways, including as insulation for fast-good containers. Then in the 1930s, scientists began finding other uses for CFCs. At the time, people would use an old-fashioned sprayer with a plunger to spray insecticides. These old cans were bulky and inefficient to use. There had to be a better way—and there was. Scientists combined CFCs and insecticides in a pressurized can. They discovered that CFCs could easily be kept as a liquid in such a device. With one touch of a spray button, the pressure in the can could be lowered, causing the CFCs to shoot out with the insect killer. The aerosol spray can was born. By 1947, 45 million aerosol cans of insecticide were sold each year.

Companies soon began putting CFCs in other products, including hair spray, deodorants, and air fresheners. CFCs did not seem to be harming anyone or anything. Everyone used aerosol spray cans and they made life easier.

In addition to CFCs, companies began manufacturing related products that contained *halogens,* a combination of five different elements including fluorine, chlorine, bromine, iodine, and astatine. Companies used halogens in fire extinguishers, dry-cleaning chemicals, and other products. As with CFCs, most people considered halogens harmless.

In the early 1970s, a scientist named James Lovelock was measuring CFCs with a machine he had built. Eventually, Lovelock took his CFC-measuring device to Antarctica. It was there, at the bottom of the world, that Lovelock began studying CFCs in earnest. He found that CFCs from industrial products were floating up into the stratosphere, where they accumulated. Lovelock thought nothing of it. In fact, he said, "The presence of these compounds constitutes no conceivable hazard."

Q & A

Question: How do we know that natural causes are not responsible for ozone depletion?

Answer: While volcanoes and oceans release large amounts of chlorine into the environment, that chlorine is washed out by rain in the lower atmosphere. CFCs are not water-soluble and are not broken down in the lower atmosphere.

THE DANGER OF CFCS

Little did anyone realize that CFCs were eating away at Earth's ozone layer. Once Lovelock found that CFCs were accumulating in the stratosphere, two other scientists, F. Sherwood Rowland and Mario Molina, decided to study what impact the compounds were having on that layer of the atmosphere.

Initially, Molina concluded that ultraviolet radiation in the stratosphere would break down CFCs. Molina said the ozone layer would not be harmed because there were simply not enough CFC molecules in the stratosphere. Then Molina revamped his numbers and came to a disturbing conclusion. Molina told his mentor Rowland what he had found: CFCs were destroying the ozone layer.

In 1974, the scientists published their findings. The pair said that if CFC production continued to increase at 10 percent a year until 1990, the ozone layer would be depleted by 5 to 7 percent by 1995, and between 30 and 50 percent by 2050. They estimated that a 5 percent reduction in the ozone layer would cause 40,000 additional cases of skin cancer each year in the United States.

Moreover, ultraviolet radiation from the Sun would causes millions of cases of cataracts, a clouding over of the eye lens. Others argued that UV radiation would harm the immune system of people, leading to widespread epidemics.

The news got worse. A disappearing ozone layer would harm animals and plants and would also disrupt Earth's weather patterns. Scientists said the lack of ozone in the atmosphere would disrupt circulation patterns, altering climate conditions in unforeseen ways.

Scientists began studying the ozone layer in earnest after Rowland and Molina published their findings. Harvard researchers predicted that the stratosphere would lose 40 percent of its ozone by 2014.

The news was so shocking and disturbing that in 1987, the nations of the world banded together to phase out the production and use of CFCs, hoping that it was not too late. CFCs already in the atmosphere can take up to 50 years to reach the stratosphere.

That is just part of the CFC story. CFCs also act as heat-trapping gases, or **greenhouse gases**, keeping heat near Earth's surface. Greenhouse gases are the cause of **global warming**, the gradual increase in Earth's temperature.

Q & A

Question: While ozone high in the atmosphere protects the planet, what happens when ozone is near Earth's surface?

Answer: Ozone near Earth's surface can be deadly. When the pollutants of burned gasoline, also known as hydrocarbons, react with sunlight and water vapor, ozone is produced; when it is near Earth's surface, ozone is a dangerous gas. The chemical reaction between the hydrocarbons and ozone creates smog, a poisonous fog.

HOLE IN THE OZONE

In 1985, British researchers studying ozone levels in the atmosphere over Antarctica announced the discovery of a hole in the ozone layer. Scientists first noticed the hole in 1982. As the years went by, the hole got bigger and bigger.

In 1985, the scientists published their findings. The news shocked the world. Earth's security blanket was in tatters. Every spring, a hole as big as the United States forms over Antarctica. A smaller hole forms over the Arctic.

See also: Air Pollution; Global Warming

FURTHER READING

Cefrey, Holly. *What If the Hole in the Ozone Grows Larger?* Danbury, Conn.: Children's Press, 2002.

Donald, Rhonda Lucas. *The Ozone Layer.* Danbury, Conn.: Children's Press, 2002.

Hare, Tony. *The Ozone Layer.* New York: Franklin Watts, 1990.

■ PESTICIDES

See also: Herbicide; Insecticide

■ POLLUTION

See also: Chemical Pollution; Clean Water; Environmental Conservation; Landfills and Superfund Sites; Recycling

■ RADIATION

Emission of energy, as high-speed particles or rays, of some atoms. Physicists associate radiation with the energy given off by radio-active elements, such as uranium and plutonium. There are many different types of radiation, however, including the energy given off by the Sun. Radiation also refers to electromagnetic radiation, which includes **radio waves, infrared light, ultraviolet light, and X-rays.**

Radioactivity from nuclear materials is an example of a nuclear reaction, or a change in the **nucleus,** or center, of an atom. Radioactivity is considered a spontaneous nuclear reaction because it takes place without the help of an outside source. Unstable nuclei will continue to emit radiation until they achieve a stable state. For example, the highly radioactive element uranium will eventually change to lead.

Radiation is a major health concern. Humans exposed to various levels of radiation from various elements may become ill with cancer as the radiation sparks the uncontrolled growth of cancer cells. Radiation can also cause changes in a person's **genetic** makeup. Genes determine a person's inherited characteristics, such as eye and hair color.

NUCLEAR REACTIONS

To understand radiation, one must first understand nuclear reactions. Every object in the universe is made up of atoms. Inside the tiny atoms are even smaller **subatomic particles.** There are negatively charged **electrons** and positively charged **protons.** There are also **neutrons.** Neutrons do not have any charge. Neutrons are found in the nucleus of most atoms. Both neutrons and protons are bound closely together. Because electrons carry a negative electrical charge and protons carry a positive charge, they attract one another. That attraction holds the atom together.

The most common way to produce nuclear energy is through a nuclear reaction, or fission. Fission is the splitting of atoms. Nuclear power plants use nuclear fission to generate electricity. Nuclear reactors use uranium-235, a powerful form of the radioactive element uranium, for this purpose. Other elements that can generate nuclear fission include plutonium or thorium.

Fission occurs when a neutron from one atom slams into the nucleus of another atom. When a uranium atom undergoes fission, it releases more neutrons. A chain reaction occurs when the released neutrons begin slamming other uranium atoms. That causes those atoms to split. As the atoms split, they change. When atoms change, they release huge amounts of energy called radiation. Radiation can take the form of alpha particles, which are positively charged, or beta particles, which are negatively charged.

Alpha particles have two protons and two neutrons. Alpha particles are high-energy particles that can travel at 1/20th the speed of light. Atoms, such as those found in plutonium-236 or uranium-238, are very large. In other words, they have a high atomic number. Beta particles are subatomic particles ejected from the nucleus of some radioactive atoms.

Three scientists first discovered radiation in 1896. Henri Becquerel, Marie Curie, and her husband, Pierre, were working in their Paris laboratory when they discovered that a black rock called **pitchblende** emitted rays of energy. The trio performed many experiments to find out which elements in pitchblende gave off the wondrous rays.

The Curies discovered that two new elements in pitchblende were giving off the energy rays. They named one of those elements polonium, after Marie's home country of Poland; they named the other radium, for the rays it gave off. The rays given off by the two elements could travel through paper, wood, and even metal. Marie Curie coined the term *radioactivity* to describe that ability. Pitchblende also contained uranium. The Curies and Becquerel showed that uranium was also radioactive, and some of that radiation had a both a positive and negative charge. It also had a neutral charge.

Marie Curie died in 1934. By that time, a few scientists had begun to theorize that if they could split, or cause a chain reaction of, a number of uranium atoms, immense energy would be released. That theory proved correct.

In 1945, as World War II (1939–1945) continued to rage in the Pacific, the United States detonated its first atomic bomb in the desert of New Mexico. Scientists had packed the bomb with more than 100 tons (91 metric tons) of explosives stitched in between tubes of plutonium. At 5:29 A.M. on July 16, 1945, the nuclear age dawned when the skies over Alamogordo, New Mexico, exploded in a giant fireball of intense heat and light. The explosion was brighter than the mid-day desert sun.

As scientists watched, they were amazed at how well their atomic bomb worked. The blast spilled harmful radiation into the surrounding area. Less than a month later, the United States dropped the first atomic bombs on the Japanese cities of Hiroshima and Nagasaki, leading Japan to surrender and ending World War II.

When Henri Becquerel and the Curies were conducting their experiments, no one knew that radiation could be harmful to the human body. Marie Curie died of leukemia, a cancer of the blood. Doctors and historians believe Marie Curie's work with radioactivity caused the disease that took her life. When American doctors went to Hiroshima and Nagasaki, they saw firsthand the devastation caused by the bomb. No one could have foreseen the extent of the injuries caused by the blast. Many of those who were not killed by the blast were badly scarred. Even those who had showed no visible effects of the detonation died weeks after because of radiation sickness. Their skin broke out in red spots, their tongues turned black, and their hair fell out. Later, women gave birth to children with defects.

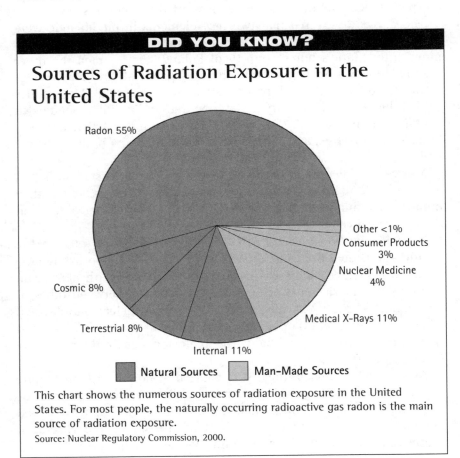

DID YOU KNOW?

Sources of Radiation Exposure in the United States

Radon 55%

Other <1%
Consumer Products 3%
Nuclear Medicine 4%
Medical X-Rays 11%
Internal 11%
Terrestrial 8%
Cosmic 8%

Natural Sources   Man-Made Sources

This chart shows the numerous sources of radiation exposure in the United States. For most people, the naturally occurring radioactive gas radon is the main source of radiation exposure.

Source: Nuclear Regulatory Commission, 2000.

SOURCES OF RADIATION

Not everyone has to be in the middle of an atomic blast to be exposed to radiation. In fact, radiation is all around. It is in the environment, and it comes from outer space in the form of cosmic rays. There's radiation in the air and radiation in the rocks.

Many foods, such as bananas and Brazil nuts, contain natural levels of radiation. Buildings built out of brick and stone have higher radiation levels than buildings made out of wood. Even the granite stones of the U.S. Capitol in Washington, D.C., contain a certain level of radiation. Exposure to natural sources of radiation varies from place to place. Radon gas, which some rocks emit, is responsible for two-thirds of natural radiation exposure. Radon can enter homes through basements or drinking water. The Sun is also a source of radiation, sending its harmful rays to Earth. Human-made sources of radiation include:

- Radioactive elements found in smoke detectors
- Food treated with radiation to destroy bacteria and other contaminants, as well as to control spoilage
- Mail treated with radiation to kill any possible bacteria, such as anthrax, which contaminated some mail in 2001
- Smoke from tobacco and cigarettes, which is by far the largest source of radiation that the public comes into contact with
- Building products, such as brick, cement blocks, granite counter tops, and glazed tiles
- Food containers that are sterilized with radiation to kill bacteria
- Various medical procedures, such as X-rays and mammograms

Although rare, accidents at nuclear power plants can release huge amounts of radiation over a wide area in a very short time. The worse release of radiation because of a nuclear accident occurred in 1986 at the Chernobyl nuclear reactor in the former Soviet Union. When the reactor exploded on April 26, 1986, it sent a plume of radioactivity into the air. Hundreds of thousands of people had to leave their homes.

The worst nuclear accident in the United States happened on March 28, 1979, when a cooling malfunction at the Three Mile Island nuclear plant in Pennsylvania caused part of the reactor's core to melt. Although some radioactive gas was released, it was not a significant amount.

Although there was no loss of life, and no adverse health effects from the accident, officials had the reactor shut down permanently.

Before people knew the hazards of radioactivity, they buried nuclear waste in the soil and dumped it in the ocean. Radiation eventually leaked into ponds or traveled to the sea. For example, in the 1940s, researchers trucked some of the nuclear waste generated from scientific experiments and buried it in only two feet of soil in a forest preserve in Palos Hills, Illinois. Over time, the radioactivity seeped into nearby water. In addition, workers dumped some radioactive waste into the ocean. In 2003, a study confirmed that scientists had found radioactivity in bird droppings.

Many industries, such as mining, nuclear power, and scientific research, as well as hospitals, produce hazardous radioactive waste. Finding a place to safely discard radioactive waste is sometimes difficult, depending on how long the waste needs to be contained. Some waste can be radioactive for only a few moments, while other materials remain radioactive for hundreds of thousands of years.

Q & A

Question: How do doctors estimate the risk from radiation exposure?

Answer: Scientists and doctors use several methods to estimate the risk of someone's being exposed to a particular radioactive substance. Scientists will often break into two groups people who have been exposed to a particular substance. One group is comprised of those experiencing health problems; the other, those who are seemingly healthy. Both groups would be similar in age, education, occupation and income. By using this method, scientists can identify other risk factors that might make one group more likely to experience a health effect due to radiation. Scientists use this method in estimating the risk of cancer in smokers. In identifying other risk factors, scientists rely on a family medical history.

Q & A

Question: How much radiation am I exposed to in the course of a day?

Answer: Exposures vary, but all humans are exposed to various levels of radon gas, cosmic rays from the Sun, and medical X-rays. The body itself carries natural radioactive elements such as isotopes of potassium. Scientists measure exposure to radiation in rems. A millirem is one-thousandth of a rem. Most people in the United States are, on average, exposed to 160 millirem of radiation per day.

HEALTH HAZARDS

Radiation causes many health problems in humans. People can inhale, ingest, and be directly exposed to radioactive materials. When a person inhales radioactive particles, those particles settle in the lungs. If the particles remain in the lungs, they will continue to decay. If some of those particles decay slowly, the person is exposed to radiation for a long time.

Some people ingest, or swallow, radioactive materials. Those materials release large doses of energy directly into the tissue, causing damage to cells and DNA. Once radiation is swallowed, a person's entire digestive system is exposed to it; so are the kidneys, bones, and other organs. Other people can come in direct contact with radioactive materials. Gamma rays can penetrate entirely through the body.

Illnesses from radiation are dependent on the duration and amount of exposure. Low-level radiation over a long period of time can cause cancer. Radiation damages the body's cells, disrupting the cell's ability to grow and reproduce. Cells also control the body's ability to repair damaged tissue. Radiation permits the uncontrolled growth of cells, also known as cancer. Radiation also affects the body's genetic makeup, that ensures that cells repair properly. Scientists call the changes in a person's DNA *mutations*.

Exposure to radiation doesn't always cause cancer. Other health effects include burns and radiation sickness, also known as radiation poisoning. Nausea, weakness, hair loss, skin burns, and lose of organ function are all examples of radiation poisoning. Radiation can also cause someone to age prematurely.

Children are more sensitive to radiation than adults, because of their fast rate of growth. There are more cells dividing and a greater opportunity for radiation to affect that process. Fetuses, too, are very sensitive to radiation. The severity of damage depends on the length of exposure and how much radiation is absorbed.

See also: Air Pollution; Carcinogens; Hazardous Wastes; Nuclear Power

FURTHER READING
Birch, Beverly. *Marie Curie: Pioneer in the Study of Radiation.* Pleasantville, N.Y.: Gareth Stevens, 1990.
Karam, Andrew P. *Radioactivity.* New York: Chelsea House, 2009.

▌ RADON

Colorless, odorless radioactive gas formed through the natural decay of uranium in rock, soil, and water. Radon occurs naturally, and low levels can be found in Earth's crust. The gas can move into the atmosphere from the ground. Some radon also stays in the soil, where it dissolves in water, which then flows under the ground's surface. High levels of radon gas are a major health problem. Radon is the second leading cause of lung cancer in the United States, behind smoking.

Radon forms through the natural decay of **radium**. First discovered in 1900, radon was classified as a health risk in the late 1980s. Scientists found the gas seeping up from the ground. When radon accumulates in enclosed spaces, such as basement or cellars, its radioactivity can be hazardous. Radon can be found in every state, although levels will vary. People can buy radon detectors to warn them of unhealthy levels of gas.

RADON IN THE HOME

Radon is a problem when it enters the home. Radon occurs naturally in several types of soil and rock, such as granite, phosphate, shale, and **pitchblende**. Radon gas can make its way up from the ground and enter a house through cracks in the foundation or walls. The gas can also find its way into a building through openings in insulation, pipes, and drains.

Water also absorbs radon gas as it moves through rock. The radon-tainted water then moves into the home through pipes. Turning the water on to wash clothes, dishes, and shower releases the gas into the air. In addition, people can ingest radon by drinking or by washing foods with contaminated water. Studies have shown that a person is more likely to develop lung cancer by inhaling radon gas than develop stomach or other digestive tract cancers by drinking radon-contaminated water.

Homes with private wells or public water supplies that use groundwater as a water source are more likely than water from a municipal or private water systems to be contaminated by radon. People who have a private well and are worried about radon-tainted water can have the water tested for radon. If the well tests positive for radon contamination, it can be fixed. Devices that remove the radon from the water before it gets to the house are available.

Fact Or Fiction?

Radon only affects certain types of houses.

The Facts: Although radon can affect all homes to some extent, home construction techniques may be able to reduce the amount of radon gas. In addition, local geology and the type of construction materials, and how the home was built, can affect radon levels. For example, buildings built mainly with wood might have lower levels of radon that buildings built of brick, stone, and block.

Building materials made out of rock and stone, such as granite countertops, fieldstone, floor tiles, and bricks might also contain radon. The U.S. Environmental Protection Agency (EPA) says that nearly one out of every 15 homes in the United States have elevated levels of radon gas.

Fact Or Fiction?

Once a contractor uses one of the radon-reduction methods, there is no need for a radon-alarm system to be installed.

The Facts: No matter what radon-reduction system you use, it is extremely important to install a warning device. That will alert you if your system does not work correctly. Place your device where you can see and hear it.

TESTING FOR RADON

Testing for radon is fairly easy. People can buy a radon test kit for their homes that creates and generates a snapshot of radon levels in both the short and the long term. Because radon levels vary from day to day, long-term tests will give residents a better indication of the amount of radon in their house. Residents can also conduct several short-term tests.

The most important step in conducting a radon test is to following the directions that comes with the test kit. According to the EPA, if people conduct a short-term test, they should remember to close all outside doors and windows and turn off any heating or air-conditioning units. Air should not be allowed to circulate during the test.

Close the windows and outside doors for at least 12 hours if doing a two- or three-day short-term test. Place the test kit in the lowest floor of the house, such as a basement or the first floor. Place the test kit at least 20 inches above the floor away from heat, exterior walls, or anything that generates high humidity, such as a vaporizer or humidifier. Follow the directions of the kit and leave it for as long as it says. Once the test is done, send the kit to the laboratory. The results should come back within a few weeks.

Long-term testing should take at least 90 days. It is more accurate than a short-term test and should give residents an indication of what the year-round exposure rate is.

Fact Or Fiction?

Scientists are really uncertain about the risks from radon.

The Facts: Scientists know more about the risks from radon than from most other cancer-causing substances. Scientists learned a great deal about radon exposure from miners.

HEALTH RISKS

What are the dangers of inhaling radon gas? When you breathe, radon gas can become trapped in your lungs. Once inside your lungs the particles are still active. They will emit short bursts of energy, or radiation. That radiation can damage the tissue in your lungs and over time, lead to lung cancer.

Fact Or Fiction?

Radon is not a problem in the air in my house. That means it is not a problem in the water.

The Facts: Just because radon levels are low in the air you breathe does not mean levels are low in the water, especially if your water comes from a well. You should have your water tested.

Smoking makes the problem even worse. Moreover, children are more likely to get cancer because the cells in their bodies are always

DID YOU KNOW?

Risks of Radon Exposure

Radon Level	If 1,000 people who smoked were exposed to this level over a lifetime*...	The risk of cancer from radon exposure is**...	WHAT TO DO: Stop smoking and...
20 pCi/L	About 260 people could get lung cancer	250 times the risk of drowning	Fix your home
10 pCi/L	About 150 people could get lung cancer	200 times the risk of dying in a home fire	Fix your home
8 pCi/L	About 120 people could get lung cancer	30 times the risk of dying in a fall	Fix your home
4 pCi/L	About 62 people could get lung cancer	Five times the risk of dying in a car crash	Fix your home
2 pCi/L	About 32 people could get lung cancer	Six times the risk of dying from poison	Consider fixing your home
1.3 pCi/L	About 20 people could get lung cancer	(Average indoor radon level)	(Reducing radon levels
0.4 pCi/L	About three people could get lung cancer	(Average outdoor radon level)	below 2 pCi/L is difficult)

Note: If you are a former smoker, your risk may be lower.

* Lifetime risk of lung cancer deaths from *EPA Assessment of Risks from Radon in Homes* (EPA 402-R-03-003).

** Comparison data calculated using the Centers for Disease Control and Prevention's 1999–2001 National Center for Injury Prevention and Control reports.

According to the EPA, the risks of getting lung cancer from radon are greater if a person is a smoker.

U.S. Environmental Protection Agency, 2001.

Risks of Radon Exposure

Radon Level	If 1,000 people who never smoked were exposed to this level over a lifetime*...	The risk of cancer from radon exposure compares to**...	WHAT TO DO:
20 pCi/L	About 36 people could get lung cancer	35 times the risk of drowning	Fix your home
10 pCi/L	About 18 people could get lung cancer	20 times the riske of dying in a home fire	Fix your home
8 pCi/L	About 15 people could get lung cancer	Four times the risk of dying in a fall	Fix your home
4 pCi/L	About seven people could get lung cancer	The risk of dying in a car crash	Fix your home
2 pCi/L	About four people could get lung cancer	The risk of dying from poison	Consider fixing your home
1.3 pCi/L	About two people could get lung cancer	(Average indoor radon level)	(Reducing radon levels below 2 pCi/L is difficult)
0.4 pCi/L		(Average outdoor radon level)	

Note: If you are a former smoker, your risk may be higher.

* Lifetime risk of lung cancer deaths from *EPA Assessment of Risks from Radon in Homes* (EPA 402-R-03-003).

** Comparison data calculated using the Centers for Disease Control and Prevention's 1999–2001 National Center for Injury Prevention and Control reports.

According to the EPA, for people who do not smoke, the risks of getting lung cancer from radon are lower.

U.S. Environmental Protection Agency, 2001.

growing. The chances of someone getting lung cancer because of radon are dependent on several factors, including the level of radon in a house; the amount of time some spends inside the house; and whether that person is a smoker.

LOWERING RADON LEVELS

Radon will always be around, but there are several steps homeowners can take to minimize its impact. In fact, a homeowner can get rid of 99 percent of the radon coming into the home. The costs of radon abatement can range from $800 to $2,500, depending on the type of system installed.

The key is to hire a qualified contractor to install the system. Here are several ways to lower your exposure:

- **Soil suction.** This method includes drawing the radon from below your house and venting it into the air through a pipe. Once the gas is in the atmosphere, it can no longer harm you.

- **Subslab depressurization.** This method works if you have a basement that has a concrete-poured floor. A contractor will install a suction pipe through the concrete floor into the soil underneath. Depending on how easily air can move, the contractor might have to install more than one pipe. Once the builder installs the pipe, he connects it to a vent. The vent draws the radon gas from below the house, releasing it into the air outside. This also creates a **vacuum** beneath the slab of concrete.

- **Passive subslab suction.** This method is the same as subslab depressurization, but it relies on air pressure and air currents to move the radon gas from beneath a house.

- **Submembrane suction.** For homes that do not have a concrete floor in the basement, contractors will cover the crawlspace's dirt floor with a plastic sheet. They will then install a pipe and fan to draw the gas up from underneath the sheet. Contractors might install simple fans to lower radon levels in the crawlspace.

- **Sealing.** Sealing cracks and openings in a building's foundation will slow the flow of radon gas. Sealing alone, however, might not be enough to reduce the gas to a healthy level.

- **House/room pressurization.** Using a fan to blow air into a basement might create enough pressure to prevent radon from making its way into the rest of the house.
- **Heat recovery ventilator (HRV).** HRV systems increase ventilation by moving outside air indoors while the air is heat or cooled.
- **Natural ventilation.** Simply opening doors and windows will increase the amount of outside air flowing into your house, resulting in reduced radon levels.

Fact Or Fiction?

Water treatment systems will move radon from water.

The Facts: Water can be treated before it enters your house by filters. Water can also be treated by filters installed at the water tap. These so-called point-of-use devices, however, do not reduce the risk of breathing in radon gas from all water you use in your home.

See also: Radiation; Hazardous Waste Disposal; Water Pollution

FURTHER READING

Gay, Kathlyn. *Silent Killers: Radon and Other Hazards.* New York: Franklin Watts, 1988.

Taylor, Ron. *Facts on Radon and Asbestos.* New York: Franklin Watts, 1990.

■ RAIN FORESTS, DEPLETION OF THE

Destruction of the world's rain forests due to decades of logging, fires, and land-clearing for farming and ranching. According to the Rainforest Action Network, humans cut down a football-sized chunk of rain forest every second.

The tropical rain forest is like no other **ecosystem** on the planet. The rain forests are important to survival of Earth. Rain forests are diverse, offering civilization medicine, food, and other forest products. Moreover, they play a major role in regulating Earth's weather. Rain forests maintain regular rainfall and help prevent erosion and drought. The rain forest also supplies the world with significant amounts of oxygen.

Q & A

Question: How much rain do rain forests receive each year?

Answer: Some rain forests receive up to 80 inches (2,000 mm) of rain a year, while other rain forests receive more than 430 inches (10,920 mm).

Although tropical rain forests once covered 14 percent of Earth's land surface, they now cover only about 7 percent. Experts say that the remaining rain forests could be gone in 40 years.

Rain forests contain more than half of the world's plant and animal species. A typical rain forest has more than 300 different kinds of trees. Scientists estimate that they have yet to discover at least 30,000 plant species.

Tropical rain forests are not only home to plants and animals; many **indigenous**, or native, people live in the region. In fact, some of the world's greatest civilizations, such as the Maya and Inca, called the rain forest home. Their civilizations thrived, and the ruins of their cities can still be seen in many areas. Most of the tribes that live in the rain forest today have been there for centuries, having learned to live off the land and understand their environment.

IMPACT ZONE

Although the world's rain forests are wondrous places, human activity has threatened to eliminate them. In West Africa, for example, humans have destroyed 90 percent of the coastal rain forests since 1900, according to the World Resources Institute.

The Amazon rain forest, which is located in parts of nine South American countries, was once teeming with plants and animals, all untouched by civilization. Several decades of farming and clear cutting, or the cutting of trees in a harvest area, have devastated the region.

In Brazil, ranchers are illegally setting acres ablaze to create pasture for livestock. Each year, humans burn more than 6,000 square miles (1,553,992 hectares) of Brazilian rain forest—an area roughly the size of Connecticut.

IN DANGER

Such deforestation is threatening thousands of plant and animal species. About 70 percent of the world's animal and plant species live in the world's rain forests. In Indonesia, for example, orangutans are in danger of **extinction** because their rain forest **habitat** is under assault by extensive logging operations. Scientists say humans have destroyed at least 80 percent of the orangutan's habitat.

The problems of devastation are many. The rain forests are important sources of water. A rain forest's climate zone generates rainfall in other areas. As humans destroy the rain forest, they are significantly altering global weather patterns. Recent studies suggest that the

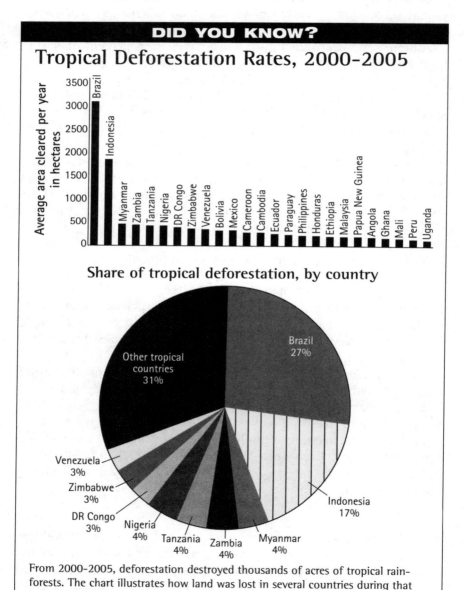

DID YOU KNOW?

Tropical Deforestation Rates, 2000–2005

Share of tropical deforestation, by country

From 2000–2005, deforestation destroyed thousands of acres of tropical rainforests. The chart illustrates how land was lost in several countries during that five-year period.

Source: The Food and Agricultural Organization of the United Nations, 2008.

destruction of rain forests along the coast of West Africa may have been responsible for two decades of drought in the interior of Africa, creating **famine** conditions in many countries.

Q & A

Question: Why are there so many plant and animal species in the rain forest?

Answer: The climate in the rain forest is perfect for animals and plants. The rain forest receives a great deal of sunlight. Plants convert sunlight into energy in a process called photosynthesis. Animals eat these energy-laden plants and reproduce. The rain forest canopy, the leafy area about 100 feet above the ground, is a great place for plants to grow and animals to live. The canopy offers shelter, food, and places to hide.

The depletion of the rain forests is also having an impact on global warming. Global warming is a gradual rise in Earth's temperature brought on by an increase in gases, such as carbon dioxide. Carbon dioxide is a **greenhouse gas**, which traps heat close to the planet's surface. Trees help clean the atmosphere by absorbing carbon dioxide. Thus, cutting down large forests increases the amount of carbon dioxide in the overall atmosphere. In addition, scientists at the National Institute of Amazon Research report that burning the world's rain forests releases 400 million tons of harmful gases into the atmosphere each year.

Fact Or Fiction?

Destroying the rain forests contributes to global warming.

The Facts: Humans are destroying the rain forests by cutting down and burning trees. Trees soak in the greenhouse gas carbon dioxide and release oxygen. Loggers burn the trees after cutting them down. The fewer trees there are, the more carbon dioxide is in the atmosphere. The more carbon dioxide there is in the atmosphere, the more the Earth warms.

POSSIBLE SOLUTIONS

Saving the rain forest from destruction is complicated, because many people depend on the rain forest for their survival. Countries with rain forests are generally among the world's poorer nations, and people in these areas need the rain forest and its natural resources to live. They cultivate the rain forest to grow food. They cut down trees and clear land for crops and pasture.

Fact Or Fiction?

The largest tropical rain forest is located in Africa.

The Facts: The largest unbroken stretch of rain forest is found in the Amazon River Basin in South America. Twenty percent of the world's remaining rain forests are located in Indonesia in Southeast Asia and the Congo in Africa.

Although many countries have laws against deforestation, enforcing those laws has proved difficult. The Brazilian government will fine and even jail ranchers and farmers who clear more than 20 percent of their land.

Another way of combating the depletion of the rain forest is to keep acres of land off-limits to people. In northern Brazil, the government turned 9.6 million acres (3,884,982 hectares) of forest into the world's largest tropical national park.

Still, closing off huge sections of the jungle has failed to protect the rain forests. Some people recommend paying rain forest nations, and the people who live there, not to chop down the trees. For example, in Sumatra, an island off the coast of Southeast Asia, an international financial company is working with the local governor and conservation groups to create a $432 million investment fund to preserve large chunks of the rain forest. In Borneo, another island in the region, an Australian banking group has set aside money to reduce forest fires and restore the portions of the rain forests that have been illegally logged.

Fact Or Fiction?

The rain forest provides us with many medicines.

The Facts: About one-quarter of all medicines come from the rain forest. Quinine, the drug doctors use to treat malaria, comes form the cinchona tree. Another plant in the rain forest contains a drug doctors use to treat leukemia, a cancer of the blood cells. Some scientists say the rain forest might provide 1,400 varieties of plants that could be used as sources to cure cancer.

See also: Environmental Conservation; Global Warming

FURTHER READING
Berminghan, Eldredge, ed. *Tropical Rainforests: Past, Present, and Future.* Chicago, Ill.: University of Chicago Press, 2005.
Knight, Tim. *Journey into the Rainforest.* New York: Oxford University Press, 2001.
Morgan, Ben. *Rainforest.* New York: DK Publishers, 2006.

■ RECYCLING

Collecting of discarded household products and processing of industrial waste so that the materials can be reused. Recycling reduces the needed for garbage to be buried in a landfill or incinerated. Recycling also decreases the emissions of **greenhouse gases** that contribute to **global warming**.

Recycling also protects natural resources, such as wood, water, and minerals. Further, it makes businesses more competitive, reducing their need for limited resources.

GARBAGE EVERYWHERE

No matter where a person is, he or she is surrounded by garbage. Cans, paper plates, candy wrappers. Technically, garbage from a house is called municipal solid waste. These are things people commonly use and then throw away, from old sofas to grass clippings.

According to the U.S. Environmental Protection Agency (EPA), Americans generate 4.6 pounds (2.1 kilograms) of trash each day per person, twice as much as any other country. What happens to all this trash? Each year, Americans throw away 254 million tons (230 million metric tons) of garbage. About 12.5 percent of that trash is burned in an incinerator. About 54 percent is buried in landfills and 33.4 percent is recycled. Out of the 254 million tons of solid waste generated in the United States in 2007, Americans recycled 63.3 million tons—3 percent (1.9 million tons) more than they did the previous year. That number does not include the amount of garbage Americans **composted**. In 2007, Americans composted 21.7 million tons of trash, an increase of more than 20.8 million tons from 2006. This means that in 2007, out of the 4.6 pounds of garbage a person generated every day, she or he also recycled or composted 1.54 pounds, an increase of 2.7 percent over 2006.

Over the past 50 years, the percentage of garbage Americans recycle has steadily increased, from just 6 percent in 1960 to 33 percent today.

Generation and Recovery of Materials

Material	Weight Generated	Weight Recovered	Recovery as % of Generation
Paper and paperboard	83.0	45.2	54.5%
Glass	13.6	3.22	23.7%
Metals			
Steel	15.6	5.28	33.8%
Aluminum	3.35	0.73	21.8%
Other nonferrous metals	1.76	1.22	69.3%
Total metals	20.8	7.23	34.8%
Plastics	30.7	2.09	6.8%
Rubber and leather	7.48	1.10	14.7%
Textiles	11.9	1.90	15.9%
Wood	14.2	1.32	9.3%
Other materials	4.43	1.16	26.2%
Total materials in products	186.1	63.3	34.0%
Other wastes			
Food, other	31.7	0.81	2.6%
Yard trimmings	32.6	20.9	64.1%
Miscellaneous inorganic wastes	3.75	Negligible	Negligible
Total other wastes	68.0	21.7	31.9%
Total municipal solid waste	254.1	85.0	33.4%

This table represents the generation of municipal trash and how much trash was recovered, or recycled, in 2007.

U.S. Environmental Protection Agency, 2008.

Paper products account for 32.7 percent of all the trash recycled in the United States. Food scraps account for 12.5 percent; yard trimmings, 12.8 percent; plastics, 12.1 percent; metals, 8.2 percent; and wood products, 5.6 percent. Americans composted or **mulched** about 20.9

million tons of yard trimmings alone, and recycled 45.2 million tons of paper products and 7.2 million tons of metals.

Recycling keeps many substances, such as plastics, which are not **biodegradable**, from harming the environment. When people recycle plastic, it is usually made into a new form that can be used in many ways. When people recycle aluminum cans, it saves 95 percent of the energy used to make new cans. It also reduces pollution caused by mining and refining bauxite, the raw material of aluminum.

There are dozens of other materials that can be recycled, including computer keyboards, monitors, and television sets. Tires can also be recycled. These are very dangerous if they are not reused, because they can catch fire and leach toxic material into the environment. Some companies shred tires and use them as landscaping mulch. Other companies grind tires up to create artificial turf for football and soccer fields.

RECYCLING METHODS

Before trash can be recycled and turned into useful goods it has to get from the home to the recycling center. Collecting recyclables varies from town to town, but there are four primary methods of recycling. They include curbside pickup, recycling drop-off centers, buy-back centers, and deposit/refund programs.

Once recyclables are collected, they must be taken to a materials recovery facility. It is at this facility that the recyclables are sorted into piles of glass, paper, cardboard, plastics, and so forth. This process gets the recyclables ready for its next leg of the journey—to the manufacturing plant. Recyclables are bought and sold just like any other product. Prices, of course, fluctuate depending on market conditions.

Once inside the manufacturing plant, workers clean and separate recyclables again. Many goods that people buy today are made from recyclable material, including newspapers; aluminum, plastic, and glass soft drink containers; tin cans; and plastic laundry detergent bottles. Some companies go one step further and create totally different products from recyclables, such as park benches, carpeting, and pedestrian bridges. Even some roadway pavement is made of recycled glass.

Putting recycled materials back on the store shelves completes the journey. Many people are demanding that companies make more of their products from recycled goods.

Not only is household garbage recycled, but scrap steel from old cars and buildings can be reused. Giant machines shred old cars and construction waste. By law, steel companies have to make sure that all new steel they make contains a certain percentage of recycled steel. New cars, trucks, and buildings all use recycled steel.

TEENS SPEAK

I'm a Recycler

My name is Carla and I'm proud to say that I recycle. I just don't recycle anything, I recycle *everything*. In fact in school, they call me "the Recycler." I always try to encourage people to recycle.

Why do I recycle? I think recycling is important to help the environment. The less garbage we bury or burn, the better it is for everyone. The water will be cleaner, the air will be easier to breathe, and even the side of the road will be prettier to look at. From beach balls to backpacks, I can recycle anything.

I like to draw pictures, and my mother likes to hang them on the refrigerator. But let's face it, after a month or two the pictures get old. What I do is take them down from the refrigerator and use them to wrap birthday presents. It also makes the gifts kind of special.

I also reuse envelopes that I get in the mail. I place a new address label over the last address label, and then mail it off. I also use old envelopes for scrap paper, and use the pictures from old calendars and make envelopes out of them. All I need is a bit of tape. Don't just throw away junk mail; use it for scrap paper or as bedding for your pets.

My dad gets sports magazines in the mail. When he's done with them, I bring them to my dentist's office, which is right around the corner. I also give them to Carl and Joe at school, because they like to read about sports.

In the springtime, my mom and I like to plant a garden. Before we begin planting, I take old egg cartons and fill them with potting soil, then plant seeds in them. By the time the garden is ready to be planted, the seeds will have already germinated. I also take broken pottery and use it as drainage for potted plants. I also use old aluminum pie trays and put them under pots and plants to hold the dripping water. Old newspapers are a great source of mulch and weed control in the garden. Just cut the newspaper up, wet it, and place it in a thick layer on the garden. Cover it with bark and stone.

I try to find a use for everything, but if I can't, I make sure that everything I used can be recycled. You can generally recycle aerosol cans by popping off the plastic cap and emptying the canister completely. Some recycling centers might not recycle deodorant sticks, but all you have to do is take the dial off the bottom and then recycle the stick. Always use rechargeable batteries. This will save you money, as well as keeping the environment safe.

If you have old books, take them to your local library, or perhaps a day-care center or senior center, depending on what titles they are. Books always make people happy. My local landfill has a book recycling hut. All people have to do is bring in old books and take home new books.

We got a new computer last year. Instead of taking our old one to the landfill, we returned it to the manufacturer, who can then recycle it. You can also donate a used computer to charity. My little brother Bobby loves to color. I took his old crayons and mailed them to the National Crayon Recycle Program. They melt the crayons down to make new ones. Leave the wrappers on, though so they can tell which colors are which.

Recycling and reusing things might seem like a lot of work, but it is fun. I'm a recycler, and I'm proud of it.

WHY RECYCLE?

Recycling helps save the environment. The environment is important because it determines whether we have enough food to eat, enough water to drink, and whether a living thing, no matter how small, will live long enough to reproduce.

Over the centuries, humans have not taken very good care of the environment. People have killed off many animals and polluted the air, water, and soil with chemicals. They have chopped down forests and destroyed the habitats of many plants and animals.

Recycling saves natural resources. People do not just create waste every time they throw something away—they create waste every time a product moves from the factory to the store and then into the home. Reusing items, or making them with fewer raw materials, decreases the amount of waste dramatically. Eventually, less material will be needed to be recycled or sent to the landfill. Recycling one plastic soda bottle saves it from 100 to 1,000 years in a landfill. Glass takes up to 4,000 years to decompose in a landfill. By recycling a glass bottle, we can use that glass indefinitely. Recycling also protects the environment from harmful emissions created when producing new bottles, and it reduces the toxicity of waste.

Additionally, recycling has an economic benefit. Cities generally have to pay by the ton to use a landfill. Recycling could save municipal budgets millions of dollars, reducing costs for communities, schools, businesses and individuals. Finally, the $4 billion a year recycling industry employs thousands of people.

See also: Hazardous Waste Disposal; Landfills and Superfund Sites

FURTHER READING
Donald, Rhonda Lucas. *Recycling.* Danbury, Conn.: Children's Press, 2002.
Inskipp, Carol. *Reducing and Recycling Waste.* Milwaukee, Wisc.: Gareth Stevens Publishing, 2005.
Cothran, Helen, ed. *Garbage and Recycling.* Chicago, Ill.: Greenhaven Press, 2002.

■ TOBACCO SMOKE
See also: Air Pollution; Carcinogens

■ TSUNAMI
See also: Earthquakes and Tidal Waves

■ ULTRAVIOLET RAYS (UV)
See also: Nuclear Energy; Ozone Layer; Radiation; Radon

■ VOLCANIC ACTIVITY
Geological forces that occur when hot magma, or molten rock, and gases well up from inside Earth and appear through cracks in the crust called volcanoes. Volcanic activity also refers to the violent eruption of molten earth. During this process a volcanic mountain forms. The mountain is generally shaped like a cone. The magma

becomes trapped inside the volcano's vent. Constant pressure causes the magma to explode in a violent eruption.

Volcanic eruptions can have a devastating impact on those living near the mountain. In 1982, more than 2,000 people were killed in Mexico when the volcano El Chichón erupted. Krakatau, a 2,667-foot volcano in Indonesia, erupted in 1883, killing 36,000 people on nearby islands. The eruption was so powerful that people could hear the mountain explode 3,000 miles away. One of the most famous eruptions in the United States occurred in 1980, when Mount St. Helens in Washington State erupted, killing 57 people.

THE EARTH'S VOLCANOES

Deep below Earth's surface the planet is a cauldron of churning super-hot gases and molten rock. Volcanoes are simply openings that allow some of the heat from inside Earth to escape. The planet's **core** is about 3,900 miles (6,300 kilometers) beneath Earth's surface and is extremely hot. Scientists estimate that Earth's outer core has a temperature of 9,000 degrees Fahrenheit (6,000 degrees Celsius). The inner core is even hotter—roughly 12,000 degrees Fahrenheit (6,600 degrees Celsius). Earth's **mantle** makes up more than 70 percent of the planet, extending from about 30 miles (50 kilometers) to 1,800 miles (2,900 kilometers) below Earth's surface.

On top of the mantle sits Earth's rocky outer layer, called the **crust.** Earth's crust is broken into many pieces, called **tectonic plates.** On top of those plates sit continents, oceans, and islands. Tectonic plates are always moving and shifting. As the plates move, they rub against one another.

Volcanoes need magma to form. In many places on Earth, hot rock from inside the mantle makes its way to the crust. As it moves, the hot rock melts into magma. Magma pools in chambers just a few short miles below Earth's surface. Magma can travel from the chamber and into fractures or simply melt a path through the surrounding rock.

As magma rises, it gets hotter, causing gases to expand. When the pressure of the magma and the gases becomes too great, it will either dribble out, or explode in a violent eruption. Once the super-hot magma reaches Earth's surface, it is called **lava.**

The planet is sprinkled with volcanoes, some of which have been dormant for millions of years. Others explode all the time, and still others wait to erupt hundreds or thousands of years.

Life would not exist on the planet if were not for volcanoes. Billions of years ago, Earth was a sea of fire. Millions of volcanic eruptions released tons of gases, lava, and rock. The spewing gases from these seething volcanoes formed Earth's atmosphere and ultimately the air humans and animals breathe. The volcanoes helped produce water vapor, clouds, and rain. The world's oceans formed when rain began to fall. As for the land itself, the lava cooled to become part of Earth's crust, forming mountains, valleys, and islands.

SPECIAL PEAKS

Volcanoes only form under special conditions. Volcanoes form near *rift zones, subduction zones,* and *hot spots.* Rift zones are areas where Earth's plates are spreading apart. The separating plates allow magma to move through fissures, or separations, in Earth's crust. Volcanoes also form under the ocean in **oceanic ridges**, which circle the planet. For example, one string of volcanoes is the Mid-Atlantic Ridge, which stretches from the Arctic Circle to the southern Atlantic Ocean. It then curls around to the Pacific Ocean.

As Earth's tectonic action forms new crust, the old crust is pushed back into the mantle in subduction zones. Subduction zones emerge when two plates collide and one plate slides under the other. The new magma created by these subduction zones rises upward to form volcanoes. That is how Mount St. Helens formed. Subduction zones surrounding the Pacific Ocean create almost half of all the world's volcanoes. Scientists sometimes call that region the Ring of Fire. The Ring of Fire borders the west coast of the United States, Japan, the Philippines, Indonesia, and other countries.

Volcanoes also form in hot spots where rising magma pushes through Earth's crust. Hot spots can occur anywhere on the planet. Hot spots always remain in place. One hot spot has been forming the Hawaiian Islands for 75 million years. How does that happen? The Hawaiian Islands sit on the Pacific Plate. When the plate passes over the hot spot it creates a **seamount**, which is a single volcano. A seamount becomes an island when its top rises from the water. Gradually, and over time, the constantly moving Pacific Plate moves the island farther away from the hot spot. The cycle repeats itself. Soon, an entire chain of islands is formed.

TYPES OF VOLCANOES

Scientists divide volcanoes in three types. They include:

- **Shield volcanoes:** Shield volcanoes form when an astounding amount of lava spreads over a wide area. As the lava spreads, it gradually builds up a low, broad, dome-shaped mountain. Mauna Loa in Hawaii is a shield volcano.

- **Cinder cone:** Cinder cone volcanoes form when pieces of rock and volcanic ash explode from the mountain and fall back around the mountain's **vent.** The accumulation of all this volcanic rock forms a cone-shaped mountain.
- **Composite volcanoes:** Composite volcanoes form when lava and rock erupt from a central vent, forming a cone-shaped mountain.

Today, somewhere in the world, a volcano is erupting. These eruptions might last only for a brief time, or they might go on for days, weeks, even months. Scientists call the ash, rock and lava that shoot up from an exploding volcano pyroclastic material. Not all lava and rock are the same. Volcanic material is dependent upon the chemical composition of the magma. For example, some magma might have high silica content and low temperature. Therefore, the pyroclastic material might move slowly. If all the material reaches the surface with a high amount of gas, the volcanic eruption will be violent. If the magma loses its gas on the way to Earth's surface, lava flows could move very slowly and not very far.

An explosive pyroclastic fall is an eruption that sends rock and lava high into the air. Scientists call that high-flying rock and lava tephra. Dust particles are the smallest tephra. Ashes are rocks that are slightly larger than dust. Cinders are bigger than ash. The largest cinders are known as blocks. Blocks can be the size of a car or a book.

TEENS SPEAK

I Live Near a Volcano

My name is Giuseppe and I live near a volcano. I live in Naples, a city in Italy. Naples is a modern city, with tall buildings and paved roads. I like living here. All my friends are from Naples. From my school window I can see Mount Vesuvius, one of the most famous volcanoes in history. Perhaps you heard of Vesuvius. It can explode at any time.

Let me tell you a story about Vesuvius and the nearby city of Pompeii. I read about it in a book. On August 24, c.e. 79,

Vesuvius exploded violently. The ash blotted out the mid-day sun. Lava and boiling mud poured down the side of the mountain. Everything in its path was burned. Superheated gas blew through the region with the speed of hurricane winds. Thousands of people in Pompeii and the city of Herculaneum raced to the sea hoping to escape the fire and the devastation. Many hid from the lava and ash in boat-houses near the beach. Others crawled into nearby caves.

When the day ended, the eruption sealed Pompeii under a blanket of ash as high as a basketball hoop. Herculaneum was buried under a thick layer of mud. About 16,000 people died that day. You can still see the bodies of some people preserved where they died, encased in hardened ash and mud.

Some people in Naples and Italy fear that Vesuvius will erupt once again. Scientists say that there is so much pressure building up inside Vesuvius that the next time the mountain blows its top it could be more devastating than the ancient eruption that August day. To help people, the government is offering to pay for each family that lives near the mountain to move to a safer place. Not too many people have taken the government up on its offer.

In 1944, Vesuvius erupted, but not as violently as it did in ancient times. Some people died of heart attacks and lava destroyed some homes. In 1995, the government created a national park near the top of the volcano. The government also made it illegal to build near the mountain.

My teacher says that that more than a half a million people live in the towns around the so-called *zona rossa*, or red zone. That includes me and my family. Many people could be in danger if the mountain erupted again. Every so often, we practice evacuating the school. We all pile into a bus and ride away from the volcano. Teacher says that two weeks before the volcano blows there will be warning signs. I do not think about Vesuvius too often. I know if Vesuvius erupts, we'll be able to leave and be safe.

VOLCANIC DANGER

A volcano that erupts has the ability to devastate the environment. Pyroclastic flows could kill wildlife, destroy acres of crops, and affect the weather. In 1815, Mount Tambora in Indonesia exploded with such ferocity that it sent more than 25 cubic miles (40 cubic kilometers) of tephra into the air. The dust and rock polluted the atmosphere so much that the summer of 1816 in North America and Europe was extremely cold. It was so cold that New England experienced snow storms in July.

Sometimes a cloud of debris will be so heavy that it cannot rise into the atmosphere. When that happens, hot gas, lava, and rock sweep over the landscape at speeds of 100 miles (160 kilometers) an hour. Lava flows can also roll through areas, burning everything in its path. Lava flows are slower than pyroclastic flows, but both are very dangerous.

On January 17, 2002, Mount Nyiragongo (nee-rah-GONG-goh), an active volcano in the Democratic Republic of Congo, sent rivers of red-hot lava flowing toward the city of Goma and its 400,000 panic-stricken residents. Sixty people died, and 500,000 were left homeless. After the eruption, many Goma residents fled across the border to Rwanda. When they came back, they found their city in ruins.

Mount Nyiragongo had a history of **seismic activity**. In 1998, **volcanologists** had noticed a buildup of lava in the mountain's crater. Two years later, Nyiragongo's crater erupted. On January 10, 1977, a wide lava lake in Nyiragongo's deep crater spilled out in less than an hour. The lava spilled from cracks in the sides of the volcano and rushed down the mountain at 40 miles an hour, killing about 70 people.

According to the United States Geological Survey (USGS), volcanic activity has killed more than 260,000 people in the past 300 years. Entire cities are sometimes destroyed, and eruptions often wreak havoc on air and water quality. Although scientists have gotten better at predicting volcanic eruptions, at least 500 million people around the world are at risk from volcanoes.

See also: Earthquakes and Tsunamis

FURTHER READING

Gates, Alexander E. *Encyclopedia of Earthquakes and Volcanoes*. New York: Facts On File, 2006.

Kusky, Timothy. *Volcanoes: Eruptions and Other Volcanic Hazards*. New York: Facts On File, 2006.

Morris, Neil. *Volcanoes*. New York: Crabtree Publishing, 1995.

■ WATER POLLUTION

Contamination, either natural or human-made, that disrupts the biological processes of bodies of water such as oceans, lakes, rivers, and streams. Nitrates, pesticides, and sewage, along with a host of industrial contaminates, such as chemical by-products created in the manufacturing process, are pollutants that can contaminate water, creating a health hazard.

WATER EVERYWHERE

More than 70 percent of our planet is made up of water.

Water might look clean, but many materials can make water unsafe. Those materials are **pollutants**, and thousands of these substances are harmful to plants, animals, and humans. Humans generate almost all of the pollution that finds its way in the environment.

Q & A

Question: How can the water in a private household well become contaminated?

Answer: Well water can become contaminated if it is located near a farm where chemicals are used, such as herbicides, insecticides, and fertilizers. If the house is near a gas station, a leaky gas tank might be contaminating the well. Sometimes wells were built in places that were used as a chemical or garbage dump. Groundwater in the area might also be contaminated by other things, such as motor oil, organic compounds, or other chemicals.

Long ago, water was able to purify itself when people dumped trash and sewage into the rivers, lakes, and streams. Most of those pollutants were **biodegradable**—bacteria in the water and soil could break down the waste into less harmful substances. Then, as the population grew, people created new sorts of products, including plastic soda bottles, laundry detergent, and other goods. Many of these products were non-biodegradable. Thus, the bacteria in the water and soil could not break these materials down into less harmful substances.

In addition, factories were often located on the banks of rivers and streams. These factories needed water in the manufacturing process. They could pump water directly from the river and dump the waste out back into the flowing waterway. Many times factories did not know what they were dumping into the water. Much of the water was tainted with harmful pollutants.

GROUNDWATER POLLUTION

Without rain, snow, and other forms of **precipitation**, Earth would wither. Every inch of rain that falls on one acre produces 27,000 gallons of water. What happens to all that water? Some of it runs off into streams, rivers, lakes, and ponds. Some water seeps into the ground. Along this journey, water picks up pollutants from the ground and the air. Carrying those pollutants, the moving water makes its way into the ground, a lake, or a river.

Much of the world's water is locked underground, in layers of loose soil, gravel, and rocks called **aquifers**. Any substance that contaminates an aquifer and makes the water unsafe to use and drink is called a groundwater pollutant.

Industrial waste sites, accidental oil spills, leaking gasoline storage tanks, chemicals used in fertilization, and the spraying of **pesticides** and **herbicides**, are just some of the substances that can pollute groundwater. **Gasoline** and **diesel** fuel are also major contaminants. **Arsenic** and **radon** will also poison groundwater.

Dangerous compounds from landfills can flow into the groundwater and reach the aquifer. In the United States, 50 percent of all people get their water from groundwater. They dig wells to access the aquifer. A long time ago, most groundwater was pure. Microbes scrubbed the water clean as it moved through the ground, breaking down any pollutants.

Q & A

Question: Why does water sometimes smell like rotten eggs?

Answer: Water rich in nutrients will cause anaerobic bacteria to become plentiful. Anaerobic bacteria do not need oxygen to survive. These bacteria produce certain gases, including hydrogen sulfide, which smells like rotten eggs.

Increased pollution contaminated much of the country's groundwater. Most people did not realize this until the 1970s, when scientists began taking a look at the water people were drinking.

Q & A

Question: How do scientists determine whether a water source is polluted or not?

Answer: Scientists detect water pollution in laboratories, where they test small samples of water for contamination. Scientists can also tell the health of a body of water by studying fish population and plant life.

SOURCES OF POLLUTION

According to the U.S. Environmental Protection Agency (EPA), 40 percent of the rivers and 45 percent of the lakes in the United States are so polluted that people cannot fish or swim in them. In fact, these waterways are too dangerous for the fish that live here.

Where does all this pollution come from? There are two categories of water-pollution sources: point and non-point. Point sources include sewage treatment plants, boats, factories, and ships that directly pollute the water.

Non-point sources include runoff from agricultural sources, mining activities, and paved roads. As the runoff moves over and through the ground, it picks up natural and human-made pollution, depositing those contaminants into waterways and underground water supplies.

The overuse of fertilizers, which help plants grow, is a major source of water pollution, as are insecticides used on farms and in homes. Other sources of non-point pollution include, oil, grease, and toxic chemical runoff.

Loose sediment from construction sites can also pollute rivers and streams. Salt, metals, and acids from mines and other industrial sources contribute to the problem, as do the bacteria and nutrients from livestock, pet waste, and faulty septic systems. How does each of these contribute to water pollution?

Sediments

Sediments are a major problem in rivers, streams, lakes, and ponds. When too much dirt gets into the water, the sediment can cause the gills of fish to clog. If that happens, the fish cannot breathe and they die. Sediments also make water cloudy, depriving aquatic plants of sunlight. Without sunlight, **photosynthesis** cannot take place. Photosynthesis allows plants to make food and plants will die without nutrients. Sediments are so unhealthy that the EPA has declared them the leading cause of surface water pollution. That is why it is important for construction crews to adequately protect against soil erosion.

Chemicals

Every year, billions upon billions of gallons of wastewater leave factories, power plants, oil refineries and mines headed for the rivers, streams, lakes, and oceans. Although some of this water has been cleaned of pollutants, much of it is loaded with hazardous waste. Scientists estimate that more than a million chemicals have already entered the world's water supplies.

The chemicals that factories use and dump as waste during the manufacturing process do not easily break down in the environment. In addition, some chemicals accumulate in the tissue of animals. Animals that are high on the food chain, such as humans, consume these chemicals when they eat animals at the lower end of the food chain such as fish.

Chemical fertilizers, household cleaners and runoff from farms also add nutrients to our waterways. Thus, plants and bacteria grow uncontrollably. While that might seem like something good, it is not. When the plants die, they use up all the oxygen in the water as they decompose. That means that fish and other aquatic life suffocate.

Metals

Industries use or produce **compounds** with various metals such as arsenic, cadmium, lead, and mercury. When these metals are dumped in the environment, they often find their way into water sources. Some of these metals are dangerous to health. They can also accumulate in the tissue of organisms.

Thermal Pollution

Much of the wastewater discharged by many factories and power plants is hot. Dumping warm water into streams, rivers, and lakes makes it difficult for fish to breathe.

Acid Rain

When factories burn **fossil fuels**, especially coal and oil, they release gases, such as sulfur dioxide and nitrous oxide, into the atmosphere. A weak sulfuric acid forms when these gases combine with water vapor in the air. When it rains, snows, or hails, the sulfuric acid falls to the ground as acid rain. Acid rain has significantly harmed lakes, streams, and ponds, especially in the Adirondacks of upstate New York. Millions of fish and aquatic plants have succumbed to acid rain.

Sewage
Every time a person takes a shower, flushes the toilet, or turns on the dishwasher, he or she is polluting the environment. Sewage contains disease-carrying bacteria and viruses. Sewage is often sent to a waste-water treatment plant, which filters the water, and allows sediment to settle at the bottom. These solids are treated to make them harmless before they are dumped into a water source. Sometimes sewage spills from wastewater treatment plants. The sewage ends up in rivers, streams, or the ocean. Many homes have on-site septic systems. Septic systems can fail, however, polluting nearby water sources.

Biological Pollution
Biological pollution can be present in the form of bacteria or viruses. Such pollution can be deadly.

EFFECTS ON HEALTH
Water pollution can have profound health effects on the environment. Pollution deforms fish and kills animal and plant life. Water pollution throws **ecosystems** off-kilter, reducing the number of plants and animals. Pollution contaminates drinking water and food, causing people to get sick.

Water pollution could cause economic hardship for many people. Oil spills hurt the recreational fishing industry and the tourism many communities rely on as an economic lifeline. Beaches may be closed because the water is too polluted.

See also: Air Pollution; Bacteria; Groundwater; Landfills and Superfund Sites

FURTHER READING
Dolan, Edward, F. *Our Poisoned Waters*. New York: Dutton Juvenile, 1997.
Strange, Cordelia. *Water Pollution and Health*. Vestal, New York: AlphaHouse Publishing, 2008.

HOTLINES AND HELP SITES

American Cancer Society
URL: http://www.cancer.org/docroot/PED/content/PED1_3x_Known_ and_Probable_ Carcinogens.asp
Phone: 1-800-ACS-2345 (1-800-227-2345), 1-404-929-6972   Fax: 1-404-327-6425
Address: 250 Williams Street, Suite 600
Atlanta, GA 30303
Mission: The American Cancer Society is a nationwide, community-based, voluntary health organization dedicated to eliminating cancer as a major health problem by preventing cancer, saving lives, and diminishing suffering from cancer through research, education, advocacy, and service.
Programs: Children's Camps; Hodge Lodge; I Can Cope; Look Good . . . Feel Better; Man to Man; Reach to Recovery

Asbestos.net
URL: http://www.asbestos.net/
Phone: 1-800-713-9791
Affiliation: Asbestos-Abatement.com
Mission: Asbestos.net provides a large and in-depth library of information not only on the many diseases and cancers caused by asbestos but also on the many other facets involved with this complex mineral.

Centers for Disease Control
URL: http://www.cdc.gov
Phone: 1-800-CDC-INFO (1-800-232-4636) TTY: 1-888-232-6348

Address: 1600 Clifton Road
Atlanta, GA 30333
Mission: The Centers for Disease Control provides users with credible, reliable health information on data and statistics, diseases, conditions, emergencies, disasters, environmental health, healthy living, injury, violence, safety, life stages, populations, travelers' health, and workplace safety and health.
Programs: CDC Disease Detective Camp; National Conference on Chronic Disease Prevention and Control; National Immunization Conference; U.S. Public Health Service, Scientific & Training Symposium

Clean Water Action Council of Northeastern Wisconsin

URL: http://www.cwac.net/index.html
Phone: 1-920-437-7304
Address: 1270 Main Street, Suite 120
Green Bay, WI 54302
Mission: The Clean Water Action Council is a non-profit citizen organization, founded in 1985, working to protect public health and the environment in Northeast Wisconsin.

County of San Mateo: RecycleWorks

URL: http://www.recycleworks.org/index.html
Phone: 1-888-442-2666   Fax: 1-650-361-8220
Address: County of San Mateo RecycleWorks Program
555 County Center, 5th Floor
Redwood City, CA 94063
Affiliation: The Public Works Department of San Mateo County
Mission: RecycleWorks creates, delivers, and promotes recycling, composting, waste prevention, procurement, sustainability and green building programs and outreach at county facilities and for residents, employees, businesses, and visitors in the unincorporated area of the county and, when appropriate, throughout San Mateo County to encourage, facilitate, and achieve resource conservation and the practice of responsible environmental stewardship and to maintain compliance with the California Integrated Waste Management Act (AB 939).
Programs: Green Building Guidelines; Green Business Program; Sustainable Building Policy

Department of Environmental Protection, State of Pennsylvania
URL: http://www.depweb.state.pa.us/justforkids/cwp/view.asp?a=3&tq
=464803
Phone: 1-717-783-2300
Address: Rachel Carson State Office Building
400 Market Street
Harrisburg, PA 17101
Mission: The mission of the Department of Environmental Protection
   is to protect Pennsylvania's air, land, and water from pollution and
   to provide for the health and safety of its citizens through a cleaner
   environment.

FamilyDoctor.org
URL: http://familydoctor.org/online/famdocen/home/common/
allergies/treatment/232.html
Phone: 1-800-274-2237 or 1-913-906-6000   Fax: 1-913-906-6075
Address: 11400 Tomahawk Creek Parkway
Leawood, KS 66211-2680
Affiliation: American Academy of Family Physicians
Mission: Familydoctor.org's mission is to improve the health of
   patients, families, and communities by serving the needs of mem-
   bers with professionalism and creativity.

Food Safety and Inspection Service
URL: http://www.fsis.usda.gov/Help/FAQs_Food_Spoilage/index.asp
Phone: 1-402-344-5000   Fax: 1-402-344-5005
Address: 1400 Independence Avenue SW
Washington, DC 20250-3700
Affiliation: U.S. Department of Agriculture
Mission: The Food Safety and Inspection Service (FSIS) is public health
   agency in the U.S. Department of Agriculture responsible for ensur-
   ing that the nation's commercial supply of meat, poultry, and egg
   products is safe, wholesome, and correctly labeled and packaged.

Federal Emergency Management Administration
URL: http://www.fema.gov
Phone: 1-800-462-7585
Address: 500 C Street SW
Washington, D.C. 20472

Affiliation: As a part of the U.S. Department of Homeland Security (DHS), FEMA also works in partnership with other organizations that are part of the nation's emergency management system. These partners include state and local emergency management agencies, 27 federal agencies, and the American Red Cross.

Mission: FEMA's mission is to reduce the loss of life and property and protect the nation from all hazards, including natural disasters, acts of terrorism, and other human-made disasters by leading and supporting the nation in a risk-based, comprehensive emergency management system of preparedness, protection, response, recovery, and mitigation.

Green Facts

URL: http://www.greenfacts.org/en/index.htm

Phone: +32 (0)2 211 34 88   Fax: +32 (0)2 218 89 73

Address: M-Brussels Village, rue des Palais 44 Paleizenstraat

b24, B-1030 Brussels

Belgium

Mission: Green Facts brings complex scientific consensus reports on health and the environment to the reach of nonspecialists.

Kids Recycling Zone

URL: http://www.kidsrecyclingzone.com

Phone: 1-202-316-3046

Address: 2000 L Street NW

Suite 835

Washington, DC 20036

Affiliation: National Trade Association; The Association of Postconsumer Plastic Recyclers

Mission: The Kids Recycling Zone mission is to expand the postconsumer plastics recycling industry through a cooperative effort aimed at identifying and eliminating barriers to successful commercial recycling.

Mayo Clinic

URL: http://www.mayoclinic.com/health/lead-poisoning/FL00068

Address: 200 First Street SW

Rochester, MN 55905

Affiliation: Mayo Foundation for Medical Education and Research

Mission: Mayo Clinic empowers people to manage their health by providing useful and up-to-date information and tools that reflect the expertise and standard of excellence of Mayo Clinic.

National Aeronautics and Space Administration
URL: http://www.nas.nasa.gov/About/Education/Ozone/ozonelayer.html
Phone: 1-650-604-4502   Fax: 1-650-604-437
Affiliation: Information Sciences and Technology Directorate
Mission: NASA develops, demonstrates, and delivers innovative, distributed heterogeneous computing capabilities to enable NASA projects and missions.

National Oceanic and Atmospheric Administration
URL: http://www.ncdc.noaa.gov
Phone: 1-828-271-4800   Fax: 1-828-271-4876
Address: National Climatic Data Center, Federal Building
151 Patton Avenue
Asheville, NC 28801-5001
Mission: The National Oceanic and Atmospheric Administration provides access and stewardship to the nation's resource of global climate and weather-related data and information and assesses and monitors climate variation and change.

National Pesticide Information Center
URL: http://npic.orst.edu
Phone: 800-858-7378
Address: National Pesticide Information Center
Oregon State University
333 Weniger Hall, Corvallis, OR 97331-6502
Affiliation: Oregon State University; United States Environmental Protection Agency
Mission: The National Pesticide Information Center serves as a source of factual, unbiased information on pesticide chemistry, toxicology, and environmental fate to all who inquire, including industry, government, medical, and agricultural personnel, in addition to the general public.

National Safety Council
URL: http://www.nsc.org/resources/issues/radon/index.aspx

Phone: 1-630-285-1121   Fax: 1-630-285-1315
Address: 1121 Spring Lake Drive
Itasca, IL 60143-3201
Mission: The National Safety Council educates and influences people
    to prevent accidental injury and death.
Programs: NSC Safety Program

National Youth Agency
URL: http://www.youthinformation.com/Templates/Internal.
asp?NodeID=90011
Phone: 0116 242 7350   Fax: 0116 242 7444
Address: Eastgate House
19-23 Humberstone Road
Leicester
LE5 3GJ
United Kingdom
Mission: The National Youth Agency provides resources to improve
    work with young people and its management; creates and demon-
    strates innovation in services and methods; supports the leadership
    of organizations to manage change; influences public perception
    and policy; and secures standards of education and training for
    youth work.
Programs: Positive Activities for Young People

Natural Resources Defense Council
URL: http://www.nrdc.org/
Phone: 1-212-727-2700   Fax: 1-212-727-1773
Address: 40 West 20th Street
New York, NY 10011
Mission: The Natural Resources Defense Council's purpose is to safe-
    guard the earth: its people, its plants and animals, and the natural
    systems on which all life depends.
Programs: Beat the Heat; Green Paws; Move America Beyond Oil;
    Simple Steps; This Green Life

Rainforest Action Network
URL: http://ran.org
Phone: 1-415-398-4404   Fax: 1-415-398-2732
Address: 221 Pine Street

5th Floor

San Francisco, CA 94104 USA

Mission: Rainforest Action Network campaigns for the forests, their inhabitants, and the natural systems that sustain life by transforming the global marketplace through education, grass roots organizing, and nonviolent direct action.

Programs: Freedom From Oil Campaign; Global Finance Campaign; Old Growth Campaign; Rainforest Agribusiness Campaign

The Water Pollution Guide

URL: http://www.water-pollution.org.uk

Address: The Guides Network Manor Coach House

Church Hill

Aldershot, Hampshire, GU12 4RQ

United Kingdom

Mission: The Water Pollutions Guide aims to explain the different types of water pollution, what causes pollution, and the potential dangers to the environment, nature, and human health.

U.S. Department of Energy

URL: http://www.ne.doe.gov

Phone: 1-800-DIAL-DOE   Fax: 1-202-586-4403

Address: 1000 Independence Avenue SW

Washington, DC 20585

Mission: The Department of Energy's mission is to lead the investment in the development and exploration of advanced nuclear science and technology.

Programs: Clean Cities Program; Federal Emergency Management Program; Fossil Energy Research & Development Program

U.S. Environmental Protection Agency

URL: http://www.epa.gov

Phone: 1-202-272-0167

Address: Ariel Rios Building

1200 Pennsylvania Avenue NW

Washington, DC 20460

Mission: The EPA's mission is to repair the damage already done to the natural environment and to establish new criteria to guide Americans in making a cleaner environment a reality.

U.S. Nuclear Regulatory Commission
URL: http://www.nrc.gov/reading-rm/basic-ref/students.html
Phone: 1-301-415-7000
Address: One White Flint North
11555 Rockville Pike
Rockville, MD 20852-2738
Affiliation: Federal Intergovernmental Matters
Mission: The NRC's mission is to regulate the nation's civilian use of by-product, source, and special nuclear materials to ensure adequate protection of public health and safety, to promote the common defense and security, and to protect the environment.

GLOSSARY

aerobic bacteria   microscopic, single-celled organisms that require oxygen to live

Agent Orange   herbicide used by the U.S. military during the Vietnam War to destroy foliage that provided cover for the enemy; term came from the colored stripe that was used to mark the drums containing the chemical

allergens   foreign substances, such as pollen or ragweed, to which the body's immune system is oversensitive and that cause allergic reactions

allergic   describes the special sensitivity of the body that makes it react with an exaggerated response of the natural immune defense mechanism

ammonia   strong-smelling gas that is lighter than air, can be dissolved in water, and is used to produce certain types of fertilizers and some explosives

anaerobic bacteria   microscopic, single-celled organisms not requiring oxygen to live

anthrax   a disease of livestock caused by a bacillus (*Bacillus anthracis*) that humans can contract

antibiotics   a group of drugs that kills or inhibits the growth of bacteria and fungi

antibody a protein made by the body to fight invading substances

antihistamines substances used to relieve allergy symptoms, such as itching, runny nose, or swelling, and to counteract the effects of histamine

aquicludes impermeable layers of rock which slow down water movement

aquifer any underground rock formation containing water

arsenic grayish-white element that is found in many ores and can be poisonous in large amounts

asbestosis disease of the lungs caused by the long-term exposure of asbestos fibers

asthma a chronic lung ailment characterized by difficulty in breathing due to spasm of the air passages

bedrock solid rock found under the soil

binary fission a form of reproduction in which a single-celled organism divides into two smaller cells

biodegradable capable of being broken down by living organisms, such as bacteria

bioremediation a process that uses organisms, such as bacteria, to attack contaminants in soil

birth defect structural, functional, or biochemical abnormality that occurs to a fetus

bubonic plague a disease caused by certain fleas on rats; also known as the black death

cadmium a highly toxic metal and environmental pollutant that is used in making batteries

calluses tissue that forms on the surface of a plant or person's skin that has been damaged

carbon dioxide   colorless, odorless gas formed by the oxidation of carbon

cataracts   a disease of the eye that causes blindness when the natural lens clouds over

chlorine   greenish-yellowish gas that is used as a bleaching agent

chlorinated phenols   a family of environmental pollutants

chlorofluorocarbons (CFCs)   ozone-destroying chemical compounds developed in the 1930s as refrigerants and later used in aerosol spray cans and other products

chlorophyll   the green pigment in plants which absorbs light energy during the process of photosynthesis

cholera   a waterborne disease the symptoms of which include violent diarrhea and vomiting

coagulation   the process by which bleeding is stopped

cocci   members of a group of circular bacteria, some of which are harmful to humans

composted   mixed organic matter, such as leaves and grass clippings, used to improve the quality of soil

compounds   two or more elements that bond to form a new substance

condense   to undergo change from a gas to a liquid state and then fall in drops

copper nitrate   chemical compound used as an oxidizing agent

copper sulfate   chemical compound used in herbicides

core   the innermost part of Earth which includes an outer core, roughly 1,800 miles (2,898 kilometers) below Earth's surface, and an inner core, which begins at a depth of 3,095 miles (4,982 kilometers)

corrosive   pertaining to a substance that eats away and eventually destroys metal

crust   the outermost portion of Earth

DDT   abbreviation for dichlorodiphenyltrichloroethane, an insecticide discovered in 1939 which was later found to be highly toxic, poisoning fish and other wildlife

decomposition   the process by which the tissue of dead animals and plants breaks down

dengue fever   a tropical fever transmitted by mosquitoes and accompanied by joint pains, headache, rash, and the swelling of the glands

deoxyribonucleic acid   also known as *DNA,* a complex molecule that contains the chemically coded information needed for a cell to function

deuterium   an isotope of hydrogen used in the nuclear industry

diesel   lightweight fuel used by certain types of engines

dioxin   a toxic chemical that can cause cancer, as well as severe reproductive and developmental problems

diphtheria   an infectious disease that damages the throat, heart, and nerves

disinfection   the process of killing bacteria and other microorganisms with chemicals

DNA   see *deoxyribonucleic acid*

drought   an extended period of months or years during which a region notes a serious reduction in rainfall

Ebola   an often-fatal illness caused by an infection with one of several viruses in the Filoviridae family

ecosystem   a community of living organisms whose relationship is so closely intertwined that the removal of any one organism could be disastrous

embryo   early developmental stage of an animal or plant following the fertilization of an egg cell; in humans, the term *embryo* is used to describe the first seven weeks of existence

emission the discharge of gases into the atmosphere

enzyme a protein in the body that induces chemical changes in other substances

epicenter the point on Earth's surface immediately above the focus of an earthquake

epidemiologic relating to the study of factors affecting the health and illness of populations

epinephrine hormone that raises blood-sugar levels by stimulating glucose production; also known as adrenaline

equator the imaginary line that separates Earth's northern and southern hemispheres

estuaries semi-enclosed coastal bodies of water with one or more rivers or streams flowing into it and which connect to the sea

evaporation process by which a liquid, such as water, is turned into a vapor or gas

extinction the dying out of a species

facultative anaerobes organisms that can live with or without oxygen

famine a severe food shortage that results in starvation and death

fault lines fractures in the earth's crust along which the two sides have moved as a result of differing strains on adjacent rock bodies

fetus the stage in the embryo development of mammals after eight weeks, when the limbs and the head are recognizable

fire retardants substances that can prevent fires from occurring

flagella small hairlike organs on the surface of some cells

formaldehyde a colorless, poisonous gas

fossil fuels nonrenewable energy sources such as coal, oil, and natural gas, formed by the fossilized remains of plants and animals that lived millions of years ago; fossil fuels will eventually run out

fungicide a chemical pesticide that can be used to prevent fungus diseases in plants and animals

gamma ray high frequency electromagnetic radiation similar to X-rays but with a shorter wave length emitted by the nuclei of radioactive substances during decay

gas one of the three states of matter (liquids and solids being the other two) where the molecules move quickly and randomly in otherwise empty space

gasoline mainly used in automobiles, a source of fuel derived from petroleum

gastrointestinal relating to the digestive tract

genetic [makeup] characteristics of an individual based on inherited qualities, such as eye and hair color, passed down from ancestor to ancestor

geothermal referring to energy harnessed from the internal heat of Earth

germination the initial stage of growth in seeds

glacier a slow-moving mass of ice formed on land by compacted layers of snow and ice

greenhouse gases gases such as carbon dioxide and nitrous oxide that trap some of the Sun's radiation and keep it close to Earth's surface, keeping the planet warm—like the inside of a greenhouse

habitat environment in which an organism lives

heavy metals metals that are dense, such as gold, mercury, and uranium

hemoglobin a blood protein that transports oxygen through the bloodstream

heterotrophs living organisms that obtain their energy from organic substances produced by other organisms; certain types of bacteria that feed on dead animal and plant material

histamines   substances released in damaged tissue which account for many of the symptoms of allergies

hydrocarbons   any class of chemical compounds containing only hydrogen and carbon

hydrogen   colorless, odorless gas that is the lightest of all elements; the most abundant element in the universe

hydrogen cyanide   a poisonous gas used for hardening steel and extracting gold and silver from their ores; also used for fumigation

hydrologic cycle   also known as the water cycle, in which water is circulated between Earth's surface and the atmosphere

hypothermia   a condition in which an organism's temperature drops below the normal level that is required for that organism to function

ice age   a period of cooling in Earth's history; several ice ages have occurred, each followed by a period of warming

indigenous   native to a particular region

influenza   any one of a number of viral infections whose symptoms include fever, chills, headache, and joint and muscle pain

infrared light   invisible electromagnetic radiation

inversion   in meteorology, the layer of air near Earth's surface which is cooler than the overlaying layer

iron sulfate   a greenish crystalline compound used in fertilizers and as a feed additive

isotope   one, two, or more atoms that have the same number of protons but a different number of neutrons

krill   tiny shrimplike creatures that live in the ocean and are a main food sources for many species, including penguins

lava   magma, or melted rock that has reached the surface of Earth

lead   a gray metallic element that can be poisonous to humans if inhaled or swallowed over time

learning disabilities a broad range of problems that result in a person's inability to acquire, retain, or use specific academic or functional skills, including the inability to read, write, or speak properly

low pressure [disturbance] the crashing of atmospheric pressure with warm moist air

malaria a parasitic disease of the tropics spread by mosquitoes

mantle the layer of Earth between the crust and the core

mast cell one of the cells that contains histamines and is involved in the production of inflammatory reactions associated with allergies

Mercalli scale instrument used to measure the intensity of an earthquake

mesothelioma a rare form of lung cancer

metabolize to convert food to energy through chemical changes in cells

methane a highly flammable natural gas that explodes when it is mixed with air or oxygen

microorganisms living organisms invisible to the naked eye

molecules groups of two or more atoms

mulch shredded vegetable or mineral matter that is used as protective covering over the top of soil

neurotransmitters chemicals in the body which relay signals between cells

neutrons subatomic particles that have no electrical charge

nitrates substances used as preservatives and as coloring agents in cured meats such as bacon and sausage

nitric acid a weak acid that decomposes quickly when mixed with water

nitrous oxide a greenhouse gas that is used with oxygen to reduce sensitivity to pain

nucleus the positively charged part of an atom

oceanic ridges mountain ranges on the seabed where tectonic plates are moving apart and magma rises to the surface

organic matter matter that has come from the decomposition of a living thing

ozone a highly reactive, foul-smelling gas that is formed when the molecule of a stable form of oxygen is split by the ultraviolet radiation of the Sun

parasites organisms that feed on or in another organism; endoparasites live inside a person or animal, and ectoparasites live on the body of a person or animal

particulates fine particles of a solid or liquid suspended in a gas; one of the categories of air pollutants monitored by the EPA

pesticides chemicals used to control a variety of pests such as fungi, insects, and weeds

petrochemical chemical derived from the processing of crude oil

phosgene gas an industrial chemical used to make plastics and pesticides

phosphorous an element in animal manure and chemical fertilizer that plants need to grow; can cause water to become polluted, killing aquatic plants and animals

photosynthesis process by which green plants use light from the Sun to make food

physicists scientists who study physics, the study of matter and energy

pitchblende brownish-black radioactive mineral that is a major component of uranium ore

pollutants   the by-products of human activity, such as noise, household trash, hazardous materials, smoke, and automobile emissions that harm the environment

polychlorinated biphenyls (PCBs)   dangerous industrial chemicals, they are extremely toxic and an environmental hazard

polyethylene   a lightweight plastic often used in packaging and insulation

precipitation   in meteorology, water that falls to the ground as rain, hail, sleet, dew, frost, and snow

protons   positively charged subatomic particle in the nucleus of all atoms

radioactive   describes energy emitted as waves by disintegrating atoms during radioactive decay

radio waves   electromagnetic waves that are used to carry voice signals over great distances

radium   radioactive element found in pitchblende and other uranium ores

regeneration   the regrowth of a new organ or tissue after the loss or removal of the original organ or tissue

renewable energy   energy sources, such as wind and solar power, which the natural world replaces in a reasonable period of time

seamount   on the seafloor, an individual mountain that is usually volcanic

seismic activity   activity related to earthquakes

seismic waves   the shockwaves given off by an earthquake

seismograph   instrument used to record the activity of an earthquake or the fracturing of rock in Earth's crust

smallpox   a highly contagious viral disease accompanied by aches, fever, vomiting, and skin eruptions

smog a mixture of smoke particles and fog which forms when the pollutants of burned gasoline, also known as hydrocarbons, react with sunlight and water vapor; can cause illnesses and loss of life, especially to those with breathing problems

species a group of organisms capable of interbreeding

spirilla spiral-shaped bacteria; can live in water and in the intestines and genital areas of animals

storm surge an offshore rise in water often associated with hurricanes and other storms or low-pressure disturbances

stratosphere the portion of Earth's atmosphere that is 50 to 80 kilometers high; the ozone layer is located in the stratosphere

subatomic particles particles such as electrons, protons, neutrons, and alpha particles that are smaller than an atom

sulfur dioxide a foul-smelling gas that is a major cause of acid rain

sulfuric acid a dense liquid that is extremely corrosive; can cause severe burning and is often used in industry in the manufacturing of fertilizers, detergents, explosives, and dyes

synthetic made by humans

tectonic plates segments of Earth's crust on which the continents, islands, and oceans sit

thermal relating to heat

thermonuclear relating to the fusion of atomic nuclei at high temperatures

tide the periodic rise and fall of the sea spurred by the gravitational pull of the Moon

tissue cellular fabric that occurs in an organism's body

tuberculosis an infectious disease, generally of the lungs, caused by the bacillus *Mycobacterium tuberculosis*; only 5 percent of those infected develop the disease

typhus   with the most serious forms affecting the brain, lungs, and kidneys, a bacterial disease transmitted by lice, fleas, mites, and ticks; symptoms can include fever, headache, and rash

ultraviolet light (ultraviolet radiation)   electromagnetic radiation invisible to the human eye

vacuum   any space completely empty of matter

vent   an opening in Earth's surface through which gases, lava, and rock explode

vibrios   any group of comma-shaped bacteria

volcanologist   scientist who studies volcanoes

West Nile Virus   a serious, and potentially fatal, disease, spread by infected mosquitoes

X-ray   a band of electromagnetic radiation between the wavelengths of gamma rays and ultraviolet radiation

INDEX

Boldface page numbers indicate extensive treatment of a topic.